Christians and Others in the Umayyad State

****

Late Antique and Medieval Islamic Near East (LAMINE)

The new Oriental Institute series LAMINE aims to publish a variety of scholarly works, including monographs, edited volumes, critical text editions, translations, studies of corpora of documents — in short, any work that offers a significant contribution to understanding the Near East between roughly 200 and 1000 C.E.

****

Christians and Others in the Umayyad State

edited by

Antoine Borrut and Fred M. Donner

with contributions by

Antoine Borrut, Touraj Daryaee, Muriel Debié, Fred M. Donner, Sidney H. Griffith, Wadād al-Qāḍī, Milka Levy-Rubin, Suzanne Pinckney Stetkevych, Donald Whitcomb, and Luke Yarbrough

2016

LAMINE 1

LATE ANTIQUE AND MEDIEVAL ISLAMIC NEAR EAST • NUMBER 1

THE ORIENTAL INSTITUTE OF THE UNIVERSITY OF CHICAGO

CHICAGO, ILLINOIS

Library of Congress Control Number: 2015956904
ISBN: 978-1-614910-31-2

Published 2016. Printed in the United States of America.

The Oriental Institute, Chicago

THE UNIVERSITY OF CHICAGO
LATE ANTIQUE AND MEDIEVAL ISLAMIC NEAR EAST • NUMBER 1

Series Editors
Leslie Schramer
and
Thomas G. Urban
with the assistance of
Rebecca Cain

With special thanks to Tasha Vorderstrasse.

Cover Illustration
St. John of Damascus, icon from Damascus, Syria (d. ca. 131/749).
19th century, attributed to Iconographer Ne'meh Naser Homsi
https://en.wikipedia.org/wiki/John_of_Damascus#/media/File:
John_Damascus_%28arabic_icon%29.gif (accessed 1/21/2016)

Printed by Thomson-Shore, Dexter, Michigan, U.S.A.

The paper used in this publication meets the minimum
requirements of American National Standard for Information
Services — Permanence of Paper for Printed Library Materials,
ANSI Z39.48-1984.
∞

Table of Contents

Acknowledgments

This volume inaugurates a new book series entitled *Late Antique and Medieval Islamic Near East* (LAMINE), published by the Oriental Institute at the University of Chicago. The editors express their gratitude to Director Gil Stein and the Oriental Institute publications committee for their support in launching this new publishing venture. LAMINE aims to publish a variety of works of scholarship, including monographs, edited volumes, critical text editions, translations, studies of corpora of documents — in short, anything that makes a significant contribution to our understanding of the Near East between roughly 200 and 1000 C.E. The primary language of the series will be English, but contributions in French and German will be considered as well. LAMINE volumes will be released simultaneously in print (softcover) and electronically (the latter available at no charge via the Oriental Institute's website[1]), to encourage dissemination of this scholarship as quickly and widely as possible.

The papers assembled below were presented at a workshop held in Chicago on June 17–18, 2011, entitled "Christians, Jews, and Zoroastrians in the Umayyad State." Two speakers were already committed to submit their work elsewhere, but the other eight papers are published here in full. The workshop was meant to foster dialogue and so papers were not read during the event, but rather pre-circulated in order to have ample time for discussion. Each paper was assigned a formal respondent, after which the floor was open to free discussion among the roughly 40 scholars who attended the workshop. Even though it was not possible to reproduce here the responses to the papers and the ensuing discussions, all participants benefited tremendously from them and they often had a significant impact as the various contributions were revised by their authors for publication. It is hoped that this gathering will be followed by others in a series of workshops dedicated to the first dynasty of Islam that will follow the same format and be subsequently published in LAMINE.

The editors are grateful to the following institutions for their generous financial support of the conference: the Franke Institute for Humanities at the University of Chicago, the Center for Middle Eastern Studies at the University of Chicago,[2] the Oriental Institute of the University of Chicago, the Department of History at the University of Maryland, the Divinity School at the University of Chicago, and the Department of Near Eastern Languages and Civilizations at the University of Chicago. Without their generosity and encouragement provided at the earliest stages of planning, it is uncertain that the conference could have materialized in such a successful manner. We also offer sincere thanks to Dr. Thomas Maguire, Associate Director of CMES, who handled most of the practical arrangements for the conference.

The editors also wish to express their profound thanks to the staff of the Publications Office of the Oriental Institute, in particular Thomas Urban and Leslie Schramer, for their efficient and highly professional handling of the many technical and other challenges posed by this manuscript once it was submitted to them. It was a pleasure to work with them and we know that this bodes well for future volumes in the LAMINE series.

[1] For more on the electronic publications initiative of the Oriental Institute, please refer to: http://oi.uchicago.edu/research/electronic-publications-initiative-oriental-institute-university-chicago

[2] CMES funding came in part from a Title VI National Resource Center grant from the U.S. Department of Education.

Abbreviations

A.D.	anno Domini (in the year of [our] Lord)
A.H.	anno Hegirae (in the year of the Hegira)
A.S.	anno salutis (in the year of salvation)
attrib.	attributed to
C.E.	Common Era
ca.	*circa*, about, approximately
ch(s).	chapter(s)
col(s).	column(s)
d.	died
ed.	edition, editor
e.g.	*exempli gratia*, for example
esp.	especially
f(f).	and following
fl.	*floruit*, flourished
gov.	governed
ibid.	*ibidem*, in the same place
i.e.	*id est*, that is
n(n).	note(s)
no(s).	number(s)
O.	ostracon
P.	papyrus
pl.	plural
r.	ruled
ref.	reference
sing.	singular
s.v.	*sub verbo*, under the word
trans.	translation, translator
v(v).	verse(s)

CSCO	Corpus Scriptorum Christianorum Orientalium
EI[1]	*Encyclopaedia of Islam*. 1st edition. Edited by M. Th. Houtsma, T. W. Arnold, R. Basset, and R. Hartmann. Leiden: Brill, 1913–1936.
EI[2]	*Encyclopaedia of Islam*. 2nd edition. Edited by P. Bearman, Th. Bianquis, C. E. Bosworth, E. van Donzel, and W. P. Heinrichs. Leiden: Brill, 2012.
EIr	*Encyclopædia Iranica*. Edited by E. Yarshater. 15 vols. London: Routledge and Kegan Paul, 1982–2011.

Introduction: Christians and Others in the Umayyad State

Antoine Borrut and Fred M. Donner

The papers in this volume were prepared for a conference entitled Christians, Jews, and Zoroastrians in the Umayyad State, held in June 2011 at the University of Chicago. The goal of the conference was to address a simple question: just what role did non-Muslims play in the operations of the Umayyad state? It has always been clear that the Umayyad family (r. 41–132/661–750) governed populations in the rapidly expanding empire that were overwhelmingly composed of non-Muslims — mainly Christians, Jews, and Zoroastrians — and the status of those non-Muslim communities under Umayyad rule and more broadly in early Islam has been discussed continuously for more than a century. It is impossible to do justice here to decades of scholarship devoted to non-Muslims in early Islam since it has become a field of its own and generated its own industry.[1] Topics such as non-Muslims' perceptions of emergent Islam, the legal status of non-Muslims under Islamic rule, theological debates between Muslims and non-Muslims, or the historiographical divide between Muslim and non-Muslim sources — to name but a few — have prompted important debates.[2]

Recent scholarship suggests, however, that the lines of division between the various "religious communities" of the Late Antique and early Islamic Middle East were more blurred than long assumed. Reducing these communities to their theological dimensions proves problematic, while the definition of legal categories was certainly not a straightforward process.[3] It has thus recently been shown how non-Muslims could resort to Islamic law when their interests were better served by it, rather than calling on their own communal jurisdictions.[4] Moreover, religiously mixed families and intermarriages contributed to shape a much more complex image of societies, not fully bound by the lines dividing religious communities.[5]

At the cultural level too, a sharp opposition between Muslims and non-Muslims should be avoided. Multilingualism was the norm, rather than the exception, among the learned.[6] This

---

[1] See now the convenient bibliography edited by Thomas and Roggema, *Christian-Muslim Relations*.

[2] See for instance the contributions of Hoyland, *Seeing Islam as Others Saw It*; Levy-Rubin, *Non-Muslims*; Wasserstein, "Conversion and the *ahl al-dhimma*"; Griffith, *The Church in the Shadow of the Mosque*.

[3] See in particular the recent discussion of Papaconstantinou, "Between *Umma* and *Dhimma*." This is of course not to say that discriminatory practices did not exist at an early stage; see Robinson, "Neck-Sealing."

[4] Simonsohn, *A Common Justice*.

[5] The *Canons* of Jacob of Edessa (d. 708) include for instance a number that address interesting questions raised by intermarriage; some of these are discussed in Hoyland, *Seeing Islam as Others Saw It*, pp. 160–67. See now Weitz's dissertation, Syriac Christians in the Medieval Islamic World.

[6] Papaconstantinou, ed., *Multilingual Experience in Egypt*. See also Johnson, "Social Presence of Greek."

is certainly best exemplified by the scholars engaged in the so-called translation movement from Syriac, Greek, and Pahlavī into Arabic that culminated in the early Abbasid period,[7] but multilingualism was already the rule in Umayyad times as evidenced by many scholars or documents, such as Egyptian papyri and even some caliphal inscriptions.[8]

More broadly, modern scholarship has also created a false dichotomy between "internal" (i.e., Muslim) and "external" (i.e., non-Muslim) sources, thus artificially separating sources along linguistic lines. Such an assumption is highly problematic given that non-Muslim scholars abounded at Muslim courts, and that many of them composed various scientific or historical works in some official capacities. The historiographical implications of this remark are quite imposing and invite us to rethink the categories we are traditionally using to approach early Islamic history and historiography.[9]

The more specific question of non-Muslims *within* the early Islamic state has received, however, much less attention. Historians have duly acknowledged the prominence of non-Muslim local élites in the aftermath of the conquest in various capacities, ranging from tax collectors to clergymen and various powerbrokers.[10] The new rulers co-opted the scribes and clerks of the former Sasanian and Byzantine empires to run their tax administration, since they lacked skilled personnel of their own who knew the terrain and the traditional procedures of revenue assessment and collection. These non-Muslim administrators, and their descendants (since such work tended to run in families), continued to serve in the Umayyad state for over a century, as is visible especially in the rich documentation offered by the Egyptian papyri.

Scholars have also duly noticed the important role of Christian secretaries later on at the Abbasid court,[11] as well as more broadly the role of Christians in the heartland of Abbasid power.[12] But paradoxically, the first dynasty of Islam has received much less attention from this perspective, even if some salient figures — first and foremost Saint John of Damascus (d. ca. 131/749)[13] — were soon singled out as exceptional. In other words, within the larger question of how non-Muslim communities fared under Umayyad rule is the more limited issue of what role non-Muslims played in the actual operations of the Umayyad government.

Two factors suggest that we cannot see this as the new Muslim regime employing non-Muslims only for menial administrative jobs in minor roles. First, there is scattered evidence that non-Muslims sometimes held positions of real importance. Not a few, it seems, did military service in the Umayyad armies.[14] Others were appointed to high-level positions as advisers and administrators; the case of the famous Yuḥannā ibn Sarjūn ibn Manṣūr (d. ca. 131/749), known more generally as Saint John of Damascus, was not unique.[15] Were these

[7] For competing chronologies of the "translation movement," cf. Gutas, *Greek Thought*, and Saliba, *Islamic Science.*

[8] The evidence of multilingual Egyptian papyri abounds; see most recently Sijpesteijn, *Shaping a Muslim State*, esp. pp. 64ff. and 229ff. A similar situation is observed in the Nessana papyri of Palestine, for instance; see Kraemer, *Excavations at Nessana*, vol. 3: *Non-Literary Papyri.* It is also worth pointing out that the first mention of the title *amīr al-muʾminīn* (Commander of the Believers) appears, at the beginning of Muʿāwiya's reign, in an inscription composed in Greek at Ḥammat Gader (42/662); see fig. 1.1, below.

[9] For a detailed discussion of this question, see Borrut, *Entre mémoire et pouvoir*, esp. pp. 137ff.

[10] See, for example, Robinson, *Empire and Elites*, esp. pp. 90ff.

[11] See especially Fiey, *Chrétiens syriaques*, and Cabrol, "Une étude."

[12] Thomas, ed., *Christians at the Heart of Islamic Rule.*

[13] See Sidney Griffith's contribution to this volume.

[14] See Wadād al-Qāḍī's paper in this volume.

[15] See Muriel Debié's contribution to this volume, especially on Athanasius bar Gūmōyē.

merely occasional collaborators with the new regime, or are they evidence that non-Muslims held significant influence in the Umayyad regime, perhaps even in the formulation of policy?

Second, we must remember that the Umayyads did not refer to themselves at first as a "Muslim regime."[16] Rather, they seem to have conceived of themselves as a regime of "Believers" (*muʾminūn*) — led by the Commander of the Believers (*amīr al-muʾminīn*) — at least for the seventh century.[17] Some of the earliest dated documents from the new era that the Believers inaugurated refer to the government as *qaḍāʾ al-muʾminīn,* the "jurisdiction of the Believers."[18] The question is whether this early self-conception as Believers meant that the Umayyads considered some Christians and other monotheists also to be Believers and incorporated them into the government more or less as equal partners (it being understood, of course, that this was typical dynastic rule, so that the highest echelons of power would remain in the hands of the Umayyad family itself, or of some lineage within it). The question of just when the regime began to consider itself one of Muslims — that is, as belonging to a new religious confession distinct from Christians, Jews, and other monotheists — also requires resolution, since the longer the Umayyads conceived of themselves mainly as Believers, the longer non-Muslim monotheists may have been included in important ways in the Umayyad state.

As indicated by its title — Christians, Jews, and Zoroastrians in the Umayyad State — the focus of the original conference in 2011 was not restricted to Christians alone, but of the papers presented, only two dealt directly with non-Christians, one with Jews and the other with Zoroastrians. Evidence — literary and documentary — for the history of Christians in the Umayyad period is scant enough, but for the Zoroastrian and Jewish communities, the basis of evidence is even more limited. In the case of the Jews, the evidence is so scarce that it is difficult to say much that is meaningful at all about them during this period.

This raises, however, the vexing conundrum that we might call the "Problem of the Vanishing Jews" in relation to Islam's beginnings. As is well known, the text of the Qurʾān mentions Jews (and Christians) on occasion as parts of Muḥammad's environment and also refers to both groups under the collective designation *ahl al-kitāb* "peoples of the Book." The Qurʾān also contains many references to key figures known from the Hebrew Bible, such Abraham, Moses, Jonah, Joseph, and David, or events in the history of the Children of Israel, such as the Exodus from Egypt, or the receiving of the Ten Commandments, which show considerable familiarity with the scriptural traditions of the Jews. The *Sīra* or sacred biography of the prophet Muḥammad, moreover, speaks of his evolving relations with the Jewish clans of Yathrib/Medina after he had undertaken his *hijra* or emigration there with his followers in 622 C.E.[19] The text of the so-called Constitution of Medina, furthermore, states explicitly that certain Jewish clans constituted part of the original community (*umma*) established by Muḥammad in Medina. From all these indications, there thus seems to be good reason to conclude that Jews were a significant presence in Muḥammad's environment. Not much is heard about Jews in the reports of the conquests that followed Muḥammad's death,[20] except

[16] On Umayyad self-definition, see Borrut and Cobb, "Toward a History of Umayyad Legacies."

[17] For a full discussion of this idea, see Donner, *Muhammad and the Believers.*

[18] Rāġib, "Une ère inconnue."

[19] On the Jewish communities of Medina in pre-Islamic and early Islamic times, see Lecker, *Muslims, Jews, and Pagans.* For a broader Arabian context, see Beaucamp, Briquel-Chatonnet, and Robin, eds., *Juifs et chrétiens*; and Robin, "Arabia and Ethiopia."

[20] Assuming, of course, that the conquests did not begin until after Muḥammad's death, as depicted by Islamic tradition. Some recent studies have proposed, however, that Muḥammad was still alive when the conquests of Palestine and Iraq began; see Crone and Cook, *Hagarism,* esp. pp. 24–28; Shoemaker, *Death of*

a few reports that mention that communities of Jews were resettled by Muʿāwiya in towns on the Syrian littoral,[21] presumably to make the population of such towns less likely to welcome any Byzantine invasion force attempting to establish a bridgehead on the coast. However, the Armenian chronicle attributed to Sebeos (fl. 660s), in describing the conquest of Palestine, claims that when the Muslims/Believers conquered Jerusalem, the *amīr al-muʾminīn* ʿUmar I b. al-Khaṭṭāb appointed a Jew as its first governor.[22] This claim is not confirmed by any Islamic or Christian source, but it may help explain why Jews, apparently, gave ʿUmar his epithet "al-Fārūq," "the redeemer."[23] At least, the fact that ʿUmar I granted Jews access to Temple Mount after decades of Byzantine persecutions may help us to understand why he was so highly praised in Jewish circles.

Beyond this famous tradition, it is also worth pointing out that several prominent Jewish scholars seem to have played a significant role in early Islam. Names of early Jewish converts to Islam such as Kaʿb al-Aḥbār (d. 32/652/653) and Wahb b. Munabbih (d. 110/728 or 114/732) immediately come to mind. (Of course, in view of the apparent fluidity or uncertainty of confessional boundaries in the earliest years of the Believers' movement, we might ask whether Kaʿb and Wahb and others were really "converts," or merely Jews who joined the new movement without giving up their former confessional ties.) Such shadowy figures, often of Yemeni origin, played at least a central part in the transmission of Jewish lore (*Isrāʾīliyyāt*) and interacted at times with the Umayyad clan.[24] At an uncertain date, traditions claiming the Jewish origins of some Umayyads were also put into circulation to denigrate family members of the first dynasty of Islam.[25]

By comparison, the presence of Christians in Muḥammad's environment is hardly attested at all. While the Qurʾān does, as noted, refer a few times to *Naṣārā*/Christians in ways that suggest that they – or at least their beliefs – were present, the *Sīra* makes no mention of any Christian communities in Medina or its environs, and Christians are not mentioned at all in the "Constitution of Medina." Christians are cited in the Muslim annals of the conquests, but mainly as tribesmen who resisted the spread of Islam or settled populations that submitted – rarely as participants in the expansion movement. And yet, by the Umayyad period, as we shall see, Christians in particular seem to be quite prominent in the Umayyad state, whereas Jews – who had evidently been prominent in Muḥammad's time – are no longer mentioned at all. So the question becomes: What happened to the Jews in the interim, and why and how have Christians risen to such prominence? Jewish communities seem to have continued to exist as before; has their relationship to the new community of Believers somehow changed? Or are we dealing with some kind of optical illusion created by lacunae in our sources that conceals the presence of Jews, making them "vanish," even as it emphasizes the presence of Christians? The first centuries of Islam were absolutely central toward the

a Prophet; Pourshariati, *Decline and Fall of the Sasanian Empire*, pp. 161–285, which does not explicitly claim that the conquest of Iraq began while the prophet was still alive, but argues that the conquest began several years earlier than allowed by the chronology of the traditional Islamic sources. On the broader challenges of the periodization of early Islam, see now Donner, "Periodization"; Borrut, "Vanishing Syria"; and Fowden, *Before and After Muḥammad*.

[21] Particularly in Tripoli; see al-Balādhurī, *Futūḥ al-buldān*,ed. p. 127, trans. Hitti and Murgotten, p. 195.

[22] The report of a Jewish governor was noted long ago by Crone and Cook, *Hagarism*, p. 6. See now Thomson, Howard-Johnston, and Greenwood, *Armenian History*, vol. 1, p. 203, and vol. 2, p. 249.

[23] Bashear, "The Title 'Fārūq'"; Donner, "La question du messianisme."

[24] See most recently Prémare, "Wahb b. Munabbih."

[25] Ward, "'You Are Only a Jew from the Jews of Sepphoris."

definition of Jewish identities, which makes this silence all the more puzzling. A study similar to what H. Lapin has conducted for Roman Jews is a much-needed desideratum, though the dearth of sources makes the situation extremely complicated.[26]

The question of Zoroastrians in early Islamic times proves also quite challenging, despite a fresh surge of studies on Sasanian and early Islamic Iran.[27] Newly discovered evidence has made the religious map of Late Antique and early Islamic Iran much more complicated, thus shedding new light on the revolts that Muslim expansion triggered in the Iranian Plateau.[28] A lot remains to be done, however, to clarify the role of the traditional élites in the emerging Muslim State, even if the dense network of *dihqāns* (village landlords) certainly continued to function.[29] Here again, the issue of the sources is a common complaint. It has indeed been shown that later narratives, from the third/ninth and fourth/tenth centuries, endeavored to rewrite the pre-Islamic and early Islamic Iranian past in order to give converts to Islam a new sense of identity and belonging, thus prompting important revisions to memory.[30] This was arguably achieved to the detriment of recollections and traces of the roles and functions fulfilled by non-Muslims in early Islamic Iran, though numismatic or sygillographic evidences are opening new perspectives.[31]

East of Iran, Central Asia raises similar problems despite the availability of some valuable archival material.[32] Here again, the exact role assigned to the local aristocracy (be it Buddhist, Zoroastrian, Manichaean, or other) in the Umayyad regime remains uncertain. It has been recently suggested that the influence of Turco-Soghdian élites in the early Abbasid world had been seriously misunderstood,[33] but the situation under the Umayyads is less clear even if the integration of Central Asian soldiers in the army in the late Umayyad period is well attested.[34] The situation in North Africa and Spain, after 92/711, is not any easier to tackle. It is tempting to assume that Umayyad control over the "peripheries" of an expanding empire was less systematic than it was, for instance, in Syria, Islam's first dynasty's heartland of power. This is, however, an immense topic impossible to address here and that we hope to cover in another volume.

The paper Fred Astren presented at the conference, which was the only one dealing with Jewish communities under the Umayyads, was already promised for publication elsewhere, and so is unfortunately not included in this volume.[35] Thus, with the exception of Touraj Daryaee's article, all the essays published here focus primarily on Christians who served in

---

[26] Lapin, *Rabbis as Romans*. See, however, Astren, "Re-reading the Muslim Sources" and "Non-Rabbinic and Non-Karaite Religious Movements."

[27] See in particular Pourshariati, *Decline and Fall of the Sasanian Empire;* and Daryaee, *Sasanian Persia*. Both considerably renewing the classic study of Christensen, *L'Iran sous les Sassanides*.

[28] Crone, *The Nativist Prophets*. See also Payne, "Cosmology and the Expansion of the Iranian Empire."

[29] Daniel, "The Islamic East," esp. pp. 462ff. See also the classic study of Morony, *Iraq After the Muslim Conquest;* and Haldon and Conrad, eds., *Elites Old and New*.

[30] Savant, *New Muslims of Post-conquest Iran*.

[31] See Touraj Daryaee's paper in this volume, and the abundant numismatic and sygillographic material published by Gyselen. See, for instance, her *Sasanian Seals and Sealings* and her edited volume, *Sources for the History of Sasanian and Post-Sasanian Iran*.

[32] Especially the Mont Mugh documents, since the recently published Afghan documents mostly date back to the Abbasid period. On the Mont Mugh documents, see Livshic, *Juridicheskie dokumenty i pis'ma* [juridical documents and letters] and *Sogdijskaja èpigrafika* [Soghdian epigraphy]; Bogoljubov and Smirnova, *Xozjajstvennye documenty* [economic documents]. The Afghan manuscripts consist of 32 legal documents ranging from 138/755 to 160/777; see Khan, *Arabic Documents*.

[33] La Vaissière, *Samarcande et Samarra*. See also Akasoy, Burnett, and Yoeli-Tlalim, eds., *Islam and Tibet*.

[34] La Vaissière, *Samarcande et Samarra*, pp. 143–45.

[35] Astren, "Non-Rabbinic and Non-Karaite Religious Movements."

the Umayyad state, or the relationships of the Umayyads to Christians (and others) who did serve as Umayyad functionaries. In doing so, each essay addresses particular aspects of the broader question of Christian participation in the Umayyad regime.

Even within this more limited framework, the chronological coverage of the Umayyad period is uneven. If the usual imbalance between Sufyanids and Marwanids has been avoided as much as possible, towering figures such has Muʿāwiya, ʿAbd al-Malik, or ʿUmar b. ʿAbd al-ʿAzīz still dominate the following pages.

Donald Whitcomb's essay deals with the first Umayyad, Muʿāwiya b. Abī Sufyān (r. 41–60/661–680), and is quite exceptional in that it relies mainly on archaeological evidence. Whitcomb makes the case that Muʿāwiya was the real founder of the new empire and emphasizes as evidence his major building projects in Damascus, Jerusalem, and Caesarea. He notes that in doing so, Muʿāwiya "coordinat[ed] a population of Christians and Jews as well as Muslims," without drawing explicit conclusions on the nature of this coordination.

Sidney Griffith's contribution sketches the career of John son of Sergius, later known in the Christian church as Saint John of Damascus, who served as a high official — essentially, head of government — for several Umayyad caliphs before resigning and retiring to a monastery, where he penned his famous Greek work "On Heresies," chapter 101 of which, devoted to "the Heresy of the Ishmaelites," has been extensively used as a source of insight into earliest Islam. Griffith cautions against taking this information about nascent Islam at face value, however, calling attention to the rhetorical strategies John employed, presumably to advance a Christian polemical agenda.

If Saint John of Damascus and his kin have long been famous in scholarly circles, Muriel Debié turns our attention to a rival and much-neglected Edessan family, the Gūmōyē. Rivalry between both families reveals the diverse Christianities practiced in Umayyad times and their shaping of inter-communal relations and power networks. Although the Gūmōyē sprang from Edessa, they flourished in Egypt while Athanasius was serving the Umayyad governor ʿAbd al-ʿAzīz b. Marwān (d. 86/705). This enviable position brought him immense power and wealth, allowing him to act as an arbitrator solving inter-communal disputes or a patron commissioning churches. Athanasius' politics and patronage thus shed fresh light on intra-Christian competition for resources and euergetism. This competition is also reflected in the sources, and so Christian texts from the first centuries of Islam ought to be read in consequence. Thus, Debié questions the transmission of Christian historiography with special emphasis on the shadowy figure of Theophilus of Edessa (d. 785).

Looking at the former Sasanian territories, Touraj Daryaee relies on numismatics to unveil the role and strategies of Persian élites in Umayyad times. The distribution of copper and silver coinages from the Iranian Plateau, and the symbolism utilized on them, reveal a logic of cooperation, rather than coercion, between the Umayyad administration and the local powerbrokers.

Wadād al-Qāḍī's richly documented contribution discusses the employment of non-Muslims in the military forces of the first Islamic state, from the beginning of the conquests to the end of the Umayyads in 132/750. She shows unequivocally that non-Muslims did serve in the Umayyad military (and also in the armies of the conquest before the rise of the Umayyads to power in 41/661). She traces in detail the many ways in which non-Muslims served the early caliphs in military capacities — making valuable use of the evidence provided by Egyptian papyri from the Umayyad period — and concludes with important historiographical observations regarding the uncertainty of many traditions dealing with early Islam.

As al-Qāḍī notes, historiographical issues — in particular, the fact that most of our literary accounts describing the Umayyads have been filtered through successive phases of redaction continuing until in the Abbasid period[36] — loom large in any discussion of the Umayyads and are especially pertinent to the remaining chapters. Suzanne Stetkevych's chapter on the Christian court poet of the Umayyads, al-Akhṭal, shows that his poetry continues many of the tribal traditions of legitimation familiar from pre-Islamic Arabian society: the ruler as a noble chief, generous, a valiant defender of his clients and allies, fierce in battle. By comparison, more clearly religious (Islamic) terms of legitimation of the ruler seem almost like an afterthought in his poetry. Nonetheless, they are present — along with the tribal traditions. This proportion of tribal to religious themes presumably reflects a time when an Islamic identity was first crystallizing and was doing so in a context that was still thoroughly imbued with a tribal ethos.[37] The question is still open, however, as to whether the later descriptions of the *Sitz im Leben* of these poems do not enshrine later (Abbasid-era) attempts to discredit the Umayyads by stressing al-Akhṭal's Christian identity and wine-bibbing habits, as well as to denigrate Christianity in general, which by Abbasid times had come to be seen as a form of *kufr*, "unbelief" — an attitude that marks a departure from the more accepting passages found in the Qurʾān, which includes at least some Christians among the Believers. So there remains some uncertainty over the status of Christians under the Umayyads in al-Akhṭal's time: Did the Umayyads continue the more accepting attitude one seems to find in some Qurʾān verses, or were they beginning to move to the more negative attitude toward Christians characteristic of Abbasid times, and if so, how far had they moved in this direction?

The last two papers take up this debate, where historiographical issues are particularly central. Both essays deal with the question of whether the Umayyads instituted policies barring Christians and other non-Muslims from employment by the government. Milka Levy-Rubin's thoroughly documented and lucidly argued chapter holds that discriminatory regulations barring employment of non-Muslims began at an early date and were later systematized in an epistle of the caliph ʿUmar II b. ʿAbd al-ʿAzīz (r. 99–101/717–720). By comparison, Luke Yarbrough's chapter argues with equal cogency that the epistle of ʿUmar II banning employment of non-Muslims may be a confection of Abbasid court circles. That the two papers can come to such strikingly different conclusions is itself evidence of the importance of historiographical source criticism in the construction of historical arguments about this period of history, and evidence of the complexity of such analysis, about which great uncertainty still reigns. In this case, we can ask: Are reports in the Arabic-Islamic sources about policies against employment of non-Muslims in the early Islamic period authentic vestiges of early attitudes, or are they interpolations reflecting the values of the Abbasid period when these sources were compiled? Are passages from Christian sources about discriminatory policies accurate, or are they, too, interpolations by later Christian authors? Are we as historians caught in the midst of an intense polemic waged by both Muslim and Christian authors of the later eighth through tenth centuries C.E., both of whom wanted to show that the discriminatory policies of Abbasid times were (for Muslims) justified by early practice that had not actually existed, or were (for Christians) evidence that Islam from its inception was discriminatory? How do these differing views fit with, and what if anything can they tell us about, the idea that Islam began as a Believers' movement in which righteous *ahl al-kitāb* were included? These and many

[36] On this process, see Borrut, *Entre mémoire et pouvoir*, pp. 61–108.

[37] See now Webb, *Imagining the Arabs*.

other questions remain to be resolved as scholars continue their efforts to unravel the story of how the early Islamic community came to be, and the role Christians and other non-Muslims played in the functioning of the Umayyad state and in the making of an "Islamic" empire.

Bibliography

Akasoy, Anna; Charles Burnett; and Ronit Yoeli-Tlalim, editors. *Islam and Tibet: Interactions along the Musk Routes*. Farnham: Ashgate, 2011.

al-Balādhurī, Aḥmad b. Yaḥyā. *Futūḥ al-buldān.*

- Edited by M. J. de Goeje, *Liber expugnationis regionum*. Leiden: Brill, 1866.
- English translation by Philip K. Hitti and Francis Clark Murgotten, *The Origins of the Islamic State*. 2 vols. Studies in History, Economics and Public Law 68/1–2. New York: AMS Press, 1916–1924.

Astren, Fred. "Non-Rabbinic and Non-Karaite Religious Movements in the Medieval Islamic World." In *The Cambridge History of Judaism*, Vol. 5: *The Medieval Era*, edited by Robert Chazan and Marina Rustow. Cambridge: Cambridge University Press, forthcoming.

————. "Re-reading the Muslim Sources: Jewish History and the Muslim Conquests." *Jerusalem Studies in Arabic and Islam* 35 (2009): 83–130.

Bashear, Suliman. "The Title 'Fārūq' and Its Association with ʿUmar I." *Studia Islamica* 72 (1990): 47–70.

Beaucamp, Joëlle; Françoise Briquel-Chatonnet; and Chistian Julien Robin, editors. *Juifs et chrétiens en Arabie aux Ve et VIe siècles: Regards croisés sur les sources*. Paris: Association des amis du Centre d'histoire et civilisation de Byzance, 2010.

Bogoljubov, Mixail, and Olga Smirnova. *Xozjajstvennye documenty: Chenie, perevod i kommentarii* [Economic documents: Edition, translation, and commentary]. Sogdijskie dokumenty s gory Mug, 3. Moscow: Nauka, 1963.

Borrut, Antoine. *Entre mémoire et pouvoir: L'espace syrien sous les derniers Omeyyades et les premiers Abbassides (v. 72–193/692–809)*. Leiden: Brill, 2011.

————. "Vanishing Syria: Periodization and Power in Early Islam." *Der Islam* 91/1 (2014): 37–68.

Borrut, Antoine, and Paul M. Cobb. "Introduction: Toward a History of Umayyad Legacies." In *Umayyad Legacies: Medieval Memories from Syria to Spain*, edited by Antoine Borrut and Paul M. Cobb, pp. 3–9. Leiden: Brill, 2010.

Cabrol, Cécile. "Une étude sur les secrétaires nestoriens sous les Abbassides (762–1258) à Bagdad." *Parole de l'Orient* 25 (2000): 407–91.

Christensen, Arthur. *L'Iran sous les Sassanides*. Copenhagen: Ejnar Munksgaard; Paris: Paul Geuthner, 1944.

Crone, Patricia. *The Nativist Prophets of Early Islamic Iran: Rural Revolt and Local Zoroastrianism*. Cambridge: Cambridge University Press, 2012.

Crone, Patricia, and Michael Cook. *Hagarism: The Making of the Islamic World*. Cambridge: Cambridge University Press, 1977.

Daniel, Elton L. "The Islamic East." In *The New Cambridge History of Islam*, Vol. 1: *The Formation of the Islamic World, Sixth to Eleventh Centuries*, edited by Chase F. Robinson, pp. 448–505. Cambridge: Cambridge University Press, 2010.

Daryaee, Touraj. *Sasanian Persia: The Rise and Fall of an Empire*. International Library of Iranian Studies 8. London: I. B. Tauris, 2009.

Donner, Fred M. "La question du messianisme dans l'Islam primitif." In "Mahdisme et millénarisme en Islam," edited by M. García-Arenal. *Revues des Mondes Musulmans et de la Méditerranée* 91–92–93–94 (2000): 17–28.

————. *Muhammad and the Believers: At the Origins of Islam*. Cambridge: Harvard University Press, 2010.

————. "Periodization as a Tool of the Historian with Special Reference to Islamic History." *Der Islam* 91/1 (2014): 20–36.

Fiey, Jean-Maurice. *Chrétiens syriaques sous les Abbassides surtout à Bagdad (749-1258)*. Corpus Scriptorum Christianorum Orientalium 420. Leuven: Secrétariat du CorpusSCO, 1980.

Fowden, Garth. *Before and After Muḥammad: The First Millennium Refocused*. Princeton: Princeton University Press, 2014.

Griffith, Sydney H. *The Church in the Shadow of the Mosque: Christians and Muslims in the World of Islam*. Princeton: Princeton University Press, 2008.

Gutas, Dimitri. *Greek Thought, Arabic Culture: The Graeco-Arabic Translation Movement in Baghdad and Early ʿAbbāsid Society (2nd-4th/8th-10th Centuries)*. London and New York: Routledge, 1998.

Gyselen, Rika. *Sasanian Seals and Sealings in the A. Saeedi Collection*. Acta Iranica 44. Leuven: Peeters, 2007.

————. *Sources for the History of Sasanian and Post-Sasanian Iran*. Res Orientales 19. Bures-sur-Yvette: Groupe pour l'Étude de la Civilisation du Moyen-Orient, 2010.

Haldon, John, and Lawrence I. Conrad, editors. *The Byzantine and Early Islamic Near East* 6: *Elites Old and New in the Byzantine and Early Islamic Near East*. Princeton: Darwin Press, 2004.

Hoyland, Robert G. *Seeing Islam as Others Saw It: A Survey and Evaluation of Christian, Jewish and Zoroastrian Writings on Early Islam*. Studies in Late Antiquity and Early Islam 13. Princeton: Darwin Press, 1997.

Johnson, Scott F. "Introduction: The Social Presence of Greek in Eastern Christianity, 200–1200 C.E." In *Languages and Cultures of Eastern Christianity: Greek*, edited by Scott F. Johnson, pp. 1–122. Surrey: Ashgate, 2015.

Khan, Geoffrey. *Arabic Documents from Early Islamic Khurasan*. London: Nour Foundation, 2008.

Kraemer, Casper J. *Excavations at Nessana*, Vol. 3: *Non-Literary Papyri*. Princeton: Princeton University Press, 1958.

La Vaissière, Étienne de. *Samarcande et Samarra: Élites d'Asie centrale dans l'empire abbasside*. Studia Iranica, Cahier 35. Paris: Association pour l'avancement des études iraniennes, 2007.

Lapin, Hayim. *Rabbis as Romans: The Rabbinic Movement in Palestine, 100-400 C.E.* Oxford: Oxford University Press, 2012.

Lecker, Michael. *Muslims, Jews, and Pagans: Studies on Early Islamic Medina*. Leiden: Brill, 1995.

Levy-Rubin, Milka. *Non-Muslims in the Early Islamic Empire: From Surrender to Coexistence*. Cambridge: Cambridge University Press, 2011.

Livshic, V. A. *Juridicheskie dokumenty i pis'ma* [Juridical documents and letters]. Sogdijskie dokumenty s gory Mug, 2. Moscow: Nauka, 1962.

————. *Sogdijskaja èpigrafika Srednej Azii i Semirech'ja* [Soghdian epigraphy from Central Asia and Semirechye]. Saint Petersburg: Filologicheskij Fakul'tet SPbGU, 2008.

Morony, Michael G. *Iraq after the Muslim Conquest*. Princeton: Princeton University Press, 1984.

Papaconstantinou, Arietta. "Between *Umma* and *Dhimma*: The Christians of the Middle East under the Umayyads." *Annales Islamologiques* 42 (2008): 127–56.

————, editor. *The Multilingual Experience in Egypt, from the Ptolemies to the Abbasids*. Farnham: Ashgate, 2010.

Payne, Richard. "Cosmology and the Expansion of the Iranian Empire, 502–628 C.E." *Past and Present* 220/1 (2013): 3–33.

Pourshariati, Parvaneh. *Decline and Fall of the Sasanian Empire: The Sasanian-Parthian Confederacy and the Arab Conquest of Iran.* London: I. B. Tauris, 2008.

Prémare, Alfred-Louis de. "Wahb b. Munabbih, une figure singulière du premier islam." *Annales. Histoire, Sciences Sociales*, 60ème année, 3 (2005): 531–49.

Rāġib, Yusuf. "Une ère inconnue d'Égypte musulmane: l'ère de la juridiction des croyants." *Annales Islamologiques* 41 (2007): 187–207.

Robin, Christian Julien. "Arabia and Ethiopia." In *The Oxford Handbook of Late Antiquity*, edited by Scott Fitzgerald Johnson, pp. 247–332. Oxford: Oxford University Press, 2012.

Robinson, Chase F. *Empire and Elites after the Muslim Conquest: The Transformation of Northern Mesopotamia.* Cambridge: Cambridge University Press, 2000.

———. "Neck-Sealing in Early Islam." *Journal of the Economic and Social History of the Orient* 48/3 (2005): 401–41.

Saliba, George. *Islamic Science and the Making of European Renaissance.* Cambridge: MIT Press, 2007.

Savant, Sarah B. *The New Muslims of Post-Conquest Iran: Tradition, Memory, and Conversion.* Cambridge: Cambridge University Press, 2013.

Shoemaker, Stephen J. *The Death of a Prophet: The End of Muhammad's Life and the Beginnings of Islam.* Philadelphia: University of Pennsylvania Press, 2012.

Sijpesteijn, Petra M. *Shaping a Muslim State: The World of a Mid-Eighth-Century Egyptian Official.* Oxford: Oxford University Press, 2014.

Simonsohn, Uriel I. *A Common Justice: The Legal Allegiances of Christians and Jews Under Early Islam.* Philadelphia: University of Pennsylvania Press, 2011.

Thomas, David, editor. *Christians at the Heart of Islamic Rule: Church Life and Scholarship in ʿAbbasid Iraq.* Leiden: Brill, 2003.

Thomas, David, and Barbara Roggema, editors. *Christian-Muslim Relations: A Bibliographical History,* Vol. 1: *600-900.* The History of Christian-Muslim Relations 11. Leiden: Brill, 2009.

Thomson, Robert W., translator; commentary by James Howard-Johnston; assisted by Tim Greenwood. *The Armenian History Attributed to Sebeos.* 2 vols. Liverpool: Liverpool University Press, 1999.

Ward, Seth. "Muḥammad Said: 'You Are Only a Jew from the Jews of Sepphoris': Allegations of the Jewish Ancestry of Some Umayyads." *Journal of Near Eastern Studies* 60/1 (2001): 31–42.

Wasserstein, D. J. "Conversion and the *ahl al-dhimma.*" In *The New Cambridge History of Islam*, Vol. 4: *Islamic Cultures and Societies to the End of the Eighteenth Century*, edited by R. Irwin, pp. 184–208. Cambridge: Cambridge University Press, 2010.

Webb, Peter. *Imagining the Arabs: The Construction of Arab Identity in Early Islam.* Edinburgh: Edinburgh University Press, forthcoming.

Weitz, Lev E. Syriac Christians in the Medieval Islamic World: Law, Family, and Society. Ph.D. dissertation, Princeton University, 2013.

1

Notes for an Archaeology of Muʿāwiya: Material Culture in the Transitional Period of Believers

Donald Whitcomb, The Oriental Institute

> Muʿāwiya [...] rebuilt some of the walls and repaved the northern part of the platform. There was even some talk of ambitious new building plans for the area.[1]

Perhaps there will always be an uncertainty whether Muʿāwiya b. Abī Sufyān became involved with the Ḥaram al-Sharīf and initiated the building known as the Qubbat al-Ṣakhra.[2] On the other hand, there is an inscription from the baths renovated at Hammat Gader in 662, a few years after Muʿāwiya became caliph (fig. 1.1). He is styled "the servant of God [...] commander

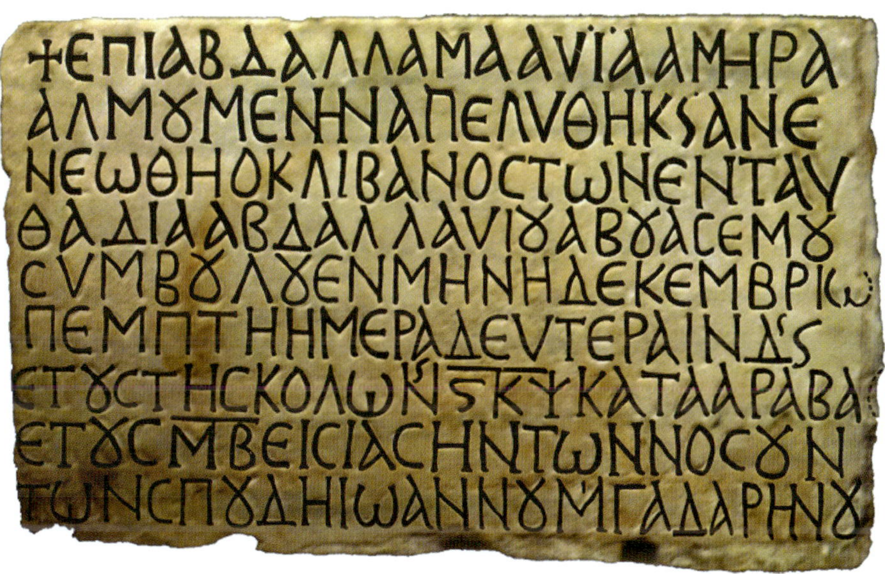

Figure 1.1. The Hammat Gader inscription (after Hirschfeld, *Roman Baths*, fig. 50)

[1] Makiya, *The Rock*, p. 154.

[2] More recent discussions suggest Muʿāwiya's involvement in the Marwānī muṣallā on the Ḥaram al-Sharīf; see St. Laurent and Awwad, "The Marwani Musalla."

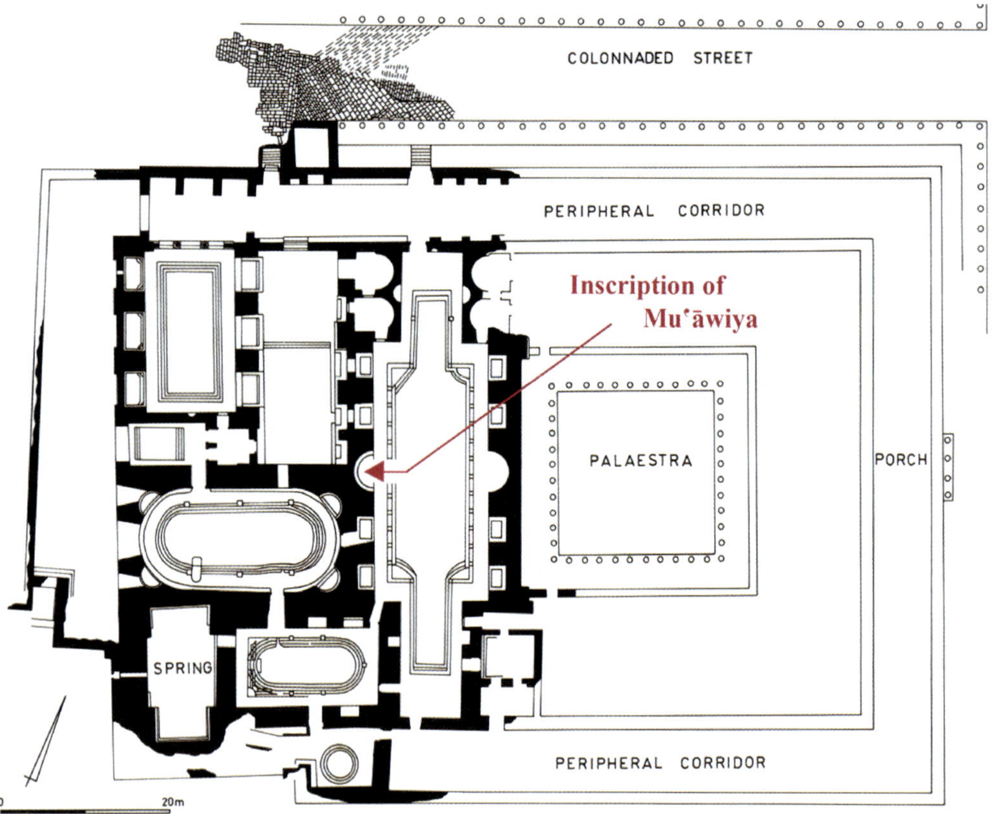

Figure 1.2. Setting of the Muᶜāwiya inscription (after Hirschfeld, *Roman Baths*, fig. 11)

of the Believers." The inscription was in Greek and not dissimilar to another of the empress Eudocia, also placed in the same hall some 200 years earlier (fig. 1.2). Both stones bear a cross and one may assume the local builder of the later to have been Christian, working under the authority of Abū Hāshim, the Muslim governor.

These two aspects of the career of Muᶜāwiya, an indirect implication of activity in Jerusalem and specific evidence of restoration in Gadara, may be taken as extremes for an "archaeology" of Muᶜāwiya. This paper explores this concept, that one may reconstruct this historical person from his effect on material culture of his time. While it is always possible to discover direct evidence relating to a person (i.e., the above inscription), this is not exactly modern archaeology, as a discipline beyond serendipitous discovery. Archaeological research is much better suited for broad questions of social and cultural history, economic and ecological development. This usually involves comparative analyses of patterns within corpora of material evidence. For an archaeologist, the study of a person is anomalous, if not counterintuitive, as a research subject.

This study stretches this understanding of modern archaeology for the sake of developing an understanding of the early Islamic period. Muᶜāwiya is a particularly appropriate subject for this experiment. He follows the crucial but nebulous period of the Rāshidūn without an obvious cultural break; he enjoyed an extraordinarily long period of power, some forty years as governor of Bilād al-Shām and caliph of the Dār al-Islām; he presided in the shift from Ḥijāz-based polity into one based in al-Shām and encompassing the Diyār al-ʿArab and Diyār al-ʿAjam; he coordinated settlement of large numbers of Believers into differing regions that remained predominantly Christian. Setting aside the nature of his political structure, that is, the vexed question of a state, he made major contributions toward the physical manifestation of Islamic structures. Parameters of this phase of development may be outlined in anticipation of a second phase, the production of ʿAbd al-Malik's sons, al-Walīd I, Sulaymān, and Hishām (705–743, another forty-year span).

A Locus of Authority?

To return to the Hammat Gader inscription and historical sources on Muʿāwiya, it is entirely possible that Muʿāwiya frequented this bath, perhaps employing the therapeutic waters for his son Yazīd, on his way to his winter quarters at Ṣinnabra (some 10 km distant).[3] The palace of Ṣinnabra may be the earliest of the so-called desert castles, here the seasonal residence of the governor of al-Shām and then commander of the Believers. The structure has specific features: a colonnaded court with a large exedra at one end. There is a series of rooms behind and around the exedra, service rooms for an audience hall.[4] Ṣinnabra bears strong similarities to the praetorium of Tiberias, which was transformed in the early Islamic period and, placed next to the *jāmiʿ* mosque, seems to have been the *dār al-imāra* of that city.[5] These structures may be in turn compared with Hishām's hall built behind the mosque at Ruṣāfa;[6] this building was adjacent to the cathedral and is usually identified as the bishop's palace. The two phases, before and after the mosque, suggest an adaptation of the structure that preserves what appears to be its ceremonial functions, foremost the seat of governance and judgment (fig. 1.3).

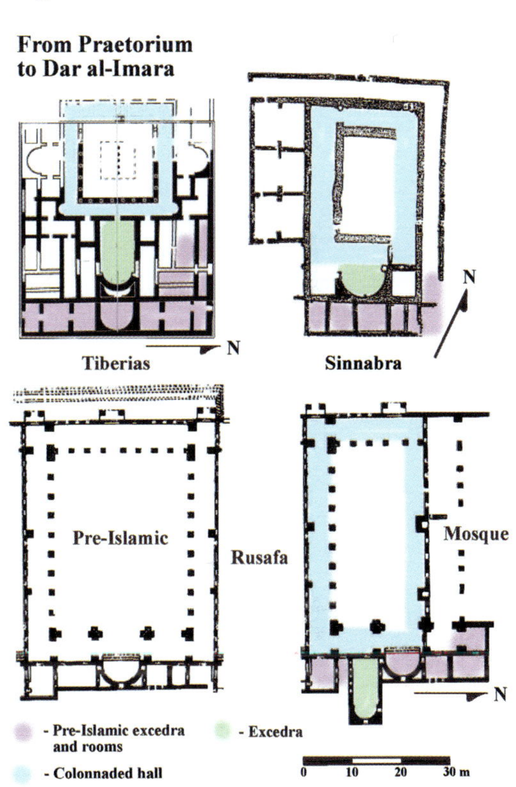

Figure 1.3. Early Islamic administrative structures at Tiberias, Sinnabra, and Rusafa (plans by D. Whitcomb)

These three examples may indicate a new architectural form for the *dār al-imāra*, which may be traced back to Muʿāwiya's rule in Bilād al-Shām and then imitated by his successors, ʿAbd al-Malik and his son Hishām. What makes this transformation interesting is the structural similarity to a church, as in the example of the building of al-Mundhir, also at Ruṣāfa, identified by Sauvaget as a praetorium, an interpretation seconded by

[3] Hasson, "Remarques," p. 99.

[4] Whitcomb, "Khirbet al-Karak."

[5] Cytryn-Silverman, "The Umayyad Mosque of Tiberias."

[6] A comparison with the audience hall at Khirbat al-Mafjar is also instructive, before that building was converted into a bath.

Shahid (contra the identification as a church by Brandt and Fowden). As Fowden points out,[7] the ambiguity itself may be significant as is the association with the Ghassanids (also of personal significance to Muᶜāwiya, as suggested by Shahid).[8]

Association of the Arab populations in Shām with these structures may reveal an element of Muᶜāwiya's organization of Qinnasrīn; as Athamina notes, "[...] during the first civil war, many tribal sub-groups left the *amṣār* of Iraq and joined the camp of Muᶜāwiya in Syria. There they were settled by Muᶜāwiya in Qinnasrīn which from then on was a *miṣr*."[9] The terms used by al-Ṭabari are *maṣṣarahā wa-jannadahā*, from *miṣr* and *jund*.[10] The combination of these terms suggests that the creation of a separate military district (*jund*) north of Ḥimṣ was an administrative operation and distinct from the creation of a new urban entity (*miṣr*), necessarily residential in nature.[11]

Appropriation of the Land

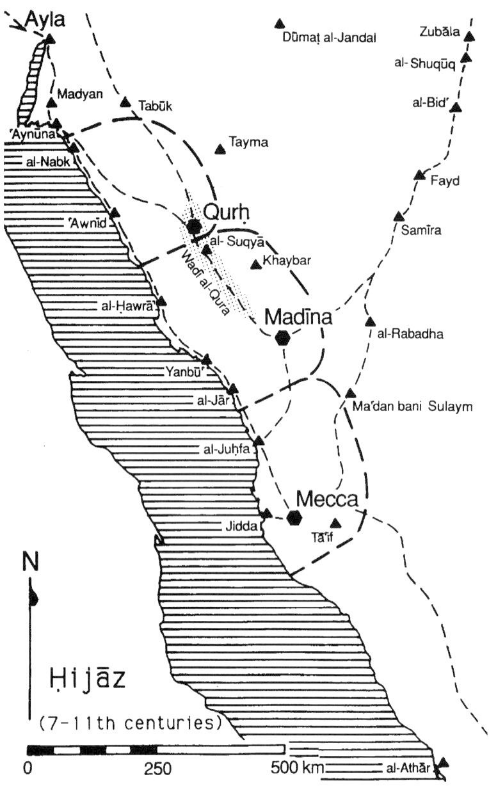

Figure 1.4. Administrative structure of the (according to Muqaddasi)

The phrase "appropriation of the land," used by Grabar in his pivotal study *The Formation of Islamic Art*, is a significant aspect of Ṣinnabra and the possible association with the Ghassanids.[12] Perhaps Humphreys misunderstands the enduring interaction with the Ḥijāz when he claims that Muᶜāwiya "not only cut his personal ties with his native Mecca but also the lingering ties of Islam's central government to its Arabian origins"; this identification was less problematic if one realizes that Muᶜāwiya (and others) did not cut personal ties with Mecca.[13] Rather it is clear that, according to al-Yaᶜqūbī, the Companions of the Prophet followed the example of ᶜUthmān, who amassed huge estates in Khaybar and Wādī al-Qurā in the Ḥijāz (fig. 1.4).[14] Indeed, one notes ᶜUmar purchased estates near Badr, perhaps to control the grain import from Egypt. The conqueror of Egypt and close associate of Muᶜāwiya, ᶜAmr b. al-ᶜĀṣ, held extensive estates between Beersheva and Hebron.[15]

[7] Fowden, "An Arab Building," p. 315.

[8] This connection is discussed in Shahid, "Ghassanid and Umayyad Structures."

[9] Athamina, "*Aᶜrāb* and *muhājirūn*." For the definition of *tamṣīr* as used recently by Kennedy, see below.

[10] Crone, "The First-Century Concept of *hiğra*," p. 360.

[11] Whitcomb, "Pastoral Peasantry," pp. 246–47.

[12] Grabar, *The Formation of Islamic Art*, pp. 43ff. As shown below, this appropriation was much more than "symbolic."

[13] Humphreys, *Muᶜawiya ibn Abi Sufyan*, p. 111.

[14] Millward, "Adaptation of Men."

[15] Lecker, "Estates of ᶜAmr b. al-ᶜĀṣ."

There are reports of Muʿāwiya b. Abī Sufyān owning ten farms in the vicinity of Mecca and Medina, as well as properties in the Wādī al-Qurā area.[16] Ghabban reports numerous palaces between al-Suqyā and Medina with Abbasid decoration and ceramics, a possible continuation of such estates.[17] The estate of al-ʿAlwīya near Mecca might have been one of these; with structures bearing similarities to Khirbat al-Mafjar (fig. 1.5).[18] Thus in both literature and archaeology evidence abounds for intense development of the Ḥijāz from the late seventh century onward.[19] The palace of al-ʿAlwīya might have been an elite residence not unlike the *quṣūr*, the so-called desert castles throughout Bilād al-Shām, of which Mafjar is counted as one.[20] These structures were the principal feature of early Islamic estates (*ḍiyāʿ*); they functioned as the center of agricultural enterprises and conceptually may be considered proto-urban establishments. Ḥijāzī agriculture developed in the early Islamic period with wealthy individuals making major investments, a practice extended into the conquered Middle East.[21]

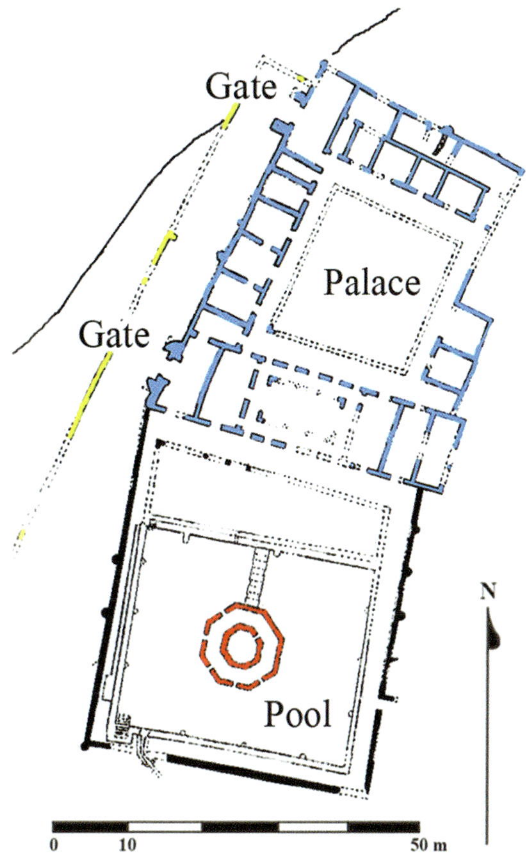

Figure 1.5. Plan of al-ʿAlwīya (plan by D. Whitcomb)

Recently al-Rāshid has reported an inscription of Muʿāwiya at Sadd al-Khanaq, a dam about 15 kilometers east of Medina on the road to the Maʿdin Banī Sulaym.[22] He places this structure in the context of other dams, such as another of Muʿāwiya near al-Ṭāʾif (fig. 1.6),[23] and notes that the caliph's interests in agriculture and estates are based on al-Samhūdī's accounts. In addition to dams, one must wonder about the use of *qanats*; these complex irrigation devices are often assumed to be much older (such as those at al-Mābiyāt);[24] but the extensive system in the Wādī ʿArabah behind Aqaba has now been carefully dated to the early Islamic period.[25]

[16] Heck, "'Arabia without Spices,'" p. 565.

[17] Ghabban, *Introduction à l'étude archéologique*, pp. 266–91 (written under the name Ali Ibrahim Hamed).

[18] Allen, "An ʿAbbāsid Fishpond Villa." Plans are found in al-Dayel and al-Helwa, "Preliminary Report," pp. 49, 60.

[19] Al-Ali, "Muslim Estates."

[20] For the most comprehensive, recent presentation of the early Islamic *quṣūr*, including many of his own discoveries, one must turn to Genequand, *Les établissements des élites.*

[21] Thus, Muʿāwiya purchased agricultural estates (*ḍiyāʿ*) "not in swampy Caesarea [... but in fertile lands, as] the low flat lands in the vicinity of Ascalon"; Whitcomb, "Qaysariya as an Early Islamic Settlement," pp. 65–82, 69–70.

[22] Al-Rāshid, "Sadd al-Khanaq."

[23] Miles, "Early Islamic Inscriptions," pl. 18A; and Grohmann, *Arabische Paläographie*, pp. 52–58.

[24] Nasif, "Qanats at al-ʿUlāʾ."

[25] Whitcomb, "Land behind Aqaba," p. 241.

Figure 1.6. First and second Kufic inscriptions on the dam of Muʿāwiyah (after Miles, "Early Islamic Inscriptions," pl. 18A)

Thus, the rise of a new, wealthy class in Medina in the seventh and eighth centuries led to irrigation and settlement in valleys by prominent families, and foremost the political leaders such as Muʿāwiya. Early disinclination toward urban markets (see below) yielded to strong commercial exchange in cosmopolitan places, such as Qurḥ or indeed the Ḥaramayn during the Ḥajj.

New Urbanism "Out of Arabia?"

The origins of urban settlements of southwestern Arabia are usually thought to be found in the classical cities of Bilād al-Shām. Mez suggested many years ago that the Arabian city should be considered a distinctive type;[26] it follows that Shabwa and Najrān might be considered urban structures most relevant to pre-Islamic experience, an important aspect of the post-conquest formation of Islam. Kennedy has recently suggested that each individual urban foundation should usually be considered "a classic piece of early Islamic speculative development,"[27] and thus the process of urban foundation (*tamṣīr*) in the early Islamic period must begin with the foundation of estates in the Ḥijāz.

The actions of Muʿāwiya and others at Mecca and Medina may indicate early aspects of this process. There are reports that "according to tradition, Muʿāwiya was the first who built in Mecca houses with baked bricks and gypsum mortar [...] He built the city into townships (*madāʾin*) and palaces (*quṣūr*). In addition, he dug wells, canals, planted gardens and orchards, and cultivated the land in Mecca."[28] These developments, whether exaggerated or not, suggest a pattern of urban development similar to the villas or estates in more rural settings. More specifically, the Dār al-Nadwa in Mecca was an old community council chamber, supposed to have been built by Quṣayy. This was purchased by Muʿāwiya and used as a caliphal residence during pilgrimages.

The restructuring of Medina seems to have begun under ʿUthmān b. ʿAffān, who reportedly pulled down all the *uṭum* (fortresses or tower-houses) that dominated the traditional settlement (fig. 1.7).[29] Southwest of the mosque was the Dār al-Qaḍāʾ, which originally belonged to ʿUmar. "Muʿāwiya bought it and made it a bureau and a treasury."[30] Near this structure was al-Ḥiṣn al-ʿAtīq, the governor's residence, and the police prefecture. This area was called al-Balāṭ, described by al-Ali as "the grand pavement 'Balāṭ Al A'dham'

---

[26] Mez, *Renaissance of Islam*, p. 412.

[27] Kennedy, "From Shahristan to Medina," p. 23.

[28] Kister, "Some Reports Concerning Mecca," pp. 84–89. Another example of transformative actions was the illumination of the Kaʿba with candles, perhaps influenced by example of Jerusalem; see Wheatley, *Places Where Men Pray Together*, p. 236.

[29] Lecker, *Muslims, Jews and Pagans*, pp. 12–13, 60.

[30] Later it was demolished and became an open space in front of the mosque (*raḥba*); al-Ali, "Studies in the Topography of Medina," fig. 3.11.

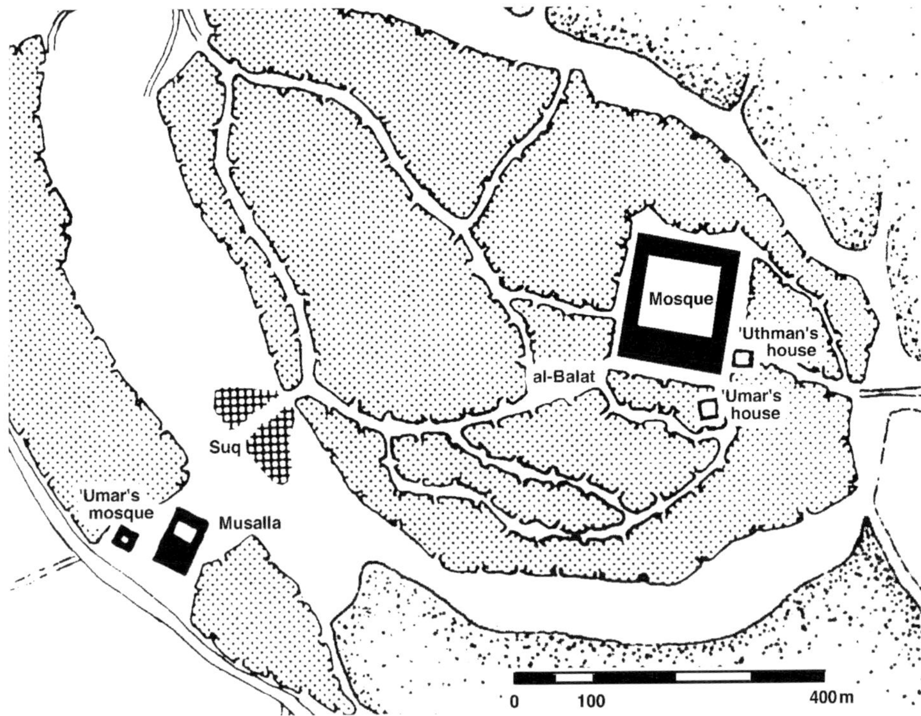

Figure 1.7. Plan early Islamic *madīna* (after AlSayyad, *Cities nad Caliphs*, fig. 3.11)

[al-aᶜẓam — D.W.] between the mosque and the *muṣallā*..."[31] Further, Muᶜāwiya built houses in the market and levied taxes, much to the chagrin of local traditionists.[32] These reports suggest his new structural organization as an attempt to make Medina the administrative center, first for all of Dār al-Islām in the earliest decades, and afterward for the central province of the Ḥijāz.

Muᶜāwiya's relationship with the Ḥaramayn and his Arabian background may have a psychological dimension. Humphreys makes note of his "great passion for the folklore and poetry of ancient Arabia";[33] he elaborates this by mentioning ᶜUbayd (or ᶜAbīd) b. Sharya al-Jurhumī (d. 686), who may have been commissioned "to compile a book on the history and antiquities of Yemen" by Muᶜāwiya.[34] One naturally must wonder whether these interests went beyond the poetics and included references to buildings and accomplishments in pre-Islamic Arabia. In her study of these traditions, Soucek mentions the alleged conversation between Muᶜāwiya and Wahb b. Munabbih about Solomon's throne "in consonance with both Muᶜāwiya's documented interest in legends [... and] the practical administration of justice."[35] Likewise, Muᶜāwiya's interaction with Kaᶜb al-Aḥbār in Ḥimṣ warrants attention in regard to the collection of traditions on antiquities.[36]

---

31 Ibid., p. 80.

32 Kister, "Market of the Prophet," p. 275; also Chalmeta, "Markets," p. 110.

33 Humphreys, *Muᶜawiya ibn Abi Sufyan*, p. 9.

34 Ibid., p. 129. See also Faris, *Antiquities of South Arabia*, pp. 2–3, 99; and Khoury, "The Dome of the Rock, the Kaᶜba, and Ghumdān," p. 59.

35 Soucek, "Solomon's Throne/Solomon's Bath," pp. 113–14.

36 Whitcomb, "Pastoral Peasantry," pp. 248–49, n. 30.

Ultimately this *Isrāʾīliyyāt* lore from Yemen seems to refer back to the Ghumdān, the high building in Ṣanʿāʾ symbolizing royal power. As Khoury puts it, "Ghumdān is too important in Arab memory not to be incorporated into Islamic history. [...] Toward the end of Ubayd's book on ancient Arabian kingdoms, Muʿāwiya proclaims that Ḥimyar's rule had been removed and transferred, through the agency of the Prophet, to a new victorious dynasty. [...] The historical scene is primed for the construction of an Arab Umayyad monument that expresses these ideals."[37] In Khoury's fascinating analysis, the object of this cultural transfer was in Damascus with the construction of the Qubbat al-Khaḍrāʾ by Muʿāwiya.

Three Cities of Muʿāwiya

A. Damascus (Dimashq)

In his study of the image of Baghdad, Wendell notes that the al-Qubbat al-Khaḍrāʾ of Muʿāwiya was imitated by al-Manṣūr's dome, perhaps through the intermediate example of another "green dome" at Wāsiṭ. He further suggests that the dome might reflect a "lingering memory of the old tribal *qubba*, the domical red leathern tent,"[38] a tempting reflection of interests in pre-Islamic traditions. Nevertheless, the immediate prototype for the form is clearly in Byzantine architecture (perhaps from Caesarea, see below).[39] Bloom provides a detailed examination of this formal relationship.[40]

The urban structure of Damascus in the time of Muʿāwiya focused on the *temenos* of the ancient temple; this area seems to have been divided so that, upon entering through the southern wall of the *temenos*, Christians turned to the left toward the cathedral of Saint John, and Muslims turned right toward the *muṣallā* or mosque.[41] Flood has analyzed evidence to suggest that the Khaḍrāʾ was on the eastern side behind the *miḥrāb* of the Companions and south of a colonnade, estimated at 50 meters south of the *qibla* wall. This configuration makes a striking topographical parallel with the Hagia Sophia and Augustaion/Chalke complex of Constantinople.[42] He continues this analysis to suggest that Muʿāwiya beautified Damascus intending it to rival Constantinople.

The palace called al-Khaḍrāʾ may have been an older Byzantine palace rebuilt by Muʿāwiya while governor (and later purchased by ʿAbd al-Malik).[43] In addition to having direct access to the mosque, al-Khaḍrāʾ formed an administrative complex with the Dār al-Khayl; the latter seems to have been located in the Ḥārat al-Balāṭa, where Saliby found inscribed mosaics (fig. 1.8).[44] The evidence for the Khaḍrāʾ assembled by Flood leads him to assume a structure more similar to Byzantine palace architecture than Umayyad desert residences (or Late Antique villas).[45] Finally he describes this area as the Ḥārat al-Qibāb, a complex of buildings likened to the Great Palace in Constantinople or those south of the

---

[37] Khoury, "The Dome of the Rock, the Kaʿba, and Ghumdān," p. 62.

[38] Wendell, "Baghdad," p. 120.

[39] Ibid., p. 118.

[40] Bloom, "'Qubbat al-Khaḍrāʾ,'" p. 135.

[41] Flood, *Great Mosque of Damascus*, pp. 122–23; Creswell, *Early Muslim Architecture*, vol. 1, pt. 1, pp. 185–96.

[42] Flood, *Great Mosque of Damascus*, pp. 165–67, fig. 80.

[43] Ibid., p. 147; Elisséeff, *Description de Damas*, pp. 227–28.

[44] Saliby, "Un palais byzantino-omeyyade à Damas." The *dār* in question was surely not "stables," but perhaps adorned with equestrian decorations.

[45] Flood, *Great Mosque of Damascus*, p. 147.

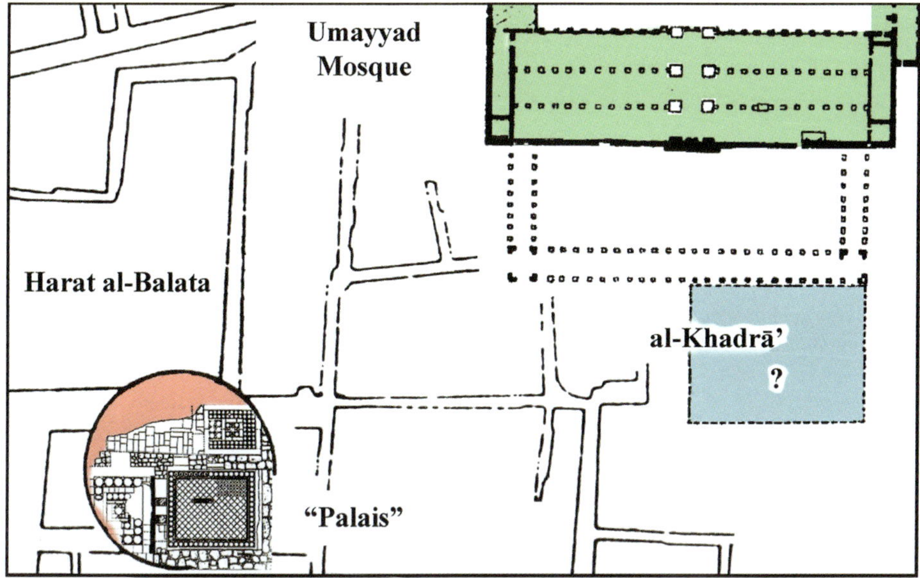

Figure 1.8. Plan of early Islamic Damascus (details after Saliby, "Un palais byzantino-omeyyade à Damas," and Flood, *Great Mosque of Damascus*)

Ḥaram al-Sharīf in Jerusalem (see below).[46] One may suggest that three buildings formed this administrative complex: the mosque, palace (*balāṭ*), and *dīwān*.[47]

B. Caesarea (Qayṣariyya)

Caesarea maritime, the capital of Palaestina Prima, was captured by Muʿāwiya b. Abī Sufyān around 640.[48] ʿUthmān b. ʿAffān appointed Muʿāwiya governor and ordered him to garrison the coastal towns. There remains some question as to whether Muʿāwiya might have followed Byzantine precedent and governed from this city, at least initially. This question belies a larger one: That the town was not destroyed during this conquest is generally accepted, but what did he find in this abandoned capital, and what changes did he make?

Al-Balādhurī relates that Muʿāwiya found a large number of Arabs living in Caesarea when he captured the city. This Ghassanid population seems to have been settled southeast of the Byzantine center and may have formed a *ḥāḍir* near the ancient hippodrome.[49] One further learns that Muʿāwiya imported a garrison of Persians when he became caliph; and one may surmise that they were installed in the former theater, made into a formidable *ḥiṣn* or fort (as it now appears). Thus, the earliest Islamic city was probably located south of and separate from the continuing urban center (fig. 1.9). This pattern would change radically under Abbasid and Fatimid rule, when the inner harbor was filled in and the *madīna* was replanned with a new mosque on the old Temple platform.

---

[46] Ibid., pp. 148–49, n. 47.

[47] Whitcomb, "Urban Structure," p. 20; see also Bacharach, "Administrative Complexes, Palaces, and Citadels," pp. 114–19.

[48] This was in A.H. 18–20, after a siege of seven years, according to Donner, *Early Islamic Conquests*, p. 153; or seven months, as in *EI*[2] s.v. "Ḳayṣariyya, Ḳayṣāriyya" (M. Sharon).

[49] Whitcomb, "Qaysariya as an Early Islamic Settlement," pp. 74–75.

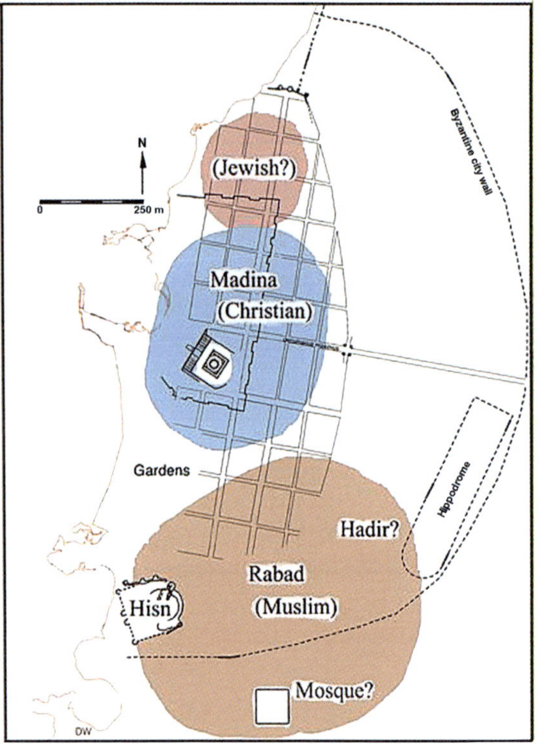

Figure 1.9. Plan of early Islamic Qayṣariyya (after Whitcomb, "Qaysariya as an Early Islamic Settlement")

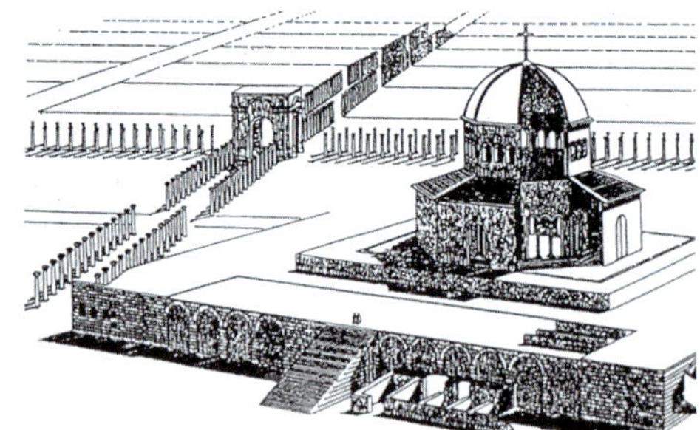

Figure 1.10. Comparative views of the Dome of the Rock (*above*) and the Temple Platform at Caesarea (*below*), after Whitcomb, "Jerusalem and the Beginnings of the Islamic City," fig. 4, and Holum, "The Temple Platform," fig. 13

Muʿāwiya may have seen there the *skrinion* (archives, tax office = *dīwān*) next to the governor's residence (*praetorium*) with a bath, a building complex serving as a model for the administrative complex.[50] Much more interesting is the great Octagonal Church on the Temple Platform. As Magness has shown, this structure dominated the skyline of Qayṣariyya well into the eighth century.[51] This building was a typical shrine of the Byzantine period, but the combination of structure and platform bears a close resemblance to the platform and Dome of the Rock (Qubbat al-Ṣakhra; fig. 1.10).[52] One may fairly ask whether this concept may have inspired Muʿāwiya to reproduce such a building on the platform of the Ḥaram al-Sharīf in Jerusalem, where he was "crowned" as caliph.[53]

C. Jerusalem (Īlyāʾ)

Rosen-Ayalon was perhaps the first archaeologist to show clearly the axial arrangement of the plan of the Ḥaram al-Sharīf, the alignment of the Dome of the Rock with the Aqṣā mosque. The axis continues as streets to the north, west (Bāb Miḥrāb Dāwūd), and south, between

[50] Whitcomb, "Urban Structure," pp. 20–21.

[51] Magness, "Pottery from Area V/4."

[52] Whitcomb, "Qaysariya as an Early Islamic Settlement," figs. 2.4 and 2.5, compared with Holum, "Temple Platform," fig. 13.

[53] Grabar, "Meaning of the Dome of the Rock"; and Blair, "Date of the Dome of the Rock."

two of the buildings south of the platform.[54] At the very least, a conceptual matrix would seem to underlie this development in the early Islamic period. Elad has assembled references to Muʿāwiya and the Aqṣā mosque and suggests an Umayyad intention to develop Jerusalem into both "a political and religious center." Further, he suggests that this process began with Muʿāwiya and ended with Sulaymān (and his transfer of the capital to al-Ramla).[55] Goitein seems to have been the first to suggest that Muʿāwiya, with his special interest in Jerusalem, was the originator of the Dome of the Rock.[56] Grabar also advanced this argument in 1990, that this organization "is not from ʿAbd al-Malik's time, but from Muʿāwiya's" (and subsequently brought to completion in 692).[57]

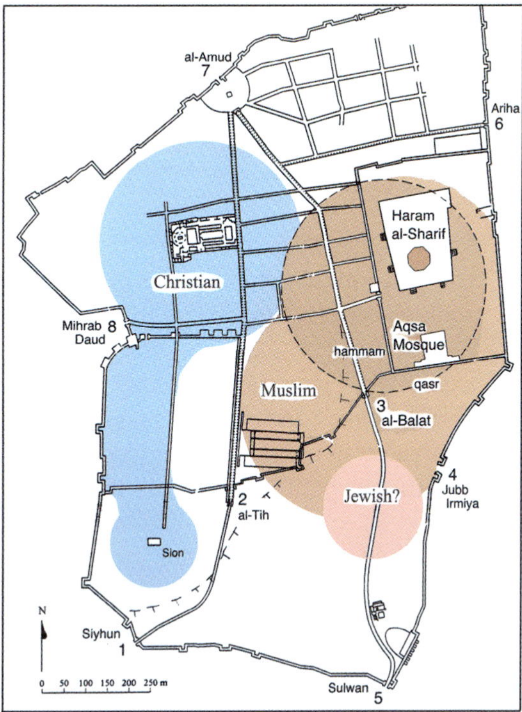

Figure 1.11. Plan of early Islamic Jerusalem (after Whitcomb, "Jerusalem and the Beginnings of the Islamic City")

Islamic occupation of Jerusalem would seem to have been focused on the Ḥaram al-Sharīf and the Bāb al-Balāṭ to the south; this would leave the Christian community in the western city focused on the Church of the Holy Sepulchre with an extension south to the Sion church. This development of Jerusalem becomes clear from the listing of its gates by al-Muqaddasī (some 300+ years later). He gives five gates in the south, then one on the east, one on the north, and one on the west, strongly indicating a predominance of Islamic occupation in the south. There are two gates on the inner wall of the south, the Bāb al-Tīh (perhaps for the Nea church) and the Bāb al-Balāṭ. This last term is most important for Jerusalem, perhaps from a local meaning or, in light of use of the term in other cities, a generic usage for an Islamic city (fig. 1.11).[58]

The excavations by Ben-Dov and Mazar, as well as earlier soundings under Kenyon,[59] revealed a series of large multi-story buildings south of the Ḥaram. The foundation is difficult to determine, though the involvement of Muʿāwiya has often been suggested.[60] The structure called Building II has been suggested as the *dār al-imāra*, accessed by a bridge from the Aqṣā mosque. Another building slightly to the north was a large bath, though very poorly

---

[54] This nodal centrality would fit well with the idea of an ompholos of the universe, and cosmological order of a ritual city as discussed by Wheatley, *Places Where Men Pray Together*, pp. 92–94, 295–98.

[55] Elad, *Medieval Jerusalem*, p. 160.

[56] Goitein, "Jerusalem."

[57] Grabar, "Meaning of the Dome of the Rock," pp. 156f.

[58] Al-Muqaddasī gives three names for Jerusalem: al-Quds, Īliyāʾ, and al-Balāṭ; al-Muqaddasī, *Aḥsan al-taqāsīm*, trans. Collins, p. 30. See interpretation in Whitcomb, "Jerusalem and the Beginnings of the Islamic City."

[59] Prag, *Excavations*, pp. 101–241.

[60] Hoyland, *Seeing Islam as Others Saw It*, pp. 222–23; Flood, *Great Mosque of Damascus*, p. 14; Whitcomb, "Urban Structure," pp. 19–20.

preserved (or at least reported). The third building should logically be the *balāṭ*, proximate to the Bāb al-Balāṭ and on analogy with other Umayyad urban settings. It may have held the offices of the *dīwān*.

A Matter of Organization

This last identification is admittedly highly speculative, but the general pattern indicates a concern with the organization of urban situations. An important restructuring of buildings took place under Muʿāwiya in Baṣra. Ziyād b. Abīhi (665–675) expanded the mosque and moved the *dār al-imāra* from the northeast to the *qibla* (southwest) side of the mosque.[61] The expansion of mosques at Iṣṭakhr,[62] Kūfa, and Baṣra has been interpreted as a tendency toward embellishment and even monumentalization well before that of al-Walīd I (705–715). The role of Ziyād may indicate a persistence of Sasanian influence in buildings and in bureaucracy. Whether or not the *balāṭ* housed the *dīwān*, it would seem that the growth of records must have been enormous. Two *dīwāns* are usually attributed to Muʿāwiya, the chancellery (*dīwān al-khātam*) and postal service (*barīd*).[63]

From the general to the more specific, a surprising number of architectural elements have been attributed to Muʿāwiya. The dome as represented in the influential Qubbat al-Khaḍrāʾ has been discussed and may also include the Qubbat al-Ṣakhra.[64] The minaret may also find its origin in Damascus, where corner towers may have led to the *sawamis* in Fusṭāṭ.[65] Within the mosque both the *maqṣūra* and *miḥrāb* have been attributed to Muʿāwiya.[66] Likewise the elevation of the Prophet's seat as a *minbar* has a tendentious but perhaps confluent history.[67] As with any corpus of reports (or narratives), one might question each report but the summary situation remains one of precedent-setting innovation, or more likely original adaptations.

Historians may be more susceptible to artifacts that contain writing, which may explain the appeal of numismatics. In Johns' eloquent summary, "Muʿāwiya [...] stands out in the archaeological record as the first Muslim ruler whose name appears on coins" (fig. 1.12).[68] This would seem a notable point in the evolution of an Islamic currency; if it were a direction toward establishment of a monarchy, the precedent did not seem to affect later caliphs, especially ʿAbd al-Malik, who adapted figural images (before "converting" to an epigraphic style). Foss has made a notable contribution to the problem of post-conquest currency by positing an earlier production under Muʿāwiya. This began with a tentative suggestion that certain coins with the image of Constans II (641–668) with bilingual inscriptions may have been issued by Muʿāwiya.[69] He has more recently refined this suggestion with a comprehensive examination of the *fals* (copper coinage). He suggests that Byzantine

---

[61] Creswell, *Early Muslim Architecture*, p. 22; the ramifications of this axial arrangement are studied in Bacharach, "Administrative Complexes, Palaces, and Citadels," p. 115.

[62] The example of Iṣṭakhr is discussed in Whitcomb, "City of Istakhr."

[63] Silverstein, *Postal Systems*.

[64] Rabbat, "The Meaning of the Umayyad Dome of the Rock."

[65] Bloom, *Minaret*, p. 29 n. 40; see also Grafman and Rosen-Ayalon, "Two Great Syrian Umayyad Mosques," p. 11.

[66] For the latter, see Whelan, "Origins of the *miḥrāb mujawwaf*," p. 60.

[67] Bloom, *Minaret*, p. 49; see also Sauvaget, *La mosquée omeyyade de Médine*, pp. 85ff.

[68] Johns, "Archaeology and the History of Early Islam," pp. 418–19, with specific references.

[69] Foss, "Syrian Coinage."

Figure 1.12. Coin of Muʿāwiya, Darabjird mint, A.H. 52–54 (672 C.E.). S. Album collection

specie continued to be imported until 658, with Arab-Byzantine imitative and derivative types including the first bilingual inscriptions.[70] This extremely complicated series of coins is described as the Bilingual series, or Umayyad Imperial Image coins.[71] In this analysis the main mints are Damascus, Baʿlabakk, and Ḥimṣ (Homs); the abundance of the latter mint production may be explained by its role as a military camp.[72] The Ḥimṣ issue (cat. no. 75) may be taken as similar to the Dārābjird dirham (above) as a conventional image with Arabic additions; the coinage emphasizes continuity (or the familiar), but with clear indications of new organization and is thus a stage in administrative development.

Foss concludes that "the Islamic government was already highly organized and bureaucratic under the great leader Muʿāwiya (661–680)."[73] What he did not emphasize was the evidence implied in landscape and especially in cities during this first forty years; that is, the attention to the urban system in the Ḥijāz, in Bilād al-Shām, and in the east was, as Wheatley might have expressed it, the organizing principle for the Islamic state.[74]

Conclusions

The question of early Islamic state formation has often devolved into the roles of Muʿāwiya and ʿAbd al-Malik. Robinson makes an important point in that ʿAbd al-Malik made this state explicitly Islamic, with strong evidence in coins and other lines of evidence.[75] On the contrary, Muʿāwiya does not appear in the same light; he seems to have been more Believer than Muslim.[76] His political role was to coordinate a population of Christians and Jews as well as Muslims and indeed might be styled the last true *amīr al-muʾminīn.*

An "archaeology of Muʿāwiya" reveals the dynamics of this transitional phase, the process of formation is revealed in the structure of the mosque, *dār al-imāra*, and urban foundations. These are material structures that may parallel characteristics of social organization in this changing culture. In sum, the larger question is whether archaeology can contribute directly to matters of ideology, and indeed, identify believers. This may be approached from the perspective of an innovative individual, the key to a transitional phase defining the Islamic polity.

---

[70] Foss, *Arab-Byzantine Coins*, pp. 20–36.

[71] Ibid., p. 40.

[72] Kennedy, *Armies of the Caliphs*.

[73] Foss, "Syrian Coinage," p. 353.

[74] Muʿāwiya initiated the transformation into "a vibrant urban hierarchy supporting the pyramidal political structure of the Umayyads and nurturing the culture, religious, intellectual, and economic dimensions of their kingdom"; Wheatley, *Places Where Men Pray Together*, p. 329.

[75] Robinson, *ʿAbd al-Malik*, esp. 49ff. A strong case is also made for development of a full state apparatus by Muʿāwiya in Foss, "Muʿāwiya's State," pp. 91–94.

[76] See the extensive discussion of Donner, *Muhammad and the Believers*, esp. pp. 170ff.

Bibliography

al-Ali, Saleh A. "Muslim Estates in Hidjaz in the First Century A.H." *Journal of the Economic and Social History of the Orient* 2 (1959): 247–61.

———. "Studies in the Topography of Medina (during the 1st Century A.H.)." *Islamic Culture* 35 (1961): 65–92.

Allen, Terry. "An ʿAbbāsid Fishpond Villa near Makkah." Sonic.net. Occidental: Solipsist, 2009. Accessed July 14, 2015. sonic.net/~tallen/palmtree/fishpond/fishpond.htm.

AlSayyad, Nezar. *Cities and Caliphs: On the Genesis of Arab Muslim Urbanism.* New York: Greenwood, 1991.

Athamina, Khalil. "*Aʿrāb* and *muhājirūn* in the Environment of the *amṣār*." *Studia Islamica* 66 (1987): 5–25.

Bacharach, Jere L. "Administrative Complexes, Palaces, and Citadels: Changes in the Loci of Medieval Muslim Rule." In *The Ottoman City and Its Parts: Urban Structure and Social Order*, edited by Irene A. Bierman, Rifa'at A. Abou-El-Haj, and Donald Preziosi, pp. 105–22. Subsidia Balcanica, Islamica et Turcica 3. New Rochelle: A. D. Caratzas, 1991.

Bienkowski, Piotr, and Katharina Galor, editors. *Crossing the Rift: Resources, Routes, Settlement Patterns and Interaction in the Wadi Arabah.* Levant, Supplementary Series 3. Oxford: Council for British Research in the Levant, 2006.

Blair, Sheila. "What Is the Date of the Dome of the Rock?" In *Bayt al-Maqdis: ʿAbd al-Malik's Jerusalem*, edited by Julian Raby and Jeremy Johns, pp. 59–87. Oxford: Oxford University Press, 1992.

Bloom, Jonathan M. *Minaret: Symbol of Islam.* Oxford: Oxford University Press, 1989.

———. "The 'Qubbat al-Khaḍrāʾ' and the Iconography of Height in Early Islamic Architecture." *Ars Orientalis* 23 (1993): 135–41.

Canivet, Pierre, and Jean-Paul Rey-Coquais, editors. *La Syrie de Byzance à l'Islam, VIIe–VIIIe siècle.* Damascus: Institut Français de Damas, 1992.

Chalmeta, Pedro. "Markets." In *The Islamic City*, edited by Robert B. Serjeant, pp. 104–13. Paris: UNESCO, 1980.

Creswell, Keppel A. C. *Early Muslim Architecture: Umayyads, Early Abbasids and Tulunids.* 2 vols. Oxford: Oxford University, 1932, 1940 (2nd ed. 1969).

Crone, Patricia. "The First-Century Concept of *hiǧra*." *Arabica* 41 (1994): 352–87.

Cytryn-Silverman, Katia. "The Umayyad Mosque of Tiberias." *Muqarnas* 26 (2009): 37–61.

al-Dayel, Khalid, and Salah al-Helwa. "Preliminary Report on the Second Phase of the Darb Zubayda Reconnaissance 1397/1977." *Atlal* 2 (1978): 51–64.

Donner, Fred M. *The Early Islamic Conquests.* Princeton: Princeton University Press, 1981.

———. *Muhammad and the Believers: At the Origins of Islam.* Cambridge: Harvard University Press, 2010.

Elad, Amikam. *Medieval Jerusalem and Islamic Worship: Holy Places, Ceremonies, Pilgrimage.* Leiden: Brill, 1995.

Elisséeff, Nikita. *La description de Damas d'Ibn ʿAsākir (historien mort à Damas en 571/1176).* Damascus: Institut Français de Damas, 1959.

Faris, Nabih A. *The Antiquities of South Arabia.* Princeton: Princeton University, 1938.

Flood, Finbarr B. *The Great Mosque of Damascus: Studies on the Makings of an Umayyad Visual Culture.* Leiden: Brill, 2001.

Foss, Clive. "A Syrian Coinage of Muʿāwiya?" *Revue numismatique* 158 (2002): 353–65.

———. *Arab-Byzantine Coins: An Introduction, with a Catalogue of the Dumbarton Oaks Collection.* Washington, D.C.: Dumbarton Oaks Research Library and Collection, 2008.

———. "Muʿāwiya's State." In *Money, Power and Politics in Early Islamic Syria: A Review of Current Debates*, edited by John Haldon, pp. 75–96. Farnham: Ashgate, 2010.

Fowden, Elizabeth K. "An Arab Building at Rusafa-Sergiopolis." *Damaszener Mitteilungen* 12 (2008): 303–24.

Genequand, Denis. *Les établissements des élites omeyyades en Palmyrène et au Proche-Orient*. Beirut: Institut Français du Proche-Orient, 2012.

Ghabban, A. I. Hamed. *Introduction a l'étude archéologique des deux routes syrienne et égyptienne du pèlerinage au nord-ouest de l'Arabie Saoudite*. Marseille: Université de Provence, 1988. [written under the name Ali Ibrahim Hamed]

Goitein, Shlomo D. "Jerusalem in the Arab Period (638–1099)." In *The Jerusalem Cathedra*, edited by L. I. Levine, vol. 2, pp. 168–96. Detroit: Wayne State University, 1982.

Grabar, Oleg. *The Formation of Islamic Art*. New Haven: Yale University Press, 1987.

————. "The Meaning of the Dome of the Rock." In *Studies in Arab History: The Antonius Lectures, 1978-87*, edited by Derek Hopwood, pp. 151–63. New York: St. Martin's, 1990.

Grafman, R., and M. Rosen-Ayalon. "Two Great Syrian Umayyad Mosques: Jerusalem and Damascus." *Muqarnas* 16 (1999): 1–15.

Grohmann, Adolf. *Arabische Paläographie*, Part 2: *Das Schriftwesen; Die Lapidarschrift*. Vienna: Böhlau, 1971.

Hasson, Isaac. "Remarques sur l'inscription de l'époque de Muʿāwiya à Hamat Gader." *Israel Exploration Journal* 32 (1982): 97–101.

Heck, Gene W. "'Arabia without Spices': An Alternative Hypothesis." *Journal of the American Oriental Society* 123 (2003): 547–76.

Hirschfeld, Yizhar. *The Roman Baths of Hammat Gader: Final Report*. Jerusalem: Israel Exploration Society, 1997.

Holum, Kenneth G. "The Temple Platform: Progress Report on the Excavations." In *Caesarea Papers 2: Herod's Temple, the Provincial Governor's Praetorium, and Granaries, the Later Harbor, a Gold Coin Hoard, and Other Studies*, edited by Kenneth G. Holum, Avner Raban, and Joseph Patrich, pp. 13–34. Journal of Roman Archaeology, Supplement Series 35. Portsmouth: Journal of Roman Archaeology, 1999.

Hoyland, Robert G. *Seeing Islam as Others Saw It: A Survey and Evaluation of Christian, Jewish and Zoroastrian Writings on Early Islam*. Studies in Late Antiquity and Early Islam 13. Princeton: Darwin Press, 1997.

Humphreys, R. Stephen. *Muʿawiya ibn Abi Sufyan: From Arabia to Empire*. Makers of the Muslim World. Oxford: Oneworld, 2006.

Johns, Jeremy. "Archaeology and the History of Early Islam: The First Seventy Years." *Journal of the Economic and Social History of the Orient* 46 (2003): 411–36.

Kennedy, Hugh. *The Armies of the Caliphs: Military and Society in the Early Islamic State*. London: Routledge, 2001.

————. "From Shahristan to Medina." *Studia Islamica* 102–103 (2006): 5–34.

Khoury, Nuha N. N. "The Dome of the Rock, the Kaʿba, and Ghumdān: Arab Myths and Umayyad Monuments." *Muqarnas* 10 (1993): 57–65.

Kister, Meir J. "The Market of the Prophet." *Journal of the Economic and Social History of the Orient* 8 (1965): 272–76.

————. "Some Reports Concerning Mecca from Jahiliyya to Islam." *Journal of the Economic and Social History of the Orient* 15 (1972): 61–93.

Lecker, Michael. "The Estates of ʿAmr b. al-ʿĀṣ in Palestine: Notes on a New Negev Arabic Inscription." *Bulletin of the School of Oriental and African Studies* 52 (1989): 24–37.

Lecker, Michael. *Muslims, Jews and Pagans: Studies on Early Islamic Medina*. Leiden: Brill, 1995.

Magness, Jodi. "The Pottery from Area V/4 at Caesarea." *Annual of the American Schools of Oriental Research* 52 (1994): 133–45.

Makiya, Kanan. *The Rock: A Tale of Seventh-century Jerusalem*. London: Constable, 2001.

Mez, Adam. *The Renaissance of Islam*. London: Luzac, 1937.

Miles, George C. "Early Islamic Inscriptions near Ṭāʾif in the Ḥijāz." *Journal of Near Eastern Studies* 7 (1948): 236–42.

Millward, William G. "The Adaptation of Men to Their Time: An Historical Essay by al-Yaʿqūbī." *Journal of the American Oriental Society* 84 (1964): 329–44.

al-Muqaddasī, Muḥammad b. Aḥmad. *Aḥsan al-taqāsīm fī maʿrifat al-aqālīm.* Translated by Basil A. Collins, *The Best Divisions for Knowledge of the Regions.* 2nd ed. Reading: Garnet, 2001.

Nasif, Abdallah A. "Qanats at al-ʿUlāʾ." *Proceedings of the Seminar for Arabian Studies* 10 (1980): 75–77.

Prag, Kay. *Excavations by K. M. Kenyon in Jerusalem, 1961-1967,* Vol. 5: *Discoveries in Hellenistic to Ottoman Jerusalem Centenary Volume: Kathleen M. Kenyon 1906-1978.* Levant, Supplement Series 7. London: Oxbow Books, 2008.

Rabbat, Nasser. "The Meaning of the Umayyad Dome of the Rock." *Muqarnas* 6 (1989): 12–21.

al-Rāshid, Saad b. Abdulaziz. "Sadd al-Khanaq: An Early Umayyad Dam near Medina, Saudi Arabia." *Proceedings of the Seminar for Arabian Studies* 38 (2008): 265–75.

Robinson, Chase F. *ʿAbd al-Malik.* Oxford: Oneworld, 2005.

Saliby, Nassib. "Un palais byzantino-omeyyade à Damas." In *Les maisons dans la Syrie antique du IIIe millénaire aux débuts de l'Islam: Pratique et représentations de l'espace domestique*, edited by Corinne Castel, Michel al-Maqdissi, and François Villeneuve, pp. 191–94. Beirut: Institut Français d'Archéologie du Proche-Orient, 1997.

Sauvaget, Jean. *La mosquée omeyyade de Médine: Étude sur les origines architecturales de la mosquée et de la basilique.* Paris: Vanoest, 1947.

Shahid, Irfan. "Ghassanid and Umayyad Structures: A Case of *Byzance après Byzance.*" In *La Syrie de Byzance à l'Islam, VIIe-VIIIe siècle*, edited by P. Canivet and Jean-Paul Rey-Coquais, pp. 299–307. Damascus: Institut Français de Damas, 1992.

Sharon, Moshe. "Ḳayṣariyya, Ḳayṣāriyya." *Encyclopedia of Islam.* 2nd edition, pp. 841–42. Leiden: Brill, 1976.

Silverstein, Adam J. *Postal Systems in the Pre-modern Islamic World.* Cambridge: Cambridge University Press, 2007.

Soucek, Pricilla P. "Solomon's Throne/Solomon's Bath: Model or Metaphor?" *Ars Orientalis* 23 (1993): 109–34.

St. Laurent, Beatrice, and Isam Awwad. "The Marwani Musalla in Jerusalem: New Findings." *Jerusalem Quarterly* 54 (2013): 7–30.

Wendell, Charles. "Baghdad: *Imago Mundi* and other Foundation-lore." *International Journal of Middle East Studies* 2 (1971): 99–128.

Wheatley, Paul. *The Places Where Men Pray Together: Cities in Islamic Lands, Seventh through the Tenth Centuries.* Chicago: University of Chicago Press, 2001.

Whelan, Estelle. "The Origins of the *miḥrāb mujawwaf:* A Reinterpretation." *International Journal of Middle East Studies* 18 (1986): 205–23.

Whitcomb, Donald. "The City of Istakhr and the Marvdasht Plain." *Akten des VII. International Kongresses für Iranische Kunst und Archäologie,* pp. 363–70. Archäologische Mitteilungen aus Iran, Ergänzunsband 6. Berlin: n.p., 1979.

————. "Khirbet al-Karak Identified with Sinnabra." *Al-ʿUsur al-Wusta* 14/1 (2002): 1–6.

————. "Land behind Aqaba: The Wadi Arabah during the Early Islamic Period." In *Crossing the Rift: Resources, Routes, Settlement Patterns and Interaction in the Wadi Arabah*, edited by Piotr Bienkowski and Katharina Galor, pp. 239–42. Levant, Supplementary Series 3. Oxford: Council for British Research in the Levant, 2006.

————. "An Urban Structure for the Early Islamic City: An Archaeological Hypothesis." In *Cities in the Pre-modern Islamic World: The Urban Impact of Religion, State and Society*, edited by Amira K.

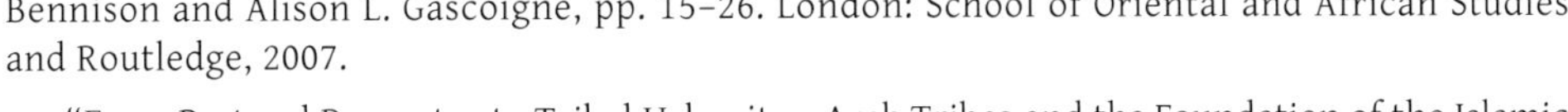

Bennison and Alison L. Gascoigne, pp. 15–26. London: School of Oriental and African Studies and Routledge, 2007.

———. "From Pastoral Peasantry to Tribal Urbanites: Arab Tribes and the Foundation of the Islamic State in Syria." In *Nomads, Tribes, and the State in the Ancient Near East: Cross-disciplinary Perspectives*, edited by Jeffrey Szuchman, pp. 241–59. Oriental Institute Seminars 5. Chicago: The Oriental Institute, 2009.

———. "Qaysariya as an Early Islamic Settlement." In *Shaping the Middle East: Jews, Christians, and Muslims in an Age of Transition*, edited by Kenneth G. Holum and Hayim Lapin, pp. 65–82. Bethesda: University of Maryland, 2011.

———. "Jerusalem and the Beginnings of the Islamic City." In *Unearthing Jerusalem: 150 Years of Archaeological Research in the Holy City*, edited by Katharina Galor and Gideon Avni, pp. 399–416. Winona Lake: Eisenbrauns, 2011.

al-Wohaibi, Abdullah. *The Northern Hijaz in the Writings of the Arab Geographers, 800–1150*. Beirut: al-Risalah, 1973.

2

The Manṣūr Family and Saint John of Damascus: Christians and Muslims in Umayyad Times

Sidney H. Griffith, The Catholic University of America

I. The Manṣūr Family

According to some accounts, when Damascus capitulated to the invading Muslims in September of the year 635 C.E., it was a local Christian and government official, Manṣūr ibn Sarjūn by name, who opened the city's Bāb al-Sharqī to the besieging Arab forces under Khālid ibn al-Walīd and received from him in return a writ of safety for the city and its inhabitants, their persons, and their goods. It was an event that later Christians remembered with chagrin. According to the Arabic *Annals* of the "Melkite" Christian historian Eutychios of Alexandria (877–940),[1] Manṣūr had been appointed a tax official (*ʿāmil al-kharāj*) in Damascus by the Byzantine emperor Maurice (582–602). During the Persian occupation (614–628), again according to Eutychios, Manṣūr had remitted the taxes collected during the occupation to the Persian authorities. When the Byzantine emperor Heraclius (610–641) came to Jerusalem in 630, he went on to Damascus and demanded restitution of these tax receipts from Manṣūr, "with blows and imprisonment," says Eutychios, in return for confirming Manṣūr in his office, a treatment that resulted in the latter becoming "angry at heart against Heraclius."[2] Manṣūr's anger reportedly later issued in his resistance to providing financial support for Heraclius' general Vahan in Syria in the campaign against the invading Arabs. Eutychios even says that Manṣūr instigated loud demonstrations in Damascus designed to frighten away Roman troops from the city.[3] In the end, as Eutychios records the events, Damascus was handed over to the Arabs with the connivance of Manṣūr, and it was this disaster that prompted Heraclius to utter his famous farewell to Syria. Eutychios wrote,

> When the people of Damascus had worn themselves out with the siege, the official, Manṣūr, went up to the Bāb al-Sharqī and spoke with Khālid ibn al-Walīd to the ef-

[1] Eutychios, *Annales*; see editions by Breydy; Cheïkho, Carra de Vaux, and Zayyat; and Pirone. A Latin translation by John Selden under the title *Contextio gemmarum* appears in Migne, ed., *Patrologia graeca*, vol. 111.

[2] Eutychios, *Annales*, ed. Breydy, CSCO 471, pp. 127–28 [Arabic]; CSCO 472, pp. 107–08 [German trans.]. See also the remarks in Kaegi, *Heraclius*, p. 231.

[3] Eutychios, *Annales*, ed. Breydy, CSCO 471, p. 135 [Arabic], CSCO 472, pp. 114–15 [German trans.]. See also the discussion of these matters in Kaegi, *Byzantium*, pp. 108–09, 120, 124–25.

fect that should he give him a writ of security for himself, for his family, and for the people of Damascus, for whoever was with him, except for the Romans, he would open the gates of Damascus. Khālid replied to what he asked and wrote the writ of security. Here is a copy of it: "This is a writ from Khālid ibn al-Walīd to the people of the city of Damascus: 'I hereby grant you security for your persons, your houses, your wealth, and your churches; they will neither be destroyed nor occupied.'" He handed the document over to him, and Manṣūr opened the Bāb al-Sharqī to Khālid. Khālid entered the city and he shouted to his companions, 'Sheathe your swords.' When Khālid's companions entered, they cried, *Allāh Akbar*! The battling Romans standing against the gates heard they cry and they knew that Manṣūr had opened the gate and let the Arabs into the city, so they left the gates and fled. [...] The Muslims kept on killing and taking prisoners. [...] The writ was publicly proclaimed by Manṣūr and Khālid announced to them the writ he had granted. [...] [After the reconciliation of differences among the Muslim leaders,] Manṣūr said to them, "Witness it right now." [...] Manṣūr then took possession of the writ. All of the Roman combatants who fled joined Heraclius in Antioch. When Heraclius heard that Damascus had been conquered, he said, "Farewell, Syria." [...] As for Manṣūr, due to the evil he had done, and what he had brought upon the Romans to the point of their being killed, all the patriarchs and bishops in the world anathematized him.[4]

So begins the story of the Christian Manṣūr family's association with the Muslims in Damascus at the very beginning of Muslim rule. As we shall see, members of the family reappear in Christian accounts of life in Damascus and in Jerusalem under the rule of the Umayyads (661–749 C.E.), extending even into Abbasid times. Sarjūn ibn Manṣūr al-Rūmī, as he was called in later Muslim sources, the son of the nemesis of Emperor Heraclius, served as a "secretary" (*kātib*) and an important official in the caliphal court up to and including sometime in the reign of ʿAbd al-Malik (685–705). But it was his son, Yuḥannā ibn Sarjūn ibn Manṣūr (d. ca. 749), who was destined to carry the family name into high repute in later Christian circles.[5] He became Saint John of Damascus, the composer of the first comprehensive summary of Christian thought in Greek and the theologian of record for the then burgeoning, Arabic-speaking, "Melkite" Christian community. He was at home in the world of Islam, and arguably he was also the first Christian thinker to seriously take account of Islam's challenge to Christianity. Two later descendants of Manṣūr would become patriarchs of Jerusalem under the Abbasids.

In all likelihood, given the evidence of their name, the Manṣūr family was of Aramaean, maybe even Arab, stock. It is notable that in his account given above of Manṣūr's delivery of Damascus to Khālid ibn al-Walīd and the invading Arabs, Eutychios of Alexandria clearly distinguishes the locals, including the Manṣūr family, from those whom he calls "the Romans" (*al-Rūm*), that is, the "Byzantines," albeit that his son would be known as "the Roman" (*al-Rūmī*) by the later Muslim chroniclers. Clearly, the Manṣūrs were an indigenous family whose members enjoyed a high civil status, both under Roman rule and under the Umayyads.

---

[4] Eutychios, *Annales*, ed. Breydy, CSCO 471, pp. 137–38 [Arabic], CSCO 472, pp. 116–17 [German trans.]. See the comments on this account in Lammens, "Études sur le règne du Calife Omaiyade Moʿawia Ier (troisième série)," pp. 250–57.

[5] It was doubtless due to his fame, and as a note of polemical chagrin, that later "Jacobite" chroniclers, writing in Syriac, confused John himself with his grandfather as the mediator between the Byzantines and the Arabs at the conquest of Damascus. In this connection, he was called "A known friend of the Ṭayyāyê"; *Chronicle of 1234*, ed. Chabot, CSCO 81, p. 248 [Syriac], and CSCO 109, p. 194 [English trans.].

The fact that they spoke and wrote Greek is no indication of Greek ancestry.[6] Rather, it was no doubt this very facility, their multilingualism and their bureaucratic experience, that made them useful to the early Umayyad caliphs in their formation of the early Islamic civil service. In all likelihood, the Manṣūr family's native language was Aramaic, along with a ready familiarity with Arabic, the language of the Arab tribes that had been dominant in the region for generations prior to the emergence of the Muslim Arabs, who would establish a new hegemony in a new political configuring of the Levant. Greek would have been the language of public affairs, and eventually of church life in Damascus, at least from the early third century C.E. onward, when the Severan emperors invested heavily in public works in the city, the metropolis of their newly declared Roman colony.[7]

According to the historian al-Yaʿqūbī, none of the caliphs before Muʿāwiya I (661–680) had employed Christians in their service.[8] Muʿāwiya is said to have inaugurated the practice, which would become a commonplace administrative arrangement among later caliphs and Muslim governors, reaching well into Abbasid times and beyond.[9] As in the case of Jews living under Muslim rule, such civil positions were not uncommon for other members of the subaltern populations as well. As for Muʿāwiya, among others, he is said to have appointed his ill-fated, Christian physician, an otherwise unknown man named Uthāl, to collect taxes in Homs, where he met his end at the hands of outraged Muslims,[10] and in Damascus Sarjūn ibn Manṣūr al-Rūmī served as the caliph's "secretary and master of affairs (*kātib* and *ṣāḥib amrhi*)";[11] his name appears with some regularity in accounts of scribal activity during Muʿāwiya's caliphate.[12] In general, Muʿāwiya was known for his politics of tolerance toward Christians.[13] There are even reports in Christian chronicles of Christians involved in doctrinal disputes with other Christians appealing to this caliph to intervene on their behalf, events that reportedly involved heavy payments on the part of the disputants on both sides.[14]

Sarjūn ibn Manṣūr came into particular favor during the lifetime of Muʿāwiya's son, Yazīd I (r. 680–683). Reports even speak of Sarjūn and the Christian court poet Akhṭal as Yazīd's table companions from his youth.[15] And the sources mention a number of events in caliphal history in this period in which Sarjūn is said to have been involved, reaching well into the reign of the caliph, ʿAbd al-Malik (685–705).[16] For example, the Syriac *Chronicle* of the "Jacobite" patriarch of Antioch, Michael the Syrian (1126–1199), reports that Sarjūn ibn Manṣūr, having been seduced by the teaching of Maximus the Confessor (ca. 580–662), a

[6] See Di Segni, "Greek Inscriptions."

[7] See *EI*² s.v. "Dimashḳ" (N. Elisséeff).

[8] See al-Yaʿqūbī, *Taʾrīkh*, vol. 2, p. 265.

[9] See Cheïkho, *Les vizirs et secrétaires* [Arabic]; See also Massignon, "La politique islamo-chrétienne," and Zaborowski, "Arab Christian Physicians."

[10] Al-Yaʿqūbī, *Taʾrīkh*, vol. 2, p. 265.

[11] Al-Ṭabarī, *Taʾrīkh*, vol. 2, p. 205.

[12] See, e.g., al-Masʿūdī, *Kitâb at-tanbîh*, pp. 302, 306–07, 312. In two places the epithet *al-naṣrānī* is appended to his name: pp. 307 and 312.

[13] See the remarks in Lammens, "Études sur le règne du Calife Omaiyade Moʿawia Ier," p. 3.

[14] See, e.g., the instances cited in Lammens, "Études sur le règne du Calife Omaiyade Moʿawia Ier (deuxième série)," pp. 143–44.

[15] In this regard, see in particular the studies of Henri Lammens: "Études sur le règne du Calife Omaiyade Moʿawia Ier (troisième série)," "Le califat de Yazid Ier," "Le chantre des Omiades." See also Suzanne Pinckney Stetkevych's chapter in this volume.

[16] See Cheïkho, *Les vizirs et secrétaires*, pp. 73–74. The Byzantine chronicler Theophanes the Confessor (ca. 760–815) reports that when ʿAbd al-Malik wanted to take some pillars away from the church at Gethsemane in Palestine to incorporate them into a building in Mecca, "Now Sergius, son of Mansour, a good Christian, who was treasurer and stood on close terms with Abimelech [i.e., ʿAbd al-Malik]," persuaded him against this course of action (Theophanes, *Chronicle*, p. 510).

doctrine adopted by the Council of Constantinople III (681 C.E.), as we shall see below, spread this teaching in Jerusalem, Antioch, and Edessa, where, says Michael, the Chalcedonians held sway from the time of the emperor Heraclius.[17] But at this point, as Henri Lammens has noted, it becomes difficult to distinguish between the activities of Sarjūn ibn Manṣūr and those of his son, Manṣūr ibn Sarjūn ibn Manṣūr, both of whom are said in the sources, both Christian and Muslim, to have served as secretary (*kātib*) to Caliph ʿAbd al-Malik.[18] Manṣūr ibn Sarjūn is the member of the family who would in due course come to be known as Saint John of Damascus;[19] it seems likely that he took the name John on becoming a monk in Jerusalem, as we shall see below.[20]

Of the subsequent members of the Manṣūr family, not much is known. There was John of Damascus' nephew, Stephen Manṣūr (d. ca. 807), a little-known writer and Hellenophile, probably a monk of Mar Saba.[21] According to the *Chronicle* of Theophanes the Confessor, in the year 734 C.E., during the reign of the caliph Hishām (724–743), for causes unknown, a certain Theodore son of Manṣūr was exiled to the desert.[22] The expanded *Annals* attributed to the "Melkite" historian, Eutychios of Alexandria,[23] mention two other members of the Manṣūr family who achieved high rank in the early Islamic period, but their preferment came much later, in Abbasid times, in service to the church in Jerusalem, and not, like their ancestors, as functionaries in the court of the Umayyad caliphs in Damascus. Of the first one, significantly named Sergios (*S-r-j-s*), the *Annals* say, "In the second year of the caliphate of al-Wāthiq (842–847) Sergios ibn Manṣūr, who had helped the Muslims to open up Damascus and who was cursed in the [four] corners of the world, was made patriarch of Jerusalem. He held office for sixteen years and died."[24] Many years later, again according to the *Annals*, in the tenth year of the caliphate of al-Muʿtamid (870–892), Īliyyā ibn Manṣūr, who had helped the Muslims to open up Damascus and was cursed in all the corners of the world, was made patriarch of Jerusalem. He held office for twenty-nine years and died."[25] It is interesting that neither Eutychios nor the expanded *Annals* make any mention of Saint John of Damascus! One can only speculate on the reason for this omission, but it stands out that Manṣūr's curse is mentioned three times in the *Annals*. And in Constantinople, as we shall see below, not only was John himself called "Saracen-minded" in the mid-eighth century, but in the course of the controversies over the veneration of the icons his enemies there seem to have delighted in calling him by his given name, Manṣūr, for polemical purposes.

II. Manṣūr ibn Sarjūn ibn Manṣūr: Saint John of Damascus

Although Saint John of Damascus was a native of Damascus, whose first career was in the civil service of the Umayyad caliphs in the city of his birth, his fame in the world of the Christians

---

[17] See Michael the Syrian, *Chronicle*, ed. and trans. Chabot, vol. 2, pp. 492–93.

[18] See Lammens, "Études sur le règne du Calife Omaiyade Moʿawia Ier (troisième série)," pp. 258–59.

[19] See Cheïkho, *Les vizirs et secrétaires*, p. 75.

[20] See Auzépy, "De la Palestine à Constantinople," p. 197.

[21] See Villa, "Stephen Manṣūr." Stories about him appear in the *Vita* of Stephen the Sabaite. See Lamoreux, ed. and trans., *The Life of Stephen of Mar Sabas*. See also Bartolomeo Pirone, "Continuità della Vita Monastica."

[22] Theophanes, *Chronicle*, p. 569.

[23] On the several recensions of the *Annales* of Eutychios, see Breydy, *Études sur Saʿīd ibn Baṭrīq*. See also Griffith, "Apologetics and Historiography."

[24] Eutychios, *Annales*, eds. Cheïkho, Carra de Vaux, and Zayyat, pp. 61–62.

[25] Ibid., p. 69.

unfolded in Jerusalem. In his day Jerusalem had already begun its journey to become after his lifetime the center of Arab Orthodox Christianity.[26] And, along with Damascus, in John's day the Holy City also became the focus of the Umayyad program to claim the public space and the civil institutions of the conquered Levant for Islam.[27]

What we know of John's biography, beyond what can be surmised from his surviving written work, comes largely from the hagiographical traditions that emerged long after his death, when his fame was at its zenith and his works were being copied and spread far and wide in the Greek-speaking world of Byzantium far outside the bounds of the World of Islam where he actually lived and wrote.[28] Perhaps for this reason the study of the Damascene's life and works has for the most part been undertaken almost entirely from the perspective of the history of Constantinople and the development of medieval Byzantine theology. It is as if he wrote primarily for an audience in the Byzantine capital, ignoring altogether or paying only lip service to the intellectual horizons and pastoral concerns of his own time and place.[29] By way of contrast, the present concern is precisely to highlight the pivotal role of Saint John of Damascus' life and work in shaping Christian thought and practice in those communities in Syria/Palestine in Umayyad times that helped formulate the "Greek Orthodoxy" that would by early Abbasid times have become the "Arab Orthodoxy" of the "Melkite" Christians living in the Islamic world.[30]

It was at some point in the reign of Patriarch John V of Jerusalem (705–735), who was the hierarch who consolidated ecclesiastical affairs in Jerusalem after the disruptions and vacancies caused by the Islamic conquest just over sixty years earlier, that John Manṣūr ibn Sarjūn left his civil servant career in Damascus to come to Jerusalem and enter the ecclesiastical life.[31] The common opinion is that the move could well have coincided with the beginning of the reign of the caliph al-Walīd (705–715), for there is no mention in the sources of significant activities on the part of members of the Manṣūr family at the Umayyad court in Damascus after the time of ʿAbd al-Malik,[32] except for the aforementioned exile in the reign of Caliph Hishām, of the otherwise unknown Theodore son of Manṣūr.[33] Caliph al-Walīd was the Umayyad caliph who reportedly effected the change from Greek to Arabic in the chancery

[26] See Griffith, "The Church of Jerusalem and the 'Melkites.'"

[27] See Griffith, "Images, Islam and Christian Icons."

[28] For the traditional account, see Jugie, "La vie de saint Jean Damascène"; Nasrallah, *Saint Jean de Damas*. The earliest extant Arabic account of John's life comes from the eleventh century. See Portillo, "The Arabic Life of St. John of Damascus." See also Flusin, "Une vie de saint Jean Damascène." For recent reassessments of the biography, see Le Coz, *Jean Damascène*; Kazhdan, "John Damaskenos." See also the very useful survey in Auzépy, "De la Palestine à Constantinople"; Kontouma-Conticello, "Jean III d'Antioche." For an authoritative account of John's theological thought, see Louth, *St. John Damascene*.

[29] See, e.g., the remarks of Louth, "Palestine under the Arabs"; idem, "The Making of the Byzantine Theological Synthesis."

[30] See works by Griffith: "Byzantium and the Christians in the World of Islam"; "'Melkites', 'Jacobites' and the Christological Controversies"; "The Life of Theodore of Edessa"; "John of Damascus and the Church in Syria."

[31] On the relationship between Patriarch John V and John of Damascus and its problems, see the important remarks of Auzépy, "De la Palestine à Constantinople," p. 198 n. 113.

[32] According to a notice reported from the Muslim historian and biographer of the notable personalities of Damascus Ibn ʿAsākir (d. 1177), the caliph ʿAbd al-Malik, in an effort to promote the use of Arabic in the *dīwān*, had replaced Sarjūn ibn Manṣūr with a man called Sulaymān ibn Saʿīd; see Auzépy, "De la Palestine à Constantinople," p. 200 n. 128.

[33] Portillo, "The Arabic Life of St. John of Damascus," p. 164; Kontouma-Conticello, "Vie de Jean Damascène," pp. 11–30; idem, "Jean Damascène."

(*al-diwān*) of the caliphate[34] and undertook the construction of the Umayyad mosque on the site of the church of Saint John the Baptist in Damascus.[35] It is interesting to note in passing that the reigns of Caliph al-Walīd I and Patriarch John V began in the same year, 705 C.E. Alternatively, a number of scholars have thought it more reasonable, both chronologically, historically, and in view of evolving Umayyad governmental policy, to date John Manṣūr's career move from Damascus to Jerusalem in the reign of Caliph ʿUmar II (717–720), citing this caliph's strong support for both the promotion of Islam in government service and the regulation of the public conduct of non-Muslims in the Muslim polity.[36] Interestingly, this caliph is remembered even in Christian, mostly Syriac sources both for his even-handed justice toward Muslims and non-Muslims alike,[37] as well as for his discriminatory regulation of Christian life in the caliphate.[38] The Arab Christian literary tradition also preserves an apologetic composition in Arabic featuring an alleged exchange of letters between the caliph ʿUmar b. ʿAbd al-ʿAzīz and the Byzantine emperor Leo III (717–741), in which the emperor responds to the caliph's summons to Islam with a reasoned defense of the claims of Christianity to be

[34] "Walīd, the king of the *Ṭayyāyê*, ordered that in his chancery, i.e., the treasury, which these *Ṭayyāyê* call the *dīwān*, one should not write in Greek but in the Arabic language, because up to that time the ledgers of the kings of the *Ṭayyāyê* were in Greek"; *Chronicle of 1234*, ed. Chabot, CSCO 81, pp. 298–99. ʿAbd al-Malik was responsible for the Arabization of the administration according to other sources; see in particular the discussion of al-Qāḍī, "The Names of Estates."

[35] "Al-Walīd wanted to build the mosque, which is [now] in Damascus. So he summoned the Christians and said to them, 'We want to extend your church into our mosque, this church of Mār John. It is an exceedingly beautiful church; there is none like it in the land of Syria. We will give you enough money to build [another] church like it wherever you want. If you want, we will give you the price of it.' He offered them forty thousand dinars. They refused and said, 'We have protection (*dhimmah*),' and they produced Khālid ibn al-Walīd's writ. Al-Walīd got angry at that. He undertook to cut away wood and bricks with his own hands and the people with him got into the demolition. He extended the mosque on the east side, and the whole enclosed space of their church remains *ʿalā hādhā*"; Eutychios, *Annales*, ed. Cheïkho, Carra de Vaux, and Zayyat, p. 42.

[36] This view is supported most recently by Le Coz, *Jean Damascène*, pp. 54–55.

[37] See, e.g., the report in the *Annales* attributed to Eutychios of Alexandria regarding ʿUmar II's settlement of a dispute between Christians and Muslims over an expropriated church in Damascus. "The Christians presented to ʿUmar b. ʿAbd al-ʿAzīz the pact they had received regarding their churches, that they would neither be destroyed nor occupied. They brought the writ of Khālid ibn al-Walīd, and ʿUmar b. ʿAbd al-ʿAzīz granted them forty thousand *dīnārs* and asked them to take the money, to leave the church, and to build a church in exchange for it in whatever place they wanted in Damascus, but they refused it. So he settled their suit to the effect that their church should be made over to them and they would restore it. The matter became a major issue for the Muslims and they said, 'Should we hand over our mosque to them after we have given the call to prayer in it, prayed and raised our prayer to God, so that it be destroyed and be made a church again?' Abū Idrīs al-Ḥulwānī said, 'The Christians have a pact only in half the city of Damascus, for the churches they have there. As for the other half of the city, it was opened by the sword. Therefore the churches and monasteries of the al-Ghūṭah suburb of Damascus belong to the Muslims because they were taken by the sword. So if the Christians would be pleased for us to return this church of theirs to them, we will return it to them on the condition that we will pull down every church in half of the city of Damascus and every church and monastery outside of the city in al-Ghūṭah. But if they leave this church to us, we will give them all that.' That was because the Muslims had settled in the churches of al-Ghūṭah and the monastery of Marwān and had occupied them. The Christians were afraid that the churches and monasteries would be pulled down, so they left them the church. But ʿUmar b. ʿAbd al-ʿAzīz signed a rescript for them that they might rest assured about their churches that were in Damascus and the churches and monasteries that were outside Damascus in al-Ghūṭah, that they would neither be destroyed nor occupied, and no Muslim would have any authority over them. And he gave his witness in their behalf in that matter"; Eutychios, *Annales*, ed. Cheïkho, Carra de Vaux, and Zayyat, pp. 43–44.

[38] See Borrut, "Entre tradition et histoire."

the true religion.[39] Given the record of this caliph's policies, it is not unreasonable to suppose that they could have provided the opportunity for John Manṣūr's move from Damascus to Jerusalem, if it was the case that his caliphal service had in fact lasted so long.

Hagiographical tradition says that John of Damascus became a monk of Mar Saba monastery in the Judean desert, but recent scholarship has called that long-held assumption into question, suggesting that having been ordained a priest by Patriarch John V, the socially high-placed John Damascene remained in the bishop's service, among the so-called *spoudaioi*, the ever vigilant and studious monks of the Church of the Anastasis in Jerusalem.[40] However this might have been, and the suggestion is based largely on the negative evidence of his name not being mentioned by other Sabaite writers, not appearing among the early notices of the heroes of Mar Saba monastery, and the lack of any mention of the monastery in his own writings, John of Damascus did spend the rest of his life in the patriarchate of Jerusalem, composing both philosophical and theological tracts, writing religious poetry and hymnody in Greek to meet the needs of the local church, for whom Greek was still the language of liturgy and scholarship;[41] the ecclesiastical shift from Greek and the local Christian Palestinian Aramaic to Arabic did not take place until after John's lifetime.[42] It took a century and more for John's reputation to be repaired in Constantinople and for his works to attain popularity in Byzantium, but by the eleventh century "John's role as the pre-eminent representative of the Byzantine theological tradition had become evident, and in the twelfth century and thereafter it made itself felt in the West."[43] But in the mid-eighth century in Constantinople and for some time thereafter, he was still being characterized as stubbornly "Saracen-minded."[44]

It is striking how readily the topical profile of John of Damascus' works corresponds both sociologically and theologically with the church-defining concerns of the Christian communities in Syria/Palestine during the time of his sojourn in Jerusalem. In particular, the refutation of Mesallians, Monotheletes, Jacobites, Nestorians, and Manichees, all active in his immediate milieu, pressingly concerned him. Nowhere else in the world of Chalcedonian Orthodoxy at the time was the press of these challenges, in the ensemble and in just this particular topical array, so acutely a problem. Even his signature topic as far as many modern scholars are concerned, the theology of the holy icons, had a local as well as a broader frame of reference, as we shall see.[45] There seems to have been a special urgency, both definitively and summarily on John's part, to present systematically coherent resolutions to these issues in a hostile environment, largely in terms borrowed from what he himself consistently represented as the teaching of the fathers of the church. In fact, John of Damascus often

[39] See the description and bibliography in Swanson, "The Arabic Letter of Leo III to ʿUmar II." See also Greenwood, "The Letter of Leo III in Ghewond."

[40] See Auzépy, "De la Palestine à Constantinople," pp. 202; idem, "Les Sabaïtes et l'iconoclasme," esp. p. 305; Kontouma-Conticello, "Vie de Jean Damascène," p. 29.

[41] See the references to the bibliographies of the works of John of Damascus and their editions in Kazhdan, "John Damaskenos." See also Geerard, ed., *Clavis Patrum Graecorum*, vol. 3, pp. 511–36, suppl., pp. 462–68. The critical edition of John's works is Kotter, *Die Schriften des Johannes von Damaskos.*

[42] See Griffith, "The Monks of Palestine" and "From Aramaic to Arabic."

[43] Louth, *St. John Damascene,* p. 16.

[44] See the text cited from the proceedings of the iconoclast council of 754 in the *Acta* of the seventh ecumenical council, Nicea II, 784, in Sahas, *Icon and Logos,* p. 168.

[45] See the extended discussion of the relevance of the works and concerns of John of Damascus to his immediate Syro/Palestinian milieu rather than to any Constantinopolitan theological agenda in Griffith, "'Melkites', 'Jacobites' and the Christological Controversies," pp. 19–38.

seems to have been more of a compiler than an original author, so much so that the epithet "plagiarist" in the modern sense of the word has even been suggested.[46] Clearly his scholarly aim was to systematically present in summary fashion and to defend the orthodoxy of the six councils, Nicea I (325) to Constantinople III (681), in the Umayyad milieu in which during his lifetime the crescendo of the twin processes of Islamicization and Arabicization were going forward under caliphal guidance.

The year of John of Damascus' death is uncertain; earlier scholars opted for the year 749 C.E.,[47] while more recently, due to difficulties and uncertainties in aligning events in John's life with the chronology of the caliphs in Damascus, contemporary historians prefer sometime between the years 750 and 753.[48] Whatever may have been the actual date of his death, for all practical purposes John's lifetime nevertheless was co-extensive with the major years of the Umayyad dynasty.

For all of his importance for Christian intellectual history in his native Syria/Palestine in early Islamic times, and given the fact that the topical profile of his work is a fair representation of the intellectual and social issues current in the Christian communities of his time and place, it is striking how little attention John of Damascus is given in the surviving works of others in the same milieu. There is little mention of him or his works in texts emanating from the Syrian milieu in either Greek or Syriac. Nor is there any significant reference to him early on in texts in Greek and Arabic coming from the wider "Melkite" world, from their centers in Alexandria, Antioch, or Edessa. Exceptions include a reference to John and to passages in his major theological work, the *Fount of Knowledge*, by a certain Elias, who read the passages, but who nevertheless became a "Jacobite" at some point in the eighth century,[49] and several notices in the *Chronicle* of Theophanes the Confessor, which I shall discuss just below. The "Melkites" seem not even to have begun the translation of John's major works from Greek into Arabic until the tenth century.[50] This state of affairs has prompted some modern scholars to suppose that in his strong anti-"Jacobite" theology, and even in his defense of the veneration of the icons, John of Damascus was actually somewhat out of step with his contemporaries in Jerusalem and even in Mar Saba monastery.[51] But one cannot avoid the thought that the real reason for the contemporary silence about John and the seemingly reluctant pace in taking up his work, or even referring to him by name, had nothing really to do with his teaching. Rather, it seems more likely that the family history and its associations were the problem. John's very name, Manṣūr, and his known ancestry gave his contemporaries, and even their successors, reasons to be cautious and perhaps even suspicious of him.

We have already noticed that the "Melkite" historian, Eutychios of Alexandria, repeats three times the remark that the bishops of the whole world had anathematized the name of Manṣūr. It was not only that it was Manṣūr who had opened Damascus to the conquering Muslims, but also the fact that he and his descendants to the third generation, seemingly

---

[46] See Louth, *St. John Damascene*, p. 26. See in this connection the important work of Studer, *Die theologische Arbeitsweise*.

[47] See Vailhé, "Date de la mort de saint Jean Damascène."

[48] See Kazhdan, "John Damaskenos," p. 75.

[49] See the discussion in Griffith, "'Meklites', 'Jacobites' and the Christological Controversies," pp. 24–25; van Roey, "La lettre apologétique."

[50] See Atiya, "St. John Damascene"; Graf, *Geschichte der christlichen arabischen Literatur*, vol. 1, pp. 377–79.

[51] See, e.g., Auzépy, "De la Palestine à Constantinople," pp. 197–99, regarding John's strong opposition to the so-called "Jacobite" addition to the *Trishagion*; and Kazhdan and Gero, "Kosmas of Jerusalem," regarding views possibly differing from John's, held by others at Mar Saba monastery about the veneration of icons.

including Manṣūr ibn Sarjūn ibn Manṣūr himself, John of Damascus, had faithfully served the Umayyad caliphs in the caliphal government at least up to the time of ʿAbd al-Malik if not further. And the Christian chronicles covering the period are full of accounts of the harsh treatment meted out to Christians and their interests at the hands of these very caliphs and their ministers. One notices a difference in the *Chronicle* of Theophanes the Confessor.

There is almost an apologetic tone to Theophanes' treatment of John of Damascus, as if the chronographer was determined to right a wrong. Theophanes (ca. 760–817/8), a Constantinopolitan, was a strong iconodule and an active adversary of the iconoclasts of Constantinople in his lifetime.[52] As a chronographer, he owed a substantial debt to the previous work of George the Synkellos (d. after 810),[53] and for the events of Umayyad times in Syria/ Palestine, much of the material in his accounts seems ultimately to derive from the now lost Syriac chronicle of Theophilus of Edessa (d. 785), which seems to have found its way into later, mostly Syriac, chronicles.[54] No doubt aware of John of Damascus' strong support of the icons, a major life commitment for Theophanes and his associates, the chronographer goes out of his way in his few references to John to put him in a positive light, especially in reaction to the characterizations of the Damascene at the iconoclast council of Hiereia (754), in the acts of which he was described by the aforementioned adjective, "Saracen-minded," and in response to the council's and the emperor Constantine V's (741–775) practice of insultingly and repeatedly calling him "Manṣūr."[55] In reference to the martyr, Peter of Maiouma, Theophanes says,

> He has been honoured in a laudation by our holy father John, rightly surnamed the Golden Stream because of the golden gleam of spiritual grace that bloomed both in his discourse and his life!
>
> John, whom the impious emperor Constantine subjected to an annual anathema because of his pre-eminent orthodoxy and, instead of his paternal name, Mansour (which means 'redeemed'), he, in his Jewish manner, renamed the new teacher of the Church Manzeros.[56]

Manzeros here, in a Greek transcription accommodated to the sound of the Arabic name Manṣūr, was undoubtedly meant by the emperor Constantine V, as Theophanes would have it in his report of the emperor's language, to evoke the Hebrew word *mamzer*, which is generally taken to mean "bastard."[57] In this passage, Theophanes is obviously trying both to rehabilitate John's reputation and to reinterpret the name Manṣūr for Greek speakers by what appears to be a flattering but false etymology of his family name. What is more, by evoking the memory of Peter of Maiouma, also known as Peter of Capitolias, sometimes even called Peter

---

[52] Kazhdan, "Theophanes the Confessor."

[53] On whom see Kazhdan, "George the Synkellos."

[54] See Hoyland, *Seeing Islam as Others Saw It*, pp. 400–09 and 428–32. See also in this connection the ground-breaking study showing the importance of the now lost chronicle of Theophilus of Edessa: Conrad, "The Conquest of Arwād." For a more restrained perspective on Theophilus, see Conterno, *La "Descrizione dei tempi,"* and Muriel Debié's contribution to this volume.

[55] See the references in Auzépy, "De la Palestine à Constantinople," p. 194 n. 84. The same information is supplied in Stephen the Deacon's life of Stephen the Younger. See Auzépy, *La Vie d'Étienne le Jeune*, p. 220 and n. 197. The text speaks of "le très honorable Jean, le prêtre damascène, surnommé par ce tyran [i.e., Constantine V] Mansour, mais pour nous saint et théophore" (p. 220). Stephen the Younger and his biographer, Stephen the Deacon, both belonged to the same iconodule circle in Constantinople, as did Theophanes the Confessor.

[56] Theophanes, *Chronicle*, p. 578.

[57] See, e.g., Jastrow, *Dictionary*, pp. 794–95.

of Damascus, and reporting that John of Damascus wrote eulogies celebrating his memory as a martyr killed on the orders of the Umayyad caliph al-Walīd in the year 715 C.E.,[58] Theophanes seems here clearly to be dissociating John's memory from any anti-Christian action on the part of the Umayyad authorities at this time, or indeed of any collusion on his part with their policies. Theophanes mentions John of Damascus two other times in his *Chronicle*. In one place he says, "in Damascus of Syria there shone forth in his life and discourse of John of the Golden Stream, son of Mansour, a presbyter and a monk, a most excellent teacher."[59] And in another place Theophanes lists "John Damascene of the Golden Stream" along with Germanos and George of Cyprus, both prominent iconodule heroes, who were "holy men and venerable teachers."[60]

It seems clear that Theophanes the Confessor intentionally meant to remedy in Constantinople the obloquy from which John of Damascus' reputation suffered in "Melkite" circles in the caliphate, due to the *damnatio memoriae* accorded to the whole Manṣūr family by many Christians in the East, with the exception of the occasional instance of voicing some invective or citing the occasions of anathemas being imposed on them as in the case of Patriarch Eutychios of Alexandria in the *Annals* attributed to him. The Orientals, including the "Melkites," appear to have regarded them all as Muslim collaborators. John himself seems to have come under the cloud of this unwelcome infamy in Syriac and Arabic sources. And perhaps there was also some bitterness in these circles in later times regarding the subsequent fame that this writer of Greek achieved in Byzantium, where Syriac- and Arabic-speaking Christians were not well regarded.

III. John of Damascus and the Muslims

Christians living in the territories of the so-called Oriental Patriarchates, Alexandria, Antioch, and Jerusalem, first took serious notice of the religious views of the conquering Arabs in texts written principally in Syriac and Greek in Umayyad times.[61] John of Damascus, writing in Greek in the ecclesiastical context of Jerusalem in the first half of the eighth century, was among the earliest of the Christian writers in the conquered territories to take the religious challenge of the Arab conquest seriously. His response to the challenge unfolded within the parameters of a threefold frame of reference: the Umayyad program to claim the body politic for Islam; the ongoing theological and ecclesiastical agendas of the Jerusalem patriarchate, including the associated, international monastic establishment; and the burgeoning confrontation between Christians and Muslims more broadly. Given the fact that in previous studies the present writer has from his own scholarly perspective already discussed John's situation within these frames of reference,[62] the focus of the present inquiry is more specifically on how John of Damascus framed a comprehensive approach to the developing

[58] On Peter and his fate, see Hoyland, *Seeing Islam as Others Saw It*, pp. 354–60; see also pp. 482–83, where Hoyland calls attention to the fact that Theophanes mistakenly included the passage quoted above under the events of the year 742.

[59] Theophanes, *Chronicle*, p. 565.

[60] Ibid., p. 592.

[61] See the systematic survey in Hoyland, *Seeing Islam as Others Saw It*. See also Griffith, *The Church in the Shadow of the Mosque*.

[62] See, in particular, "Images, Islam and Christian Icons"; "The Signs and Wonders of Orthodoxy"; "'Melkites', 'Jacobites' and the Christological Controversies;" "John of Damascus and the Church in Syria"; "Christians, Muslims and the Image of the One God"; and "Crosses, Icons and the Image of Christ in Edessa."

religious thinking among Muslim intellectuals in his day. Their thinking would have impacted the Christian communities by way of the confidence their writings would have imparted to Muslims in their interactions with contemporary Jews and Christians and their increasing tendency to call others to the profession of Islam.

As a member of the Manṣūr family, John of Damascus came to his participation in the religious confrontation between Christians and Muslims as a one-time political insider, from within the governing circles of the Umayyad caliphate. Given this important dimension of his own biography, and the likelihood of his continuing participation in his family's social network, albeit now from a probably more pronounced religio-cultural distance in Jerusalem, there is every reason nevertheless to think that he must have been well aware not only of the Umayyad policies of his day, both civil and religious, but also that his knowledge of Islam and current Muslim thinking must have been somewhat unique among contemporary Christians, more accurate and more reflective of the current intellectual concerns of Muslims. And although the present focus is widely concerned with his presentation of Islam from his church's distinctive, Christian doctrinal perspective, it is the hypothesis lying behind the present inquiry, advanced also in earlier essays, not only that John's larger perception of the religious challenge of Islam was a determining factor operative in those of his texts that have specifically to do with Islam in some fashion, but also that it was a motivating concern informing his whole intellectual project. This concern of his with the wider intellectual challenge of Islam, along with his knowing critique and even his heresiographical parody of Islam in one place, as we shall see, sets him apart somewhat from his colleagues in the "circle" of Syro-Palestinian thinkers and writers, also from Damascus and more clearly associated with Mar Sabas monastery than was John, who are seen by modern Byzantinists to have been engaged along with John in advancing Greek-speaking, Byzantine church life within the world of Islam.[63] In this milieu, his very concern with Islam, in addition to the adumbrations caused by his family name and the family's social circumstances, may well have been an aggravating factor in the Byzantine chill affecting John's memory in eighth-century Constantinople and even in local "Melkite" circles.

The first half of the eighth century witnessed a notable development in Islamic religious thinking in two places in particular, Damascus in Syria and Baṣrah in Iraq, as the very mention of the names of Ghaylān ad-Dimashqī (d. 749), Jahm ibn Ṣafwān (d. 745), Ḥasan al-Baṣrī (642–728), and Waṣīl ibn ʿAṭa' (d. 748), among others, immediately brings to mind. The debates among Muslim intellectuals associated with these names about the range of human willing and what to think about God's attributes among other topics formed the backdrop for the development in due course of the wide-ranging Muʿtazilah school of thought.[64] It would not be stretching matters too far to suppose that the socially well-connected, Arabic-speaking John of Damascus would have been aware of this notable development and of its potential to articulate a systematic, religious, and philosophical view of this world and the next. The particular intellectual concerns of these and other Muslim scholars also found a place *mutatis mutandis* in his own thinking, and their modes of discussion and organization of topics bear an uncanny resemblance to the patterns of John's own work. It is clear, for example, that with the component parts of his *Pēgē Gnoseōs*, he too intended to present a comprehensive and summary presentation of the Orthodox Christian faith, complete with the definitions

[63] See, e.g., Sahas, "The Arab Character"; and idem, "Cultural Interaction."

[64] The now standard study of this intellectual history is van Ess, *Theologie und Gesellschaft*, esp. vols. 1 and 2.

of the philosophical and logical terms in which it was articulated, and a guide to the errors of thought and practice that had plagued the church in the past and the present. The work in the ensemble, composed in the aforementioned manner of quoting large sections from the earlier works of the "Orthodox Fathers," seems geared to serve an apologetic and even a polemic purpose all at once and in a summary fashion, a first in Greek theology. What is more, over thirty years ago Shlomo Pines called attention to the fact that the compositional pattern of the early Islamic *kalām* works, particularly those of the Muʿtazilah, match the order of topics as they are presented in John's *De Fide Orthodoxa*. He wrote:

> In all the texts that have been cited, [...] the first section deals with the sources of knowledge. The exposition of theological doctrine begins in all these texts with the demonstration that the world, i.e., all things directly known to man are created and must have a Creator. This proof is followed by an argumentation proving that God is one, which is succeeded by a discussion of the question of what God is or may be said to be; this involves the problem of the divine attributes.[65]

Pines concluded that inasmuch as the conventional compositional pattern of the works of Islamic *kalām* mirrored the order of topical exposition in such works as the *De Fide Orthodoxa*, and even its methods of reasoning, the conventions of Muslim scholars "reflected to a considerable extent those employed (in writing or in oral instruction) by Christian theologians who lived in the Islamic empire."[66] He is not so much claiming a direct influence as pointing out the fact that the Muslim thinkers to some degree may be seen to have joined a conversation that was already underway and that they were required to make the case for their own beliefs in somewhat the same idiom of the ongoing conversation. To some extent the same may be said of the task undertaken by John of Damascus. He undertook the defense of Chalcedonian Orthodoxy not only in response to the challenges of "Jacobites," "Nestorians," "Iconoclasts," and other Christian communities, but also over against Jews, Manichees, and Muslims. To borrow an apt phrase from a commentator on the shaping of early Islamic thought, John worked in a newly franchised "Sectarian Milieu"[67] to present a comprehensive, systematically reasoned defense of the faith of his church community, and he did it at the very time when Muslim scholars were beginning to undertake the same kind of a project in their own communities. From this perspective, one might well consider his whole intellectual project, especially with the *Pēgē Gnoseōs*, but not excluding even his three orations in defense of the icons (as one has suggested elsewhere), as a reasoned response to the intellectual and religious challenge of a burgeoning Islam. The corollary of this position is that it is a methodological mistake to consider only John's explicitly anti-Islamic writing as exhausting his response to the call to Islam.

Among the several texts having explicitly to do with Islam that are attributed to John of Damascus, only one of them, albeit with some dissenters, is generally considered by current scholars to be authentic.[68] It is chapter 100 of the century "On Heresies," a component of John's larger project, the compendium of Christian orthodoxy entitled *Pēgē Gnōseōs*, or

[65] Pines, "Some Traits of Christian Theological Writing," pp. 112–13.

[66] Ibid., p. 115.

[67] Not only is the title phrase highly suggestive, but so is the hermeneutical principle operative in the study of the formulation of religious discourse in an interreligious context in Wansbrough, *The Sectarian Milieu*.

[68] See the list of the several texts discussed in Khoury, "Jean Damascène et l'Islam." Regarding authenticity, see Le Coz, *Jean Damascène*, pp. 183–203.

"Fount of Knowledge." A surviving "Conversation between a Saracen and a Christian," also attributed to John of Damascus, is now thought to be a later composition by someone else that nevertheless reports the Damascene's thinking about Islam.[69]

A. Chapter 100 of the Century "On Heresies"

The century "On Heresies," like the other parts of the *Fount of Knowledge*, is largely composed on the basis of earlier texts by other writers, in this case with a heavy reliance on the *Panarion*, a comprehensive heresiography by the originally Palestinian writer Epiphanius of Salamis (ca. 310/20–403).[70] But, as Andrew Louth has explained, in two instances of his reaction to other religious traditions, outside of what we might call the "main-line churches" of his day, John of Damascus is more personally involved; they are his responses to Manichaeism and Islam.[71] In the case of Manichaeism, while he included in Chapter 100 what Epiphanius had presented, he also composed an independent dialogue against what are presented as the teachings of Mani (216–276) and his followers in a manner that suggests to Louth a contemporary conversation.[72] There is indeed evidence that in Umayyad times Manichees did once again emerge into public life in the Syro-Mesopotamian milieu, once the more repressive rule of the Byzantines in the area had ended.[73] Louth suggests that John of Damascus took advantage of this situation to combat dualism and in the course of the dialogue also to combat the typically Islamic objections to the doctrines of the Trinity and the Incarnation. He even suggests that John wrote the dialogue while he was still in Damascus.[74]

As for the presentation of Islam in Chapter 100, here John speaks of what "we say" in response to what he calls "the now ruling, misleading religion (*thrēskeia*) of the Ishmaelites," presaging the coming of the Antichrist. He says that it was introduced by the false prophet Muḥammad (*Mamed*), who founded his own "heresy" (*hairesin*) having taken cognizance of the Old Testament and the New Testament and having frequented the company of a seemingly Arian monk and being in receipt of a "scripture" (*graphēn*) revealed by God that came down to him from heaven. He put together some laughable teachings in a book of his own and thus he handed over to them this particular manner of "worship" (*to sebas*).[75]

Here is not the place to provide yet another reading of Chapter 100; a number of scholars have already done this in great detail.[76] What one wants to highlight is twofold: the language John used to characterize Islam as he knew it, and the overtly polemical way in which he evokes passages from the Qur'ān and Islamic lore in general, in a manner that he must have known was distorted, from the point of view of an accurate portrayal. As for his characterization of Islam, he calls it a "religion," a "heresy," and a "way of worship." Two of these terms would seem to put Islam outside the circle of the religious insiders with whom he is largely

[69] Both of these texts are published with Kotter's critical edition of the Greek text and a French translation in Le Coz, *Jean Damascène*, and in Glei and Khoury, *Johannes Damaskenos und Theodor Abū Qurra*. They are published with the earlier, uncritical edition from Migne, ed., Patrologia graeca, vol. 94, cols. 764–73, 1336–48, and an English translation in Sahas, *John of Damascus on Islam*.

[70] Epiphanius of Salamis, *The Panarion*.

[71] Louth, *St. John Damascene*, pp. 54–83.

[72] See the text of John's "Against the Manichees," in Kotter, *Die Schriften des Johannes von Damaskos*, vol. 4, pp. 333–98.

[73] Lieu, *Manichaeism*, pp. 82–83.

[74] Louth, *St. John Damascene*, p. 71.

[75] Le Coz, *Jean Damascène*, pp. 210–12.

[76] Most notably Le Coz, *Jean Damascène*, pp. 89–133; see also Sahas, *John of Damascus on Islam*, pp. 67–95.

concerned in most of his work, that is, those whom he thinks of as Orthodox, along with their so to speak "in-house," but erring adversaries, the contemporary "Monothelites," the "Jacobites," and the "Nestorians." He calls Islam a "religion," using the Greek term (*thrēskeia*) that in the patristic parlance with which he was most familiar means "religion" in the sense of the general practice of worship offered to God, or even to creatures,[77] an understanding that John reaffirms with his subsequent use of the correlatively general term "worship" or "adoration" (*to sebas*).[78] As for the designation "heresy," it was generally used in patristic texts in contradistinction to the term "schism,"[79] to mean, from a given author's or church's point of view, a wrong understanding of the nature of Christ. This meaning in the present context is reaffirmed by John's mention of a "seemingly Arian monk," with whom Muḥammad is said to have been in contact. Accordingly, by explicitly using the term "heresy," John of Damascus is signaling his view that what is principally wrong with Islam is its heretical understanding of Jesus Christ.

In connection with John's mention of the "seemingly Arian monk," commentators have often recalled the monk Baḥīrā,[80] so named in the early biography of Muḥammad by the Damascene's younger contemporary, Muḥammad ibn Isḥāq (d. 767); Baḥīrā was said to have recognized Muḥammad's status as a prophet already in his youth.[81] But John's remark seems to be meant theologically and not historically. While he may well have known of the story of Baḥīrā, or at least of Muḥammad's alleged encounters with a monk or monks (there are several such stories in the Prophet's biography), John's point is that Islam's teaching is seemingly Arian, in Christian parlance. In other words, he is thereby categorizing the "heresy" of Islam as Christological in character.[82]

Commentators have long noticed the basic accuracy of John of Damascus' knowledge of Islam and of the Qurʾān, but seldom have they taken cognizance of his rhetoric and its polemical intent. They have had a tendency to think of his polemical twists of text or interpretation as indicative of a lack of accurate knowledge of the details of Islamic thought, lore, or practice. But the opposite is probably the case; effective rhetoric for the sake of persuasion, especially in the cases of invective or religious polemic, requires that the well known be given a demeaning reiteration or interpretation. Examples of this basically unfair manner of argument can be seen in Chapter 100 in the suggestion that the Qurʾān's identification of Christ as the Word of God and a Spirit from him (IV *an-Nisāʾ* 171) bespeaks the text's acceptance of the doctrine of the Trinity, which is explicitly rejected in the same verse, along with the divinity of Christ as Son of God, something one must think John knew very well. The same could be said of his account of Abraham, Hagar, Ishmael, and the Kaʿbah, his recollection of the affair of Zayd's wife, as well as his belittling reference to "the book (*graphē*) of God's Camel." Similarly, John several times mentions with demeaning intent that Muḥammad's inspiration came to him in sleep or in dreams. It is hard not to conclude that he was well aware of the mention of dreams and portents in early Islamic accounts (already in Ibn Isḥāq) of Muḥammad's experiences of revelation, and John singles them out, to the exclusion of

[77] See Lampe, *Patristic Greek Lexicon*, p. 654.

[78] Ibid., p. 1227.

[79] Ibid., p. 51.

[80] See, e.g., Le Coz, *Jean Damascène*, pp. 97–98.

[81] See Guillaume, *The Life of Muhammad*, pp. 79–82. The later Christian legend of Baḥīrā, and his designation in some recensions of his story as a "Nestorian," is a Christian composition that takes its cue from the original Islamic story. See Roggema, *The Legend of Sergius Baḥīrā*.

[82] See in this connection Valkenberg, "John of Damascus"; Valkenberg and Davids, "John of Damascus."

other features of the experience, precisely in view of their polemical potential. Here is not the place to discuss in detail this polemical dimension of John's rhetoric in Chapter 100; suffice it to have called attention to this seldom recognized dimension of his account of Islam.

B. The "Conversation of a Saracen and a Christian"

It is difficult not to think of this text as an early exercise in the genre of dialectical theology, called *al-kalām* in Arabic, a term very adequately translated by the Greek word *diálexis* used in the title of this composition. As mentioned above, the scholars who study the works of John of Damascus are convinced that while this work is not, strictly speaking, authentic, in that it was not written by John, it nevertheless adequately reflects his teaching as found in his authentic works, and not least in the aforementioned "Against the Manichees."[83] Indeed, Theodore Abū Qurrah (ca. 755–ca. 833), who includes much of the discourse in a "Conversation" of his own, speaks of having composed it "*dià phōnēs Iōánnou Damaskēnou.*"[84] A notable feature of the text is its evocation of the current controversy between those who in contemporary Islamic texts are called "Qadarites," the partisans of the doctrine of the human capacity for free willing, and the "Mujbirites," those who thought that the human power of willing is constrained by God's prior knowledge. John's teaching in this regard as presented in the "Conversation," seemingly drawn principally from his "Against the Manichees," presents a line of argument reprised and developed to a considerable extent in a later Arabic composition by Abū Qurrah, who likewise aims his arguments against Mani.[85] It is not unreasonable to think that it was in fact Abū Qurrah who put together the "Conversation of a Saracen and a Christian" now attributed to John of Damascus.

The other topics in the "Conversation," such as discussions of God's justice, creation, God's will and tolerance, a long disquisition on Christology, incarnation, the death of Mary, and the sacrament of baptism, while redolent of later conversations between Christians and Muslims composed largely in Arabic, nevertheless also evoke both the topics of discussion and the idiom of their expression in the Islamic *ʿilm al-kalām*.[86] One finds the beginnings of this development already in the work of John of Damascus.

IV. Christians and Muslims in Umayyad Times

The Manṣūr family occupied an unusual position in Umayyad society; in some ways it anticipated on a smaller scale the role other well-known Christian families would come to play in Baghdad in its heyday from the ninth to the mid-eleventh century.[87] Their fortunes were uncharacteristic of those of most Christians in their own day, although others had careers not totally unlike theirs, as we learn from the chronicles.[88] The long memory of the role of the *paterfamilias* in the conquest of Damascus undoubtedly helps explain the family's tarnished reputation among Christians, even "Melkites," as well as the wariness with which John of Damascus and his works were initially approached.

---

[83] See Le Coz, *Jean Damascène*, pp. 136–82.

[84] Ibid., p. 200 n. 5.

[85] See Griffith, "Free Will in Christian Kalām."

[86] See the discussion in Griffith, *The Church in the Shadow of the Mosque*, pp. 75–105.

[87] See n. 9, above.

[88] See in particular, Cheïkho, *Les vizirs et secrétaires*. Muriel Debié discusses the example of the Gūmōyē family in this volume.

A notable feature of Christian life in Umayyad times is the number of martyrs whose trials under the Umayyads found expression in both Greek and Arabic accounts of their sufferings. We have already taken notice of the eulogy composed by John of Damascus for the martyr, Peter of Capitolias.[89] But there were many others especially in "Melkite" sources.[90] It is interesting to note that conversion emerges as a factor in these narratives, some of them having to do with alleged cases of the conversion of Muslims to Christianity, while others feature the Christian protagonists reviling Islam, the Qurʾān, or the person of Muḥammad in the attempt to persuade Muslims to convert to Christianity, particularly those who had recently apostatized from the church. This is a little-studied chapter of early Islamic history.

It was not only in Syria/Palestine or only in proto-"Melkite" circles that Christian intellectual life took a novel turn in Umayyad times. The most well-studied development, especially in "Jacobite" circles, was the production in Syriac in the early decades of the eighth century of apocalyptic texts designed to make Christian sense of the arrival of Islam, with the now well-known *Apocalypse of Pseudo-Methodius* leading the way. This literature provided Christians with what one might call a theologically or biblically inspired, historiographical adjustment to their vision of current affairs that would have a long life in Eastern Christian circles and beyond. Not only did it help explain how the tragedy of the conquest came about, but it also proposed the vision of a future when against all odds Christianity would once again prevail in its homeland.[91]

At the same time, also writing in Syriac, other "Jacobite" scholars, building on the apocalyptic vision of the future, were presenting the teachings of their church in a newly phrased idiom that would in due course become the standard expression of the church's theological identity, while making practical adjustments to their conduct of church life to meet the new challenge of Islam. Arguably, the "Jacobite" thinkers of Umayyad times were the ones who brought their community to its full maturity as a distinctive Christian church, building on the foundations laid by their forbears in the sixth century.[92] A case in point is the work of Jacob of Edessa (ca. 640–708),[93] still largely unpublished and under-studied, who was perhaps the most significant intellectual of his community until the time of Bar Hebraeus (1226–1286) in the thirteenth century. And one must not forget the "Jacobite" George, bishop of the Arabs (ca. 640–724), who was active in the translation movement of Greek texts into Syriac in Umayyad times that would pave the way for the well-known Abbasid translation movement of the ninth and tenth centuries.[94] In his letters he was also among the first in his community to devise strategies for responding to the multiple religious challenges of Muslims, becoming in this way one of the forerunners of Christian *kalām* in Arabic.[95]

After overcoming some serious divisions in their communities in Umayyad times, especially in Qatar and the Persian Gulf regions,[96] a striking development among the Syriac-speaking "Nestorians," due perhaps in some part to the pressure of Islam, was the flowering

[89] See n. 58, above.

[90] See Hoyland, *Seeing Islam as Other Saw It*, pp. 336–86; Griffith, "Christians, Muslims, and Neo-Martyrs."

[91] For discussion and bibliography, see Griffith, *The Church in the Shadow of the Mosque*, esp. pp. 32–39.

[92] See in this connection the work of Menze, *Justinian and the Making of the Syrian Orthodox Church*. See also Ibrahim, "The Syrian Churches."

[93] See Drijvers, "Jakob von Edessa"; idem, "The Testament of our Lord"; Kruisheer and Van Rompay, "A Bibliographical Clavis"; ter Haar Romeny, "From Religious Association to Ethnic Community"; Tannous, "You Are What You Read."

[94] See Hugonnard-Roche, *La logique d'Aristote*.

[95] See now the important article by Tannous, "The Life and Letters of George."

[96] See Le Coz, *Histoire de l'Église d'Orient*, pp. 139–43.

of the monastic life, inspired by the translation of Greek monastic classics into Syriac. The high-water mark of this movement was achieved in the middle years of the seventh century with the publication of the classic *Paradise of the Fathers*, a compilation of the classics of Egyptian desert spirituality in Syriac translation by the Church of the East monk ʿEnānīshōʿ (fl. ca. 630–670) of the monastery of Mount Izla, near Nisibis.[97] Meanwhile, under the impetus of these translated texts, a long and wondrous tradition of east Syrian ascetical and mystical writing got underway.[98] It was not without importance for the soon-to-be-developing tradition of Islamic Sufism.[99]

Perhaps not surprisingly in this period of monastic growth, the missionary activity of the "Nestorian" Church of the East was flourishing, especially in Central Asia and China.[100] But it would not be until the last years of the eighth century, in early Abbasid times, that the intellectuals of the community would engage religiously seriously with the challenge of Islam. And it is interesting to note that just as John of Damascus responded with a compendious summary of his community's doctrine, so too did the "Nestorian" Theodore bar Kōnī (fl. ca. 792) in his *Scholion*, clothed in the form of a commentary on the Old and New Testaments.[101] In the next generation, the long-lived patriarch Timothy I (727/8–823) became the first in the field of a long line of Church of the East intellectuals who would significantly energize the interreligious life of Baghdad in years of her intellectual flowering.[102]

Bibliography

Atiya, A. S. "St. John Damascene: Survey of the Unpublished Arabic Versions of His Works in Sinai." In *Arabic and Islamic Studies in Honor of Hamilton A. R. Gibb*, edited by George Makdisi, pp. 73–83. Leiden: Brill, distributed by Harvard University Press, Cambridge, 1965.

Auzépy, Marie-France. "De la Palestine à Constantinople (viiiᵉ–ixᵉ siècles): Étienne le Sabaïte et Jean Damascène." In *Travaux et Mémoires* 12, pp. 183–218. Travaux et mémoires du Centre de recherche d'histoire et civilisation de Byzance. Monographies 12. Paris: De Boccard, 1994.

———. "Les Sabaïtes et l'iconoclasme." In *The Sabaite Heritage in the Orthodox Church from the Fifth Century to the Present*, edited by Joseph Patrich, pp. 305–14. Orientalia Lovaniensia Analecta 98. Leuven: Peeters, 2001.

———. *La vie d'Étienne le Jeune, par Étienne le Diacre*. Birmingham Byzantine and Ottoman Monographs 3. Aldershot: Ashgate, 1997.

Baum, Wilhelm, and Dietmar W. Winkler. *The Church of the East: A Concise History*. London and New York: RoutledgeCurzon, 2003.

Beulay, Robert. *La lumière sans forme: Introduction à l'étude de la mystique chrétienne syro-orientale*. Chevetogne: Éditions de Chevetogne, 1987.

[97] The work has long circulated in the edition and English translation of Budge, *The Paradise, or Garden of the Holy Fathers*.

[98] See especially Beulay, *La lumière sans forme*.

[99] See Blum, *Die Geschichte der Begegnung christlich-orientalischer Mystik*.

[100] See Baum and Winkler, *The Church of the East*, pp. 46–51; Tang, *Nestorian Christianity in China*.

[101] See Griffith, "Theodore bar Kônî's *Scholion*"; idem, "Chapter Ten of the *Scholion*."

[102] See Griffith, "The Syriac Letters of Patriarch Timothy I."

Blum, Georg Günter. *Die Geschichte der Begegnung christlich-orientalischer Mystik mit der Mystik des Islams.* Orientalia Biblica et Christiana 17. Wiesbaden: Harrassowitz, 2009.

Borrut, Antoine. "Entre tradition et histoire: genèse et diffusion de l'image de ʿUmar II." *Mélanges de la faculté orientale de l'Université Saint-Joseph de Beyrouth* 58 (2005): 329–78.

Breydy, Michel. *Études sur Saʿīd ibn Baṭrīq et ses sources.* Corpus Scriptorum Christianorum Orientalium 450. Leuven: Peeters, 1983.

Budge, E. A. Wallis. *The Paradise, or Garden of the Holy Fathers.* 2 vols. London: Chatto & Windus, 1907.

Cheïkho, Louis. *Les vizirs et secrétaires arabes chrétiens en Islam (622-1517).* Patrimoine Arabe Chrétien 11. Jounieh: Librairie Saint-Paul; Rome: Pontificio Istituto Orientale, 1987.

Chronicle of 1234 (Anonymous). Edited by Jean-Baptiste Chabot, *Anonymi Auctoris Chronicon ad Annum Christi 1234 pertinens, I.* Corpus Scriptorum Christianorum Orientalium 81 and 109. Leuven: L. Durbecq, 1952 (first published Paris: Gabalda, 1920).

Conrad, Lawrence I. "The Conquest of Arwād: A Source-Critical Study in the Historiography of the Early Medieval Near East." In *The Byzantine and Early Islamic Near East*, Vol. 1: *Problems in the Literary Source Material*, edited by Averil Cameron and Lawrence I. Conrad, pp. 317–401. Studies in Late Antiquity and Early Islam 1. Princeton: Darwin Press, 1992.

Conterno, Maria. *La "Descrizione dei tempi" all'alba dell'espansione islamica: Un'indagine sulla storiografia greca, siriaca e araba fra VII e VIII secolo.* Berlin: De Gruyter, 2014.

Di Segni, Leah. "Greek Inscriptions in Transition from the Byzantine to the Early Islamic Period." In *From Hellenism to Islam: Cultural and Linguistic Change in the Roman Near East*, edited by Hannah M. Cotton, Robert G. Hoyland, Jonathan J. Price, and David J. Wasserstein, pp. 352–73. Cambridge: Cambridge University Press, 2009.

Drijvers, Han J. W. "Jakob von Edessa (633–708)." In *Theologische Realenzyklopädie*, vol. 16, pp. 468–70. Berlin: De Gruyter, 1993.

———. "The Testament of Our Lord: Jacob of Edessa's Response to Islam." *ARAM* 6 (1994): 104–14.

Epiphanius of Salamis, *The Panarion.* Translated by Frank Williams, *The Panarion of Epiphanius of Salamis.* 2 vols. Nag Hammadi Studies 35, Nag Hammadi and Manichaean Studies 36. Leiden: Brill, 1987–1994.

Eutychios of Alexandria (Saʿīd b. Baṭrīq). *Annales.* [*Taʾrīkh al-majmūʿ ʿala al-taḥqīq wa-al-taṣdīq* or *Naẓm al-jawhar*]

- Edited by Louis Cheïkho, Bernard Carra de Vaux, and Habib Zayyat, *Eutychii patriarchae Alexandrini annales*, Part 2. Corpus Scriptorum Christianorum Orientalium 51. Leuven: Peeters, 1909.
- German translation by Michael Breydy, *Das Annalenwerk des Eutychios von Alexandrien: Ausgewählte Geschichten und Legenden, kompiliert von Saʿid ibn Baṭrīq um 935 A.D.* Corpus Scriptorum Christianorum Orientalium 471–72. Leuven: Peeters, 1985.
- Italian translation by Bartolomeo Pirone, *Gli annali.* Studia Orientalia Christiana, Monographiae 1. Cairo: Franciscan Centre of Christian Oriental Studies, 1987.

Flusin, B. "De l'arabe au grec, puis au géorgien: une vie de saint Jean Damascène." In *Traduction et traducteurs au moyen âge*, edited by Geneviève Contamine, pp. 51–61. Paris: Éditions du Centre National de la Recherche Scientifique, 1989.

Geerard, Maurice, editor. *Clavis Patrum Graecorum.* Corpus Christianorum. 5 vols. and supplement. Turnhout: Brepols, 1974–1998.

Glei, Reinhold, and Axel Theodor Khoury. *Johannes Damaskenos und Theodor Abū Qurra, Schriften zum Islam.* Corpus Islamo-Christianum, Series Graeca 3; Würzburg: Echter, 1995.

Graf, Georg. *Geschichte der christlichen arabischen Literatur.* 5 vols. Città del Vaticano: Biblioteca Apostolica Vaticana, 1944–1953.

Greenwood, Tim. "The Letter of Leo III in Ghewond." In *Christian-Muslim Relations: A Bibliographical History,* Vol. 1: *600-900*, edited by David Thomas and Barbara Roggema, pp. 203–08. The History of Christian-Muslim Relations 11. Leiden: Brill, 2009.

Griffith, Sidney H. "Chapter Ten of the *Scholion*: Theodore bar Kônî's Apology for Christianity." *Orientalia Christiana Analecta* 218 (1982): 169–91.

———. "Theodore bar Kônî's *Scholion*: A Nestorian *Summa contra Gentiles* from the First Abbasid Century." In *East of Byzantium: Syria and Armenia in the Formative Period,* edited by Nina G. Garsoïan, Thomas F. Mathews, and Robert W. Thomson, pp. 53–72. Washington, D.C.: Dumbarton Oaks, 1982.

———. "Free Will in Christian Kalām: The Doctrine of Theodore Abū Qurrah." *Parole de l'Orient* 14 (1987): 79–107.

———. "The Monks of Palestine and the Growth of Christian Literature in Arabic." *The Muslim World* 78 (1988): 1–28.

———. "Images, Islam and Christian Icons: A Moment in the Christian/Muslim Encounter in Early Islamic Times." In *La Syrie de Byzance à l'Islam: VIIe-VIIIe siècles,* edited by Pierre Canivet and Jean-Paul Rey-Coquais, pp. 121–38. Damascus: Institut Français de Damas, 1992.

———. "Byzantium and the Christians in the World of Islam: Constantinople and the Church in the Holy Land in the Ninth Century." *Medieval Encounters* 3 (1997): 231–65.

———. "From Aramaic to Arabic: The Languages of the Monasteries of Palestine in the Byzantine and Early Islamic Periods." *Dumbarton Oaks Papers* 51 (1997): 11–31.

———. "Christians, Muslims, and Neo-Martyrs: Saints' Lives and Holy Land History." In *Sharing the Sacred: Religious Contacts and Conflicts in the Holy Land; First-Fifteenth Centuries C.E.*, edited by Arieh Kofsky and Guy G. Stroumsa, pp. 162–207. Jerusalem: Yad Izhak ben Zvi, 1998.

———. "The Signs and Wonders of Orthodoxy: Miracles and Monks' Lives in Sixth-Century Palestine." In *Miracles in Jewish and Christian Antiquity: Imagining Truth,* edited by John C. Cavadini, pp. 139–68. Notre Dame Studies in Theology 3. Notre Dame: University of Notre Dame Press, 1999.

———. "'Melkites', 'Jacobites' and the Christological Controversies in Arabic in Third/Ninth-Century Syria." In *Syrian Christians under Islam: The First Thousand Years,* edited by David Thomas, pp. 9–55. Leiden: Brill, 2001.

———. "The Life of Theodore of Edessa: History, Hagiography and Religious Apologetics in Mar Saba Monastery in Early Abbasid Times." In *The Sabaite Heritage in the Orthodox Church from the Fifth Century to the Present,* edited by Joseph Patrich, pp. 147–69. Orientalia Lovaniensia Analecta 98. Leuven: Peeters, 2001.

———. "Apologetics and Historiography in the *Annals* of Eutychios of Alexandria: Christian Self-definition in the World of Islam." In *Studies on the Christian Arabic Heritage: In Honour of Father Prof. Dr. Samir Khalil Samir S.I. at the Occasion of his Sixty-fifth Birthday,* edited by Rifaat Ebied and Herman Teule, pp. 60–89. Eastern Christian Studies 5. Leuven: Peeters, 2004.

———. "The Church of Jerusalem and the 'Melkites': The Making of an 'Arab Orthodox' Christian Identity in the World of Islam (750–1050 C.E.)." In *Christians and Christianity in the Holy Land: From the Origins to the Latin Kingdoms,* edited by Ora Limor and Guy G. Stroumsa, pp. 175–204. Cultural Encounters in Late Antiquity and the Middle Ages 5. Turnhout: Brepols, 2006.

———. "Christians, Muslims and the Image of the One God: Iconophilia and Iconophobia in the World of Islam in Umayyad and Early Abbasid Times." In *Die Welt der Götterbilder,* edited by Brigitte Groneberg and Hermann Spieckermann, pp. 347–80. Beihefte zur Zeitschrift für die alttestamentliche Wissenschaft 376. Berlin: Walter de Gruyter, 2007.

———. "The Syriac Letters of Patriarch Timothy I and the Birth of Christian Kalām in the Muʿtazilite Milieu of Baghdad and Baṣrah in Early Islamic Times." In *Syriac Polemics: Studies in Honour of Gerrit Jan Reinink*, edited by Wout Jac van Bekkum, Jan Willem Drijvers, and Alexander Cornelis Klugkist, pp. 103–32. Orientalia Lovaniensia Analecta 170. Leuven: Peeters, 2007.

———. "John of Damascus and the Church in Syria in the Umayyad Era: The Intellectual and Cultural Milieu of Orthodox Christians in the World of Islam." *Hugoye: Journal of Syriac Studies* 11 (2008). http://syrcom.cua.edu/Hugoye/Vol11No2/HV11N2Griffith.html.

———. *The Church in the Shadow of the Mosque: Christians and Muslims in the World of Islam*. Princeton: Princeton University Press, 2008.

———. "Crosses, Icons and the Image of Christ in Edessa: The Place of Iconophobia in the Christian-Muslim Controversies of Early Islamic Times." In *Transformations of Late Antiquity: Essays for Peter Brown*, edited by Philip Rousseau and Manolis Papoutsakis, pp. 63–84. Farnham: Ashgate, 2009.

Guillaume, Alfred, translator. *The Life of Muhammad: A Translation of Isḥāq's Sīrat rasūl Allāh*. Karachi: Oxford University Press, 1978.

Hoyland, Robert G. *Seeing Islam as Others Saw It: A Survey and Evaluation of Christian, Jewish and Zoroastrian Writings on Early Islam*. Studies in Late Antiquity and Early Islam 13. Princeton: Darwin Press, 1997.

Hugonnard-Roche, Henri. *La logique d'Aristote du grec au syriaque: études sur la transmission des textes de l'Organon et leur interpretation philosophique*. Textes et Traditions 9. Paris: Librairie Philosophique J. Vrin, 2004.

Ibrahim, Mar Gregorios Yohanna. "The Syrian Churches during the Umayyad Era." In *Syriac Churches Encountering Islam: Past Experiences and Future Perspectives*, edited by Dietmar W. Winkler, pp. 48–65. Pro Oriente Studies in the Syriac Tradition 1. Piscataway: Gorgias Press, 2010.

Jastrow, Marcus. *A Dictionary of the Targumim, the Talmud Babli and Yerushalmi, and the Midrashic Literature*. New York: The Judaica Press, 1982.

Jugie, M. "La vie de saint Jean Damascène." *Échos d'Orient* 23 (1924): 137–61.

Kaegi, Walter E. *Byzantium and the Early Islamic Conquests*. Cambridge: Cambridge University Press, 1992.

———. *Heraclius, Emperor of Byzantium*. Cambridge: Cambridge University Press, 2003.

Kazhdan, Alexander P. "George the Synkellos." In *The Oxford Dictionary of Byzantium*, edited by Alexander P. Kazhdan, vol. 2, p. 839. New York and Oxford: Oxford University Press, 1991.

———. "John Damaskenos." In *A History of Byzantine Literature: 650–850*, edited by Alexander P. Kazhdan, pp. 75–94. Research Series 2. Athens: National Hellenic Research Foundation, Institute for Byzantine Research, 1999.

———. "Theophanes the Confessor." In *The Oxford Dictionary of Byzantium*, edited by Alexander P. Kazhdan, vol. 3, p. 2063. New York and Oxford: Oxford University Press, 1991.

Kazhdan, Alexander P., and Stephen Gero. "Kosmas of Jerusalem: A More Critical Approach to His Biography." *Byzantinische Zeitschrift* 82 (1989): 122–32.

Khoury, Paul. "Jean Damascène et l'Islam." *Proche Orient Chrétien* 7 (1957): 45–63; 8 (1958): 313–39.

Kontouma-Conticello, Vassa. "Jean Damascène." In *Dictionnaire des philosophes antiques*, edited by R. Goulet, vol. 3, pp. 1001–27. Paris: Éditions CNRS, 2000.

———. "Jean III d'Antioche (996–1021) et la *Vie de Jean Damascène* (BHG 884)." *Revue des Études Byzantines* 68 (2010): 127–47.

———. "Vie de Jean Damascène." In *Jean Damascène, La foi orthodoxe*, translated by P. Ledrux, pp. 11–30. Sources Chrétiennes 535. Paris: Éditions du Cerf, 2010.

Kotter, P. Bonifatius. *Die Schriften des Johannes von Damaskos.* 5 vols. Berlin: De Gruyter, 1969–1988.

Kruisheer, Dirk, and Lucas Van Rompay. "A Bibliographical Clavis to the Works of Jacob of Edessa." *Hugoye* 1 (1998). http://www.bethmardutho.org/index.php/hugoye/volume-index/92.html.

Lammens, Henri. "Études sur le règne du Calife Omaiyade Moʿâwia Ier." *Mélanges de la faculté orientale de l'Université Saint-Joseph de Beyrouth* 1 (1906): 1–108.

———. "Études sur le règne du Calife Omaiyade Moʿawia Ier (deuxième série)." *Mélanges de la faculté orientale de l'Université Saint-Joseph de Beyrouth* 2 (1907): 1–172.

———. "Études sur le règne du calife omaiyade Moʿâwia Ie (troisième série: la Jeunesse du Calife Yazid Ier)." *Mélanges de la faculté orientale de l'Université Saint-Joseph de Beyrouth* 3 (1908): 143–312.

———. "Le califat de Yazîd Ier." *Mélanges de la faculté orientale de l'Université Saint-Joseph de Beyrouth* 4 (1910): 233–312.

———. "Le califat de Yazîd Ier (4e et dernier fascicule)" *Mélanges de la faculté orientale de l'Université Saint-Joseph de Beyrouth* 6 (1913): 401–92.

———. "Le chantre des Omiades: Notes bibliographiques et littéraires sur le poète arabe chrétien Akhṭal." *Journal Asiatique* 4, 9th series (1894): 94–176, 193–241, 381–459.

Lamoreux, John C., editor and translator. *The Life of Stephen of Mar Sabas.* Corpus Scriptorum Christianorum Orientalium 578–79. Leuven: Peeters, 1999.

Lampe, G. W. H. *A Patristic Greek Lexicon.* Oxford: Clarendon Press, 1961.

Le Coz, Raymond. *Histoire de l'Église d'Orient: Chrétiens d'Irak, d'Iran et de Turquie.* Paris: Éditions du Cerf, 1995.

———. *Jean Damascène: écrits sur l'Islam.* Sources Chrétiennes 383. Paris: Éditions du Cerf, 1992.

Lieu, Samuel N. C. *Manichaeism in the Later Roman Empire and Medieval China: A Historical Survey.* Manchester: Manchester University Press, 1988.

Louth, Andrew. "John of Damascus and the Making of the Byzantine Theological Synthesis." In *The Sabaite Heritage in the Orthodox Church from the Fifth Century to the Present,* edited by Joseph Patrich, pp. 301–04. Orientalia Lovaniensia Analecta 98. Leuven: Peeters, 2001.

———. "Palestine under the Arabs, 650–750: The Crucible of Byzantine Orthodoxy." In *The Holy Land, Holy Lands, and Christian History,* edited by R. N. Swanson, pp. 67–77. Studies in Church History 36. London: The Boydell Press for the Ecclesiastical History Society, 2000.

———. *St. John Damascene: Tradition and Originality in Byzantine Theology.* Oxford Early Christian Studies. Oxford: Oxford University Press, 2002.

al-Masʿūdī. *Kitâb at-tanbîh wa'l-ischrâf.* Edited by M. J. de Goeje, *Kitâb at-tanbîh wa'l-ischrâf auctore al-Masûdî.* Bibliotheca Geographorum Arabicorum 8. Leiden: Brill, 1894.

Massignon, Louis. "La politique islamo-chrétienne des scribes nestoriens de Deir Qunna à la cour de Bagdad au ixe siècle de notre ère." *Vivre et Penser* 2 (1942): 7–14.

Menze, Volker-Lorenz. *Justinian and the Making of the Syrian Orthodox Church.* Oxford and New York: Oxford University Press, 2008.

Michael the Syrian, *Chronicle.* Edited and translated by Jean-Baptiste Chabot, *Chronique de Michel le Syrien, patriarche jacobite d'Antioche (1166–1199).* 4 vols. Paris: E. Leroux, 1899–1924.

Migne, Jacques-Paul, editor. *Patrologia graeca.* 162 vols. Paris: Garnier Fratres, 1857–1886.

Nasrallah, J. *Saint Jean de Damas: son époque, sa vie, son œuvre.* Souvenirs chrétiens de Damas 2. Harissa: Imprimerie Grecque Melchite de Saint Paul, 1950.

Pines, Shlomo. "Some Traits of Christian Theological Writing in Relation to Moslem Kalām and to Jewish Thought." *Proceedings of the Israel Academy of the Sciences and the Humanities* 5 (1976): 112–15.

Pirone, Bartolomeo. "Continuità della Vita Monastica nell'Ottavo Secolo: S. Stefano Sabaita." In *The Sabaite Heritage in the Orthodox Church from the Fifth Century to the Present*, edited by Joseph Patrich, pp. 49–62. Orientalia Lovaniensia Analecta 98. Leuven: Peeters, 2001.

Portillo, Rocio Daga. "The Arabic Life of St. John of Damascus." *Parole de l'Orient* 21 (1996): 157–88.

al-Qāḍī, Wadad. "The Names of Estates in State Registers Before and After the Arabization of the 'Dīwāns.'" In *Umayyad Legacies: Medieval Memories from Syria to Spain*, edited by Antoine Borrut and Paul M. Cobb, pp. 255–80. Leiden: Brill, 2010.

Roggema, Barbara. *The Legend of Sergius Baḥīrā: Eastern Christian Apologetics and Apocalyptic in Response to Islam*. Leiden: Brill, 2009.

Sahas, Daniel J. "The Arab Character of the Christian Disputation with Islam: The Case of John of Damascus (ca. 655–ca. 749)." In *Religionsgespräche im Mittelalter*, edited by Bernard Lewis and Friedrich Niewöhner, pp. 185–205. Wolfenbütteler Mittelalter-Studien 4. Wiesbaden: Harrassowitz, 1992.

———. "Cultural Interaction during the Ummayad Period: The 'Circle' of John of Damascus." *ARAM* 6 (1994): 35–66.

———. *Icon and Logos: Sources in Eighth-Century Iconoclasm*. Toronto: University of Toronto Press, 1986.

———. *John of Damascus on Islam: "The Heresy of the Ishmaelites."* Leiden: Brill, 1972.

Studer, B. *Die theologische Arbeitsweise des Johannes von Damaskus*. Studia Patristica et Byzantina 2. Ettal: Buch-Kunst, 1956.

Swanson, Mark N. "The Arabic Letter of Leo III to ʿUmar II." In *Christian-Muslim Relations: A Bibliographical History*, Vol. 1: *600–900*, edited by David Thomas and Barbara Roggema, pp. 377–80. The History of Christian-Muslim Relations 11. Leiden: Brill, 2009.

al-Ṭabarī, Muḥammad b. Jarīr. *Taʾrīkh al-rusul wa-al-mulūk*. Edited by M. J. de Goeje, *Annales quos scripsit Abu Djafar Mohammed ibn Djarir at-Tabari*. 16 vols. Leiden: Brill, 1879–1901.

Tang, Li. *A Study of the History of Nestorian Christianity in China and Its Literature in Chinese; Together with a New English Translation of the Dunhuang Nestorian Documents*. 2nd rev. ed. Frankfurt am Main: Peter Lang, 2001.

Tannous, Jack. "Between Christology and Kalām? The Life and Letters of George, Bishop of the Arab Tribes." In *Malphono w-Rabo d-Malphone: Studies in Honor of Sebastian P. Brock*, edited by George A. Kiraz, pp. 671–716. Piscataway: Gorgias Press, 2008.

———. "You Are What You Read: Qenneshre and the Miaphysite Church in the Seventh Century." In *History and Identity in the Late Antique Near East*, edited by Philip Wood, pp. 83–102. Oxford: Oxford University Press, 2013.

ter Haar Romeny, Bas. "From Religious Association to Ethnic Community: A Research Project on Identity Formation among the Syrian Orthodox under Muslim Rule." *Islam and Christian-Muslim Relations* 16 (2005): 377–99.

Theophanes the Confessor. *Chronicle*. Translated by Cyril Mango and Roger Scott, *The Chronicle of Theophanes Confessor: Byzantine and Near Eastern History, A.D. 284–813*. Oxford: Oxford University Press, 1997.

Vailhé, S. "Date de la mort de saint Jean Damascène." *Échos d'Orient* 9 (1906): 28–30.

Valkenberg, Pim. "John of Damascus and the Theological Construction of Christian Identity vis-à-vis Early Islam." *Jaarboek Thomas Instituut te Utrecht* 20 (2001): 8–30.

Valkenberg, Pim, and Adelbert Davids. "John of Damascus: The Heresy of the Ishmaelites." In *The Three Rings: Textual Studies in the Historical Trialogue of Judaism, Christianity, and Islam*, edited by Barbara Roggema, Marcel Poorthuis, and Pim Valkenberg, pp. 71–90. Publications of the Thomas Instituut te Utrecht 11. Leuven: Peeters, 2005.

van Ess, Josef. *Theologie und Gesellschaft im 2. und 3. Jahrhundert Hidschra: Eine Geschichte des religiösen Denkens im frühen Islam.* 6 vols. Berlin: De Gruyter, 1991–1995.

van Roey, A. "La lettre apologétique d'Élie à Léon, syncelle de l'évêque chalcédonien de Ḥarrān: une apologie monophysite du viiie–ixe siècle." *Le Muséon* 57 (1944): 1–52.

Villa, David H. "Stephen Manṣūr." In *Christian-Muslim Relations: A Bibliographical History,* Vol. 1: *600-900,* edited by David Thomas and Barbara Roggema, pp. 388–89. The History of Christian-Muslim Relations 11. Leiden: Brill, 2009.

Wansbrough, John. *The Sectarian Milieu: Content and Composition of Islamic Salvation History.* London Oriental Series 34. Oxford: Oxford University Press, 1978.

al-Yaʿqūbī, Ahmad. *Taʾrīkh.* Edited by M. Th. Houtsma, *Ibn Wādhih qui dicitur al-Jaʿqūbī, Historiae.* 2 vols. Leiden: Brill, 1883.

Zaborowski, Jason R. "Arab Christian Physicians as Interreligious Mediators: Abū Shākir as a Model Christian Expert." *Islam and Muslim-Christian Relations* 22 (2011): 185–96.

3

Christians in the Service of the Caliph: Through the Looking Glass of Communal Identities

Muriel Debié, École Pratique des Hautes Études

We know from experience that when we are told a story about a person or an event we ought to listen to the point of view of several independent witnesses or protagonists in order to get a more objective picture of what happened. This is all the more true in the case of a criminal trial or of any controversial issue. As historians we cannot but be aware of this, and yet at the same time we are often dependent on the sources available to us, which give, most of the time, a one-sided account of history and past events. We all know how important it is to compare and contrast our sources, and yet, not only because of traditional academic frontiers but also because of our inability to deal with multiple languages, corpora, and bibliographies, we tend to restrict ourselves to those materials with which we are familiar. That is why an initiative such as this one — the work of Fred Donner and Antoine Borrut, thanks to whom we are having these exchanges — is so important.

We also know that we ought to be more aware of the position from which the historian is speaking, and his or her cultural, academic, and ideological background. Being heirs of a Western conception of antiquity as having been Greek and Roman, our mental map has long been shaped by the image of a Roman *oikoumene*, a Roman vision of the Mediterranean region as *Mare nostrum*, excluding those territories that lay outside the frontiers of what was considered the civilized world. Late antiquity was long considered as the history of the decline and fall of "the" empire — the coming of Islam putting a definite end to the ancient world. But now, terms such as "the post-classical world" or "bas empire" have been abandoned, and it is in the context of decolonization, the questioning of cultural hegemony, and the search for identities in a more globalized world where nation-states are challenged and a "clash of civilizations" announced, that modern historians are engaging with what is now termed late antiquity. The aim of this paper is to show that when studying the role played by the Christians in the Umayyad state, modern historians ought to be aware that their predecessors were also affected by their own cultural and ideological contexts, and so we must go beyond the images created by the historical sources, which so often mirror the religious affiliations of their authors, in order to gain a better and more trustworthy picture of actual events and their explanations.

The Edessan Family of the Gūmōyē

The variety and complexity of interrelations among the Christian churches in the Near East are as confusing for modern observers as they were for the newly arrived "Muslims," who were themselves in the process of defining their own socio-religious identity.[1] But it should not be forgotten that the definitive identity formation of these churches, and of their internal sects and subdivisions, also took place in the context of the new Islamic rule,[2] when they each had to assert their independence from the other Christian denominations and their own unique identity. Modern historians far too often tend to consider that these inter-communal differences are relevant only for ecclesiastical history, or for the study of Christian doctrine. The christological debates that continued after the fifth century, concerning the nature of the union between the human and divine natures of Christ, are considered as "byzantine" disputes — in the pejorative, rather than political, sense of the term — and thus of no interest except for broad-brush portraits of the Eastern Christian world into which the Muslim-Arab conquests irrupted. Few historians of the period, except those who work on Christian sources, actually bother to engage with what look like complex theological issues with little impact on historical events, except to make simplistic claims that this theological complexity may explain the success of the comparatively simpler religious message of Islam regarding the nature of the divinity.

This paper will argue that these differences among Christian groups, however pointless and complex they may appear, should not be discounted or ignored since they deeply shaped the social networks of the indigenous groups. They also had consequences for the ways that the sources about these groups were written by contemporary historians, or by later historians, who were themselves not only members of these groups but also key figures in the process of identity formation. And perhaps more importantly, the expression of the differences of these "sectarian" milieux, as they are aptly described, continues to shape the way we read these very same sources today. So, it is to the distortions introduced by the fragmented identities of the Christian groups in the Umayyad state that this paper would like to draw attention, by casting some light on the little-studied milieu of the Syriac Orthodox and Chalcedonian Christians in Edessa, the metropolis of northern Mesopotamia. Inter-communal and sectarian relations here were already complicated at the time of the conquest, due not only to the long-running christological and ecclesio-political controversies, but also to the consequences of the recent lengthy occupation of the Near East (ca. fifteen years) by the Sasanians.

The importance of the Chalcedonian milieux of the Judean monasteries has been well studied, and in particular the influence of the Christian Manṣūr family in Damascus has been drawn to the attention of historians. In his paper in this volume, Sydney Griffith has traced their influence over several generations. Another contemporary family, however, distinguished itself during the same period (although for a shorter time span), and yet has so far received very little attention. The Gūmōyē family of Edessa are the counterpart of the Manṣūr family of Damascus, as well as their religious adversaries, since they were Syrian Orthodox

---

[1] On the making of a discrete Muslim identity, see Donner, *Muhammad and the Believers*.

[2] Cf. Griffith, *The Church in the Shadow of the Mosque*. On the Syrian Orthodox, cf. ter Haar Romeny, ed., "Religious Origins of Nations?" and idem, "Ethnicity, Ethnogenesis and the Identity of Syriac Orthodox Christians."

and the Manṣūrs were Chalcedonian Melkites. Although they were in touch, were part of the same Umayyad administration, and probably had at some point to worked together, the Manṣūrs at the caliph's court in Damascus and the Gūmōyē in Egypt, the Gūmōyē are hardly mentioned in the Melkite sources, and the Syro-Orthodox sources do not reflect the same image of the Manṣūrs that we get from the Melkite sources.[3]

The Syriac chronicle of Michael the Syrian[4] and the anonymous *Chronicle up to the Year 1234*[5] borrowed from the chronography of the Syrian Orthodox patriarch Dionysius of Tell-Maḥrē[6] the history of this noble family of Edessa that was linked by matrimony to the Tellmaḥrōyē, the family of Dionysius himself. He in turn had borrowed material concerning the Gūmōyē from the accounts written by his maternal grandfather, Daniel son of Moses of Ṭur ʿAbdin. The Tellmaḥrōyē had thus in their midst a dynasty of historians: Moses (Dionysius' great-grandfather), his son Daniel (Dionysius' grandfather), Dionysius himself, and his older brother Theodosius, the metropolitan of Edessa. They were, among other things, the historians of their own family and of the other related noble Syrian Orthodox families of Edessa.

Dionysius' fairly long account of the life and career of Athanasius bar Gūmōyē in the caliph's service is preserved in the later chronicle of Michael the Syrian and that up to 1234. It can be summarized as follows:

> This Athanasius, called Bar Gūmōyē, was from Edessa. He was a noble and an intelligent man. He had studied a lot, both ecclesiastical and secular books, and was famous everywhere. When he heard that he was such a learned man, ʿAbd al-Malik summoned him to Damascus and entrusted him with his younger brother ʿAbd al-ʿAziz, who became the emir of Egypt, and asked him to be his secretary and his preceptor. "To put it briefly, all the countries submitted to the Arabs (*Ṭayyāyē*) were placed under the direction of Athanasius."[7] He was in charge of the tribute in Egypt. Since in addition to the money and honors he received from the king he and his sons received each year one dinar for each soldier in Egypt, and knowing that there were 30,000 soldiers stationed in Egypt and that he stayed there for 21 years, it is not surprising that he became immensely rich. He was zealous for the orthodox faith. He repaired and built churches, gave to the poor and the orphans. He owned 4,000 slaves, villages, houses, gardens, gold, silver, and gemstones. In Edessa he owned 300 shops and 9 hospitals. His elder son Peter was in charge of his possessions in Edessa and the others helped him in the region of Gunada (?). In Egypt he built several churches and monasteries and in the city of Fosṭat he built two churches. He built in Edessa the beautiful church of the Mother of God. He also built a baptistery with channels of water such as those established by the bishop Amazonios in the great and old church of Edessa. He adorned it with marble, gold, and silver.[8]

This history, as summarized from the later sources, reveals the clear pride of the Edessans concerning the high position Athanasius reached in the caliph's service. It is instructive on several grounds, for it shows that at the same time that ʿAbd al-Malik (685–705) allegedly

[3] The Gūmōyē have also been largely neglected in modern scholarship, but see now Mikhail, *From Byzantine to Islamic Egypt*.

[4] The Syrian Orthodox Patriarch of Antioch (1166–1199), and among other things a distinguished historian. Michael the Syrian, *Chronicle*, ed. Chabot, hereafter cited as MS *Chronicle*.

[5] *Chronicle up to the Year 1234*, ed. Chabot, hereafter cited as *Chronicle of 1234*. See now Hilkens, The Anonymous Syriac *Chronicle up to the Year 1234*.

[6] Syrian Orthodox Patriarch of Antioch, 818–845.

[7] MS *Chronicle* XI, 16, t. IV, p. 447 T, II, p. 475 V.

[8] MS *Chronicle* XI, 16, t. IV, pp. 447–48 T, II, p. 475 V; *Chronicle of 1234* I, pp. 229–30 T, 294–95 V.

ordered his men to tear down crosses and to kill all pigs,[9] he also entrusted a Christian with the education of his younger brother and with the administration, or at least the taxation, of Egypt.

The Educational Issue

The mention of Athanasius having studied secular as well as ecclesiastical books clearly indicates that he knew Greek as well as Syriac, like all educated Edessans (including Dionysius of Tell-Maḥrē and his brother, later on in the ninth century). From his role as preceptor of the caliph's brother, we can reasonably surmise that he knew Arabic too. We can also conclude that the caliph singled him out because he was an outstanding scholar — although even here, perhaps we should not dismiss the possibility that his family also had influential court connections.

More generally, we know that the Syrian Orthodox strongly encouraged education both in their monasteries and in their numerous schools at all levels,[10] in contrast to the miaphysite Copts, for instance. If we are to believe Dionysius of Tell-Maḥrē, a *Tetrapylion* outside the Old Church of Edessa served, until its destruction by the emir Muḥammad in 823/4, as a place of gathering where every morning the nobles and the priests of Edessa would meet to discuss and expound both secular and ecclesiastical books.[11] It is, at least as far as I know, the only mention of such a practice, and it is particularly noteworthy that this included laymen and was not restricted, as we might have imagined, to clerics and monks. Such high levels of education and literacy among the elites would explain how over several generations high civil and church servants came from the same noble Edessan families, whether as secretaries of the caliph (such as Athanasius and his sons) or, a little later on, as patriarchs like Dionysius, who was no less well connected to and intimate with the caliphal court of his own day. The position held by Athanasius bar Gūmōyē also clearly had consequences for the rest of his family, and in particular his sons: the elder was in charge of the private business of the family in Edessa, while the others held office as assistants to their father.

In this period and place, as in many others, education was clearly seen as a necessary means of preparing young and wealthy aristocrats to take over the family business. The historian and bishop John of Ephesus in the sixth century already portrayed in his Syriac *Lives of the Eastern Saints* a noble Armenian called Thomas whose father spent large sums of money in order to provide him with a first-rate education, and so prepared him for a successful career, during which he became a leader of men, took over the position of his father at court, and administered the family properties with the aid of his own sons.[12] The heirs of the rich and noble families of northern Mesopotamia were thus educated and trained in order to perform the duties associated with their social position. There can be little doubt that it was precisely because of these skills, developed by a careful education, that at the time of the nascent Umayyad empire when competent civil servants were urgently required, these Christian nobles were employed as secretaries and administrators despite their religion.

[9] Hoyland, *Theophilus of Edessa's Chronicle*, p. 189.

[10] Debié, "Livres et monastères."

[11] MS *Chronicle* XII, 13, t. IV, p. 514 T, III, pp. 61–62 V.

[12] John of Ephesus, *Lives of the Eastern Saints*, XXI, pp. 283–98.

The Practical Forms of Identity

It is interesting to note that among the various activities of Athanasius the construction of churches is singled out for mention, not only in Edessa but also in Egypt where he was stationed. This was one of the key social issues in the early years after the conquest, as it had already been during the period of the Sasanian occupation. Church buildings were prominent public monuments throughout the cities of Syria and Mesopotamia, although of varying degrees of splendor and grandeur, and so their ownership was an obvious public affirmation of the prosperity, prestige, and local social status of the relevant Christian denomination which could not be ignored by the new political powers. Church buildings also played an important role within the Christian communities, where the question of identity was not only based on theological differences as expressed in controversial texts or christological treatises, but was also a question of daily religious practices and the recognition of socio-religious groups in the public sphere of the city, not least in response to the basic question: Who prays where? The possession of the churches may have been one of the first issues at play in the encounter of the new conquerors and the numerous Christian denominations, with multiple groups asserting their rights of ownership over specific places of worship, and frequently the same places of worship. In these confrontations it was not simply a matter of Christians versus Muslims — although the size and central location of the most splendid urban churches would eventually frequently encourage their confiscation and conversion into mosques for reasons of Muslim political and social affirmation — but more frequently in our period, confrontation between the various Christian denominations, such as the Syrian Orthodox, the Chalcedonians, and the "Nestorians," or indeed between sub-divisions within these denominations: the Syrian Orthodox, for example, were still divided into Julianists and Severians,[13] and the Chalcedonians into "melkites" and "monothelites." Since their identity was essentially a socio-religious one, the possession of the churches was its most visible dimension since it was inconceivable for these groups to share a common altar and partake in the same mysteries. The Muslim rulers were thus immediately confronted by the mosaic of Christian denominations in the very geography of the conquered cities and had to legislate about the use of the churches.

What we learn from the Syriac chronicles is that under the Sasanians the Syrian Orthodox appear to have been favored by the occupying administration: their bishops were allowed by King Khusrō II to return to their sees from the exile imposed upon them by the Byzantine emperor because of their miaphysite adherence.[14] In Edessa they regained possession of the main church, known as the Old Church. During the Byzantine reconquest, however, when Emperor Heraclius (r. 610–640) came to Edessa, the miaphysite bishop Isaiah forbade him to communicate unless he anathematized the Council of Chalcedon. The emperor was so outraged that he decided to give the cathedral back to the Chalcedonians. The most important Syrian Orthodox families (including the Tellmaḥrōyē and the Reṣaphōyē) immediately decided to leave "their" church (to which they had given money and precious donations, and which they had adorned), with the secret hope that after the departure of the emperor they would be able to return with "their" bishop (presumably one coming from their ranks) and regain their church.[15]

---

[13] See Penn, "Julian of Halicarnassus," on the controversy between Julian and Severus of Antioch.

[14] MS *Chronicle* X, 26, t. IV, p. 391 T, II, p. 381 V.

[15] MS *Chronicle* XI, t. IV, p. 409 T, II, p. 412 V.

More generally, since Heraclius after the reconquest was unable to impose unity upon the Syro-Orthodox and the Chalcedonians, he allowed the Chalcedonians to plunder the possessions of their adversaries. As a consequence, many churches and monasteries actually changed hands and came under Chalcedonian control, especially in Mabbug, Emesa, and the "regions in the south" (southern Syria), and this also affected property belonging to the monks of the monastery of Mar-Maron.[16] Induced by the possibility of material gains, a number of Syrian Orthodox groups seem to have switched sides in these regions and to have become Chalcedonians. So during the period of the Byzantine reconquest, a new confessional geography was unfolding, reflecting the recent shift in the political influence and governmental support of the various Christian denominations. Contemporaries seem to have presumed that this was only temporary, and that it would no doubt shift again with a change of imperial policy, or leadership, whereas in fact, as events turned out, it was to be crystallized by the Muslim conquests.[17] Dionysius of Tell-Maḥrē thus complains bitterly about the fact that churches remained in the hands of the Chalcedonians after the Muslim conquests because the conquerors decided to leave the churches in the possession of the denomination that held them when the cities made their submission. He thus particularly regrets that the Great Church in Edessa, and also that in Ḥarrān, were lost to the Syrian Orthodox and became the permanent property of the Chalcedonians who happened to hold them when the Muslims took control of the cities. But at the same time he also emphasizes the positive side of the new regime, namely that the Syrian Orthodox were at last freed from persecutions by the Byzantine Chalcedonian power.[18]

Other examples of the importance of the issue of the possession of religious buildings can be found in the Syriac *Life of Simeon of the Olives*, a monk of the celebrated monastery of Mar-Gabriel/Qartmin, who later became the bishop of Ḥarrān.[19] While still a monk, but one with a private fortune, Simeon decided to build churches for the Syrian Orthodox in the city of Nisibis (modern Nusaybin in southeast Turkey), which had traditionally been a stronghold of the Nestorians. He gained support from the local Muslim governor through his generous gifts and asked permission to go and see (and bribe) the caliph in order to be granted an official permit for the building of religious buildings (namely a monastery outside the gate of the city and two churches, to be endowed with an inn, gardens, mills, and orchards, ca. 706). The opposition he encountered did not come, as we might have expected, from the Muslim authorities but from the Nestorians, who were at that time the dominant Christian group in the city and who were hostile to the local implantation of the Syrian Orthodox with the support of the Muslim authorities.

Simeon allegedly also built a mosque in the city with a "*madrasa*," just as he had founded a school with the church in his native village of Habsenas. It is not clear whether this is intended simply to be another example of Simeon's worldly wise actions — to be reckoned

[16] MS *Chronicle* XI, t. IV, p. 410 T, II, p. 412 V.

[17] For a summary of the successive changes, see MS *Chronicle* XI, 5, p. 414 T, II, p. 419 V.

[18] MS *Chronicle* XI, t. IV, p. 411 T, II, p. 413 V; *Chronicle of 1234*, p. 287 T, II, pp. 185–86 V.

[19] This fascinating life is still unpublished (A. Palmer announced its edition in his book *Monk and Mason*), but thanks to the generosity of Jack Tannous I have had access to the images of two manuscripts of this *Life*, as well as to Jack's draft English translation. A translation into French is in progress and one into English in Oxford. Fiey and Conrad, *Saints syriaques*, p. 175, no. 412; see Brock, "The Fenqitho," for a summary of the *Life*, and Palmer, *Monk and Mason*, pp. 159–65, 256.

alongside his shrewd financial investment in shops, mills, and inns, as well, of course, as in his trademark, olives — or whether this is a memory of a political deal, in which, in exchange for being allowed to renew some old Christian buildings and also to build new ones, he also had to build a mosque. It is interesting to see that he associated with it a Muslim *madrasa*, following the well-established tradition in the region that the founding of a church always went with the founding of a school.

This life also offers a striking example of what Antoine Borrut called "historiographical filters" of Abbasid times that led, later on under the Abbasids, to a re-writing of what happened at the time of the Umayyads.[20] We do not have here an official re-writing but obviously the image, not to say the legend, of the Abbasid period that had an impact on the shaping of this Christian hagiographical discourse in the context of controversies with other Christian denominations on the one hand, and Islam on the other. Although Simeon lived in the Umayyad period (he died in 724), it is the Abbasid-era reality that is superimposed on his story by the later anonymous author who narrated his life. The fame of the religious disputations at the caliph's *majlis* in Baghdad (founded in 762) was such that the author of the life imagined a religious debate between Simeon and representatives of the Nestorians, Jews, and Muslims in Baghdad at the court of al-Maʾmūn (r. 813–833, that is, nearly a hundred years after Simeon's death) as if it were the only way in which Simeon's visit to the caliphal court could have taken place. The model for this religious disputation is probably that said to have been conducted by Theodore Abū Qurrah (ca. 750–ca. 823),[21] and so appears to be an appropriation of the history of a Melkite hero by the Syrian Orthodox hagiographer, a well-known practice in hagiographic literature, where it is customary to borrow literary motifs, situations, miracles, and even characters.[22] We have here then an anachronistic account of a typical practice of Abbasid times transposed to the time of the Umayyad empire, and also an example of the translation of a holy man (or, at least, his deeds) from one Christian denomination to another. Both are due to the great scholarly prestige of the learned Abū Qurrah and of his having become the very type of the Christian disputer with Islam.

Disputes between Christians were not only private matters but could also draw the attention of the emirs, especially if they led to public order problems. For example, the internal schism among the Chalcedonians concerning the number of wills in Christ — with on one side the dyothelete supporters of Maximus the Confessor (who acknowledged the Council of Constantinople II), and on the other the monotheletes (who opposed Maximus and accepted the longer version of the *Trisagion*) — produced open conflict and sometimes violent disorder. In Aleppo, for instance, the two factions fought over the main church. The emir had to intervene in order to enforce peace between them. He ordered that a movable partition be constructed in the middle of the church to separate the two parties, but they still fought over the top of this, and so he had the two bishops punished (their hair and beards were shaved), and he put armed (Muslim?) guards on each side of the altar, who were to ensure that the priests of the two factions would celebrate together each day and would each give communion to their own faithful.[23] Thus the emir, as the civic authority in charge of enforcing the law, also had to play the role of arbiter between the Christian factions, like a father with unruly children.

---

[20] Borrut, *Entre mémoire et pouvoir*, esp. pp. 79ff.

[21] Cf. Bertaina, An Arabic Account of Theodore Abu Qurra. Lamoreaux, "The Biography of Theodore Abū Qurrah Revisited."

[22] Palmer, *Monk and Mason*, p. 161.

[23] MS *Chronicle* XI, 20, t. IV, pp. 460–61 T, II, pp. 495–96 V.

Destruction of churches certainly took place, but they were never a rule, and such actions occurred either at the initiative of individual governors or under special circumstances. Indeed, as exemplified by the stories of Athanasius and Simeon, the Christians were even allowed to build new churches, provided appropriate financial provisions were made: they had to pay for the costs of building the churches, of course, but they also needed to gain the favor of the rulers by means of well-chosen gifts, or even by building mosques or other public buildings in addition to the Christian building. In the beginning the attitude of the new masters was a pragmatic one: they did not have a predetermined plan, or a well-established ideological position on this subject, and so they simply continued with the *status quo ante*. The wealth of Athanasius' family in Edessa, as well as his new fortune accumulated during his stay in Egypt, enabled him to increase the number of churches available for his own community. Since his activity did not affect the Melkites directly, it is not mentioned in Melkite sources, but only in those histories written by members of the related aristocratic Syrian Orthodox families in Edessa.

The Gūmōyē and the Manṣūr

Every political regime depends upon financial income from the territory ruled to enable the functioning of the state, and this is a particularly sensitive matter for new rulers following military conquest, who still need to pay for the maintenance of large military forces, and who lack the detailed knowledge of local wealth necessary to enable the imposition of their own tax collectors. Once again, what happened in the Umayyad state is remarkably similar to that which occurred earlier during the Sasanian occupation. The leading Christian families who had acted as tax collectors for the Byzantine empire continued to fulfil this same function under the new regimes, and so collected taxes first for the Sasanian shah and then for the caliphs. From Melkite sources we learn that this was the role played by the Manṣūr family, Sergius and his better-known son John, as secretaries of the caliph ʿAbd al-Malik (685–705), but were it not for the Syrian Orthodox chronicles we could easily be misled into thinking that they were the only Christians at the same level in the administration of the Umayyad state. The Gūmōyē, however, occupied the same type of position in the new administration, but in Egypt in the service of the governor. Both families were in charge of collecting taxes, and, at least in the case of the Gūmōyē, their redistribution.

The image of the Gūmōyē that emerges from the testimony of the Syriac sources is one of a family as powerful as the Manṣūr, and maybe even richer, due to their previous fortune in Edessa being supplemented by what they accumulated in Egypt. The account of Dionysius and his family archives gives a unique insight into the way the tax collectors were paid, since it is said that they received a dinar for each soldier stationed in Egypt. Not surprisingly the tax was linked to the armed forces since it was primarily used to pay the soldiers.

It also reveals how the affairs of the caliphate were geographically decentralized, each emir being in charge of the administration of a portion of the state. The links between Edessa and Egypt are attested here for the first time at an administrative level. It is well known that Syrian ecclesiastical leaders — notably patriarch Severus of Antioch (513–518) but also crowds of ordinary priests, bishops, and monks — were exiled to Egypt during the Byzantine campaigns against the miaphysites. This special link between the ecclesiastical milieux in Syria and in Egypt may also explain why Athanasius was chosen for administering Muslim affairs there. His intervention on behalf of the miaphysite bishop in Alexandria confirms that membership of a specific religious community had practical consequences, no doubt because of the existence of networks of social contacts inside the communities. This situation proved to be an enduring one since, at the turn of the eighth and ninth centuries, Patriarch Dionysius of Tell-Maḥrē was summoned to Egypt by the contemporary emir in order to take care of a peasants' revolt in the south.[24] It was not the local Alexandrian patriarch but the Syrian one who was given responsibility for regulating internal difficulties of the caliphate in Egypt. This may perhaps have been due to the same logic that forbids French Gendarme officers from being posted to their home regions, thus preventing local sympathies from interfering with the exercise of their duty, but other factors doubtless also played a role. Dionysius, as well as his brother Theodosius, who was the bishop of Edessa, may well have been singled out by the caliph and the emir of Egypt because of their high level of education, received in the celebrated monastery of Qenneshre in Syria, where they were educated in Greek as well as in Syriac, and Dionysius, at least, also spoke Arabic fluently. Upon his arrival Dionysius was received as a high-ranking official, almost as an ambassador of the Christians, not only of his own church, but more broadly of all the Christians for whom he interceded, whether from Egypt, Mosul, or Edessa. He was even allowed to enter into the presence of the caliph on horseback and was admitted to the caliph's private gardens.[25] But this is another era and another paper. What is described then in Athanasius' history is not that exceptional, and the same circumstances had the same result more than a century later.

So while he was enforcing the Islamization of the Umayyad state and initiating the transformation of the Arabic state into an Islamic one,[26] ʿAbd al-Malik chose for the education of his brother, as well as for the administration of the finances of the empire, highly qualified individuals from the indigenous Christian families. He is the caliph who built the Dome of the Rock in Jerusalem with a strongly anti-Trinitarian purpose, and yet simultaneously of all the caliphs he was perhaps the one who was most surrounded by Christians at the highest level of the state. The global picture is thus far from being black and white. A dose of realism, as well as a strong sense of the needs of the state, may explain why he chose competent and well-educated men for the sake of the administration whatever their religion and their primary language and culture.

In the Mirror of the Sources

The picture gained from the sources can be mistaken and strangely distorted if all the available sources are not taken into account. Although Melkite sources remember the Manṣūr family as traitors who delivered Damascus into the hands of the Muslims,[27] this aspect does not appear at all in the Syrian Orthodox sources. In the *Chronicle up to 1234*, it is John bar Sarjūn (and not Sarjūn/Sergius) who is mentioned as the "intermediary" between the inhabitants and the conquerors, but nowhere is his attitude condemned in any way. For the Syrian Orthodox, fleeing to the Byzantine empire was not an option since Byzantium could hardly be considered as a shelter or refuge, due to its intrinsic hostility to the miaphysite secession. (Earlier attempts to reunite Chalcedonians and anti-Chalcedonians were strongly motivated by the need to reunify the empire, especially in the aftermath of its reconquest

---

[24] *Chronicle of 1234*, II, pp. 266–67 T, pp. 200–01 V.

[25] Barhebraeus, *Chronicon ecclesiasticum*, pp. 367–68.

[26] See Donner, "Qurʾânicization."

[27] See Sydney Griffith's contribution in this book.

from the Sasanians. Heraclius with his religious *Ekthesis* — which was ultimately, and ironically, brought to a standstill by the monothelete controversy — as well as his policy of forced baptism of Jews, actually tried to enforce on religious grounds a unity much needed on political and military ones.) Treason was not an issue, and the Manṣūr are never presented as traitors to an empire that, admittedly, was often portrayed by the Syrian Orthodox more as an enemy than the Muslim conquerors themselves. Opening a city to the enemy was considered a reasonable thing to do in order to avoid the massacre of the population and the subsequent acts of destruction, especially of the churches.[28] Moreover, the recent experience of the Sasanian occupation and the Byzantine reconquest may well have suggested to many that the new conquest too might well be temporary, and so peaceful occupation would be preferable to violent destruction. Far too often modern historians handle the events of this period without compensating for hindsight; from our perspective it is obvious that the Arab conquest was going to change the region permanently, but this was far from being obvious to contemporaries.

Local issues were also at play: according to Dionysius of Tell-Maḥrē the Egyptians surrendered Alexandria and the whole country to the Arabs because of the persecution by the Chalcedonians; in Damascus, however, it is a Chalcedonian, Sarjūn ibn Manṣūr, who surrendered the city; elsewhere the Syrian Orthodox or Melkite governors did the same, whereas in yet other places they refused to admit defeat. If there was a nationalistic or ethno-religious issue in the decision about whether or not to surrender a city, it was not a simple and homogeneous one. The later commentaries of Byzantine Orthodox sources, as well as of Syrian Orthodox sources, may also have construed interpretations of the events that were acceptable to the readers of their age, but which were quite different from what really happened at the time. A comparison of the available sources produced in the different socio-religious circles shows how religious affiliations have a significant impact on the interpretation of the same events and circumstances. Modern historians may not need to be theologians, but they should at least be aware that the sources they use are profoundly shaped by the pervading religious ideas of the period, not only on a theoretical level but also on a very practical one, since they were part of the process of identity construction by the various groups, often in contradistinction against the others. The immediate consequence is that the rendering of the present and of the past of the communities, whether Muslim, Christian, Jewish, or Zoroastrian, is distorted by the sectarian lens of communal affiliations.

To take another example, while John of Damascus is labeled as "Saracen-minded"[29] in the Byzantine sources, his father is positively appreciated in the Syriac chronicles for being well known and highly considered by the Arabs.[30] Socio-religious affiliation also affected more general attitudes toward the Muslims, and so the Syrian Orthodox were for obvious reasons more positive in their comments about them than some of their Melkite counterparts, especially later on in Byzantium. Sydney Griffith has brilliantly highlighted the fact that Melkites in Palestine should not be confused with the Byzantine Orthodox in Constantinople, even though they shared the same strict Chalcedonian adherence. Theology, and more broadly religion, is only one of the many aspects of the Christian identities considered: culture, language, geographical origins, and religious practices are just as important. We may not have

[28] MS *Chronicle* XI, 7, t. IV, p. 421 T, II, p. 426 V about the rendition of Edessa, whereas Tella and Dara refused to surrender and the Romans were killed.

[29] See Sydney Griffith in this volume.

[30] *Chronicle of 1234*, I, p. 248 T, 194 V.

sources sufficiently detailed and precise to be certain, but it is not improbable that there also existed differences between the urban Melkite milieux in Damascus and the monastic ones in Palestine.

Although the surrender of Damascus is not a charge laid against the Manṣūr family by the Syrian Orthodox sources, nevertheless the rivalry between them and the Gūmōyē is mentioned. Dionysius of Tell-Maḥrē tells how, when the emir ʿAbd al-ʿAzīz died in Egypt, Athanasius bar Gūmōyē did not go back to Edessa but to the capital, Damascus, with his family, all his slaves, possessions, and immense riches. But the Manṣūr were apparently far from happy to see competitors move in to their hometown, and they seem to have been jealous of the wealth of these fellow Christians. Sergius Ibn Manṣūr is said to have denounced Athanasius to the caliph on the grounds that he had plundered Egypt and robbed its resources. However true the denunciation may have been (the caliph may not have needed somebody to draw his attention to the outstanding wealth of Athanasius), the caliph reacted gently, saying that it was not fair that a Christian should be so rich, and he asked him to give him a portion of his wealth and to keep the rest. The conclusion of the chronicler is that even after that Athanasius still had plenty.[31] The challenge, as in other similar examples, was to restrict the visible wealth of Christians to an acceptable level.[32] Their wealth was thus not dissimilar to other outward signs of pride and prosperity (garments, riding on horseback, etc.) or practices (use of *simandras* and bells, processions with crosses); in order to be acceptable to the Muslims they should take care not to stand out, nor to be too visible. In this case the wealth of Athanasius was extraordinary, but the reaction of the caliph was benevolent as well as practical. He did not take sides in the rivalries between the two Christian families, but reacted as was proper to remind Athanasius that he was a Christian subject and was not allowed to do whatever he wanted. At the same time he took financial advantage of the situation and maintained the equilibrium in his administration, keeping the cooperation of his Christian high-ranking officials.

We would have almost no hint of the existence of the Gūmōyē if we relied only upon Melkite sources. Similarly, the Syrian Orthodox sources highlight other aspects of the history of the Manṣūr than do the Melkite ones. The family is thus presented in the Syrian Orthodox sources as agents of a "re-Chalcedonization" of Syria and even Mesopotamia, but we find no mention of this in the Melkite sources. Dionysius of Tell-Maḥrē (or again one of his sources) says that Sergius ibn Manṣūr was greatly oppressing the "Orthodox" in Damascus and in Emesa.[33] He had them erase the addition to the *Trisagion* liturgical prayer which was a sign of the communal identity not only of the anti-Chalcedonians but also of the monothelete Chalcedonians and "neo-Chalcedonians" in Syria and Palestine. This move may in part reflect the growth in numbers of the dyotheletes in Syria due to the conquest and the subsequent arrival in Syria of Roman prisoners, who were mostly dyothelete Chalcedonians. The bishops in the main cities of Jerusalem, Antioch, and even Edessa became, or remained, dyothelete and opposed the christocentric addition to the *Trisagion*. The author of the passage preserved in Michael states that in addition to monotheletes many "Orthodox" also switched sides and became dyothelete Chalcedonians. The campaign of Sergius ibn Manṣūr, supported by the

---

31 *Chronicle of 1234*, I, p. 295 T, 230 V.

32 This was of course a major difficulty faced by the Church more generally, as brilliantly discussed in Brown, *Through the Eye of a Needle*.

33 MS *Chronicle* XI, 20, t. IV, p. 458 T, II, p. 492 V.

influx of refugees, seems to have been successful and to have moved the boundaries between the Christian denominations.

From the opposite point of view, Athanasius bar Gūmōyē is not a complete stranger in other sources, but in these he is only known by his first name and can not easily be identified as a member of the great Gūmōyē family. Outside of these Edessan families, his lineage does not seem significant. According to *The History of the Patriarchs of Alexandria*, Athanasius actually assisted the patriarch John III (681–689) in retrieving the goods put under seal by the Chalcedonian governor of Alexandria, Theodosius, after the death of the patriarch Agathon, his predecessor.[34] It is as a miaphysite that he helped the patriarch against the Chalcedonian governor, taking advantage of his position at the emir's court. It is because of his religious affiliation and of his prominent position that he is thus mentioned in an Egyptian miaphysite source.[35]

Athanasius bar Gūmōyē may also be one and the same as the Athanasius mentioned in the *Hodegos* of Anastasius of Sinai as his opponent during a dispute between miaphysites and dyophysites. Although not a cleric, his involvement in this debate may have been a consequence of his high level of education and culture and the simple accident of his presence in Egypt.

Here again the information drawn from a Chalcedonian Greek and a Miaphysite Copto-Arabic source are utterly different and do not overlap, each having selected the piece of information that was of interest to its own purpose and perspective. It is only through the confrontation of sectarian sources that we can get a sense of the diverging interpretations of the same events due to the varied concerns of different socio-religious and regional communities. The fragmented groups mirrored almost exclusively their own reactions and positions, and so awareness of this requires the modern historian to go beyond the reflection offered by each of them in order to reconstitute a broader and more accurate image of the complexity of the situation.

Even among sources written within the same tradition, modern historians have to face the problem of the transmission of information. The passage quoted below sheds light on yet another aspect of the history of Athanasius and comes from the *Chronicle* of Michael the Syrian and ultimately from Dionysius of Tellmaḥre and his ancestors, but it was not copied by the *Chronicle up to 1234* even though it too made extensive use of Dionysius.

> The baptistery was built in order to house the famous Portrait of Edessa.[36] The Edessans were unable to pay the tribute so somebody suggested to Muḥammad, the tax collector, that he should threaten to take the Portrait because they would then sell all their possessions, even their children and their own life, in order to keep it. Muḥammad did so and the terrified Edessans went and asked the prince Athanasius to lend them the money and to keep the Portrait at home as a guarantee. Athanasius readily accepted and during that time had a copy made by a skilled painter. When the inhabitants gave him the money back, he put the copy back in the baptistery and only later did he exchange it against the real one.[37]

[34] Sévère ibn al-Muqaffaʿ, *History of the Patriarchs*, pp. 4–5.

[35] I owe this reference as well as the following one to André Binggeli.

[36] This image was considered a protector of the City blessed by Jesus; see Griffith, "Crosses, Icons and the Image of Christ in Edessa."

[37] MS *Chronicle* XI, 17, t. IV, pp. 448–49 T, II, pp. 476–77 V.

This anecdote presents a unique insight into the symbolic value of the famous portrait of Jesus kept in Edessa and supposedly painted either by King Abgar's secretary Ḥannan or not by human hands at all (*acheiropoietes* in Greek), and either on a cloth or, according to the later development of the story, as an icon.[38] It seems that a Christian explained to the Muslim tax collector the immense value of this image for the local Christian population and how it could be used to blackmail them into paying their overdue taxes. There is no question here of iconoclasm or problems with icon worshipping. The story, however, sheds light on the outstanding position of Athanasius, who acts as the protector and benefactor of the local Christian population, although presumably with a special bias in favor of the Syrian Orthodox faction. He acts like a local prince, and he was rich enough to be able to pay all the overdue tax until the inhabitants were in a position to pay him back. Once again the anecdote is placed in the broader context of the local communal rivalries, since according to Dionysius the outcome of these events was that the image was at this time transferred from the custody of the Chalcedonians to that of the Syrian Orthodox.[39] Here again the Muslim conquest prompted changes in the balance between the communities. The Syrian Orthodox were no longer considered as heretics, as they had been under Byzantine rule, but they could now affirm their own identity and advance their status and prestige in the same way as any other Christian denomination. And they did not miss the opportunity!

Theophilus of Edessa: A Distorted Image of the Transmission Channels

A final striking example of the importance of communal affiliations in the transmission of historical information within the Christian communities as much as between Christians and Muslims is provided by the person and work of Theophilus of Edessa. The famous Theophilus (ca. 695–785) was another prominent character also of Edessan origin, and a new star of modern Islamic and Byzantine studies. He has attracted much attention in recent decades and exemplifies how the transmission of knowledge was much more dependent on the Christian affiliations than on translation from one language to another or, for that matter, from one religion to another. But it is also a case study of our own modern biases and preconceptions when dealing with late antique sources. Theophilus has been known for a long time to specialists of astrology as one of the leading Christian astrologers, whose works written in Greek entered the great Byzantine collections and also had a strong influence on Islamic astrology.[40] He only really came to the attention of historians, however, with the seminal study of Lawrence Conrad, which focused attention on the "intercultural transmission" between he Byzantine chronography of Theophanes (813), several Syriac chronicles, and the lost text of Theophilus' history. It was the first study since E. W. Brooks' articles at the end of the nineteenth century,[41] and then those of A. S. Proudfoot[42] and N. V. Pigulevskaja[43] in the twentieth century, that drew attention to the existence of a so-called common source used

[38] On the successive developments of this story, see Brock, "Transformations of the Edessa Portrait."

[39] Debié, "Les apocryphes et l'histoire," pp. 72–73.

[40] Pingree, "Astrology"; idem, "From Alexandria to Baghdād to Byzantium," pp. 13–21; Tihon, "L'astronomie à Byzance." See now Borrut, "Court Astrologers and Historical Writing," esp. pp. 477ff.

[41] Brooks, "The Sources of Theophanes."

[42] Proudfoot, "The Sources of Theophanes."

[43] Pigulevskaja, "Theophanes' *Chronographia*."

both by Theophanes in his Greek chronicle and also by a number of Syriac chronicles. Conrad focused on the episode of the conquest of the small island of Arwad and argued that the common source might be Theophilus.[44] Since then this hypothesis has steadily gained ground to the point that in subsequent publications on the subject it is treated as though it were a certainty, especially since it was adopted in the very useful work of Robert Hoyland.[45] At the risk of upsetting some of those who have grown attached to this convenient and familiar hypothesis, I would like here to challenge this well-established consensus and argue for some caution in the attribution of almost all the material of the Umayyad period to Theophilus by reassessing the data we have concerning the author in the later sources.[46]

In many ways Theophilus seems like the perfect candidate for the transmission of the common material derived from Islamic sources found in Christian texts. He was attractive to modern Islamic historians because his career was more familiar to them than that of the other well-known Christian writers of the region who wrote in Syriac and were all monks and bishops, and who were thus not part of the canon of Islamic or Arabic historical sources. Theophilus was the — or one of the — official astronomers of the caliph al-Mahdī (775–785) in Baghdad and may previously have been in the service of Marwān II (744–750) in the same capacity.[47] Not only was he in the service of the caliph, but as a professional astrologer in charge of establishing horoscopes, and with a particular specialization in predictive military astrology, he followed the caliph during his campaigns. It thus comes as no surprise that the historian Agapius of Membidj reports that he was an eyewitness of the battle fought by the caliph Marwān II against the army of Khurāsān led by ʿAbdallāh ibn ʿAlī on the left bank of the Greater Zāb between 15 and 25 January 750,[48] and then goes on to quote him. The trouble is that this is the only passage explicitly attributed to him.

Theophilus is the ghost of Syrian Orthodox historiography, since he haunts it without ever becoming visible. He is cited by Dionysius of Tell-Maḥrē in his preface (copied by Michael the Syrian) as one of his sources, although a distorted one because of his Chalcedonian bias.[49] Barhebraeus praises his chronicle too, which he says was written in Syriac.[50] Since the *Chronography* of Dionysius is not preserved as an independent work but only through the adaptations made by later chroniclers who do not explicitly acknowledge their source, it is a methodological challenge to retrieve Theophilus of Edessa's material from this double layer of lost texts (his own and Dionysius'). And this is all the more true since Dionysius, the only one using Theophilus' chronicle directly, accuses his Chalcedonian counterpart of distorting the truth in matters regarding the Syrian Orthodox and claims that he would cite only what he considered accurate.

Ancient historiography consisted in compiling a text from extracts taken from earlier sources, and the original contribution of any author lay in the way he selected, combined, and organized these extracts. This process showed absolutely no respect for the original

---

[44] Conrad, "Conquest of Arwād."

[45] Hoyland, *Seeing Islam as Others Saw It*, pp. 631–71 (with a tentative reconstitution in English), and more recently Hoyland, "Agapius, Theophilus and Muslim Sources," pp. 355–64.

[46] See Debié, *L'écriture de l'histoire en syriaque*. See also the recent discussion of Conterno, *La "Descrizione dei tempi."*

[47] Pingree, "From Alexandria to Baghdād to Byzantium," p. 15.

[48] Agapius of Manbij, *Kitāb al-ʿunwān*, p. 525.

[49] MS *Chronicle* X, 20, t. IV, p. 378 T, II, p. 358 V.

[50] Barhebraeus, *Chronicon ecclesiasticum*, pp. 126–27; Budge, ed., *Chronography of Gregory Abû'l-Farag*, pp. 116–17; Barhebraeus, *History of the Dynasties*, trans. Pococke, pp. 219–20 T, 147 V.

sources, which could be cut and pasted in any way desired. It is thus often impossible, even if two sources offer parallel passages, to reconstitute the original text, and this is especially true in the case of Theophilus since his work can only be accessed in Syriac sources through the double barrier of its use by Dionysius, who never mentions him as his source for the passages borrowed from his chronicle, and the use of Dionysius by later chroniclers (who do not always mention him as their source, either). It is only through the careful study of passages likely to come from Theophilus given the date of the events referred to, and given what we know of Theophilus' interests and career, that some material might be attributed to him with even minimal confidence. Sifting extant chronicles and histories for information deriving from Theophilus is not an impossible task, but it requires a careful labor of *Quellenforschung*. It is thus a concern that the recent book published by Robert Hoyland under the title *Theophilus of Edessa's Chronicle and the Circulation of Historical Knowledge in Late Antiquity and Early Islam* will in effect appear to make incarnate the work of an author who is, to say the least, evanescent. Many historians will use the book to discover what Theophilus said, when in reality it is simply a collection of passages of uncertain origin that deal with a particular period of history in a particular region. It is clear that the translation by Hoyland in his two books (*Theophilus of Edessa's Chronicle* and *Seeing Islam as Others Saw It*) of the passages dealing with the first years of the caliphate are very useful and provide access to sources that non-specialists would otherwise probably have ignored, but it is far from certain that it actually represents Theophilus' text. Such a reconstitution is highly problematic and each common passage should be discussed in detail in order to provide even the slightest chance of correctly identifying what actually comes from Theophilus.

A recent study of the textual passages common to Theophanes, the Syriac chronicles, and Agapius in their original languages goes in the same direction and argues for a more careful attribution to Theophilus of shared information.[51] It is far from sure that Theophilus was the actual conduit for the circulation of historical knowledge between Theophanes and the Syriac and Arabic sources. As Maria Conterno convincingly argued, the so-called common source also used by the Syriac chronicles, at least for the reign of Emperor Constans II, was more probably written in Greek, and not in Syriac, and so this appears to exclude Theophilus, who wrote his chronicle in Syriac and other potential candidates among the Syriac chroniclers, such as Cyrus of Batnan. The unknown John bar Samuel, however, from the "Western regions," which means Syria and the islands, may have been an intermediary, but we know too little about him, and the language of composition of his work, to be able to build on this hypothesis. The Byzantine chronicler George Syncellus might also have played a role in the transmission of historical material to Constantinople since he is supposed to have handled something like notes to Theophanes. Syncellus shares with Syriac tradition a great number of sources, especially for ancient history, and he might be the George mentioned by Dionysius of Tell-Maḥrē as one of his sources. It is difficult to go beyond what must remain a hypothesis in the meantime, but the circulation of historical material should certainly be envisioned more broadly,[52] especially since it seems that Theophanes had access to Muslim sources directly or from a Greek source, rather than from a Syriac one such as Theophilus.[53]

---

[51] Conterno, *La "Descrizione dei tempi."*

[52] Debié, *L'écriture de l'histoire en syriaque*; idem, "Theophanes' 'Oriental Source.'" See also in the same volume Hoyland, "Agapius, Theophilus and Muslim Sources" and Conterno, "Theophilos, 'The More Likely Candidate?'"

[53] Conterno, *La "Descrizione dei tempi."*

On the Syro-Orthodox side, it can be added that other Chalcedonian authors were used (they are mentioned in the plural), but as usual their names are not given. The question of the sources is thus much more complicated than it would seem at first glance, or as is implied by some recent studies. This is not the place for a detailed source-critical study, but we have to keep in mind that all we know for sure is the short citation of Theophilus himself saying that he was a witness of the events relating to the Abbasid revolution. Everything else is mere speculation. We do not even know exactly about which periods he wrote. We have mentions of his "World era," that is, the number of years elapsed from the creation to the Seleucid or Christian era, but that does not mean that his chronicle actually spanned the period from creation to his own time. Such calculations were very popular and were meant as an aid for other historians to calculate and systematize their dates. Moreover, Dionysius classified Theophilus' work as "accounts similar to ecclesiastical history" and added that he wrote only a "summary and partial" history, "without paying careful attention to the times neither to the succession of events." This commentary would suggest that it is indeed historical accounts more than a universal chronicle that Theophilus authored. Barhebraeus calls it a "chronicle" but without saying when it started.[54]

Theophilus remains a likely candidate, and I do not deny that historical material actually came from his chronicle, but he may not be the "common source" behind Theophanes and the Syriac and Arabic chronicles. He certainly, however, transmitted material dealing with Abbasid times to the later Syriac chronicles (through Dionysius) and Arabic chronicles. More work is needed on the sources of what is identifiable of Dionysius in later texts and on the sources of Agapius in order to reach more secure conclusions.

What we know of Theophilus comes from his own work as an astronomer more than from what the Syrian Orthodox Syriac sources say about him, which is very brief on account of his being a Chalcedonian. His legacy is a discreet one, hardly acknowledged by the Syrian Orthodox authors who used his chronicle without explicitly acknowledging this. In this case of source criticism, as well as in the earlier examples concerning the filtering and selection of information provided in historical texts, the communal and ecclesiastical affiliations of the authors and compilers strongly influenced the ways in which sources and information made their way to us. It is thus only when going through the looking glass of the sectarian sources that we can acquire a more complete image of what was really going on at the time of the confrontation between Muslims and Christians in all their denominations.

Abbreviations

Chronicle of 1234 — *Chronicle up to the Year 1234*, ed. Chabot
MS *Chronicle* — Michael the Syrian, *Chronicle*, ed. Chabot

[54] MS *Chronicle* X, 21, IV, p. 378 T, II, p. 358 V.

Bibliography

Agapius of Manbij. *Kitāb al-ʿunwān*. Edited and translated by Alexandre Vasiliev, *Kitab al-Unvan, Histoire universelle*. Patrologia Orientalis 7. Paris: Firmin-Didot, 1911.

Barhebraeus. *Chronicon ecclesiasticum*. Edited and translated by Jean-Baptiste Abbeloos and Thomas Joseph Lamy, *Gregorii Barhebræi Chronicon ecclesiasticum*. 3 vols. Paris: Maisonneuve; Leuven: Peeters, 1872–1877.

————. *History of the Dynasties*.

- Edited by Anton Salhani, *Tārīkh mukhtaṣar al-duwal*. Beirut: Imprimerie catholique, 1890; reprint 1958.
- Latin translation by Edward Pococke, *Historia compendiosa dynastiarum*. Oxford: Excudebat H. Hall, 1663; reprint 1984.

Bertaina, David. An Arabic Account of Theodore Abu Qurra in Debate at the Court of Caliph al-Maʾmun: A Study in Early Christian and Muslim Literary Dialogues. Ph.D. dissertation, Catholic University of America, 2007.

Borrut, Antoine. *Entre mémoire et pouvoir: l'espace syrien sous les derniers Omeyyades et les premiers Abbassides (v. 72–193/692–809)*. Leiden: Brill, 2011.

————. "Court Astrologers and Historical Writing in Early ʿAbbāsid Baghdād: An Appraisal." In *The Place to Go: Contexts of Learning in Baghdād, 750–1000 C.E.*, edited by J. Scheiner and D. Janos, pp. 455–501. Princeton: Darwin Press, forthcoming.

Brock, Sebastian P. "The Fenqitho of the Monastery of Mar Gabriel in Tur 'Abdin." *Ostkirchliche Studien* 28 (1979): 168–82.

————. "Transformations of the Edessa Portrait of Christ." *Journal of Assyrian Academic Studies* 18/1 (2004): 46–56.

Brooks, Ernest W. "The Sources of Theophanes and the Syriac Chroniclers." *Byzantinische Zeitschrift* 15 (1906): 578–87.

Brown, Peter. *Through the Eye of a Needle: Wealth, the Fall of Rome, and the Making of Christianity in the West, 350–550 A.D.* Princeton: Princeton University Press, 2012.

Budge, Ernest Alfred Wallis, editor. *The Chronography of Gregory Abû'l-Farag (1225–1286)* (*Chronicon syriacum*). 2 vols. London: Oxford University Press, 1932; reprint Amsterdam, 1976.

Chronicle up to the Year 1234 (Anonymous).

- Edited by Jean-Baptiste Chabot, *Chronicon ad A.C. 1234 pertinens*. Vol. I, CSCO 109 ser. III, 14 T, Leuven: Peeters, 1920 (reprint CSCO 81/Syr. 36 T, Leuven: Peeters, 1953), CSCO 109, ser. III, 14 V, Leuven: Peeters, 1937 (reprint CSCO 109/Syr. 56 V, Leuven: Peeters, 1952); Vol. II, CSCO 82/Syr. 37 T, Paris: Gabalda, 1920.
- French translation by Albert Abouna, *Anonymi auctoris Chronicon ad A.C. 1234 pertinens, II*. CSCO 354/Syr. 154 V, Leuven: Peeters, 1974 (with introduction, notes, and index by Jean-Maurice Fiey).

Conrad, Lawrence I. "The Conquest of Arwād: A Source-Critical Study in the Historiography of the Early Medieval Near East." In *The Byzantine and Early Islamic Near East*, Vol. 1: *Problems in the Literary Source Material*, edited by Averil Cameron and Lawrence I. Conrad, pp. 317–401. Studies in Late Antiquity and Early Islam 1. Princeton: Darwin Press, 1992.

Conterno, Maria. *La "Descrizione dei tempi" all'alba dell'espansione islamica: un'indagine sulla storiografia greca, siriaca e araba fra VII e VIII secolo*. Berlin: De Gruyter, 2014.

———. "Theophilos, 'The More Likely Candidate?' Towards a Reappraisal of the Question of Theophanes' Oriental Source(s)." In *Studies in Theophanes*, edited by Marek Jankowiak and Federico Montinaro, pp. 383–400. Travaux et Mémoires 19. Paris 2015.

Debié, Muriel. "Livres et monastères en Syrie-Mésopotamie d'après les sources syriaques." In *Le Monachisme syriaque*, edited by Florence Jullien, pp. 123–68. Études syriaques 7. Paris: Geuthner, 2010.

———. "Les apocryphes et l'histoire en syriaque." In *Sur les pas des Araméens chrétiens: mélanges offerts à Alain Desreumaux*, edited by Françoise Briquel Chatonnet and Muriel Debié, pp. 63–76. Cahiers d'études syriaques 1. Paris: Geuthner, 2010.

———. "Theophanes' 'Oriental Source': What Can We Learn from Syriac Historiography?" In *Studies in Theophanes*, edited by Marek Jankowiak and Federico Montinaro, pp. 365–82. Travaux et Mémoires 19. Paris 2015.

———. *L'écriture de l'histoire en syriaque: transmissions interculturelles et constructions identitaires entre hellénisme et islam*. Late Antique History and Religion 12. Leuven: Peeters, 2015.

Donner, Fred M. *Muhammad and the Believers: At the Origins of Islam*. Cambridge: Harvard University Press, 2010.

———. "Qur'ânicization of the Religio-Political Discourse in the Umayyad Period." *Revue des mondes musulmans et de la Méditerranée* 129 (2011): 79–92.

Fiey, Jean Maurice, and Lawrence I. Conrad, editors. *Saints syriaques*. Studies in Late Antiquity and Early Islam 6. Princeton: Darwin Press, 2004.

Griffith, Sidney H. *The Church in the Shadow of the Mosque: Christians and Muslims in the World of Islam*. Princeton: Princeton University Press, 2008.

———. "Crosses, Icons and the Image of Christ in Edessa: The Place of Iconophobia in the Christian-Muslim Controversies of Early Islamic Times." In *Transformations of Late Antiquity: Essays for Peter Brown*, edited by Philip Rousseau and Manolis Papoutsakis, pp. 63–84. Farnham: Ashgate, 2009.

Hilkens, Andy. The Anonymous Syriac Chronicle up to the Year 1234 and Its Sources. Thesis, University of Ghent, 2014.

Hoyland, Robert G. *Seeing Islam as Others Saw It: A Survey and Evaluation of Christian, Jewish and Zoroastrian Writings on Early Islam*. Studies in Late Antiquity and Early Islam 13. Princeton: Darwin Press, 1997.

———. *Theophilus of Edessa's Chronicle and the Circulation of Historical Knowledge in Late Antiquity and Early Islam*. Translated Texts for Historians 57. Liverpool: Liverpool University Press, 2011.

———. "Agapius, Theophilus and Muslim Sources." In *Studies in Theophanes*, edited by Marek Jankowiak and Federico Montinaro, pp. 355–64. Travaux et Mémoires 19. Paris, 2015.

John of Ephesus. *Lives of the Eastern Saints*. Edited by E. W. Brooks. Patrologia Orientalis 17/1. Paris: Firmin-Didot, 1923.

Lamoreaux, John C. "The Biography of Theodore Abū Qurrah Revisited." *Dumbarton Oaks Papers* 56 (2002): 25–40.

Michael the Syrian, *Chronicle*. Edited and translated by Jean-Baptiste Chabot, *Chronique de Michel le Syrien, patriarche jacobite d'Antioche (1166–1199)*. Paris: Academie des inscriptions et belles-lettres, 1899–1924. Reprinted in 4 vols. Brussels: Culture et Civilisation, 1963; and Toronto: Gorgias Press, 2008.

Mikhail, Maged S. A. *From Byzantine to Islamic Egypt: Religion, Identity and Politics after the Arab Conquest*. Library of Middle East History 45. London: I. B. Tauris, 2014.

Palmer, Andrew. *Monk and Mason on the Tigris Frontier: The Early History of Ṭur ʿAbdin*. University of Cambridge Oriental Publications 39. Cambridge: Cambridge University Press, 1990.

Penn, Michael P. "Julian of Halicarnassus." In *Gorgias Encyclopedic Dictionary of the Syriac Heritage*, edited by Sebastian P. Brock, Aaron M. Butts, George A. Kiraz, and Lucas Van Rompay, p. 236. Piscataway: Gorgias Press, 2011.

Pigulevskaja, Nina V. "Theophanes' *Chronographia* and the Syrian Chronicles." *Jahrbuch der Österreichischen Byzantinischen Gesellschaft* 16 (1967): 55–60.

Pingree, David. "Astrology." In *Religion, Learning and Science in the ʿAbbasid Period*, edited by M. J. L. Young, J. D. Latham, and R. B. Serjeant, pp. 291–300. Cambridge: Cambridge University Press, 1990.

———. "From Alexandria to Baghdād to Byzantium: The Transmission of Astrology." *International Journal of the Classical Tradition* 8/1 (2001): 3–37.

Proudfoot, Ann S. "The Sources of Theophanes for the Heraclian Dynasty." *Byzantion* 44 (1974): 367–439.

Sévère ibn al-Muqaffaʿ. *History of the Patriarchs of the Coptic Church of Alexandria*, Vols. I–IV, edited by Basil Evetts. Patrologia Orientalis I.2, I.4, V.1, and X.5. Paris: Firmin-Didot, 1906–1915.

ter Haar Romeny, R. Bas. "Ethnicity, Ethnogenesis and the Identity of Syriac Orthodox Christians." In *Visions of Community in the Post-Roman World: The West, Byzantium and the Islamic World, 300-1100*, edited by Walter Pohl, Clemens Gantner, and Richard E. Payne, pp. 183–204. Farnham: Ashgate, 2012.

———, editor. "Religious Origins of Nations? The Christian Communities of the Middle East." Special issue, *Church History and Religious Culture* 89 (2009): 1–3.

Tihon, Anne. "L'astronomie à Byzance à l'époque iconoclaste." In *Science in Western and Eastern Civilization in Carolingian Times*, edited by Paul L. Butzer and Dietrich Lohrmann, pp. 181–203. Basel and Boston: Birkhäuser, 1993.

4

Persian Lords and the Umayyads: Cooperation and Coexistence in a Turbulent Time

Touraj Daryaee, University of California, Irvine

In Memory of M. I. Mochiri

The Arab Muslim conquest of *Iranshahr* (Middle Persian *Ērānšahr* "Realm of the Iranians") and its aftermath have only recently begun to receive attention.[1] Still, we are ill informed on the real nature of the dealings and interactions that took place between the Umayyad overlords and the Iranian ruling elite in different provinces.[2] Were the relations between the Umayyads and the inhabitants of the Iranian Plateau in this era mainly marked by resistance and conflict, or did they also – or sometimes – reflect cooperation between the two sides? In this paper I would like to highlight the numismatic evidence for such interaction and show that (1) for a variety of reasons, including local Arab rivalries and the power of the local Iranian nobility, the Umayyads depended on, and the Iranian nobility cooperated with, the Arabs in ruling over Iran; and (2) the Umayyads were much more flexible in their encounter with the Iranians and often cooperated with the local elites.[3] This tactic was needed by the Umayyads in order to rule over *Iranshahr* effectively, as there were not only major cities, but many feudal-type settlements and smaller cities on the Iranian Plateau, which the small Arab Muslim army could not control directly. The Middle Persian signs and symbols, and in general the iconography of the coins that were circulated in this period, suggest that while they were understandable and carried on the old Iranian worldview and tradition, they were made in such a way as to avoid offending the sensibility of the new Muslim overlords, and so as to be in line with the Umayyad coinage reform. Furthermore, the coinage demonstrates the beginning of the Islamicization of the plateau through familiar Zoroastrian terminology and tradition. As evidence, a coin of ʿAbd al- ʿAzīz ʿAbdallāh b. ʿĀmir, who was the governor of Sīstān during the late seventh century C.E., will be studied. The importance of the coinage is that it demonstrates the impact of Islamic monotheistic tradition on the terminology and

[1] For a convenient narrative of the conquest, see Donner, *Early Islamic Conquests*; Kennedy, *The Great Arab Conquests*, pp. 169–99. See also the classic discussion of Zarrīnkūb, "The Arab Conquest of Iran."

[2] See, however, the recent discussion of Crone, *The Nativist Prophets*, esp. pp. 1–11.

[3] On the articulation of elite power in Late Antique and early Islamic Iran, see Pourshariati, *Decline and Fall of the Sasanian Empire*, to be read in light of Daryaee, "The Fall of the Sasanian Empire."

Figure 4.1. Coinage of the caliph ʿAbd al-Malik (courtesy of the British Museum)

worldview of Zoroastrian Iran. This tradition can now be supplemented with the Pahlavī documents from the central Iranian Plateau, which use similar language in relation to religious vocabulary.

There is little literary evidence for the existence of what we may call independent Iranian local lords in the early Islamic era. In fact it is only the numismatic evidence that provides the names of certain individuals along with dates, some speculative and others more firm.[4] While most of the copper coinage of Fārs is difficult to date, based on stylistics and comparison with dated coins we are able to establish an approximate chronological range for them. These copper coins continue to be minted throughout the second *fitna*, mainly in Fārs, and as late as the time of ʿAbd al-Malik's caliphate (685–705) (fig. 4.1). These coins contain names and slogans that hint at the persuasion of the people who struck them. They appear for the major districts of Fārs, more than for any other province on the Iranian Plateau. This could mean that the fiercest resistance was put against the Arab Muslim conquerors in this province.

The Copper Coinage of Fārs during the Umayyad Caliphate

Several sub-provinces in Fars minted very interesting copper coinage, which most probably belonged to the local elites. These coins hint at a form of cooperation that is rare for this period anywhere in the Umayyad caliphate. In the sub-province of Bēšābuhr, we encounter a coinage with the legend *āzād bēšāpūr*.[5] The legend can be translated as "Bēšābuhr is free,"[6] which suggests that the city is in the hands of local nobility or is being ruled freely and is not directly under Umayyad control. Although it has been suggested that the legend cannot be read as such,[7] I believe that the reading *āzād* should be maintained, as a uniform orthography for the Pahlavī legend did not exist in late Sasanian and early Islamic Iran. Already on the coins of Yazdgerd III minted in Sīstān, we come across a legend on the margin where the Pahlavī word is written unconventionally. I have argued that this is a post-Yazdgerd III coinage, minted by his sons when they established a second Sasanian kingdom in southeastern Iran, stating that the region was autonomus.[8]

In the district of Iṣṭakhr we have three copper coins minted with the name of a lord named Manṣūr. Most of these coins are from the time when al-Ḥajjāj b. Yūsuf was controlling

[4] The most important works in this regard are Curiel and Gyselen, *Une collection de monnaies*, and Gyselen, *Arab-Sasanian Copper Coinage.*

[5] Gyselen, *Arab-Sasanian Copper Coinage*, p. 122.

[6] Curiel and Gyselen, *Une collection de monnaies*, p. 4.

[7] Gyselen, *Arab-Sasanian Copper Coinage*, p. 122.

[8] Daryaee, "Yazdgerd III's Last Year," pp. 26–27.

Figure 4.2. Coin of Manṣūr (after Gyselen, *Arab-Sasanian Copper Coinage*, type 20)

some of the Iranian provinces. While al-Ḥajjāj b. Yūsuf was the governor, we have the striking of coins sometimes with both the names of Manṣūr and al-Ḥajjāj b. Yūsuf and sometimes with the name of Manṣūr alone. I would like to suggest that Manṣūr was a member of a local elite and that al-Ḥajjāj b. Yūsuf may have given autonomy to Manṣūr, while Manṣūr would have come to an agreement with the governor. This type of "co-regency" on a local level would have reduced local native resistance in the province and at the same time given the Umayyads a chance to deal more effectively with other Arab Muslim contenders such as the Zubayrids and the Khawārij. This suggestion is evident from the coinage of the district of Iṣṭakhr, where the name of Manṣūr is written on the margin as holding the office of (Middle Persian) *ōstāndār* / (Arabic) *ʿāmil* "governor" or "subordinate governor."[9] It is quite possible that Manṣūr was also a sub-governor of Dārābgerd (fig. 4.2).

The rival caliph, ʿAbdallāh b. al-Zubayr, and his followers also struck coins in Fārs, especially in the western part in the district of Weh-az-Amid-Kawād. This is evident from their silver coins with the mint mark WYHC from 688 to 692.[10] The Zubayrids were active in the province until 692, when al-Ḥajjāj b. Yūsuf defeated and killed ʿAbdallāh b. al-Zubayr. The Khawārij had become active already from 657, when ʿAlī agreed to arbitration with Muʿāwiya after the battle of Ṣiffīn. The Umayyads tried to control the province by appointing various governors, beginning with Ziyād b. Abīhi, who had also been a governor for ʿAlī. The Azāriqa also tried to control the province during and after the second *fitna*. On the Persian side, two names need to be mentioned. First, Manṣūr, who was from an Iranian family, and, more importantly, Farroxzād, who controlled various parts of the province and who may have come to a final agreement with al-Ḥajjāj b. Yūsuf as the co-ruler of the local area. One of Farroxzād's dated coins is from Gōr, which suggests that the city was one of his strongholds.[11]

The reasoning for the idea that during this period there was very little local anti-Umayyad rebellion on the Iranian Plateau[12] may be that some of the local Iranian elite (Middle Persian *xwadāyān*) cooperated with the Arab overlords and were given some autonomy in the area over which they held power. We should remember that during the late seventh century it was some of the Arab Muslims, notably the Khawārij, who rebelled against ʿAlī and then against the Umayyads in Fārs.

---

[9] Curiel and Gyselen, *Une collection de monnaies*, p. 33.
[10] Ibid., p. 25.
[11] Gyselen suggest the date A.H. 79; Gyselen, *Arab-Sasanian Copper Coinage*, p. 73.
[12] Kennedy, *The Prophet and the Age of the Caliphates*, p. 117.

Figure 4.3. Al-Muhallab b. Abī Ṣufra copper coinage based on Khusrō II type (http://db.stevealbum.com/php/chap_auc.php?site=2&lang=1&sale=8&chapter=2&page=1 [accessed 1/14/2016], Sale 8, Lot 52, Item 93996 = Gyselen, *Arab-Sasanian Copper Coinage*, type 23)

The Khawārij began to rule Iṣfahān from 679 onward and did so until 690. But there is also evidence that they may have controlled other parts of Fārs, such as Jahrom after 687, and Tawwaj from 675 to 682.[13] In Dārābgerd, copper coins were struck in the year 687, after the death of a certain ᶜUbaydallāh, who may also have been of Iranian ancestry based on Mochiri's reading of his full name on a coin: *mwcʾb y ʾbydwlʾ y štlyʾlʾn* "Muṣᶜab ī ᶜUbaydallāh ī Shahriyārān."[14] This may also mean the he was promoted against the Khawārij by the Umayyads. The Azāriqa continued to mint coins until 698 in Fārs in the districts of Ardaxšīr-xwarrah and Bēšābūhr.[15] They were among the opponents of the Umayyads who caused much trouble in the province of Fārs, but they were not alone. It makes perfect sense for the Umayyads to have given power to the local elites to withstand and help in their campaigns against the rebel Arab groups throughout the plateau (fig. 4.3).

We also encounter a group of copper coins with the name of Farroxzād at the time when al-Muhallab b. Abī Ṣufra (d. 82 or 83/702 or 703) was the governor of Fārs, either independently or with the name of an Arab governor between 693 and 698. This may mean that during the disorder, especially during the time of the Zubayrid revolt, Farroxzād was a member of the local elite cooperating with the Umayyads against the Zubayrids. It is important to note that Farroxzād's first coinage appears with that of al-Muhallab b. Abī Ṣufra, the ex-general of

Figure 4.4. Coin of Farroxzād (after Gyselen, *Arab-Sasanian Copper Coinage*, type 2)

[13] Mochiri, *Arab-Sasanian Civil War Coinage*, p. 61.

[14] Ibid., p. 59.

[15] Ibid., p. 73.

ᶜAbdallāh b. al-Zubayr, who after the defeat of Muṣᶜab b. al-Zubayr had given his allegiance to the Umayyads.[16] All of the mints issuing coinage in the name of Farroxzād alone were active in Fārs, namely Ardaxšīr-xwarrah, Bēšābuhr, Gūr, Dašt, Tawwaj, and Tūj (fig. 4.4).[17]

The reason for this action on the part of the Umayyads may be that they could not control Fārs, and so the idea of co-regency, of one Arab and one local Persian, would have been the only possible means of rule over the province. This also indicates the power and importance of the local Persian elites in the area even after the initial uprising in the first half of the Islamic century, when many of the nobility and the military either had been killed or joined the Arab forces. The power of the local Persians in Fārs is manifest when we consider that the last coinage of Farroxzād was struck with none other than the powerful Arab governor al-Ḥajjāj b. Yūsuf. They were issued at Bēšābuhr after the *fitna* of Ibn al-Zubayr had ended and the Umayyad caliphate had been stabilized (fig. 4.5).

Farroxzād's coinage is devoid of Arabic legends or Islamic symbols.[18] He appears to have become the *ᶜāmil*, and copper coins from the following mints were struck with his name:

Governor	*Mint*	*Date*
Al-Muhallab b. Abī Ṣufrā	TART	75–76 (695–696 C.E.)
Al-Muhallab b. Abī Ṣufrā	ART	76 (696 C.E.)
Al-Ḥajjāj b. Yūsuf	BYŠ	79 (699 C.E.)

What is also of interest is the stylistic type of Farroxzād's coinage. While the obverse is a recognizable Sasanian coinage type, the reverse has a new image, which has been called Sīmorγ (Middle Persian *Sēnmurw*),[19] the mythical bird of the Iranians who in the *Book of Kings* aids the Iranian hero Rustam and his family against the enemies of Iran. One can only guess at Farroxzād's choice of the *Sēnmurw* as a religious and an ideological statement, but it is certainly possible that the iconographical symbol resonated with the Zoroastrian population, who were well aware of its significance. This symbol in turn did not go against the new Muslim sensibility, as the fire temple was now deleted in favor of an animal image. However, most recently, it has been suggested that this symbol really stands for the idea of divine or

Figure 4.5. Farroxzād's copper coinage (Daryaee, *Iranian Kingship*, p. 71, no. 6)

[16] Ibid., p. 70.

[17] Ibid., p. 71.

[18] Curiel and Gyselen, *Une collection de monnaies*, p. 68.

[19] Schmidt, "*Sēnmurv*: Of Doges, Birds and Bats."

Figure 4.6. Khusrō II type with the so-called *Sēnmurw* countermark on the fourth quadrant over the Middle Persian *Xwarrah*. Mint GW =Kermān. Arab-Sasanian Coinage: http://grifterrec.rasmir.com/islam/arab_sas/cmk_sas/i_asas_GW_35_cmk.jpg [accessed 1/14/2016]

royal glory (Middle Persian *Xwarrah*). In fact, M. Compareti has shown that this could be the case when we take the numismatic evidence from Sogdiana, where some of the images of *Sēnmurw* have the Sogdian legend *prn/Farn* (glory) struck on them.[20] One can provide further evidence in this regard, where on some of the Arab-Sasanian silver coinage we find the image of the so-called *Sēnmurw* struck exactly at the quadrant where the Middle Persian legend *Xwarrah* appears. This may be a further clue that the bird stands for the idea of Divine Glory, which is so intimately linked with the notion of rulership in *Iranshahr* (fig. 4.6).

Our other local lord, Dārāy, also minted coins in Bēšābuhr. The typology of his coinage is different from that of Manṣūr and Farroxzād. Furthermore, his name certainly suggests that it is not a slogan, as is the possibility with the other two names. This fact should persuade us to give more credence to the idea that Manṣūr, Farroxzād, and Dārāy all are proper names and not slogans. Dārāy's coinage has the slogan "increase in glory" (*GDH ʾpzwt/xwarrah abzūd*) with frontal image, reminiscent of Khusrō II's coinage. On the obverse is the important legend "Bēšābuhr is free" (*ʾcʾd byšʾpwhr/āzād bēšābuhr*). Dārāy's coins suggest that he was able to hold on to Bēšābuhr, although it is not clear at what exact time, as the coins do not have a date (fig. 4.7).

The obverse of Dārāy's coinage is also interesting in that a ram-like figure is struck instead of a fire alter. Here I would suggest we are encountering another avatar of the concept

Figure 4.7. Coin of Dārāy (illustration by T. Daryaee)

[20] Compareti, "The So-Called Senmurv," p. 192.

of *Xwarrah* or Divine Glory. This is clear from the surviving Middle Persian literature, of which the best known is the *Kārnāmag ī Ardaxšīr ī Pābagān*. In a part of the story when the founder of the Sasanian dynasty is in flight from the Arsacid forces, a ram appears. When a ram (*warrag*) is seen going along with his horse, the meaning of this occurrence is explained as follows (*Kārnāmag* IV.24): *Ardaxšīr xwarrah ī kayān awiš rasīd* "the Kayānid glory has reached Ardashīr."[21] The Kayānids are the mythical Avestan dynasty who are the model for rulership in the ancient Iranian world. Their most famous rulers were Kay Wištasp, who accepted the religion from the Prophet Zarathushtra, and Kay Khusrō, who was victorious against the enemies of Iran. They are given further attention in the Persian epic, the *Shāhnāmeh* of Ferdowsi, as the kings of old whom the Sasanians tried to emulate, as some Islamic dynasties would later do. The Kayānids were considered to hold the *Xwarrah*, that is, the power to rule over the Iranian world; hence those who later claimed to be rightful rulers used the symbols associated with the Kayānid Glory.

ʿAbd al-ʿAzīz b. ʿAbdallāh b. ʿĀmir, Governor of Sīstān

One of the most interesting coins struck in the eastern half of the Umayyad caliphate belongs to ʿAbd al-ʿAzīz b. ʿAbdallāh b. ʿĀmir (fig. 4.8). This coin was struck five years before the Umayyad coinage reform of ʿAbd al-Malik, which, as Mochiri states, involved "removing all symbolism associated with the former Byzantine and Sasanian rule, and its replacement with a purely inscriptional coin-type, giving in Arabic the Muslim confession of faith, and various Qur'anic verses."[22] The legend on ʿAbd al-ʿAzīz b. ʿAbdallāh b. ʿĀmir's coin is typical Sasanian style with the addition of *bism Allāh* on the margin, as well as *al-ʿAzīz*, but the reverse is unique and very interesting.

Even here we see that while Islam and its tradition are being introduced, it was done through familiar Zoroastrian terminology. Allāh was represented by the Middle Persian *yazd/yazad*, which normally appears in the plural in relation to Ohrmazd in Middle Persian literature (*yazdān*). While the aim was to emphasize the monotheism of Islam in the legend

Figure 4.8. Coin of ʿAbd al-ʿAzīz b. ʿAbdallāh b. ʿĀmir, Governor of Sīstān (after Mochiri, "Pahlavi Forerunner of Umayyad Reformed Coinage," p. 169)

[21] Grenet, *La geste d'Ardashir*, p. 72.

[22] Mochiri, "A Pahlavi Forerunner," p. 168.

yazad-ēw "one god," Zoroastrian terminology was utilized to convey the message to the local population. The legend does not mention Allāh, but simply states that there is "no other god" (*any yazad nēst*). Finally, the most interesting blend of Islamic and Persianate tradition is on the third line, where Muḥammad is designated the messenger of *yazad* "god" (*Muḥamad paygāmbar ī yazad*). I would translate the reverse of the coinage in the following manner:

> *yazad-ēw bē oy, any yazad nest, mahmat paygāmbar ī yazad*
>
> There is one God, without any other, (and) Muhammad is the prophet of God[23]

Certainly in the Iranian tradition either the specific name of the god or its plural form would have been provided. Not only the coinage but ʿAbd al-ʿAzīz b. ʿAbdallāh b. ʿĀmir himself appears to be one who co-opted the local elites into the Umayyad system, no doubt this silver coin being the material example. We are told in the *Tārikh ī Sīstān* that he was friendly to the local population and made important gestures of friendship toward the local population.[24] This change from *yazdān* to *yazad* in the Iranian world is also found in the newly found Pahlavī documents from the region of Qom from the early eighth century, where the opening line of the papyrus reads,

> *pad nām ī yazad ī kardakkar*
>
> In the name of god who (is) powerful[25]

Conclusion

I believe that the evidence from Fārs and Sīstān suggests an interesting way in which the Umayyads attempted to rule over the Iranian Plateau. This was not the harsh and draconian caliphate about which one reads in modern Persian historical works, but rather a more tolerant and friendlier regime. No doubt the co-option of the local elites after the fall of the Sasanians and the conquests of the Rāshidūn period brought a *modus vivendi* that put both sides in a better position vis-à-vis the other. At the same time, their cooperation allowed the Umayyads to deal more effectively with the anti-caliphal movements.

While the copper coinage of Fārs demonstrates the dealings of the Umayyad caliphate with individual elites in the province, the silver coinage of the governor of Sīstān suggests a subtle religious propagation by a friendly local ruler in the language understood by the population. On the other hand, the use of Iranian symbolism such as the *Sēnmurv* and the ram suggests a laxity and openness by the Umayyads on the local level. I believe it was this form of Perso-Arab cooperation on the local level that cemented the interests of both sides and disallowed any local uprisings and havoc. Umayyads were much more flexible than may be thought in the Iranian world, and the Arab rulers worked more closely with the local population and their traditions.

---

[23] Mochiri ("A Pahlavi Forerunner," p. 170) translates it as: "One God, but He another god does-not-exist. Muhammad (is) the messenger of God."

[24] Ibid., p. 171.

[25] Weber, "Arabic Activities," pp. 180–81.

Bibliography

Compareti, M. "The So-Called *Senmurv* in Iranian Art: A Reconsideration of an Old Theory." In *Loquentes linguis: Studi linguistici e orientali in onore di Fabrizio A. Pennacchietti (Linguistic and Oriental Studies in Honour of Fabrizio A. Pennacchietti)*, edited by Giorgio Borbone, Alessandro Mengozzi, and Mauro Tosco, pp. 185–200. Wiesbaden: Harrassowitz 2006.

Crone, Patricia. *The Nativist Prophets of Early Islamic Iran: Rural Revolt and Local Zoroastrianism.* Cambridge: Cambridge University Press, 2012.

Curiel, Raoul, and Rika Gyselen. *Une collection de monnaies de cuivre Arabo-Sasanides.* Paris: Association pour l'avancement des études iraniennes, 1984.

Daryaee, Touraj. "Yazdgerd III's Last Year: Coinage and History of Sīstān at the End of Late Antiquity." *Iranistik* 9–10 (Festschrift für Erich Kettenhofen) (2006–2007): 21–30.

———. "The Fall of the Sasanian Empire to the Arab Muslims: From Two Centuries of Silence to Decline and Fall of the Sasanian Empire: The Partho-Sasanian Confederacy and the Arab Conquest of Iran." *Journal of Persianate Studies* 3 (2010): 239–54.

———. *Iranian Kingship, The Arab Conquest and Zoroastrian Apocalypse: The History of Fārs and Beyond in Late Antiquity (600-900 CE).* Mumbai: The K. R. Cama Oriental Institute, 2012.

Donner, Fred M. *The Early Islamic Conquests.* Princeton: Princeton University Press, 1981.

Grenet, Frantz. *La geste d'Ardashir fils de Pâbag.* Die: A. Die, 2003.

Gyselen, Rika. *Arab-Sasanian Copper Coinage.* Vienna: Verlag der Österreichischen Akademie der Wissenschaften, 2009.

Kennedy, Hugh. *The Prophet and the Age of the Caliphates: The Islamic Near East from the Sixth to the Eleventh Century.* London and New York: Longman, 1986.

———. *The Great Arab Conquests: How the Spread of Islam Changed the World We Live in.* London: Weinfeld & Nicolson, 2007.

Mochiri, Malek Irakj. *Arab-Sasanian Civil War Coinage.* Paris: n.p., 1987.

———. "A Pahlavi Forerunner of the Umayyad Reformed Coinage." *Journal of the Royal Society of Great Britain and Ireland* 2 (1981): 168–72.

Pourshariati, Parvaneh. *Decline and Fall of the Sasanian Empire: The Sasanian-Parthian Confederacy and the Arab Conquest of Iran.* London: I. B. Tauris, 2008.

Schmidt, Hans-Peter. "*Sēnmurv*: Of Dogs, Birds and Bats." *Persica* (1980): 1–85.

Weber, Dieter. "Arabic Activities Reflected in the Documents of the 'Pahlavi Archive.'" In *Documents, argenterie et monnaies de tradition sassanide*, edited by Rika Gyselen, pp. 179–89. Res Orientales 22. Bures-sur-Yvette: Groupe pour l'Étude de la Civilisation du Moyen-Orient, 2014.

Zarrīnkūb, ʿAbd al-Ḥusain. "The Arab Conquest of Iran and Its Aftermath." In *The Cambridge History of Iran, Vol. 4: From the Arab Invasions to the Saljuqs*, edited by Richard Nelson Frye, pp. 1–56. Cambridge: Cambridge University Press, 1975.

5

Non-Muslims in the Muslim Conquest Army in Early Islam

*Wadād al-Qāḍī, The Oriental Institute**

This paper deals with the question of whether non-Muslims served in the Muslim army, including the fleet, from the beginning of the conquests until the end of the Umayyad period in 132/750, when the conquests came virtually to a halt. It will use both Islamic and non-Islamic sources, as the conquests touched the lives of both the Muslims and the indigenous non-Muslim populations of the Near East. This mixture of sources, appended whenever possible by documentary materials, should allow us not only to form a more complete picture of the topic, but also to see it in a comparative context, given that the conquests were seen very differently by the conquerors (in the Islamic sources) than by the conquered (in the non-Islamic sources). It should also allow us once more to reflect, among other things, on the issue of the continuity between the pre-Islamic and Islamic Near East and the question of the authenticity of the Islamic sources. As an introduction, and for further comparative purposes between the theoretical and the practical, I shall begin with a brief survey of the legal information we have on the subject in early Islamic times. The major areas of non-Muslim participation in the Muslim army in the historical record will then be discussed in three parts under three rubrics: the roles played by the Arab Christian tribes, the roles played by the non-Arab non-Muslim groups and individuals, and the nature of the service of non-Muslims in the Muslim fleet. The paper will be based largely on original texts as they are reported and will be limited to the discussion of the activities of the Muslim armies against non-Muslims; hence no attempt will be made to explore non-Muslim participation in inner-Muslim hostilities.

Introduction: The Muslim Jurists on the Participation of Non-Muslims in the Muslim Army

The Muslim jurists discussed the subject of having non-Muslims serve in the Muslim army fairly extensively, mostly in the chapters on *jihād* and *siyar* of their legal compendia. The law

* This is a thoroughly revised version of my earlier study entitled "Non-Muslims in the Muslim Army in Early Islam: A Case Study in the Dialogue of the Sources" and printed in an extremely poor form in Khaṣāwinah, ed., *Conference on Orientalism*, pp. 109–59. I am grateful to my colleagues at the conference on Christians, Jews, and Zoroastrians in the Umayyad State (Chicago, June 2011) for giving me a number of valuable comments. My thanks go also to Bilal Orfali for helping me secure sources that I could not have secured on my own.

presented there claims to be based, first, on the *sunna* of the Prophet, and, second, on the practice of prominent early Muslims.

The corpus of Prophetic traditions deals with two main issues: did the Prophet actually allow non-Muslims to fight in his campaigns; and if so, did he compensate them, and in what manner? There are two contradictory answers to the first question in this corpus, one showing that the Prophet's *sunna* was not to permit non-Muslims to participate in his expeditions, and one showing the opposite. Regarding non-participation, five traditions are cited:

a. ʿĀʾisha's *ḥadīth* from ʿUrwa: in its longest form, it says that when the Prophet headed to Badr, he was met at a named place by a man known for his courage and resourcefulness, and that made the Companions rejoice. The man told the Prophet he wanted to follow him and gain [spoils] with him. The Prophet asked him whether he believed in God and His Messenger. The man said no, whereupon the Prophet sent him back, saying: "I shall not seek the assistance of a polytheist" (*fa-lan astaʿīna bi-mushrik*).[1] The man then met the Prophet at another named place, and the same dialogue went on between them. When they met at a third named place, the man said he believed in God and His Messenger, whereupon the Prophet told him: "Go ahead!" (*fa-inṭaliq*).[2]

b. The *ḥadīth* from Saʿīd b. al-Mundhir says that, on his way out to Uḥud, the Prophet looked back when he was at a named place and saw a fine squadron (*katība ḥasnāʾ*). He asked about its people and was told they were ʿAbd Allāh b. Ubayy b. Salūl and his clients of the Jews. He asked whether they had converted to Islam and was told they had not. He said: "We do not seek the assistance of unbelievers [in fighting] against polytheists" (*fa-innā lā nastaʿīnu bi-l-kuffār ʿalā al-mushrikīn*).[3]

c. The *ḥadīth* from al-Zuhrī says that the Anṣār asked the Prophet at Uḥud whether to seek the assistance of their allies from the Jews. The Prophet said: "We do not need them" (*lā ḥājata lanā fīhim*).[4]

d. The *ḥadīth* of Khubayb b. Yasāf, on the authority of his grandson, says that the Prophet went out toward an unnamed place (*yurīdu wajhan*) and the narrator, Khubayb, and another man from his people came to him and said: [Is it conceivable] that our people should attend a battle (*mashhadan*) while we do not? The Prophet asked them whether they had become Muslims (*aslamtumā*), and they said they had not. He thus said: "We do not seek the assistance of polytheists [in fighting] against polytheists (*fa-innā lā nastaʿīnu bi-l-mushrikīn ʿalā al-mushrikīn*). The narrator then said that Khubayb and his fellow tribesman later converted and participated in battle with the Prophet.[5]

[1] On this *ḥadith*, with its variants, see the valuable study of Yarbrough, "I'll not Accept Aid from a *mušrik*." Yarbrough tries to situate these *ḥadīth* narratives, using their *isnāds*, in a common temporal and geographical setting — that of early second/eighth-century Medina.

[2] The report is in its fullest form in Muslim b. al-Ḥajjāj, *Ṣaḥīḥ*, vol. 3, pp. 1449–50 ("al-jihād wa-l-siyar," 1870); Saḥnūn, *Mudawwana*, vol. 2, p. 617. It occurs in shorter forms in Ibn Abī Shayba, *Muṣannaf*, vol. 6, p. 487 ("al-jihād," 33162); al-Tirmidhī, *Sunan*, vol. 3, pp. 58–59 ("al-siyar," 1601); Abū Dāwūd, *Sunan*, vol. 3, p. 173 ("al-jihād," 2732); Ibn Ḥazm, *Muḥallā*, vol. 7, p. 335. See also al-Shāfiʿī, *Umm*, vol. 4, p. 261, where the report is only referred to.

[3] Ibn Abī Shayba, *Muṣannaf*, vol. 6, p. 487.

[4] Saḥnūn, *Mudawwana*, vol. 2, pp. 617–18. This is a rather strange and isolated *ḥadīth*; al-Zuhrī advocated a completely different position, as we shall see.

[5] Ibn Abī Shayba, *Muṣannaf*, vol. 6, p. 487.

e. A related *ḥadīth* from Abū Hurayra says that the Prophet said, in a longer tradition: "Booty has not been made licit for anyone before us" (*fa-lam taḥilla al-ghanāʾim li-aḥadin min qablinā*). This has been interpreted to mean that no one other than Mulsims are allowed to take booty.[6]

These proof texts were convincing for two major scholars, Saḥnūn and Ibn Ḥazm, and thus they represent the positions of the Mālikī and Ẓāhirī schools.[7] It is interesting to note, though, that both scholars had caveats added to their position, as will be noted below.

The *ḥadīth* corpus that shows the Prophet accepting the participation of non-Muslims with Muslims in battle consists again of five *sunnas*:

a. The *ḥadīth* from al-Zuhrī, narrated via four different channels, says that some Jews used to raid with the Prophet, and he would give them and the Muslims the same shares of the booty (*kāna yahūd yaghzūna maʿa al-nabī fa-yushim lahum ka-siham al-muslimīn*).[8]

b. The *ḥadīth* from al-Wāqidī says that the Prophet took along with him to Khaybar ten Jews from Medina and gave them and the Muslims the same shares of the booty.[9] This possibly deals with the same occasion spelled out less clearly in the *ḥadīth* from Abū Mūsā al-Ashʿarī, which says: "I came with a party of the Ashʿarīn to the Prophet at Khaybar and he gave us shares like those who conquered it."[10]

c. The *ḥadīth* from Ibn ʿAbbās that the Prophet sought the assistance of the Banū Qaynuqāʿ (of the Jews) in an unidentified battle; he gave them a little but did not give them shares (i.e., as he did to the Muslims; *istaʿāna rasūl Allāh bi-yahūd Qaynuqāʿ faraḍakha lahum wa-lam yushim*).[11]

d. It is narrated that Ṣafwān b. Umayya participated in the battle of Ḥunayn after the conquest of Mecca while he was still a polytheist.[12]

e. A related *ḥadīth* from Abū Hurayra says that the Prophet and Abū Bakr hired a man from the tribe of al-Diʾl as a skilled guide (*khirrīt*) when that man was still a polytheist. They gave him their two camels and made an appointment with him to meet them at the Thawr cave (*ghār*) three days later. He did, and went with them, together with another man, along the coastal road.[13]

---

[6] Muslim b. al-Ḥajjāj, *Ṣaḥīḥ*, vol. 3, p. 1367 ("al-jihād wa-al-siyar," 1747); Ibn Ḥazm, *Muḥallā*, vol. 7, p. 335.

[7] To them must be added a certain Abū Sulaymān, who must be Dāwūd b. ʿAlī b. Khalaf al-Ẓāhirī, the founder of the Ẓāhirī school of law to which Ibn Ḥazm belonged — which, in itself, is quite interesting. I am indebted to Luke Yarbrough for this identification. According to Ibn Ḥazm, Abū Sulaymān used to believe that polytheists ought not to fight with the Muslims and ought not to receive anything from their booty.

[8] ʿAbd al-Razzāq, *Muṣannaf*, vol. 5, pp. 188–89; Ibn Abī Shayba, *Muṣannaf*, vol. 6, p. 487; al-Tirmidhī, *Sunan*, vol. 3, p. 59; Ibn Ḥazm, *al-Muḥallā*, vol. 7, p. 334. See also al-Bayhaqī, *al-Sunan al-kubrā*, vol. 9, pp. 53, 92.

[9] See al-Bayhaqī, *al-Sunan al-kubrā*, vol. 9, pp. 53, 92.

[10] Al-Tirmidhī, *Sunan*, vol. 3, p. 59.

[11] Abū Yūsuf, *Radd*, p. 40; al-Bayhaqī, *al-Sunan al-ṣughrā*, vol. 3, p. 393.

[12] Al-Shāfiʿī, *Umm*, vol. 4, pp. 167, 261. This is confirmed by the *sīra* and the Companions' tradition; see Guillaume, trans., *The Life of Muhammad*, pp. 567, 569; Ibn Ḥajar al-ʿAsqalānī, *al-Iṣāba fī tamyīz al-ṣaḥāba*, vol. 2, p. 187.

[13] Al-Bukhārī, *Ṣaḥīḥ*, vol. 3, pp. 181–82; Ibn Ḥazm, *Muḥallā*, vol. 7, p. 335.

This body of *sunnas* convinced all of the early jurists, except for those mentioned above, that the Prophet condoned the participation of polytheists/unbelievers in his campaigns. This was the position of al-Shaʿbī, Qatāda, Abū Ḥanīfa, al-Awzāʿī, Sufyān al-Thawrī, Abū Yūsuf, Muḥammad b. al-Ḥasan al-Shaybānī, al-Shāfiʿī,[14] Abū ʿUbayd al-Qāsim b. Sallām, and probably Mālik personally.[15] Even the jurists who were against this participation could not but see that there was a point to it. Thus, Saḥnūn had the following caveat: "unless they were sailors (*nawātiyya*) or servants (*khadam*); there I find no objection." And Ibn Ḥazm dwelt at length on the Prophetic *ḥadīth*s favoring participation, finding them compelling,[16] allowing for the hiring of guides,[17] and giving the impression that he would have accepted them had they not violated his strict rules about which *ḥadīth* qualifies as valid. As for the discrepancy between the two sets of Prophetic *ḥadīth*s, one prohibiting and one permitting the participation of non-Muslims with the Muslims in battle, only al-Shāfiʿī seemed to care to comment on it, attributing it to abrogation (*naskh*): the prohibition reports came only from the very early period (Badr, Uḥud), whereas the permission ones came from thereafter.[18]

In general, though, the jurists favoring the participation of non-Muslims in the Muslim armies based their legal opinion not solely on the Prophet's *sunna* but also on the practice of the early leading Muslims. Here also we find a large body of reports, all of which speak in favor of participation.[19] These "leading Muslims," as I have called them, were either commanders in battle or "people in charge," meaning either commanders or caliphs.

a. It is related that Saʿd b. Mālik (= Saʿd b. Abī Waqqāṣ) led a campaign in which there were Jews. After the battle, he gave them a little of the booty (*raḍakha lahum*).[20] This report elicited the following comment from Ibn Ḥazm: "We know of no one of the Companions who went against Saʿd in this [matter]."[21]

b. It is related that Salmān b. Rabīʿa al-Bāhilī, one of the conquerors of Khurāsān, invaded Balanjar in one of his campaigns. There he sought the assistance of people from the polytheists to fight against the polytheists, saying: "Let the enemies of God fight the enemies of God (*li-yaḥmil aʿdāʾ Allāh ʿalā aʿdāʾ Allāh*)."[22]

c. It is narrated on the authority of al-Awzāʿī that the basis for his position is not only that the Prophet gave shares (of the booty) to those who fought with him from the Jews, but also that the people in charge of the Muslims (*wulāt al-muslimīn*) after the Prophet gave shares to the Jews and Magians (*majūs*) whose assistance they sought against their enemies.[23]

---

[14] For a summary with most of the names mentioned above, see Ibn Ḥazm, *Muḥallā*, vol. 7, p. 334. For specific jurists, see Abū Yūsuf, *Radd*, p. 39; idem, *Kharāj*, p. 391; al-Shaybānī, *Siyar*, with the commentary of al-Sarakhsī, vol. 2, pp. 680–82; vol. 3, pp. 995–1000; al-Shāfiʿī, *Umm*, vol. 4, pp. 166–67, 261, 269–70; Abū ʿUbayd, *Kharāj*, p. 431.

[15] This is what Ibn Ḥazm says. Cf. Saḥnūn, *Mudawwana*, vol. 2, p. 617 (where the author is not decisive about Mālik's position).

[16] See Ibn Ḥazm, *Muḥallā*, vol. 7, pp. 334–35, particularly his comment on al-Zuhrī's *ḥadīth*, saying it is among the best of the *mursal ḥadīth*.

[17] Ibn Ḥazm, *Muḥallā*, vol. 7, p. 335.

[18] Al-Shāfiʿī, *Umm*, vol. 4, p. 261.

[19] Indeed, one of the things that seemed to sway Ibn Ḥazm almost to the point of accepting the participation of non-Muslims is this corpus; see his *Muḥallā*, vol. 7, p. 334, particularly his comment on al-Shaʿbī and Saʿd b. Mālik.

[20] Ibn Abī Shayba, *Muṣannaf*, vol. 6, p. 488; Ibn Ḥazm, *Muḥallā*, vol. 7, p. 334; al-Bayhaqī, *al-Sunan al-kubrā*, vol. 9, pp. 37, 64.

[21] Ibn Ḥazm, *Muḥallā*, vol. 7, p. 334.

[22] Ibn Abī Shayba, *Muṣannaf*, vol. 2, p. 487; Ibn Ḥazm, *Muḥallā*, vol. 7, p. 334.

[23] Abū Yūsuf, *Radd*, p. 39. Abū Yūsuf's comment on this report is interesting: "I did not think that any

d. Finally, and perhaps most importantly, we have a saying of al-Shaʿbī's which is broader and more detailed than the previous reports. In its most expanded form, it says that Jābir [b. ʿAbd Allāh al-Anṣārī] asked al-Shaʿbī about his opinion regarding the Muslims leading a campaign in which there were People of the Book. He said: "The *imāms* whom I have witnessed (*adraktu al-aʾimmata*), those knowledgeable in the law and those not knowledgeable in it (*al-faqīh minhum wa-ghayr al-faqīh*), conducted campaigns in which there were *ahl al-dhimma*. [After the battle,] the *imāms* would give them a portion [of the booty] (*yaqsimūna lahum*), and would remove their tribute (*jizya*); this is a good spoil (*nafl*) for them."[24] Qatāda is also reported to have transmitted a similar saying.[25] Though he disagreed with the legal position ensuing from this report, Ibn Ḥazm could not but evaluate it positively; "al-Shaʿbī was born at the beginning of ʿAlī's days and he lived long enough to witness Companions after ʿAlī."[26]

The above allows us to conclude that the vast majority of the early Muslim jurists condoned the participation of non-Muslims in the battles of the Muslims. Two things have to be noted, though. The first is that historical precedence, undertaken by pious early Companions, and even reportedly by the Prophet himself, was a primary reason for the jurists' acceptance of non-Muslims in the ranks of the Muslim armies. The second is that many of those jurists did not embrace non-Muslim participation with open arms, but were rather uncomfortable with it, as if feeling more or less obliged to accept it on the strength of the evidence. In some cases, they put restrictions on that participation, limiting it only to the cases in which the non-Muslims bring some "benefit" (*manfaʿa*) to the Muslims' cause, as was stated by Abū Yūsuf, Muḥammad b. al-Ḥasan al-Shaybānī, al-Shāfiʿī, and Abū ʿUbayd al-Qāsim b. Sallām.[27] The first added that if their presence was not beneficial, no reward should be given to them;[28] the second insisted that they show their contribution by action, not merely by word;[29] and the third said that the *imām* should prohibit them from joining the Muslims in combat if they proved to be hypocrites who could use their participation to lie to the Muslims, assist the enemy against them, or put down their spirits, all of which brings harm to the Muslims' cause.[30]

There is furthermore the question of the reward that the non-Muslims are to receive. Here only two jurists, al-Awzāʿī and Sufyān al-Thawrī, said that they are to receive shares (i.e., *yusham lahum*), just like the fighting Muslims, while the vast majority said that they are to be given a little of the booty (i.e., *yurḍakh lahum*; also, but much less frequently, *yuḥdhā lahum*).[31] At issue here, I believe, is the matter of equality or lack thereof between Muslims and non-Muslims, in view of the fact that some Muslim participants in battle (minors, women, or slave converts) do not receive regular shares of the booty, but, rather, little is given to them, if at all.[32] In addition, more than one jurist thought it to be unfair that Muslims be penalized

---

one of the jurists (*ahl al-fiqh*) was ignorant of this and did not fall into doubt!"

[24] Ibn Ḥazm, *Muḥallā*, vol. 7, p. 334. For shorter versions, see ʿAbd al-Razzāq, *Muṣannaf*, vol. 5, p. 189; Ibn Abī Shayba, *Muṣannaf*, vol. 6, p. 488.

[25] Ibn Ḥazm, *Muḥallā*, vol. 7, p. 334, where *ahl al-ʿahd* (people of treaty) occurs in lieu of *ahl al-dhimma* (people of protection).

[26] Ibn Ḥazm, *Muḥallā*, vol. 7, p. 334.

[27] Abū Yūsuf, *Kharāj*, p. 392; al-Shaybānī, *Siyar*, vol. 3, p. 995; al-Shāfiʿī, *Umm*, vol. 4, p. 270; Abū ʿUbayd, *Amwāl*, p. 431.

[28] Abū Yūsuf, *Kharāj*, p. 391.

[29] Al-Shaybānī, *Siyar*, vol. 3, p. 995.

[30] Al-Shāfiʿī, *Umm*, vol. 4, pp. 269–70.

[31] For a summary, see Ibn Ḥazm, *Muḥallā*, vol. 7, p. 334.

[32] See, for example, al-Shaybānī, *Siyar*, vol. 2, p. 681; al-Shāfiʿī, *Umm*, vol. 4, p. 261.

for matters they have no control over while non-Muslims are penalized for something they do have control over.[33] This is one of the reasons, as it seems, for some jurists' expression of preference that non-Muslims be "hired" (*ustuʾjirū*),[34] that is, be bound by a hire contract. This would make them subject to the preset conditions of the contract (normally monetary and small), give them no claim on the potentially substantial booty that the campaigning army might fall upon, and eliminate any perception of equality between them and the Muslims. Overall, the jurists leave a great deal of room for the discretion of the leader (*imām/amīr*).[35] But these are matters that take us out of our immediate concern in this study. Suffice it to say that a reading of the legal, theoretical compendia of the early Muslim jurists leaves no room for doubt that the vast majority of them considered the participation of non-Muslims in the Muslim army as licit, and all of them admitted that it was widely practiced from the earliest times and throughout the conquests. This last point is certainly supported by historical evidence, as we shall see next.

The historical record, both Islamic and non-Islamic, takes it for granted that non-Muslims participated in the Muslim army in the period of the conquests and throughout the Umayyad period; thus no discussion is undertaken as to whether this participation is legitimate or not. In each of the following three parts, the evidence from the Islamic sources is presented first, followed by the evidence from the non-Islamic sources. In the third part, on the Muslim fleet, the evidence of the papyri will be presented last.

I. The Christian Arab Tribes

It is important to state right from the start that one must be careful when one approaches the historical reports that deal with Christian Arab tribes and not assume that the discussion is always about Christians when mention is made of the Taghlib, Iyād, al-Namir b. Qāsiṭ, or other Arab tribes who were known to have been Christian at the beginning of the conquests, and who converted only very slowly to Islam later on. We are, of course, at our safest when the sources mention literally that the Arabs involved were Christian, and the sources do that not infrequently. But we can also judge by context that the Arabs being discussed were Christians. Examples of such contexts are when the sources mention that the Muslims requested the *jizya* from these Arabs,[36] or when they identify a time and place for a battle in which Islam did not exist prior to the conquest of that place at that time,[37] or when they clarify the Christianity of the participating Arabs in a certain battle when discussing the subsequent battle that resulted from the first.[38]

---

[33] See, in particular, al-Shaybānī, *Siyar*, vol. 2, p. 681, and al-Shāfiʿī, *Umm*, vol. 4, p. 261. See also Abū Yūsuf, *Kharāj*, p. 391; al-Bayhaqī, *al-Sunan al-ṣughrā*, vol. 3, p. 392.

[34] Al-Shāfiʿī, *Umm*, vol. 4, p. 261. Al-Shaybānī, *Siyar*, vol. 3, pp. 997–1000, has a long and detailed section on hiring non-Muslims as spies and guides. See also Ibn Ḥazm, *Muḥallā*, vol. 7, p. 335, for his preference of a hire contract for guides.

[35] This is especially clear in al-Shaybānī, *Siyar*, vol. 2, pp. 680–82; vol. 3, pp. 997–1000, but also in Abū Yūsuf, *Kharāj*, p. 391, and al-Shāfiʿī, *Umm*, vol. 4, p. 267.

[36] See, for example, the people of al-Ḥīra, the names of whose leaders are Arabic, in the agreement between them and Khālid b. al-Walīd in 12/633–634; see al-Ṭabarī, *Tārīkh*, ed. Ibrāhīm, vol. 3, p. 464 / ed. de Goeje, vol. I, pp. 2044–45.

[37] See, for example, the raids the Muslims conducted on various Arab tribes in Iraq in 12/633. See also Donner, *Early Islamic Conquests*, p. 198, and p. 335 n. 152.

[38] Like the battle of al-Walaja, in Iraq, which is placed by al-Ṭabarī (*Tārīkh*, vol. 3, pp. 353–54/vol. I, pp. 2029–31) under the year 12/633. In the reports on this battle, Khālid b. al-Walīdʾs enemies, whom he

It is well known that the Christian Arab tribes in Syria, Iraq, and northern Mesopotamia (al-Jazīra) played an important part in the early conquests, sometimes siding with the Byzantines or the Sasanians, and others with the Muslims before they converted to Islam. It is also well known that, already during the caliphate of ʿUmar b. al-Khaṭṭāb (r. 13–23/634–644), the Christian Arabs, in particular the Taghlib, were granted a special tax status conducive to winning them over to the side of the Muslims. What is of interest for the topic under discussion is how the Islamic sources presented the information on this participation: Did they try to avoid mentioning the confessional difference or did they articulate it, and if they did articulate it, did they express any qualms or embarrassment about it?

An examination of the reports on this subject indicates that, whereas the information is not abundant, it is straightforward in delineating the difference in religion between the fighting Muslims and the assisting Christian Arabs; it is relatively generous in reporting names and conversations at times; and it is unapologetic about the whole matter, in no way trying to find what could be construed as a justification on the part of the Muslims for doing "irregular" things.

The Islamic sources are clear that the Muslims observed Christian Arab tribes fighting alongside the Byzantines[39] and the Sasanians,[40] and that they fought them as enemies, and that they sometimes dealt harshly with them.[41] The sources are sometimes clear in indicating the confessional aspect of the Christians fighting with their enemies against them, and do not hesitate to name the specific Arab tribes and individuals involved in the fighting. We see this in al-Ṭabarī's main reports on the battles of al-Walaja and Ullays in southern Iraq in 12/633;[42] the Muslims were then fighting under the leadership of Khālid b. al-Walīd.[43] The reports have it that the Persians and their Christian Arab supporters were defeated by the Muslims at the battle of al-Walaja, and many of them were killed and others captured, including the sons of two Christian Arabs from the tribe of Bakr b. Wāʾil: Jābir b. Bujayr and ʿAbd al-Aswad [al-ʿIjlī], the latter belonging to the tribe of ʿIjl, as his name indicates. Some Christians of the Bakr b. Wāʾil (*min Bakr ibn Wāʾil min naṣārāhum*) were angered by what had happened to their Christian kin (*naṣārā qawmihim*). They thus corresponded with the Persians (*al-aʿājim*) and subsequently gathered together at Ullays under the command of ʿAbd al-Aswad al-ʿIjlī. The Sasanian leader Ardashīr sent an army to Ullays to join "those who have come to you from the Persians (*fāris*) and the Christian Arabs (*naṣārā al-ʿarab*)." The Arab garrisons gathered there came from the tribes of ʿIjl, Taym al-Lāt, and Ḍubayʿa, in addition to some outlaying Arabs from the people of al-Ḥīra (*wa-ʿarab al-ḍāḥiya min ahl al-Ḥīra*) and the above-mentioned Christian Arab leaders, Jābir b. Bujayr of the Bakr b. Wāʾil and ʿAbd al-Aswad from the ʿIjl.

eventually defeats, are called collectively Persians (*aʿājim*), led by a Persian (*fārisī*) and assisted by the *dihqāns* and the "Arabs of the neighborhood" (*ʿarab al-ḍāḥiya*); no identification of those Arabs is provided. If the text had stopped at that, it could not have been used for the Christian Arabs' role in this battle. However, since in the following battle, that of Ullays, those Arabs are identified both as Christian Arabs and as participants in the previous battle of al-Walaja, the report on al-Walaja can be used for that purpose.

[39] As in the battle of Marj al-Ṣuffar, where the Ghassān, under the leadership of al-Ḥārith b. al-Ayham, were routed by Khālid b. al-Walīd in 13/634; al-Ṭabarī, *Tārīkh*, vol. 3, p. 410/vol. I, 2114–15.

[40] As in the battle of al-Walaja, mentioned above.

[41] As in the case of ʿAqqa b. Abī ʿAqqa, among other Arab prisoners of war taken at the battle of ʿAyn al-Tamr in Iraq in 12/633; al-Ṭabarī, *Tārīkh*, vol. 3, pp. 376–77/vol. I, 2062–64.

[42] I shall discuss the two battles in chronological order here for the purpose of clarity (cf. n. 38 above).

[43] For the two battles, see al-Ṭabarī, *Tārīkh*, vol. 3, pp. 353–58/vol. I, 2029–36.

Interestingly, one report highlights that the Muslims who fought most fiercely against the Arab Christians were the Muslims from the ʿIjl.[44] Clearly at that point in time, part of the tribe of ʿIjl had converted to Islam, and part was still Christian.[45]

Along similar lines, the Islamic sources give the names of the Arab Christian tribes and some of their leaders who participated in the more famous battle at al-Yarmūk less than two years later, in 14/635. Thus we learn that there was with Heraclius, the Byzantine emperor, "of the Arabs (*mustaʿriba*), the tribes of Lakhm, Judhām, Balqayn, Balī, ʿĀmila, Quḍāʿa, and Ghassān [...] 12,000 [fighters], led by Jabala b. al-Ayham."[46] The Islamic sources also unapologetically record many raids conducted by the Muslims against Christian Arab tribes in Byzantine[47] and Sasanian[48] territory during the early conquests of Syria and Iraq. In such cases, they do not specify the confession of the tribes, but, when captives are taken from them, the sources sometimes identify the captives' faith, normally Christian.[49] The sources mention an instance in 15/637 in which the Muslims left in peace the Arabs of Ḥāḍir Qinnasrīn in northern Syria. These were certainly Christians, because the sources state that they had been forcibly drafted by the Byzantines to fight when they actually did not want to fight (*annahum ʿarab ḥushirū wa-lam yakun min raʾyihim al-ḥarb*).[50] The sources, furthermore, mention instances in which Christian Arabs requested peace agreements from conquering Muslim leaders.[51]

According to the Islamic sources, it was during these raids that the Muslims began to recruit guides and spies from the local Arab Christians in order to assist them in their wars in lands unknown to them. That some of the recruitment was undertaken intentionally is clear from al-Ṭabarī's saying that, after the battle of al-Thiny in 12/633, Khālid b. al-Walīd put Suwayd b. Muqarrin in charge of taxation and recruiting spies (*wa-aqāma li-ʿaduwwihi yatajassas al-akhbār*).[52] In the same year, Khālid b. al-Walīd built into the peace agreement with the chiefs of al-Ḥīra a condition that the Ḥīrites "be spies for him" (*ʿalā an yakūnū lahu ʿuyūnan*).[53] Much of the intelligence that the Muslims received, however, seems to have come voluntarily from the local population, with some reward attached to it, as the sources intimate. A man from the Taghlib, presumably a Christian, who was taken prisoner in one of the early raids of Iraq, is reported to have bought his freedom from the Muslims by volunteering to guide them to a place where a group of the (presumably Christian) Rabīʿa resided; he did so and got his freedom.[54] Another Taghlibī, a guard who was captured with two other guards near al-Anbār, asked the raiding Muslims to grant him, his family, and his goods safe conduct in

[44] Al-Ṭabarī, *Tārīkh*, vol. 3, pp. 355/vol. I, p. 2032: *wa-kāna ashaddu al-nas ʿalā ūlāʾika al-naṣārā muslimū Banī ʿIjl.*

[45] See on this Donner, "The Bakr b. Wāʾil Tribes."

[46] Al-Ṭabarī, *Tārīkh*, vol. 3, p. 570/vol. I, p. 2347.

[47] As in the raid conducted by Khālid b. al-Walīd in 13/634 against the Ghassān in Marj Rāhiṭ "on their day of Easter (*yawma fiṣḥihim*)" and against a branch of the Quḍāʿa in Quṣam; see al-Ṭabarī, *Tārīkh*, vol. 3, p. 407/vol. I, p. 2209.

[48] See a series of those raids in Iraq in 13/634, particularly against the Taghlib, but also against the al-Namir b. Qāsiṭ, Kalb, Bakr b. Wāʾil, and groups of the Quḍāʿa; see al-Ṭabarī, *Tārīkh*, vol. 3, pp. 475–76/vol. I, pp. 2206–08; al-Balādhurī, *Futūḥ al-buldān*, pp. 246, 248.

[49] See al-Ṭabarī, *Tārīkh*, vol. 3, p. 352/vol. I, p. 2029, where the father of al-Ḥasan al-Baṣrī is identified as a captive in the battle of al-Thiny that took place in 12/633; the text adds: "and he was a Christian" (*wa-kāna naṣrāniyyan*).

[50] Al-Ṭabarī, *Tārīkh*, vol. 3, p. 601/vol. I, p. 2393.

[51] See, for example, al-Balādhurī, *Futūḥ al-buldān*, p. 149: "the Christians of Khunāṣira" asked Abū ʿUbayda for a peace agreement; Khunāṣira was so named after Khunāṣir b. ʿAmr b. al-Ḥārith, of the Arab tribe of Kalb, of the Kināna, who was its chief.

[52] Al-Ṭabarī, *Tārīkh*, vol. 3, p. 352/vol. I, p. 2029.

[53] Ibid., vol. 3, p. 346/vol. I, pp. 2019–20.

[54] Al-Balādhurī, *Futūḥ al-buldān*, p. 248.

return for his guiding them to a place nearby where some of the Taghlib lived, for he had been there that very same day. The Muslims granted him his request, raided the Taghlib, and returned with a lot of booty.[55]

Indeed, several of the accounts we have in the sources about the Muslims' raids in Iraq in the early phase of the conquests are reported as having been propelled by volunteering almost enthusiastic local Arab (presumably Christian) guides, for no immediate reward. The accounts of the battle of al-Khanāfis in 13/634 are filled with such information. A report has it that after al-Muthannā b. Ḥāritha was through with the battle of al-Buwayb, two presumably Christian men, one from al-Anbār and the other from al-Ḥīra, importuned him, each desiring to guide him to rich marketplaces, the first to al-Khanāfis and the second to Baghdād [= Ctesiphon]. Al-Muthannā raided and plundered al-Khanāfis on its market day; it was guarded by two cavalry units from the Rabīʿa and the Quḍāʿa, both of whom seem to have been Christian, since the name of the Quḍāʿī leader is not Arabic (Rūmānūs b. Wabara). The man from al-Ḥīra guided al-Muthannā to a village frequented by the merchants of Ctesiphon and other cities and in which a great deal of money and goods exchanged hands. The guide then gave him detailed instructions as to how to proceed toward al-Anbār. There he should seek the assistance of some *dihqāns* in assigning guides (*adillāʾ*). Al-Muthannā did according to the information provided by the Ḥīrite and took guides who went with him on the last leg of five or six parasangs until he reached his destination, where he gained a great deal of valuable spoils. He returned and with him the guides, across deserts and canals, until they arrived in al-Anbār, where the *dihqāns* received them with hospitality and joy.[56]

In the same year, 13/634, the Islamic sources begin to speak about a higher level of support from the Christian Arabs to the conquering Muslim armies: they start fighting the Byzantines and the Sasanians with them, among their armies. Two such activities are reported. The first took place during the battle of al-Buwayb in Iraq, which was led by the same al-Muthannā b. Ḥāritha; the report about it is so explicit in delineating the confessional difference between the conquering Muslims and the cooperating Christian Arabs that we have to dwell on it at length.[57] The report has it that when two Christian Arab leaders saw the Persians camp against the Muslims, they said, "We shall fight with our people (*qawminā*)," meaning the Arabs, that is, the conquering Muslims in this case. The first of these two was Anas b. Hilāl al-Namarī; he came "to reinforce al-Muthannā with men from the Namir *who were Christians*, and traders (*jullāb*) who brought horses." The second was Ibn Mirdā al-Fihrī al-Taghlibī, whose name was ʿAbd Allāh b. Khālid; he came "with men from the Banū Taghlib *who were Christians* and traders who brought horses." After the battle had become prolonged and severe, the report continues, al-Muthannā approached Anas b. Hilāl and said, "O Anas, you are an Arab man *even if you do not follow our religion*. When you see me attack Mihrān [the Persian general], attack with me." He then approached Ibn Mirdā al-Fihrī and said to him the same thing. Both Christians and their men fought in battle with the Muslims, and Anas was carried wounded from the battlefield. But these two men were not the only Christians who fought with the Muslims in the battle of al-Buwayb. It is reported that a group of young Taghlibīs joined the battle at al-Buwayb after it had started, saying, "We shall fight the Persians with the Arabs." One of them, "a boy of the Taghlibīs *who was a Christian*," slew Mihrān b. Bādhān al-Hamadhānī, whom the Persians had put forward to fight the Muslims. The boy

[55] Al-Ṭabarī, *Tārīkh*, vol. 3, pp. 475–76/vol. I, pp. 2206–07.

[56] Ibid., vol. 3, pp. 473–75/vol. I, pp. 2203–06.

[57] Ibid., vol. 3, pp. 461–70/vol. I, pp. 2184–98.

mounted his horse and started chanting, tracing his ancestry, "I am the Taghlibī boy! I have killed the *marzbān*!"

The second incident in which the Christian Arabs went into active combat with the Muslims took place in 17/638 in Mesopotamia. Again here the report is clear in indicating that some of the Arabs fighting the Byzantines alongside the Muslims had not converted. The text has it that when the commander of the Muslim army, al-Walīd b. ʿUqba, came to Mesopotamia, the Christian Arab tribe of Iyād b. Nizār had crossed to Byzantine territory, but the Taghlib and the rest of the Arabs in Mesopotamia joined him in the battle and pushed into Byzantine land, "both Muslims and unbelievers" (*bi-muslimihim wa-kāfirihim*).[58] After the Muslim victory in that battle, the caliph ʿUmar b. al-Khaṭṭāb wrote to the Byzantine emperor to send back the Christians who had taken refuge in his territory, otherwise he, ʿUmar, would expel the Arab Christians living in Muslim territory. Some 4,000 of them returned to their lands while others lagged behind.[59] And when al-Walīd b. ʿUqba insisted that the Arab Christians, particularly the Taghlib, should convert to Islam since they were Arab, the caliph ʿUmar overruled him, saying that the law that each Arab must become Muslim applied only to the inhabitants of the Arabian Peninsula, not to anywhere else.[60]

But did the Christian Arabs, while still Christian, fight with the Muslims in the latters' campaigns against Byzantium other than from their own lands in Syria, Iraq, and Mesopotamia? The answer is uncertain, for we hear of only one, rather unusual, such case; it concerns a poet who went out with the expedition of Maslama b. ʿAbd al-Malik to al-Ṭiwāna in 85/704. This is the Taghlibī al-Nuʿmān b. Najwān, better known as Aʿshā Banī Taghlib.[61] That he was a Christian and remained so is certain, for we know that, whereas he was close to the Umayyad caliph al-Walīd b. ʿAbd al-Malik (al-Walīd I; r. 86–96/705–715) and received grants from him, when ʿUmar b. ʿAbd al-ʿAzīz (ʿUmar II) became caliph in 99/717–718, long after Maslama's campaign, ʿUmar withheld money from him, saying, "I do not see a right for poets in the (Muslims') treasury (*bayt al-māl*); even if they had such a right, you do not, because you are a Christian man (*li-annaka umruʾun naṣrānī*)."[62] What is uncertain is the purpose of his joining Maslama's campaign. The only report we have on this matter is a conversation between the two men in which Maslama requested the Taghlibī poet to compose verses satirizing a certain man from the ʿAbs, a thing that the poet promptly did. Could the Christian poet then have gone out with Maslama not to fight (especially if he was actually *aʿshā*, dim-sighted) but to provide companionship and entertainment to the expedition's leader? This question must remain unanswered.

Let us now go to the non-Islamic sources and see what they have to say about the Christian Arab tribes' role in the Muslim conquests. The material there is meager, but, overall, it confirms the general picture painted in the Islamic sources about Christian Arabs fighting with the Byzantines and Sasanians at the beginning of the conquests and the subsequent change in the loyalties of some of them, with devastating effects on both the Byzantine and

---

[58] Ibid., vol. 4, p. 54/vol. I, p. 2507.

[59] Ibid., vol. 4, p. 55/vol. I, pp. 2508–09.

[60] Ibid., vol. 4, p. 55/vol. I, p. 2509. See also al-Balādhurī, *Futūḥ al-buldān*, p. 182, where ʿUmar is said to have overruled ʿUmayr b. Saʿd in his desire to force the Taghlib to convert to Islam. Another, more specific episode concerning Jabala b. al-Ayham is in ibid., p. 136.

[61] On Aʿshā Banī Taghlib, see Ibn al-ʿAdīm, *Zubdat al-ḥalab fī tārīkh ḥalab*, vol. 8, pp. 3619–20.

[62] Ibid., vol. 8, pp. 3619–20.

Sasanian empires.[63] These sources provide us with four new pieces of valuable information that enrich our understanding of the Christian Arabs' role in the conquests without contradicting the Islamic historical record about it. Furthermore, these sources provide a link with the pre-Islamic past with regard to some of the actions of the Christian Arabs after the conquests.

The first is a short and rather strange report that says that Abū Bakr [caliph 11–13/632–634] sent out four generals, one to Moab en route to Palestine, one to Egypt, one to the Persians, and one to "the Christian Arabs who were subject to the Romans."[64] Although the report is unclear as to the destination of this last army, it is noteworthy that it betrays a perception on the part of the Byzantines that the Christian Arabs, aside from the Byzantines and the Sasanians, were military targets of the Muslims at the very beginning of the conquests. The second report adds to our information about the battle of al-Yarmūk. Its says that the messenger who brought to the emperor Heraclius, who was then in Antioch, the news about the defeat there was a Christian Arab; for "no one of his soldiers had lived to tell the tale."[65] The third report unveils the motives that made some Christian Arabs change sides, dropping their support to the Byzantines and aiding the invading Muslims with information. According to Theophanes, in the year 631–632 (= A.H. 10), there were some Arabs who received small payments from the emperors to guard the entrances of the desert. But at that time, a eunuch came to pay the soldiers' wages and the Arabs came to receive their pay. The eunuch, however, drove them out, saying, "The emperor barely pays his soldiers their wages, much less these dogs!!" Aggrieved, the Arabs went "to their fellow-tribesmen" (meaning the invading Muslims) and showed them the route to the rich land of Gaza, which is the entrance to the desert in the direction of Mount Sinai.[66] And the last report portrays the sense of misplaced tranquility some of the residents of Byzantine territory had with regard to Christian Arabs, taking their loyalty to their empire for granted and swiftly falling victim to Muslim attacks. The event described is not dated, but its place in the *Chronicle of 1234* puts its date at A.H. 17 or 18 (A.D. 646–648). It goes as follows.

> Muᶜāwiya's next goal was the heartlands of the Romans, so he advanced to Euchaita [...] leaving a trail of destruction behind him. No one sounded the alarm. The Euchaitans were scattered over the countryside, harvesting the crops and working the vineyards. They had seen the aggressors all right; but they were under the impression that they were Christian Arabs, from one or other tribe allied with the Roman. So they saw no reason to alter their dispositions, let alone run away. The Arabs found the gates of the unhappy city open and the people sitting around without the slightest fear. The next moment they were entering it, plundering it, piling up great mounds of booty [...].[67]

[63] On this, see Kaegi, *Byzantium*, pp. 52–54, 62, 100, 121, 144, 173–75, 272. See also Donner, *Early Islamic Conquests*, pp. 116–19, 251–71.

[64] *Chronicle of A.D. 1234*, in Palmer, *West-Syrian Chronicles*, p. 146. The report occurs in Theophanes, *Chronicle*, trans. Mango and Scott, p. 466, but is confused there. Cf. al-Ṭabarī, *Tārīkhī*, vol. 3, p. 406/vol. I, pp. 2107–08.

[65] *Chronicle of 1234*, in Palmer, *West-Syrian Chronicles*, p. 158.

[66] Theophanes, *Chronicle*, p. 467. Kaegi, *Byzantium*, p. 91, comments that "[t]he Byzantine government's cancellation of payments to the federated Arabs was not unique. There was a sharp retrenchment in military expenditures, including soldiers' pay, all over the empire."

[67] *Chronicle of A.D. 1234*, in Palmer, *West-Syrian Chronicles*, p. 166; more briefly in Michael the Syrian, *Chronicle*, vol. 2, p. 431.

II. The Non-Arab Non-Muslims and the Muslim Army

When we come to the non-Arab non-Muslims and the Muslim army, the information increases in the sources and becomes more complex. This makes it necessary to break up the topic into sections that answer the following questions: Who were those non-Arab non-Muslims? How did they come to have a relation to the Muslim army? And what did they do in the Muslim army?

a. Who Were Those Non-Arab Non-Muslims?

The Islamic sources mention several non-Arab groups who, while non-Muslim, served in one way or another with the Muslim army. Since some of these groups eventually did convert to Islam at some point, the information about them could be hazy and perhaps difficult to ascertain.

Starting with the east, one such group is the Asāwira, the formerly elite cavalry unit of the Sasanian army.[68] We first hear about them in the conquest of al-Madāʾin in ca. 17/638, that is, two or three years after the battle of al-Qādisiyya;[69] at that point, the sources have it that the caliph ʿUmar b. al-Khaṭṭāb wrote to the leaders of the conquests in Iraq to "seek the assistance of whomever they needed from the Asāwira," and that they should "drop their tribute" (*wa-yaḍaʿū ʿanhum al-jizāʾ*).[70] The mere mention of the *jizya* indicates that the Asāwira had not yet converted at the conquest of al-Madāʾin, and that at least some of them had fallen under Muslim rule. Did any of the Asāwira then fight with the Muslims in return for being exempted from paying the *jizya*? The sources are silent on this matter. Some years later, however, shortly before the conquest of Tustar, the Asāwira reappear, now offering Abū Mūsā al-Ashʿarī to convert to Islam and join his forces, which they did, participating in the siege of Tustar.[71] One would think, then, that the Asāwira who fought alongside the Muslim army at the latest in 20/640 were Muslims. And yet, many years later, in 64/683, the leader of the Asāwira still has a Persian name: Māh Afrīdhūn.[72] This, along with what we hear in the sources about the Asāwira's admission of being weak in Islam at the beginning of their conversion,[73] leads us to conclude that the Asāwira were, at least for part of the time they fought with the Muslims, still not Muslim. And the same can be said about three other groups who

---

[68] On the Asāwira, see Morony, *Iraq after the Muslim Conquest*, pp. 198, 271–72, and *passim* (see index); Zakeri, *Sāsānid Soldiers*; ʿAthamina, "Non-Arab Regiments and Private Militias," pp. 348–55.

[69] For the various dates mentioned for the battle of al-Qādisiyya, see Donner, *Early Islamic Conquests*, p. 212.

[70] Al-Ṭabarī, *Tārīkh*, vol. 4, p. 49/vol. I, p. 2497.

[71] See al-Balādhurī, *Futūḥ al-buldān*, pp. 373–74; al-Ṭabarī, *Tārīkh*, vol. 4, pp. 90–91/vol. I, pp. 2562–63. The conquest of Tustar is placed somewhere between 16/637 and 20/640; see Donner, *Early Islamic Conquests*, p. 217.

[72] See Crone, *Slaves on Horses*, p. 237 n. 362, based on al-Ṭabarī, *Tārīkh*, vol. 5, pp. 518–19/vol. II, pp. 452, 454. ʿAthamina, "Non-Arab Regiments and Private Militias," p. 349, offers a plausible explanation: "the *Asāwira* who converted to Islam and joined the Arabs in the year 638/17 were no more than a small segment of the *Asāwira* in the Persian imperial army. There were still other groups of *Asāwira* who had become normal subjects like the other citizens of the occupied territory."

[73] In al-Ṭabarī, *Tārīkh*, vol. 4, p. 90/vol. I, p. 2563, it is reported that when the Asāwira were blamed by Abū Mūsā al-Ashʿarī for not fighting well in the conquest of Tustar, their leader explained that by citing several reasons, the first of which was "we are not like you in this religion, nor are our insights like yours."

converted to Islam at some point but not at the beginning of the conquests of Iraq, namely the Indian Zuṭṭ, Sayābija, and Indighār, all of whom had served in the Sasanian army, since al-Balādhurī says that they did like the Asāwira.[74]

Another group that is slightly less problematic is the Daylam, or al-Ḥamrāʾ (or Ḥamrāʾ al-Daylam), who were also an elite unit, probably of the infantry, in the Sasanian army at the beginning of the conquest of Iraq. One source says that they fought with the Sasanians during the battle al-Qādisiyya in 14/635, but after the Sasanians' defeat there and after Rustamʾs death, they became neutral. They then converted to Islam and participated in the conquest of al-Madāʾin and the battle of Jalūlāʾ.[75] Another source, however, has a different story: after al-Qādisiyya, "the Daylam and the chiefs of the advance garrisons *who had responded to the Muslims and fought with them while still having not embraced Islam* said: Our brethren who entered this religion (*al-amr*) from the beginning had better judgment and were better than we were. By God, no, the Persians will not succeed after Rustam — except those of them who enter this religion."[76] The latter text is explicit in indicating that the Daylam at an early stage of the conquests fought alongside the Muslims before converting. One can assume, however, that they converted fairly early, perhaps not too long after al-Qādisiyya.[77]

Another two groups about whom the material in the sources is not problem free are the Ḥamrāʾ and the Fārisiyyūn, who participated in the conquest of Egypt. In the earliest report about them, they are identified as non-Arabs (*al-ʿajam*), the latter being Persians (*furs*), allegedly from the Persians of Ṣanʿāʾ, while the former were Greeks (*rūm*), of whom are the Banū Yanna, Banū Rūbīl, and Banū al-Azraq.[78] Furthermore, it is reported that ʿAmr b. al-ʿĀṣ brought the two groups with him to Egypt *from Syria*.[79] Four centuries later, this report is repeated, but with the following addition: "[...] *min ʿajam al-Shām mimman kāna raghiba fī al-islām min qabl al-Yarmūk*" (from the non-Arabs of Syria who had been inclined to [accept] Islam from before [the battle of] al-Yarmūk).[80] Although the report does not state clearly that the two groups had already converted to Islam when they participated in the conquest of Egypt, it certainly insinuates that. But this seems to be unlikely, given the names of the Greek families cited by the first report. Furthermore, in the published extracts from Ibn Yūnus' history, one person from each of those groups is profiled, and both have non-Arabic names: Yanna al-Ḥamrāwī and Sunbukht al-Fārisī;[81] only in the next generation do we get Arabic names for people from these groups.[82] When the conversion of these Greek and Persian units took place is difficult to pin down, but it happened certainly before 39–41/659–661, when, according to Sebeos, the "army which was in Egypt [...] made a treaty" with the Byzantine emperor, and "the host of troops, about 15,000, converted to Christianity."[83]

---

[74] Al-Balādhurī, *Futūḥ al-buldān*, p. 375. On these three groups, see Morony, *Iraq after the Muslim Conquest*, pp. 271–72; Zakeri, *Sāsānid Soldiers*, *passim*; ʿAthamina, "Non-Arab Regiments and Private Militias," pp. 355–58. See also *EI*[2] s.vv. "Sayābidja" and "al-Zuṭṭ" (both C. E. Bosworth).

[75] Al-Balādhurī, *Futūḥ al-buldān*, p. 280.

[76] Al-Ṭabarī, *Tārīkh*, vol. 3, p. 566/vol. I, p. 2341.

[77] Morony, *Iraq after the Muslim Conquest*, p. 197, synthesizes the problematic material on the Daylam by saying that some of them converted before al-Qādisiyya, some after it.

[78] Ibn ʿAbd al-Ḥakam, *Futūḥ Miṣr*, p. 129.

[79] Ibid., p. 129.

[80] Ibn Duqmāq, *al-Intiṣār li-wāsiṭat ʿiqd al-amṣār*, pp. 4–5.

[81] See Ibn Yūnus, *Tārīkh*, vol. 1, *Tārīkh al-miṣriyyīn*, pp. 317, 224, respectively.

[82] Ibid., vol. 1, p. 317 (ʿAbd al-Raḥmān b. Yanna), and cf. "ʿAbd al-Raḥmān b. Yuḥannis" in al-Kindī, *Kitāb al-wulāt*, p. 51, and al-Maqrīzī, *Khiṭaṭ*, vol. 1, p. 210.

[83] Sebeos, *The Armenian History*, vol. 1, p. 154; and see vol. 2, p. 287.

Remaining in Egypt, the non-Muslim group about whose participation in the Muslim army's activities there is clear evidence is the Christian Copts. The Islamic sources do mention a few such instances, although these come always particularly clearly in the form of individuals.[84] As a group, the Copts' contribution to the Islamic conquests is articulated more in the papyri, as we shall see in the discussion of the fleet, below.

In Syria, the Islamic sources are clear in indicating that two groups, the Jarājima (Mardaites) and the Anbāṭ, assisted the Muslim armies while remaining Christian.[85] Another group identified by confession as an ally who collaborated with the Muslims was the Samaritans.[86] There is a passing reference in the sources to Slavs (*al-Ṣaqāliba*) helping the conquering Muslims.[87] Other unidentified local groups in northern Syria and Mesopotamia are also referred to.[88]

In the northeast frontier region, and more so in the east, the Islamic sources provide indirect evidence to the participation of all kinds of non-Arab and non-Muslim peoples in Muslim military activities.[89] This can be gleaned from the peace agreements that the Muslims concluded in these regions, where one of the conditions of the agreements is that the locals should provide military assistance to the Muslims upon demand, sometimes in return for dropping the *jizya* required of them.[90] The key text that is relevant here is the one describing the negotiations that took place between the "king" of al-Bāb and the commander of the Muslim forces, ʿAbd al-Raḥmān b. Rabīʿa. These ended with a peace agreement, sanctioned, it is reported, by no less than the caliph ʿUmar b. al-Khaṭṭāb; it stipulated that there be, among other things, potential military assistance to the Muslims from the people of al-Bāb. The text then continues, "and it became common practice (*sunna*) regarding those fighting the enemy from the polytheists (*al-mushrikīn*): [...] if they were called upon to fight (*yustanfarū*), the tribute (*jizya*) of that year would be removed from them."[91] Such was the case with the Armenians,[92] the people of Jurjān and Dahistān,[93] Ādharbayjān,[94] and

[84] One Copt is reported to be with the first Muslim campaign against Ifrīqiya; see al-Mālikī, *Riyāḍ al-nufūs*, vol. 1, pp. 17–18; al-Dabbāgh, *Maʿālim al-īmān*, p. 34. See also Ibn ʿAbd al-Ḥakam, *Futūḥ Miṣr*, pp. 165–66, for the assistance another Copt provided to ʿAmr b. al-ʿĀṣ. More details will be provided below.

[85] On the Jarājima/Mardaites having remained Christian, see al-Balādhurī, *Futūḥ al-buldān*, p. 161: *ʿalā allā yukrihū wa-lā aḥad min awlādihim wa-nisāʾihim ʿalā tark al-naṣrāniyya*. On the Anbāṭ, see Ibn Aʿtham al-Kūfī, *Kitāb al-futūḥ*, vol. 1, p. 144: *wa-kāna hāʾulāʾ al-anbāṭ qawman naṣārā*. See also *EI*[2] s.vv. "Djarādjima" (M. Canard) and "Nabaṭ" (T. Fahd).

[86] Al-Balādhurī, *Futūḥ al-buldān*, p. 158. See on the Samaritans *EI*[2] s.v. "al-Sāmira" (S. Noja Noseda).

[87] Al-Balādhurī, *Futūḥ al-buldān*, p. 150.

[88] See al-Balādhurī, *Futūḥ al-buldān*, p. 150, for the people of Dulūk and Raʿbān, and ibid., pp. 156–57, for the people of Arabissos.

[89] See in particular de La Vaissière, *Samarcande et Samarra*, pp. 44ff.

[90] For these peace agreements, see al-Qāḍī, "Madkhal." Many of the texts of the agreements have been reproduced in Ḥamīdullāh, *al-Wathāʾiq al-siyāsiyya*, see index.

[91] Al-Ṭabarī, *Tārīkh*, vol. 4, p. 156/vol. I, p. 2664 (*sub anno* 22).

[92] Al-Ṭabarī, *Tārīkh*, vol. 4, pp. 156–57/vol. I, pp. 2665–66 (*sub anno* 22). The agreement stipulates that those Armenians who cannot fight with the Muslims must pay the *jizya*. The Armenians should also provide the Muslims with guidance (*dilāla*) and lodging for one day and one night (*nuzl*). Cf. al-Qāḍī, "Madkhal," pp. 242, 265–66.

[93] Al-Ṭabarī, *Tārīkh*, vol. 4, p. 152/vol. I, p. 2658 (*sub anno* 22). The agreement is dated 18/[639] and seems to request payment of the *jizya* from those who do not fight alongside the Muslims. They are also requested to provide the Muslims with advice (*naṣaḥū*) and feeding (*qirā*). Cf. al-Qāḍī, "Madkhal," pp. 242, 263.

[94] Al-Ṭabarī, *Tārīkh*, vol. 4, p. 155/vol. I, p. 2662 (*sub anno* 22). The agreement is dated 18/[639]. Here also those who do not fight with the Muslims have to pay the *jizya*. Exempted from paying any *jizya* are prepubescent children, women, the sick, and the reclusive pious (*mutaʿabbid mutakhallin laysa fī yadayhi shayʾ min*

Marw al-Rūdh.[95] Other conditions of cooperation were established also in the peace agreements of Mūqān,[96] Iṣfahān,[97] and al-Rayy.[98] In the northeast, too, help to the Muslims is reported to have come from Soghdia; but here there is also a report about an individual,[99] not a group, as in the case of an Armenian.[100] Both will be discussed below.

Finally, another group that was mostly non-Muslim (and certainly non-Arab) and yet fought with the Muslims is the slaves (*mamālīk*; also *ʿabīd*),[101] of which the Muslims must have captured enormous numbers during the conquests.

Going to the west, one would expect that the Berbers would be the main group to participate in the activities of the Muslim armies in Ifrīqiya, the Maghrib, and Andalusia. This matter, however, is rather difficult to pin down with accuracy:[102] when the sources[103] say that the Berbers offered the Muslims both "Islam" and "obedience,"[104] that seems to mean that the Berber tribes involved converted. But what about when they say that Berbers offered the Muslims "obedience" only:[105] does that mean they did *not* convert? This is far from clear. Above all, if some Berbers helped the Muslims, did they do so before they converted? And what did they convert *from* in the first place?

The sources talk about the population of the west as made up of Rūm (Romans, Greeks) and Berbers,[106] sometimes adding Magians (*majūs*).[107] At the beginning of the conquest, they sometimes call all these collectively *kuffār* (unbelievers)[108] or *mushrikūn* (polytheists).[109] They are, however, aware that the "Romans" are Christian,[110] and that there were some Christians among the Berbers.[111] The Berbers to them are though, by and large, simply pagan, especially

al-dunyā). They are requested to guide the "Muslim soldiers" (*junūd al-muslimīn*) and feed them for one day and one night. Cf. al-Qāḍī, "Madkhal," pp. 242, 264.

[95] Al-Ṭabarī, *Tārīkh*, vol. 4, pp. 310–11/vol. I, pp. 2898–99 (*sub anno* 32). Interestingly, the agreement states that if the people convert to Islam and follow the Messenger, they would receive from the Muslims stipends (*ʿaṭāʾ*), allowance of food (*rizq*), and status (*manzila*), and would be their "brothers" (*wa-anta akhūhum*). Cf. al-Qāḍī, "Madkhal," pp. 264–65.

[96] Al-Ṭabarī, *Tārīkh*, vol. 4, p. 157/vol. I, p. 2666 (*sub anno* 22). The agreement is dated 21/[642] and stipulates that the people of Mūqān provide the Muslims with guidance and lodging for one day and one night. Cf. al-Qāḍī, "Madkhal," p. 266.

[97] Al-Ṭabarī, *Tārīkh*, vol. 4, p. 141/vol. I, p. 2641 (*sub anno* 21). The agreement requests the people of Iṣfahān to provide the Muslims with guidance, feeding for one day and one night, repairing their roads, and transporting Muslim unmounted riders (infantrymen?) for a distance of about one day's journey (*ḥumlān al-rājil ilā marḥala*). Cf. al-Qāḍī, "Madkhal," pp. 243, 262.

[98] Al-Ṭabarī, *Tārīkh*, vol. 4, p. 151/vol. I, p. 2655 (*sub anno* 22). The agreement stipulates that the people of al-Rayy and its environs provide the Muslims with guidance and feeding for one day and one night. Cf. al-Qāḍī, "Madkhal," pp. 262–63.

[99] On the agreement with the Soghdians, see Ibn Aʿtham, *Kitāb al-futūḥ*, vol. 7, pp. 244–46. Cf. al-Qāḍī, "Madkhal," pp. 239, 242, 246–47, 266–67. On the individual, see al-Ṭabarī, *Tārīkh*, vol. 7, p. 7/vol. II, p. 1442 (*sub anno* 104).

[100] In al-Ṭabarī, *Tārīkh*, vol. 6, pp. 530–31/vol. II, pp. 1315–16 (*sub anno* 98).

[101] Al-Ṭabarī, *Tārīkh*, vol. 6, p. 532/vol. II, p. 1318.

[102] The literature I have consulted does not tackle the topic in which we are interested here, namely when the Berber tribes converted to Islam, and whether they were Muslims when they helped the conquering Arabs in the conquest of the Maghrib and Andalusia.

[103] I will be using mainly Ibn ʿIdhārī al-Marrākushī's (d. after 706/1306) relatively late history, *Kitāb al-bayān al-mughrib*, vol. 1, since he cites a variety of earlier Islamic sources, some of which have not survived.

[104] See ibid., p. 38.

[105] See ibid., pp. 42, 60.

[106] See ibid., pp. 24, 28, 32, 35.

[107] See ibid., p. 24. Ibn ʿIdhārī mentions another group: *al-Afāriqa* "the Africans" (pp. 12, 36). The term seems to mean simply the indigenous people of the province of Ifrīqiya, without specifying a particular group.

[108] See ibid., p. 25.

[109] See ibid., pp. 27, 32.

[110] See ibid., pp. 24, 25.

[111] See ibid., p. 24.

those living in the mountains.[112] In addition, the sources impart that the conquering Muslims knew that the Berbers were divided into tribes, each of which controlled a different part of the Maghrib, and that they dealt with them accordingly.[113] But when and how did that extend to converting them to Islam?

The sources intimate that the Islamization of the Berbers went through two phases. It began in the form of the personal zeal of some Muslim officials, then became a government policy, the critical events separating the two phases being the decisive victory of the Muslims over the Byzantines in the battle of Carthage in 73/692 and over the formidable Berber rebel al-Kāhina (the Sorceress) in ca. 82/701.[114] ʿUqba b. Nāfi al-Fihrī, the governor of Ifrīqiya in 49–55/669–674 and 62–63/681–683, represents the first, personal phase. He is said to have established at least three mosques in various parts of the Maghrib, and to have left there "some of his associates to teach the Qurʾān and Islam, among them Shākir of the *ribāṭ*." As a result, most of the Maṣmūda tribe of the Berbers in the farthest Maghrib converted voluntarily to Islam (*aslamū ṭawʿan*).[115] After that, the sources start talking about more systematic efforts at Islamization,[116] so that the year 85/704 is said to be the year in which "the conversion of the people of the farthest Maghrib was completed."[117] The Islamization efforts continued and took in 100/718 an even more official form, when the highest Islamic authority, the Umayyad caliph ʿUmar II, sent a group of Muslim religious scholars (whose names have been preserved) to Ifrīqiya and the Maghrib in what amounts to a missionary operation.[118] The result was that the rest of the Berbers of Ifrīqiya converted.[119] All these efforts, the sources say, led various Berber tribes of the Maghrib to convert to Islam.[120] That did not prevent some Berber uprisings, some quite successful,[121] including the "defection" of some Berber groups to Muslim sectarian Khārijism.[122]

---

[112] See ibid., pp. 27, 32, 37, 61. See also the negative description of the Berbers attributed to Julian, Count of Ceuta (on whom see below), in ibid., p. 26: they are "like animals (*al-bahāʾim*)"; they have espoused no religion, including Christianity, and are thus *kuffār*; they eat corpses; and they eat their cattle and drink their blood. The famous Berber rebel al-Kāhina (the Sorceress; see below) is associated with the Awrās mountains (ibid., pp. 35–39). See also *EI*[2] s.v. "al-Kāhina" (M. Talbi).

[113] See Ibn ʿIdhārī, *al-Bayān al-mughrib*, vol. 1, pp. 26–28, 38.

[114] See ibid., p. 38. The governor of Ifrīqiya in ca. 73–86/692–705, i.e., during these two momentous series of battles, was Ḥassān b. al-Nuʿmān al-Ghassānī. The subsequent consolidation of Muslim power in Ifrīqiya made Ḥassān set up government offices/records (*dawwana al-dawāwīn*) and conclude written agreements about taxes with the non-Arab population (*ʿajam*) of Ifrīqiya who had remained Christian.

[115] See ibid., pp. 27, 38. What gives such accounts reasonable credibility is that the sources mention several failures by the Arabs to Islamize the Berbers, with the latter preferring to fight the Arabs instead; see, for examples, ibid., p. 28 (regarding the tribes of Dukkāna and Haskūra).

[116] See ibid., p. 42: Mūsā b. Nuṣayr (gov. ca. 86–90/705–709) "ordered the Arabs to teach the Berbers the Qurʾān and [...] the religion"; in Tangier, Mūsā left behind seventeen men to teach the Qurʾān and "the laws (*sharāʾiʿ*) of Islam." On Tangier, see also Anonymous, *Akhbār majmūʿa*, p. 4.

[117] See Ibn ʿIdhārī, *al-Bayān al-mughrib*, vol. 1, p. 43: they thus "turned the mosques that the polytheists had built to [the direction of] the *qibla*, and they built *minbars* in the congregational mosques."

[118] On this mission and its members, see Abū al-ʿArab al-Qayrawānī, *Ṭabaqāt ʿulamāʾ Ifrīqiya*, pp. 54–87; Ibn ʿIdhārī, *al-Bayān al-mughrib*, vol. 1, p. 48.

[119] See ibid., p. 48: *ḥattā aslama baqiyyat al-Barbar bi-Ifrīqiya ʿalā yadayhi.*

[120] See ibid., pp. 26–27, 38 (where the Berbers involved converted and agreed to support the Arabs with 12,000 troops).

[121] See Ibn al-Qūṭiyya, *Iftitāḥ al-Andalus*, pp. 40–44 (for Andalusia); Ibn ʿIdhārī, *al-Bayān al-mughrib*, vol. 1, pp. 28–31, 52–59, 60–61; Anonymous, *Akhbār majmūʿa*, pp. 31–37, also 38–39 (for Andalusia).

[122] See Ibn ʿIdhārī, *al-Bayān al-mughrib*, vol. 1, pp. 52–54, 55, 56–59; Anonymous, *Akhbār majmūʿa*, pp. 31–37.

With this in mind, the question that concerns us here is whether the Berbers who fought with the Muslims were Muslim. It is reported that 12,000 Berbers converted to Islam immediately after the defeat of al-Kāhina and fought with the Muslims in the conquest of the Maghrib, but three (key) individuals did not convert, as will be discussed below.[123] As for the first large army[124] that started the conquest of al-Andalus, its rank and file were almost certainly Muslims. This is clear from the distinctions the sources make between them and the population of the Iberian Peninsula, and from sheer common sense: all the sources agree that this army, led by Ṭāriq b. Ziyād in 91/711, was entirely, or almost entirely, composed of Berbers.[125] These Berbers could not have been non-Muslims.[126] And when, shortly thereafter, Mūsā b. Nuṣayr, the next conqueror of Andalusia, had serious problems with Ṭāriq,[127] none of them even touched on the religion of the first conquerors.

Andalusia brings us to the last non-Muslim group that participated with the Muslims in the conquest of the west, namely the Rūm (Romans). But here again the Islamic sources provide information mainly about individuals, some of whom commanded small groups who helped the Muslims, as will be shown later.[128]

Going to the non-Islamic sources, we find some overlapping information with the material of the Islamic sources, though at times with greater elaboration, and some supplementary information.

The most striking text is the Syriac one that comes from John bar Penkayē, who was writing in Mesopotamia in 68–69/687 and hence was a witness to the Muslim conquests.[129] After saying that the Muslim armies annually raided distant lands, bringing back captives "from all peoples under the heavens," he adds, "and there were among them not a few Christians, some belonging to the heretics, and some to us,"[130] meaning by "the heretics" the Monophysites, and by "us" the Nestorians. This is a truly stunning contemporary testimony from within the Christian community that there were Christians of practically all denominations fighting with the Muslims — and this confirms what the Islamic sources had said. There is also some evidence, albeit quite controversial, that there were Jews who collaborated with the conquering Muslim armies.[131]

---

[123] See below the case of the two sons of al-Kāhina (Ibn ʿIdhārī, *al-Bayān al-mughrib*, vol. 1, pp. 35–39). Fearing defeat, their mother sent them to the Muslims. Whether they converted is never stated, but each of them led almost immediately thereafter 6,000 convert Berbers in battle with the Arabs (ibid., p. 38). The third key individual is Ḥubāḥiba al-Rūmī of Ifrīqiya, to whom no conversion is attributed; see ibid., pp. 16–17.

[124] This army was composed of many thousand Berbers; the sources cite 7,000 and 12,000. See, e.g., al-Raqīq al-Qayrawānī, *Tārīkh Ifrīqiya*, p. 71; Anonymous, *Akhbār majmūʿa*, pp. 6, 7. See also *EI*[2] s.v. "al-Andalus" (É. Lévi-Provençal, J. D. Latham, L. Torres Balbás, and G. S. Colin).

[125] See al-Raqīq al-Qayrawānī, *Tārīkh Ifrīqiya*, p. 74; Anonymous, *Akhbār majmūʿa*, p. 6.

[126] The authors of the article "al-Andalus" in *EI*[2] assume that the conquering armies were all composed of Muslims.

[127] See examples of these problems in Ibn al-Qūṭiyya, *Iftitāḥ al-Andalus*, pp. 35–37; al-Raqīq al-Qayrawānī, *Tārīkh Ifrīqiya*, pp. 87–91; Anonymous, *Akhbār majmūʿa*, pp. 29–30. See also *EI*[2] s.v. "Mūsā b. Nuṣayr" (É. Lévi-Provençal).

[128] Julian and his retinue are the most famous; see Ibn al-Qūṭiyya, *Iftitāḥ al-Andalus*, pp. 33–34; al-Raqīq al-Qayrawānī, *Tārīkh Ifrīqiya*, pp. 73–74; Ibn ʿIdhārī, *al-Bayān al-mughrib*, vol. 2, pp. 4–5, 7; Anonymous, *Akhbār majmūʿa*, pp. 4–5, 7, 10, 16; "al-Andalus," in *EI*[2], s.v.

[129] On John bar Penkayē, see Hoyland, *Seeing Islam as Others Saw It*, pp. 194–200.

[130] See John bar Penkayē, *Chronicle*, ed. Mingana, vol. 2, pp. 147/175. See also Brock, "Syriac Views," p. 17; Donner, "From Believers to Muslims," p. 44; idem, *Muhammad and the Believers*, p. 176.

[131] Hoyland, *Seeing Islam as Others Saw It*, p. 528: "A number of Jews would even seem to have participated in the Arab armies." To support this claim,

The non-Islamic sources not only confirm but also provide more details about two groups that the Islamic sources mention. The first is the Slavs, to whom the Islamic sources briefly refer. Under two separate years, 44/664–665 and 73/692–693,[132] Theophanes mentions the defection of large numbers of Slavs from the Byzantine army to the Muslim army, 5,000 of them in the first year, and 20,000 in the second;[133] Michael the Syrian gives the figure 7,000 for the second year.[134] In the first instance, Theophanes says that the Slavs were taken by the Muslims to Syria and settled in the village of Seleukobolos near Apamea; in the second, Michael the Syrian says that they were also taken to Syria but were settled in Antioch and Cyrrhus. He adds that they were given women, money, and provisions.[135] The second group is the Armenians. The most interesting thing here is that Sebeos, who was a contemporary of the Muslim conquests, mentions the peace treaty between the Muslims and the Armenians (possibly using a documentary source),[136] and it includes a condition that "I (= the Muslim commander) shall not request the cavalry for Syria; but *wherever else I command they shall be ready for duty*"[137] — which is similar to what we had seen in the Islamic version of that treaty.[138] Other information provided by the non-Islamic sources about the Armenians includes a defection to the Muslim side by a certain partríkios of theirs,[139] and by the still-Christian leaders and soldiers of the embryonic Armeniak theme.[140] Thus, as Kaegi has noted, "Armenia represented the first instance of the defection of the armed leadership of some Christians, and the soldiers and civilians under their authority, to Muslim authority, without any immediate expectation of their conversion to Islam."[141]

The non-Islamic sources add another "foreign" group to the army of the Muslims, namely mercenaries — although the only text I have found in this respect calls them "hirelings." This is the *Maronite Chronicle* (A.D. 664), which was contemporaneous with the early conquests. It narrates the story of the Muslim campaign led by Yazīd b. Muᶜāwiya (Yazīd I; r. 60–64/680–684), that is, in 47/667,[142] into Thrace. While the Muslims encamped there, the "Arabs" scattered seeking to plunder what they can, and they left behind in the camp their sons and their hirelings "to pasture the cattle." Thus left, the camp was vulnerable to the attack of some people there, who killed "a great many young men/children and hirelings and some of the Arabs too." On the next day, the Arabs, "in tribal formation," calling "in the way

---

Hoyland cites the *Doctrina Jacobi* and other sources. But Kaegi, *Byzantium*, p. 109, while admitting that the Jews had "special incentives to withhold support from the Byzantines and possibly to give active aid to the Muslims," adds (p. 116) that "no source specifically mentions any actions whatever on the part of these Jewish communities at that time."

[132] Both these campaigns are documented in the Islamic sources; for the first, led by ᶜAbd al-Raḥmān b. Khālid b. al-Walīd, see al-Yaᶜqūbī, *Tārīkh*, vol. 2, p. 239; for the second, led by Muḥammad b. Marwān, see al-Balādhurī, *Futūḥ al-buldān*, p. 188. There is no mention of any Slav defection there, though.

[133] See Theophanes, *Chronicle*, pp. 487, 511.

[134] See Michael the Syrian, *Chronicle*, vol. 2, p. 470. The discrepancy in the number of the Slavs is striking, but clearly the numbers involved were enormous.

[135] See also now Hoyland, *Theophilus of Edessa's Chronicle*, p. 186. I am indebted to the author for allowing me to use the text before its publication.

[136] See Hoyland, *Seeing Islam as Others Saw It*, pp. 125–26.

[137] Sebeos, *The Armenian History*, vol. 1, p. 136.

[138] See above, at n. 90.

[139] See *Chronicle of A.D. 1234*, in Palmer, *West-Syrian Chronicles*, p. 205.

[140] See Kaegi, *Byzantium*, p. 203. For the motives of the Armenians, see ibid., pp. 199–200. Kaegi believes that a few Armenians did collaborate with the Muslims from the beginning (p. 199).

[141] Ibid., p. 203.

[142] This campaign is known in the Islamic sources. See, for example, al-Yaᶜqūbī, *Tārīkh*, vol. 2, p. 229.

of their language 'God is great!'" attacked, killed many people, and took many captives.[143] It is in the light of this element of "foreigners" in the army of Yazīd I that we should understand Theophanes' description of the army as consisting of "an armed force of numerous barbarians."[144] Theophanes certainly did not mean by "barbarians" the Arabs/Muslims, for whom he always uses the words "Arabs," "Saracens," or "Agarenes" (= Hagarenes). What he must have meant by his statement is that there were many "foreign" peoples in that army, possibly including slaves, whose participation in the Muslim armies was mentioned by the Islamic sources, as we have seen.

Finally, the non-Islamic sources mention the threat to the monks of the Egyptian church to serve on the ships of the Muslim fleet,[145] in addition to supporting it financially;[146] this information is not mentioned in the Islamic sources. On the other hand, the non-Islamic sources confirm what came in the Islamic ones regarding individual Copts assisting the Muslim war effort.[147] Both these matters will be discussed below.

b. How Did Non-Arab Non-Muslims Come to Have a Relation with the Muslim Army?

The Islamic sources suggest two ways. The first is the voluntary movement to the Muslims' camp by various groups. This is how they portray the actions of the Asāwira, the Daylam, the Zuṭṭ, the Sayābija, and the Indighār, as we have seen. The second is related to the Islamic state's policy to provide enticements for the non-Muslims to join the Muslims. This could be done on an individual basis, as we saw in ʿUmar b. al-Khaṭṭāb's first policy statement about the Asāwira, namely to remove the tribute requirement from them if their aid was needed by the Muslims. It can also be seen in the case of the village of Arabissos: ʿUmar decreed that, in order to secure the cooperation of its population, "give them two ewes in the place of one, two cows in the place of one, and two things in the place of every other thing."[148] More frequently, though, the Islamic sources put those policy-related enticements in the form of formal peace agreements, treaties that specify what the contracting parties require of each other. We have seen above how this policy was enacted with regard to many districts in the northeast and east. But the sources also mention that such treaties were also concluded with the Jarājima[149] and the Anbāṭ of Syria.[150] These concessions given by the Muslims to the local peoples varied from place to place, although they always included safety and protection of life, children, and property; in some cases they included provisions and promise of military assistance, of non-enforcement of conversion, and of exemption from the *jizya*.[151]

---

[143] The *Maronite Chronicle*, in Palmer, *West-Syrian Chronicles*, pp. 32–33.

[144] Theophanes, *Chronicle*, p. 490.

[145] In [pseudo-]Severus, *History of the Patriarchs*, Patrologia Orientalis 5 (henceforth PO 5), p. 71.

[146] Ibid., pp. 70–71.

[147] See the case of Sanutius in [pseudo-]Severus, *History of the Patriarchs*, Patrologia Orientalis 1 (henceforth PO 1), pp. 408–09. He is probably the same person mentioned in John, Bishop of Nikiu, *Chronicle*, pp. 194–95, with the name Sinôda (= Shenūda).

[148] Al-Balādhurī, *Futūḥ al-buldān*, p. 157.

[149] Al-Balādhurī, *Futūḥ al-buldān*, p. 161. The agreement was concluded in 89/708. It specifies that the Jarājima should fight alongside the Muslims and to receive booty in particular circumstances. See also ibid., p. 159.

[150] Al-Balādhurī, *Futūḥ al-buldān*, p. 159. This agreement must have taken place about the same time as that with the Jarājima, and its conditions were identical to it. This is why al-Balādhurī's local source says that the Anbāṭ and the villagers of the area were called *al-rawādif*, the appendages [to the Jarājima]; see a further explanation below, n. 195.

[151] See al-Qāḍī, "Madkhal," pp. 230–43, 251–69.

There is, perhaps, a third way in which the Muslim state tried to reinforce its army through the assistance of local populations, except that the Islamic sources do not link it with army activities. By that I mean the transfer of entire groups and populations and their settlement in frontier areas or coastal cities. The sources report several such resettlements. In 42/662, Muʿāwiya moved a group (*qawm*) of Persians from Baalbeck, Ḥimṣ, and Antioch to Tyre and Acre, of the coast of Jordan, very possibly for maritime defense purposes.[152] Around the same year, he moved a group of the Asāwira from Baṣra and Kūfa and a group of Persians from Baalbek to Ḥimṣ and Antioch.[153] In 49/669 or 50/670, he moved a group of the Zuṭṭ and Sayābija from Baṣra to Antioch.[154] Al-Walīd I moved to Antioch a group of the Zuṭṭ and Sindīs who were brought to al-Ḥajjāj in Iraq by Muḥammad b. al-Qāsim, the conqueror of India; al-Ḥajjāj then sent them to al-Walīd.[155] Many years later, al-Walīd b. Yazīd (al-Walīd II; r. 125–126/743–744) moved Cypriots from their home island to the coast of Syria, but after serious legal objections from local jurists headed by al-Awzāʿī, his action was reversed by his successor, Yazīd b. al-Walīd (Yazīd III; r. 126/744), who sent them back to Cyprus.[156] It is true that some Arab Muslims and new converts were made by the state to populate frontier towns, but these were either soldiers whose stipends were kept active, or local Syrian converts for whom the movement north did not entail a great deal of adjustment.[157] As for the "foreign" groups who were settled in faraway places, their resettlement could not have been voluntary,[158] and the government could not have done that except for very good reasons. Given that the resettlements were mostly to frontier areas, the military component of the policy cannot be overlooked.

The non-Islamic sources confirm, albeit indirectly, the Muslim state's policy of population settlement in frontier areas, for, as we have seen, they mention the Muslims' settlement of the Slav defectors from the Byzantine army near Apamea and in Antioch and Cyrrhus. They also mention the settlement by al-Walīd II of the Cypriots on the Syrian coast, and the revocation of that settlement by Yazīd III, adding that that settlement was in a town called al-Māḥūr/Māḥūz, on the coast between Sidon and Tyre,[159] a site that has been confirmed by archaeology.[160] They also add another frontier settlement undertaken by the Muslims and not mentioned in the Islamic sources, namely that of the Armenians expelled by the Byzantines in Malaṭya and Sumaysāṭ, during the caliphate of al-Walīd I.[161] They further mention two rather unusual settlements by the Muslims of some of the people of Sicily in Damascus in 43/663,[162] and of some of the people of Arwād in Syria under Muʿāwiya;[163] in both these cases the settlement was voluntary, undertaken at the wish of the people themselves. The non-Islamic sources are furthermore informative in indicating that resettlement of groups was a policy that was used also by the Byzantines, often for military purposes. In 68/687–688, Justinian campaigned against Sclavinia and Bulgaria, took a multitude of Slavs, some in battle but some went over to him, and settled them in Opsikion.[164] In 72/691–692, he "transplanted

[152] Al-Balādhurī, *Futūḥ al-buldān*, p. 117. See Lammens, "Les Perses du Liban"; Borrut, "L'espace maritime."

[153] Al-Balādhurī, *Futūḥ al-buldān*, pp. 117, 142.

[154] Ibid., p. 162.

[155] Ibid., p. 162.

[156] Ibid., pp. 154, 156.

[157] See ibid., pp. 147, 148, 150.

[158] See Morony, *Iraq after the Muslim Conquest*, p. 198.

[159] Agapius of Manbij, *Kitāb al-ʿunwān*, pp. 511–12.

[160] See Sauvaget, "Notes de topographie omeyyade."

[161] Agapius, *Kitāb al-ʿunwān*, p. 500.

[162] Theophanes, *Chronicle*, p. 487.

[163] Agapius, *Kitāb al-ʿunwān*, p. 482.

[164] Theophanes, *Chronicle*, p. 508.

30,000 Slavs, armed them, and named them the 'Chosen People'";[165] it was from these Slavs that a large group defected to the Muslim side, as we have seen. A year earlier, the same Justinian decided to move the population of Cyprus to Byzantium "to prevent them from paying tribute to the Arabs." As the Cypriots were crossing, the ships sank. Many of them drowned or died of illness on the way, and the remainder returned to Cyprus. Only some settled in the city of Cyzicus.[166]

The non-Islamic sources are also aware of the enticements that the Muslims offered groups to have their loyalties shift to them; it is, after all, a method the Romans themselves had been using for centuries.[167] The Slavs who crossed over to the Muslims did so after Muḥammad b. Marwān sent to the general of the Slavs "a pouch full of gold pieces."[168] They also mention the peace agreements concluded between the Muslims and the local people, as we have seen in the one concluded with the Armenians. As for the voluntary crossing over of the local peoples to the Muslim side, it is mentioned there frequently but, understandably, in terms different from those used in the Islamic sources: now we hear of "deceit," "betrayal," and "treachery."[169]

c. What Did the Non-Arab Non-Muslims Do in and for the Muslim Army?

The Islamic sources highlight six major activities: using them as couriers, spies, guides, advisors, garrisoned frontier posts, and fellow combatants. Those they employed as workmen were almost certainly non-Arab non-Muslims.

Most of the information we have about using local non-Muslims as couriers (*fuyūj*) comes from the earliest period of the conquests. The group mostly used in this capacity is identified as the Syrian Anbāṭ,[170] since "the Byzantines did not suspect them."[171]

These Anbāṭ played another auxiliary role for the Muslim armies, namely to spy for them (*jawāsīs*; *ʿuyūn*), at one point informing them that there were 20,000 fighters in Baalbeck, for example.[172] In this activity, they were not alone, for the Samaritans of Jordan and Palestine are also reported to have spied for the Muslims.[173] One particular Christian who played a seminal role in encouraging the Muslims to conquer Andalusia is Julian, Count of Ceuta. Why he did that is mired in legend and varies in varying narratives, but it boils down to his wish to exert revenge on the Visigothic king of Spain, Roderic.[174] He and his men are reported to have accompanied the first major Muslim thrust into Andalusia under the leadership of Ṭāriq b. Ziyād in 91/711 and recruited local Andalusians (*ahl al-balad*) who would "guide them to the weak spots [of the enemy] and bring intelligence to them" (*yadulluhum ʿalā al-ʿawrāt*

---

[165] Ibid., p. 511.

[166] Ibid., p. 509; Michael the Syrian, *Chronicle*, vol. 2, p. 470; *Chronicle of A.D. 1234*, in Palmer, *West-Syrian Chronicles*, p. 205. See also Hoyland, *Theophilus of Edessa's Chronicle*, p. 187.

[167] See Whitby, "Recruitment in Roman Armies," p. 66.

[168] Theophanes, *Chronicle*, p. 511.

[169] See examples in Theophanes, *Chronicle*, p. 527; Michael the Syrian, *Chronicle*, vol. 2, p. 442; *Chronicle of A.D. 1234*, in Palmer, *West-Syrian Chronicles*, p. 205. See also Hoyland, *Theophilus of Edessa's Chronicle*, p. 186.

[170] See examples in Ibn Aʿtham, *Kitāb al-futūḥ*, vol. 1, pp. 144, 175, 187–88.

[171] Ibid., vol. 1, p. 144.

[172] Ibid., vol. 1, p. 175.

[173] Al-Balādhurī, *Futūḥ al-buldān*, p. 158.

[174] Ibn al-Qūṭiyya, *Iftitāḥ al-Andalus*, pp. 33–34; Anonymous, *Akhbār majmūʿa*, pp. 4–5; al-Raqīq al-Qayrawānī, *Tārīkh Ifrīqiya*, p. 73; Ibn ʿIdhārī, *al-Bayān al-mughrib*, vol. 1, p. 26; vol. 2, p. 6. See also "al-Andalus," in *EI*², s.v.

wa yatajassas lahum al-akhbār).[175] Later in the conquest, one of the main generals leading the conquest, Mughīth al-Rūmī, is said to have used the services of "spies and guides" (*ʿuyūnahu wa adillāʾahu*) during the conquest of Cordoba.[176]

Spying, or, more accurately sometimes, intelligence gathering, was one of the main requirements demanded of the local people in the peace agreements the Muslims made with them, as in the case of the Jarājima[177] and the people of Cyprus;[178] in the case of the agreement with the people of Dulūk and Raʿbān in northern Syria, the treaty specifically called for their "seeking the news of the Byzantines and informing the Muslims about it *in writing*."[179] Conversely, the biggest problem the Muslims had with the frontier town of Arabissos was that its people were "informing our enemy about our weak spots (*ʿawrātinā*) but not us of our enemy's weak spots." The commander of the Muslim army was thus ordered by ʿUmar to use diplomacy with them, give them double what they used to receive from the Muslims, and give them also time, one year, to change their ways; if they had not done so by then, their town should be destroyed. All said and done, the townsfolk did not change, and their town was destroyed.[180] It is to be noted that, conversely, some of the agreements concluded between the Muslims and the indigenous populations stipulated that the latter not give refuge to the spies of the Muslims' enemies[181] or to those wanted by the Muslims (*bughya*).[182]

Acting as guides for the Muslims in lands unfamiliar to them — such as routes, mountain passes, and river crossings — was also another form of help that the Muslim armies must have often found invaluable, as is reported about the Samaritans;[183] the Arab Christians, as we recall, had done the same before. And providing *dilāla* for the Muslims was one of the conditions built into several of the peace agreements the Muslims concluded with the peoples of the northeast and east;[184] in the pledge of the people of Damascus to the Muslims, the former committed themselves to guide the latter "in their paths and roads."[185]

On a more concrete level, we have seen how some local Andalusians guided the Muslims in the conquest. Three specific cases are additionally reported. In the first, and after Ṭāriq had conquered some Andalusian cities, Julian of Ceuta is reported to have advised him to head to Toledo and take with his army guides from Julain's men to conquer other cities. Ṭāriq agreed, and Julian's guides went with three Muslim armies that headed to Cordoba, Rayya, and Granada.[186] In the second, we get a much more detailed report. The leader of the army heading to Cordoba, Mughīth al-Rūmī, stopped at a village called Shaqunda and sent out his guides (*adillāʾahu*) to scout the area. They found an informed shepherd grazing his sheep and brought him to Mughīth. The shepherd informed Mughīth that the elite of the people of Cordoba (*ʿuẓamāʾ ahlihā*) had fled to Toledo, leaving only its king (*malikahā*) with 400 troops and a weak citizenry (*ḍuʿafāʾ ahlihā*). In answer to Mughīth's question about the strength of the city's walls, the shepherd asserted that they were strong but had a breach (*thaghra*), which he went on to locate above a particular gate of the city and to describe it. Mughīth followed the shepherd's instructions and reached the city's walls but could not locate the breach. They brought back the shepherd; he showed them the breach, and Mughīth was able to enter the

175 Anonymous, *Akhbār majmūʿa*, p. 7; see also al-Raqīq al-Qayrawānī, *Tārīkh Ifrīqiya*, p. 73.

176 Anonymous, *Akhbār majmūʿa*, p. 12.

177 Al-Balādhurī, *Futūḥ al-buldān*, p. 158.

178 Ibid., p. 154.

179 Ibid., p. 150, reading *yabḥathū* for *yanjathū*.

180 Ibid., pp. 156–57.

181 See al-Qāḍī, "Madkhal," pp. 219, 268, 269.

182 Cf. ibid., pp. 243, 264.

183 Al-Balādhurī, *Futūḥ al-buldān*, p. 158.

184 See above, nn. 92, 94, 96, 97, 98.

185 See al-Qāḍī, "Madkhal," pp. 220, 268.

186 See Anonymous, *Akhbār majmūʿa*, p. 10.

city "with his associates, spies, and guides."[187] In the final report, Ṭāriq's superior, Mūsā b. Nuṣayr, also used the services of Christain guides (*al-ʿulūj al-adillāʾ*) from the local people, when he disembarked in Andalusia after hearing about the successes that Ṭāriq had achieved and had become envious of him. It was these guides who told Mūsā they could guide him to a better road than Ṭāriq's and to greater cities than those conquered by Ṭāriq — which is what he did, and was very successful.[188]

Were the spies and guides paid? The historical record does not provide an answer. But there is a rather striking text that occurs in an early *ḥadīth* collection. A person who had participated in the early conquests was purportedly asked, "Did you use to subject the non-Arabs [to any particular service]" (*hal kuntum tusakhkhirūn al-ʿajam*)? The answer was, "We used to subject them to showing us the road from one village to another, then we would let them go."[189] The use of the word *tusakhkhirūn* in the text almost certainly means "unpaid labor." Whether this can be generalized to cover all or most guiding activities would be too risky to conclude from this single report, and payment in return for this and similar services cannot be dismissed.

In the above we have seen glimpses of the third activity in which the non-Muslims aided the military effort of the Muslims, namely as advisors; but the Islamic historical sources provide more tangible instances, some with interesting results. In Andalusia, where we left off, Julian was the one to advise Ṭāriq to conquer Andalusia,[190] and, as we have seen, the guides who helped both Ṭāriq and Mūsā were acting not merely as guides but as advisors, too, as he was indeed "a very old man who had wrapped his eyebrows with a band because of old age" who advised Mūsā to proceed with the conquest of Andalusia to the finish.[191] We also have reports in the Islamic sources about Copts helping the Muslims as advisors. A Copt is said to have been with the army of ʿAbdallāh b. Saʿd b. Abī Sarḥ, Egypt's governor, which invaded Ifrīqiya in 27/647; he is identified in the Islamic sources only as "a man of the Copts (of Egypt)" (*rajul min al-Qibṭ/Qibṭ Miṣr*). The sources have it that when Ibn Abī Sarḥ could not overcome the resistance of the army of Ifrīqiya's strongman, Patriarch Jurjīr, the Copt came forward and gave Ibn Abī Sarḥ military advice: a strategy by which he can break the enemy. He should not, the Copt said, face the enemy (merely) with his army lined up in rows. Rather, he should (couple that with) setting up ambushes for him and attack him stealthily first. Ibn Abī Sarḥ followed the Copt's advice, rattled the enemy's men, and won the battle.[192] Another Copt is reported to have advised ʿAmr b. al-ʿĀṣ on how to re-open the Canal of Trajan (in Arabic, *khalīj Amīr al-muʾminīn*) after it had silted and became blocked. Since this canal opened up one of the branches of the Nile and linked it to the Red Sea and to the Mediterranean, it was an important waterway for the ships of the fleet and other traffic-related purposes. The Copt asked that the *jizya* be dropped from him and his household. ʿAmr followed the Copt's advice, succeeded in re-opening the canal,[193] and, one assumes, was only too happy to accede to the Copt's request about the *jizya*.

---

[187] Anonymous, *Akhbār majmūʿa*, pp. 10–12; Ibn ʿIdhārī, *al-Bayān al-mughrib*, vol. 2, p. 10.

[188] Anonymous, *Akhbār majmūʿa*, p. 15; Ibn ʿIdhārī, *al-Bayān al-mughrib*, vol. 2, p. 13.

[189] ʿAbd al-Razzāq, *Muṣannaf*, vol. 5, p. 279.

[190] Ibn al-Qūṭiyya, *Iftitāḥ al-Andalus*, pp. 33–34; al-Raqīq al-Qayrawānī, *Tārīkh Ifrīqiya*, pp. 73–74; Anonymous, *Akhbār majmūʿa*, p. 5.

[191] See al-Raqīq al-Qayrawānī, *Tārīkh Ifrīqiya*, p. 80.

[192] See al-Mālikī, *Riyāḍ al-nufūs*, vol. 1, pp. 17–18; al-Dabbāgh, *Maʿālim al-īmān*, p. 34.

[193] See Ibn ʿAbd al-Ḥakam, *Futūḥ Miṣr*, pp. 165–66. At that time, the canal was used for transporting food from Egypt to Medina. The canal is, however, also mentioned in a papyrus in a context related to the fleet; see n. 282, below.

There are two other cases reported about non-Muslims advising Muslims during the conquests; they come from the northeast and are not straightforward. In the first, the cousin of the king of Farghāna informed al-Ḥarashī, the leader of the campaigns in Soghdia in 114/732, about the Soghdians' military situation and advised him to attack them before they reached a certain pass. Al-Ḥarashī instructed his lieutenants to proceed according to this advice, but then had afterthoughts: it was an infidel (*ʿilj*) who had advised him, and he does not know whether the man spoke the truth. Fearing that he had endangered his troops, he tried to stop his lieutenants from attacking the Soghdians, but other factors intervened, and the advice of the "infidel" proved to be right.[194] In the second case, the Muslims received advice from a non-Muslim that led to complete disaster. During Maslama b. ʿAbd al-Malik's siege of Constantinople in 98/716, he received advice from the Armenian Leo the Isaurian. Leo, promised to be made emperor by the Byzantine commanders, met with Maslama and advised him to burn his food, so that the people of Constantinople would think he, being without food, was going to attack them boldly and would submit to him. Maslama made the mistake of following Leo's advice and brought misery on his men and utter defeat to his campaign.[195]

In one of the earliest peace agreements in the conquests, the Muslims required the Jarājima to man garrisoned frontier posts (*masāliḥ*) for the Muslims in Mount al-Lukām, their frontier home territory,[196] and the same agreement was extended to the peasant population (*al-anbāṭ*) of the villages in the area, whence they were called *al-rawādīf* "appendages."[197] What exactly that entailed is not clear from our text.[198] Although they were not allowed to develop into lasting "buffer states,"[199] it is safe to assume that they were expected to be on the frontline of defense in case of attacks on Muslim territory, that is, they are expected to fight.

Being fellow fighters with the Muslims in their campaigns is actually one of the conditions cited in the peace agreement between the Muslims and the Jarājima. There, the words used for the call to participate in active combat alongside the Muslims are all derived from "to raid": *an yaghzū maʿa al-muslimīn* and *idhā ḥaḍarū maʿahum ḥarban fī maghāzīhim*.[200] The same condition is cited in the peace agreements that the Muslims concluded with the peoples of the northeast and east mentioned above: whenever the Muslims deem it fit that they should be called upon to fight with them, they should respond by fighting. There, however, the words are much more diversified: *yuḥsharū*, *ḥashr* (to be mobilized),[201] *yustanfarū*, *yanfurū* (to be called upon to fight or go to war),[202] and the more general *nuṣra* (support, succor, help

[194] See al-Ṭabarī, *Tārīkh*, vol. 7, pp. 7–8/vol. II, pp. 1442–44.

[195] See al-Ṭabarī, *Tārīkh*, vol. 6, pp. 530–31/vol. II, pp. 1315–17. On Maslama's siege of Constantinople, see most recently Borrut, *Entre mémoire et pouvoir*, pp. 229ff.

[196] Al-Balādhurī, *Futūḥ al-buldān*, p. 159.

[197] Ibid., p. 159. There, the reason for the name is given as either because they "followed" (*talaw*) the Jarājima but were not of them, or because the Jarājima brought them to the army of the Muslims while they physically walked behind them (*wa-hum ardāf lahum*).

[198] What makes it more difficult to determine in the case of the Jarājima is their erratic behavior, since they often sided with the Byzantines, with the latters' encouragement, as is well known. For a good text in this regard, see al-Balādhurī, *Futūḥ al-buldān*, pp. 159–60: *wa-kāna al-jarājima yastaqīmūna li-l-wulāt marratan wa-yaʿwajjūna ukhrā fa-yukātibūna al-rūma wa-yumāliʾūnahum.*

[199] See Kaegi, *Byzantium*, p. 256.

[200] Al-Balādhurī, *Futūḥ al-buldān*, p. 161; see also p. 159.

[201] Al-Ṭabarī, *Tārīkh*, vol. 4, p. 155/vol. I, p. 2662 (Ādharbayjān), p. 157/p. 2665 (Armenia).

[202] Al-Ṭabarī, *Tārīkh*, vol. 4, p. 156/vol. I, p. 2664 (al-Bāb), p. 157/p. 2665 (Armenia).

make victorious),[203] and *maʿūna, istaʿannā* (assistance);[204] perhaps also the words *naṣīḥa, nuṣḥ, naṣaḥū* (advice)[205] and *ḍalʿ* (side with, make common cause with)[206] were also intended to convey the same meaning. As we have seen above, in almost all of these cases, fighting alongside the Muslims is rewarded by exemption from the tribute in the particular year such fighting occurs, so that, as one of the treaties put it, fighting is considered a recompense or compensation (*ʿiwaḍ*) for the *jizāʾ*. Some agreements further specify that those who do not rise and fight with the Muslims (*nahaḍa*) but rather stay back (*aqāma*) will have to pay the tribute.[207]

Did these non-Arab non-Muslims actually fight with the Muslims? They certainly did at times, according to the Islamic sources, as we know from several cases we have encountered above: the Asāwira in the conquest of Tustar, the Daylam in the battle of al-Qādisiyya and in the conquest of Khānaqīn,[208] and the Ḥamrāʾ and Persians in the conquest of Egypt. Regarding the Jarājima, we have a rather unique case of an individual who, when he was still a Christian, fought bravely under the banner of Islam and was killed in Byzantine territory while fighting. This is Maymūn al-Jurjumānī, whose story, as recorded by the Islamic sources, goes as follows. He was a Greek (*rūmī*) slave of the family of Umm al-Ḥakam, Muʿāwiya's sister. When ʿAbd al-Malik (r. 66–86/685–705) heard about his courage and resourcefulness, he asked his patrons (*mawālīhi*) to manumit him, which they did. ʿAbd al-Malik then gave him command over a group of soldiers and stationed him in Antioch. In 85/704, he raided al-Ṭiwāna under the command of Maslama b. ʿAbd al-Malik, heading 1,000 soldiers from the people of Antioch. He was "martyred" (*ustushhida*) in battle after fighting bravely. ʿAbd al-Malik is said to have been so distressed at his death that he decided to launch a major attack against Byzantium "in revenge" for Maymūn.[209]

The Islamic sources are not as forthcoming about non-Arab non-Muslims fighting with them in the northeast and east, so that we do not hear them say something like, then the Muslims and the polytheists (or unbelievers) charged forward. And the above-mentioned statement attributed to Salmān b. Rabīʿa al-Bāhilī in one of the legal compendia, "Let the enemies of God fight the enemies of God," when he attacked Balanjar, does not occur in the historical narratives when they report on his attack on Balanjar.[210] Given, however, the state of frequent turmoil and ever more distant and unfamiliar territory in that region for many decades, it would be unlikely, indeed surprising, if the Muslims had not asked the local people for military assistance of various kinds. One probably non-local group is reported to have

---

[203] Al-Ṭabarī, *Tārīkh*, vol. 4, p. 162/vol. I, p. 2675 (Tiflīs), p. 311/p. 2899 (Marw al-Rūdh); Abū ʿUbayd al-Qāsim b. Sallām, *Amwāl*, p. 299; al-Balādhurī, *Futūḥ al-buldān*, p. 201; Yāqūt, *Muʿjam al-buldān*, vol. 2, p. 36.

[204] Al-Ṭabarī, *Tārīkh*, 4, p. 152/vol. I, p. 2658 (Jurjān and Dahistān).

[205] Al-Ṭabarī, *Tārīkh*, vol. 4, p. 152/vol. I, p. 2658 (Jurjān and Dahistān), p. 157/p. 2666 (Mūqān), p. 162/p. 2675; Abū ʿUbayd al-Qāsim b. Sallām, *Amwāl*, p. 299; al-Balādhurī, *Futūḥ al-buldān*, p. 201; Yāqūt, *Muʿjam al-buldān*, vol. 2, p. 36 (Tiflīs).

[206] Al-Ṭabarī, *Tārīkh*, vol. 4, p. 162/vol. I, p. 2675; Abū ʿUbayd, *Amwāl*, p. 299; al-Balādhurī, *Futūḥ al-buldān*, p. 201; Yāqūt, *Muʿjam al-buldān*, vol. 2, p. 36 (Tiflīs).

[207] Al-Ṭabarī, *Tārīkh*, vol. 4, p. 155/vol. I, p. 2662 (Ādharbayjān), p. 157/p. 2665 (Armenia), and also see above, at nn. 89–96.

[208] Al-Ṭabarī, *Tārīkh*, vol. 4, p. 34/vol. I, p. 2473.

[209] See al-Balādhurī, *Futūḥ al-buldān*, pp. 160–61; Ibn ʿAsākir, *Tārīkh madīnat Dimashq*, vol. 61, p. 369; see also Khalīfa b. Khayyāṭ, *Tārīkh*, p. 291. Al-Ṭabarī (*Tārīkh*, vol. 6, p. 429/vol. II, p. 1185) was certainly wrong when he made Maslama fight against Maymūn in the battle of al-Ṭiwāna.

[210] See, for example, al-Balādhurī, *Futūḥ al-buldān*, pp. 203–04, 259; al-Ṭabarī, *Tārīkh*, vol. 4, pp. 158–59/vol. I, pp. 2667–69; pp. 304–05/pp. 2889–93. Salmān was killed, along with 4,000 of his troops, at Balanjar. For Salmān's statement, see above, n. 22.

participated in the conquest of Jurjān and Ṭabaristān with Yazīd b. al-Muhallab in 98/716, namely slaves (*mamālīk*).[211]

In the west, non-Muslim participation in combat is also attested. On a general level, it would be unlikely that all the Christian spies, guides, and advisors who worked with the Muslims in Andalusia did not participate in the fighting. In fact, in the conquest of Carmona, the Muslims could not win the city except after "infidels (*ʿulūj*) from the associates of Julian and others" pretended they had been defeated and were allowed into the city. Having entered it with their weapons, they attacked the guards of one of the city's gates and opened it for the Muslims at nightfall.[212] In Ifrīqiya, we also hear about two cases in which non-Muslims fought with the Muslims, or at least assisted them in starting the fighting. In the first, the two sons of the Berber rebel al-Kāhina, who had been sent to the Muslims by their mother shortly before her defeat, are reported to have led two Muslim armies that conquered parts of the Maghrib. Obviously it is possible that they had converted, but since nothing is mentioned about that in the sources, and that they seem to have immediately taken up their military command, one may assume that they did not.[213] Something similar happened in the second case, that of Ḥubāḥiba al-Rūmī. This Ḥubāḥiba is identified as a leader in Ifrīqiya (*al-qāʾim bi-amrihim*) who rejected the Byzantine emperor's request of more taxes in about 45/665 and expelled the emperor's emissary. He then went to Syria and asked Muʿāwiya to send an Arab army with him. Muʿāwiya did send an army, but gave its leadership to an Arab, Muʿāwiya b. Ḥudayj, and Ḥubāḥiba accompanied him until they reached Alexandria. The account then says that Muʿāwiya b. Ḥudayj appointed Ḥubāḥiba governor of Alexandria and proceeded to campaign in Ifrīqiya. Whether Ḥubāḥiba participated in those campaigns is not stated. Again in this case, no conversion to Islam is attributed to him.[214]

Finally, the Islamic sources mention an interesting report from which one gathers that the Muslim army took along workmen. This is mentioned in the same report about the campaign of Yazīd b. al-Muhallab referred to above. It says that in his march to Ṭabaristān, Yazīd took with him "workers (*faʿala*) who would cut trees and repair roads."[215] No other information is provided about this group, but it is safe to assume that they were non-Arab non-Muslim prisoners of war accompanying the Muslims in their military campaigns, providing them with various labor-related services such as this one. This is not unexpected, given that in at least one peace agreement that was concluded between the Muslims and the people of Iṣfahān, repairing the roads was one of the requirements of the agreement, as we have seen.[216] Another agreement, with the people of al-Ruhā, workmen for the construction of bridges were required,[217] and in still another, with the people of Herat, maintaining the land (for agriculture; *iṣlāḥ* [...] *al-araḍīn*) was required.[218] In the same Iṣfahān agreement, the Iṣfahānīs were requested also to provide transportation for unmounted Muslim riders, possibly infantrymen.[219] This means that the indigenous population could also be requested to come up with service people with access to mules, horses, or other riding animals for

[211] See al-Ṭabarī, *Tārīkh*, vol. 6, p. 532/vol. II, p. 1318.

[212] See Ibn ʿIdhārī, *al-Bayān al-mughrib*, vol. 2, pp. 13–14; Anonymous, *Akhbār majmūʿa*, pp. 15–16.

[213] See, for example, Ibn ʿIdhārī, *al-Bayān al-mughrib*, vol. 1, pp. 35–39. The entry "al-Kāhina" in *EI*[2] mentions the crossing over of the two sons but does not discuss the issue of their conversion.

[214] Ibn ʿIdhārī, *al-Bayān al-mughrib*, vol. 1, pp. 16–17.

[215] Al-Ṭabarī, *Tārīkh*, vol. 6, p. 534/vol. II, p. 1320.

[216] See above, n. 97.

[217] See al-Qāḍī, "Madkhal," pp. 233, 243, 351, 260.

[218] Cf. ibid., pp. 243, 265.

[219] Cf. above, n. 97.

members of the Muslim armies on the move in their lands. Perhaps we can put under this title also the assistance — voluntary in this case — that Julian and his men gave to the Ṭāriq b. Ziyād's soldiers on their way to the conquest of Andalusia. In some reports, these men almost "smuggled" Ṭāriq's soldiers by placing them, a group at a time, on the commercial ships sailing to Andalusia, as if they were merchants.[220]

Going to the non-Islamic sources, we find important information that clarifies what the Islamic sources were unclear about, confirms some of what they did mention, and brings new and valuable information. In addition, we have documentary evidence for the participation of non-Muslims in the Muslim army in an auxiliary, service-related capacity.

Not unexpectedly, we hear nothing about the Muslims using the local people as couriers, spies, guides, or advisors, but we learn for the first time that the Armenians were recruited by the Muslims to gather information about Byzantine troop movements for them,[221] and that such a role had been solicited from the Armenians by the Sasanians long before.[222] We also become clear from the reports about the twice-defecting Slavs what a frontier garrisoned post (*maslaḥa*) consisted of, and we get confirmation for non-Arab non-Muslim groups actually fighting alongside the Muslims. Regarding the first issue, it is to be recalled that the second group of Slav defectors were settled in Antioch and Cyrrhus and given women, money, and provisions. Leaving aside women for obvious reasons, the fact that the Muslims gave them money and provisions, and that the latter are called in Syriac *rūziqā*,[223] that is, the equivalent of the Arabic *rizq*, allows one to conclude that they were treated like the other regular Muslim soldiers who receive *rizq*, in addition to stipends (*ʿaṭāʾ*), from the government.[224] It is noteworthy also that the text does not state that the Muslims gave them weapons; this probably means that they used their own weapons with which they defected. Regarding the second issue, we have a unique text from Theophanes in which he says that in 694–695 (A.H. 75), two years after the defection of the second batch of Slavs, Muḥammad b. Marwān attacked "the Roman land," taking with him the Slavs who had fled, as they "were acquainted" with the land."[225]

The non-Islamic sources also confirm that there were workmen in the Muslim armies, along with the soldiers. A contemporary Syriac source to the conquests affirms this about the campaign of 91–92/709–711 in Byzantium;[226] and in the campaign of ʿAbdallāh b. ʿAbd al-Malik in 85/704, the workmen accompanying the army were used to rebuild the town of Mopsuestia in Galicia.[227] One recalls also that, in the text cited above from the Maronite chronicle about Yazīd I's campaign against Thrace, the "hirelings" mentioned there are said to be involved with pasturing the Muslim fighters' cattle and tending to their children.[228] This may confirm the image one has of the local populations providing the Muslim armies with various menial and general services.

---

[220] See al-Raqīq al-Qayrawānī, *Tārīkh Ifrīqiya*, p. 74; Ibn ʿIdhārī, *al-Bayān al-mughrib*, vol. 2, p. 6.

[221] See Kaegi, *Byzantium*, p. 202.

[222] See ibid., p. 198.

[223] Michael the Syrian, *Chronicle*, vol. 2, p. 470 (translated there as "provisions"); see Palmer, *West-Syrian Chronicles*, p. 205 n. 511.

[224] Cf. the promise the Muslims made to the people of Marw al-Rūdh (see above, n. 95): if they convert they would receive both *rizq* and stipends *ʿaṭāʾ*, just like the Muslim fighters.

[225] Theophanes, *Chronicle*, p. 513.

[226] *Chronicle of* A.D. *819*, in Palmer, *West-Syrian Chronicles*, p. 80.

[227] Ibid., p. 78.

[228] See above, at n. 143.

The non-Islamic sources add three other ways in which local people assisted the Muslim army. The first consists of providing transportation of weapons on ships. We have one report from Egypt on this subject that occurs in (Pseudo-)Severus.[229] In a part of a longer narrative, it says that the duke Sanutius, who is probably John of Nikiu's Sinôda (= Shenūda),[230] was "with the *amīr*" (i.e., ʿAmr b. al-ʿĀṣ) in Alexandria, from where ʿAmr was heading to Tripoli, when one of the ships was grounded. The ship contained "the provisions and heavy equipment[231] of the troops," along with Sanutius' baggage. Clearly Sanutius was providing the Muslims with means of maritime transportation of their heavier equipment. The text does not mention whether Sanutius' ship(s) were also to transport the troops themselves, but this is not impossible.[232]

The second consists of offering technical assistance. This occurs in a report in the Maronite chronicle mentioned above. It says that when ʿAbd al-Raḥmān b. Khālid conquered Amorium and came to the fortress of Smyrna, "a master-carpenter from Paphlagonia" told him, "If you give me and my household your word (that our lives will be spared), I will make you a catapult (Greek *manganikē*) capable of taking their fortress." ʿAbd al-Raḥmān agreed and had logs brought. The man then made a catapult "such as [the Muslims] had never seen before," and they used it in forcing their way into the fortress, killing a large number of men.[233]

The third way in which local people assisted the Muslim army comes not from literary sources but from the papyri, and it consists of providing auxiliaries to perform compulsory public service for that army. This valuable information is based on one of the Nessana Greek papyri, no. 74, from the desert area of southern Palestine. The papyrus, which dates to about 66/685, the first year of ʿAbd al-Malikʾs caliphate, consists of a letter addressed to the administrator of Nessana, George (whom we know from other papyri in the Nessana collection, nos. 68 and 70), from a superior, asking him for the following:

> [...] make sure that you have ready two camels and two laborers who are to perform compulsory service from Caesarea to Scythopolis. Keep in mind also that he wants good camels, and workmen who have pack-saddles and straps [...][234]

The letter, thus, is asking the Nessanites to provide two expert camel drivers who would ride or lead two good camels for service on the road from Caesarea to Scythopolis — a long distance of 260 miles, according to Kraemer.[235] Since the letter mentions "compulsory service," it is certain that those providing the service are non-Muslims: this service, as is well known, is part of the tribute they paid to the Muslim state. But what is more important for our purposes here is the occurrence in the letter of the word *stolou*, which means expedition or equipment, especially for war-related purposes, thus indicating military preparation, as Kraemer has pointed out.[236] This makes this papyrus parallel to another papyrus in the

[229] See [pseudo-]Severus, *History of the Patriarchs*, PO 1, pp. 408–09.

[230] See John, Bishop of Nikiu, *Chronicle*, pp. 194–95. He is condemned for collaborating with the invading Arabs. See also n. 148, above.

[231] The Arabic text has *anfāl* (spoils), which does not make sense in the above context. I have read the word as *athqāl* (heavy equipment).

[232] Cf. Muhammad, "Role of the Copts," p. 3. Muhammad does not provide a source for this episode, and asserts that Sanutius was transporting "Arab troops" without mentioning anything about the provisions and the spoils/heavy equipment.

[233] The *Maronite Chronicle*, in Palmer, *West-Syrian Chronicles*, pp. 34–35.

[234] Kraemer, *Excavations at Nessana*, vol. 3, p. 210.

[235] Ibid., p. 209.

[236] Ibid., p. 209.

Nessana collection, no. 37, which goes back to Byzantine times (ca. 560–580 C.E.)[237] and which is an account of camels and men requested of the Nessanites for military or police transport rather than action; after all, compulsory service was in effect in Byzantine times, too. From all this we can conclude that there is documentary evidence to the service of non-Muslims in the Muslim army in the form of auxiliary support, such as transporting camel drivers in the case of people of Nessana. It indeed reminds us of what was mentioned in the Islamic sources about the Iṣfahānīs being requested to provide transportation for unmounted Muslim riders, possibly infantrymen, as was mentioned above.[238]

Before closing this part, I would like to mention an interesting report that occurs in a Syriac source and claims that the Muslims, very early in the conquests, could have received the support in combat from the son of a Sasanian defector to the Byzantines, but eventually decided not to. The report concerns the son of Shahrbarāz, the Sasanian commander who was killed in al-Ḥīra. This son, called Rōmēzān, became the Byzantines' companion at arms and was given the command of an army that was supposed to head to Damascus but was defeated by Khālid b. al-Walīd at Ḥimṣ. The commanders of the army were killed in battle except for Rōmēzān, to whom the Muslims gave amnesty when they settled in Ḥimṣ.[239] The report continues that Rōmēzān sent to the caliph ʿUmar b. al-Khaṭṭāb the following letter: "Give me command of a tribe of Arabs to go to Persia and fight my enemies and I will make the whole country your subjects and tributaries." The story goes on to say that Chosroes' daughter and son, having heard of Rōmēzān's letter to ʿUmar, appealed to ʿUmar, "[...] He has no scruples about killing his fellow-countrymen and his lords as if they were foreigners. If he cannot keep faith with his own flesh and blood, is he going to keep faith with you? [...] As soon as he has seized power he will defy you and become your enemy." ʿUmar was convinced, and he sent instructions that the son of Shahrbarāz be impaled. He was executed summarily at the gate of Ḥimṣ.[240]

III. Non-Muslims in the Muslim Fleet

Most of the information I have come across about the service of non-Muslims in the Muslim fleet comes from non-Islamic sources and from the papyri, but the Islamic sources do provide a small amount of valuable information in basically three areas. The first is that about the arsenals for making ships, in Egypt, particularly at Alexandria and *jazīrat/ṣināʿat al-Rawḍa*, near Fusṭāṭ;[241] in Syria, at Acre and Tyre;[242] and in Ifrīqiya, specifically in Tunis.[243] Except for Tunis,

---

[237] Ibid., pp. 114–17.

[238] Cf. above, at nn. 97 and 219.

[239] *Chronicle of A.D. 1234*, in Palmer, *West-Syrian Chronicles*, p. 149.

[240] *Chronicle of A.D. 1234*, in Palmer, *West-Syrian Chronicles*, p. 151; Michael the Syrian, *Chronicle*, vol. 2, p. 421.

[241] See al-Maqrīzī, *Khiṭaṭ*, vol. 2, pp. 189–91. See also Fahmy, *Muslim Sea-Power*, pp. 23–50.

[242] Al-Balādhurī, *Futūḥ al-buldān*, pp. 117–18. See also Fahmy, *Muslim Sea-Power*, pp. 51–54.

[243] There is a reliable account and an unreliable one on the foundation of the arsenal at Tunis. The unreliable account, which must be discarded, occurs in a suspicious Eastern source, [pseudo-]Ibn Qutayba's *al-Imāma wa-l-siyāsa*, vol. 2, p. 57. Unlike the reliable account, it attributes that foundation to Mūsā b. Nuṣayr, governor of Ifrīqiya in ca. 86–90/705–709, without any caliphal initiative, and for no particular reason. It then connects this foundation, blatantly artificially, with the ill-fated naval Egyptian expedition of ʿAṭāʾ b. Abī Rifāʿa (on which see below), making a mistake even in his name — calling him ʿAṭāʾ b. Abī Nāfiʿ al-Hudhalī, about whom the sources obviously know nothing. It is thus no surprise that E. Lévi-Provençal ignored the allegation of Mūsā's foundation of the arsenal at Tunis in his article about him in *EI*^{2}. This account has nothing on non-Muslims participating in this project.

the material about these arsenals includes little of significance about non-Muslims. But in the more reliable of its two accounts on the arsenal at Tunis,[244] the material is relatively detailed and identifies two non-Muslim groups who were involved in its foundation. The caliph ʿAbd al-Malik instructed his brother and governor over Egypt, ʿAbd al-ʿAzīz b. Marwān, to send to Tunis from Egypt one thousand Copts, together with their wives and children, and to provide them with all their needs on their trip to Tunis. He also wrote to his governor over Ifrīqiya, Ḥassān b. al-Nuʿmān al-Ghassānī (gov. ca. 73–86/692–705), about this arsenal, emphasizing that he wanted it to last forever as a source of power for the Muslims. He further instructed him to have another group, the Berbers, that is, the indigenous population of Ifrīqiya — almost certainly the non-Muslims among them — to bring wood to the place of the arsenal for the building of ships. The purpose of all this, ʿAbd al-Malik said, was to fortify Muslim lands and to launch *jihād* against the Byzantine coasts, so that the Byzantines' attention would be averted from the capital of Ifrīqiya, al-Qayrawān. The Copts arrived in Tunis: the governor drew water to the port of Tunis from nearby Rādes; the Berbers brought the wood; and the Copts, obeying the governor's command, built many ships.[245]

The second area for which the Islamic sources provide information on the Muslim fleet is that of the non-Muslim workmen working in the arsenals. In addition to the Copts and Berbers mentioned in Tunis' arsenal, the sources mention the skilled workmen (*ṣunnāʿ*) and carpenters (*najjārūn*) whom Muʿāwiya settled in the coastal cities (*al-sawāḥil*), clearly non-Muslims, albeit without further identification.[246] Only in one instance do we learn that there were with them some Greeks (*rūm*) in addition to the Arab troops (*jund min al-ʿarab*).[247] It is also very possible that some of the population transfers that the Umayyads undertook and that were mentioned above had a maritime dimension, particularly those to the coastal areas, like the transfer of Persians from Antioch, Ḥimṣ, and Baalbek to the coast of Jordan.[248]

The third area in which the Islamic sources provide some information consists of various descriptions of the Muslims' naval battles, particularly Cyprus, Arwad, and Dhāt al-Ṣawārī. Only the last of these battles, which took place in 34/655 at the coast of Phoenix (today's Finike),[249] includes information on non-Muslims. This comes in a rather opaque report in al-Ṭabarī's history, narrated on the authority of al-Wāqidī; it hence needs interpretation. The leader of the Muslim fleet was the governor of Egypt, ʿAbdallāh b. Saʿd b. Abī Sarḥ, who had had deep-seated political problems with the Qurashī Companion of the Prophet Muḥammad b. Abī Ḥudhayfa.[250] After his disagreement with him on a matter pertaining to prayer ritual, Ibn Abī Sarḥ scolded Muḥammad and swore he could not sail "with us" in the naval campaign at hand. The report goes on to say,

[244] See the reliable account on this arsenal in Abū ʿUbayd al-Bakrī, *al-Mughrib*, pp. 37–39; al-Raqīq al-Qayrawānī, *Tārīkh Ifrīqiya*, p. 66. See also Fahmy, *Muslim Sea-Power*, pp. 69–72; Muhammad, "Role of the Copts," pp. 4–5.

[245] See the sources cited in the previous note. Some decades later, the Umayyad finance director of Egypt, ʿUbaydallāh b. al-Ḥabḥāb (in office 116–124/734–741), renovated this arsenal and added to its fortifications. See Abū ʿUbayd al-Bakrī, *al-Mughrib*, p. 39.

[246] Al-Balādhurī, *Futūḥ al-buldān*, p. 117. Probably related to this is the well-known fact that the funeral of al-Awzāʿī, which took place in the Syrian coastal town of Beirut in 157/773, included Copts, Christians, and Jews; see Ibn Abī Ḥātim al-Rāzī's *taqdima* to his *al-Jarḥ wa-al-taʿdīl*, vol. 1, p. 202.

[247] Al-Balādhurī, *Futūḥ al-buldān*, p. 117.

[248] See above, at n. 152; see also Fahmy, *Muslim Sea-Power*, p. 52.

[249] See *EI*[2] s.v. "Ḏh̲āt al-Ṣawārī" (C. E. Bosworth).

[250] On these problems, see the concise yet detailed biography of Muḥammad b. Abī Ḥudhayfa in al-Ṣafadī, *al-Wāfī bi-l-wafayāt*, ed. Dedering, vol. 2, pp. 328–40.

> He (Muḥmammad) responded: "Shall I sail with the Muslims [at all]"? He (Ibn Abī Sarḥ) said: "Sail wherever you want." He (al-Wāqidī) said: So he (Muḥammad) sailed on a ship (*markab*) alone with no one with him except Copts, until they reached Dhāt al-Ṣawārī.[251]

Aside from the problems in pronouns,[252] one has to figure out what the Copts were doing on a ship all alone by themselves, without any Muslim being with them. There are two possibilities: either they were fighters or they were not. The first possibility is, I think, not viable: without any kind of direct, physical oversight by the Muslims, the entire ship could slip away, and the Copts would disappear in the sea or on land and take refuge with their fellow Christians. Indeed, the Islamic government, especially in Egypt, had constant problems with fugitives: Copts who fled their ships, not only their villages, as we shall see. Thus, if the Copts manning an entire ship in the Egyptian fleet heading to the battle of Dhāt al-Ṣawārī were not fighters, they must have been sailors or workmen, and their ship must be one carrying resources needed by the fighters, like provisions, equipment, and weapons.[253]

Let us now go to the literary non-Muslim sources. There we find two important pieces of information. The first comes from (pseudo-)Severus. It says that Usāma b. Zayd, the financial director of Egypt in 96/714, assembled the leading monks and requested one *dīnār* of each of them.[254] This part of the report is confirmed by al-Maqrīzī.[255] But then (pseudo-)Severus' report goes on to say that Usāma told the monks that if they did not do that, he would, among

---

[251] Al-Ṭabarī, *Tārīkh*, vol. 4, p. 291/vol. I, pp. 2869–70 (*sub anno* 31).

[252] I do not see an alternative to understanding the pronouns differently from what I have written in the translation above; the text in Arabic reads: *qāla: fa-arkabu maʿ al-muslimīn? Qāla: irkab ḥaythu shiʾta. Fa-rakiba fī markab waḥdahu, mā maʿahu illā al-qibṭ, ḥattā balaghū Dhāt al-Ṣawārī.* This understanding agrees with that of the translator of this volume of al-Ṭabarī, R. Stephen Humphreys, in his *History of al-Ṭabarī*, p. 76. The translation of Muhammad, "Role of the Copts," p. 4, makes Ibn Abī Sarḥ (rather than Muḥammad b. Abī Ḥudhayfa) sail alone on a ship with only Copts accompanying him. This is obviously wrong, since Ibn Abī Sarḥ was the leader of the entire Egyptian fleet. Fahmy, like several modern scholars, does not talk about this part of the report in his discussion of the battle of Dhāt al-Ṣawārī (*Muslim Sea-Power*, pp. 103–04).

[253] Both Fahmy (*Muslim Sea-Power*, pp. 103–04) and Muhammad ("Role of the Copts," pp. 4, 6–7) agree with this conclusion, as does Hourani in his *Arab Seafaring*, p. 59, who says that the battle was won by "a combination of Coptic seamanship and Arab swordplay [...]." Muhammad's explanation, however (p. 4), is untenable, as we have seen from the above: "because the Arabs did not allow the Christians or Jews (*ahl adhimma; sic*) to fight in the Islamic armies." Humphrey's statement, in his *Muʿawiya ibn Abi Sufyan*, p. 57, is inconclusive. After saying (pp. 55–56) that the "shipbuilders and sailors of the new fleet were Christians from the coast (especially Lebanon [...])," he says: "The Muslim fleet probably had ships and soldiers from both Lebanon and Egypt." Does that mean that the soldiers at the battle of Dhāt al-Ṣawārī were (at least in part) Christians?

[254] [Pseudo-]Severus, *History of the Patriarchs*, PO 5, pp. 70–71. Cf. Fahmy, *Muslim Sea-Power*, pp. 106–07 n. 1; and Muhammad, "Role of the Copts," p. 4 n. 26. Fahmy claims that, according to Severus, the monks were not only threatened with service on ships by Usāma b. Zayd during Sulaymān's caliphate, but also, and much earlier, "Theodore, the governor of Alexandria during the caliphate of Yazíd ibn Muʿâwiya [i.e., 60–64/680–684] compelled the monks in Egypt to build ships for the fleet [...]." Fahmy gave as his source Severus, pp. 70–71. Muhammad then copied this material from Fahmy, acknowledging him and Severus in a footnote. But these pages of [pseudo-]Severus have nothing on the caliphate of Yazīd I, and thus Fahmy's (and Muhammad's) conclusion cannot stand. This is a pity, since Fahmy's book, despite its age, remains among the best work we have on Muslim naval activities in the first few Islamic centuries, as is indeed Muhammad's article. I must add that there is actually a piece of information about the caliphate of Yazīd I in [pseudo-]Severus, PO 5, p. 5. But there Theodore is said to have taken from Abba Agathon a 36-*dīnār jizya* annually, and, in addition, "made him pay for whatever he (Yazīd) spent on the sailors in the fleet."

[255] Al-Maqrīzī, *Khiṭaṭ*, vol. 2, p. 492.

other things, "make you serve on board of the ships of the fleet (*wa-jaʿaltukum fī marākib al-usṭūl*)." This troubled the monks immensely.[256] Two things can be concluded from this report: that the monks were exempted from service in the fleet while the other, lay Copts were not; and that it was a hateful thing to serve in the fleet for the monks, but possibly also for the Copts in general.[257] The second piece of information comes from Theophanes and concerns Maslama b. ʿAbd al-Malik's ill-fated naval campaign against Constantinople in 98/716. According to Theophanes, two Muslim fleets coming from Egypt and Africa (= Ifrīqiya) hid in a bay, and the Byzantines were not aware of them. Then the Egyptian component stepped in: "the Egyptians of these two fleets took counsel among themselves and, after seizing at night the skiffs of the transports, sought refuge in the City and acclaimed the emperor [...] The emperor had been informed by them of the two fleets hidden in the bay."[258] This report, then, claims that Egyptian Copts served in the Muslim fleet; it does not say, however, in what capacity. The two translators of Theophanes' *Chronicle*, Mango and Scott, thought they served as "crews" in the fleet.[259]

Let us now turn to the papyri, which are documentary sources. These papyri not only confirm that Egyptian Christians served in the Muslim fleet, but also provide us with further valuable details about the role played by non-Muslims in the Muslim fleet. Most of this information comes from the Aphrodito (Ashqawh) collection of Greek papyri in the British Museum, mostly datable to the 90s/710s, and has been perceptively studied by H. I. Bell at the beginning of the twentieth century.[260] A few decades later, in 1950, Aly Mohamed Fahmy made very good use of these and other Egyptian Greek papyri from other libraries in his University of London doctoral dissertation, Muslim Sea-Power in the Eastern Mediterranean from the Seventh to the Tenth Century A.D.[261] His work influenced writers on the subject in European languages, especially Xavier de Planhol[262] and, more recently, Tarek Muhammad, who used additional Coptic and Arabic papyri.[263] The most abundant scholarship on Muslim navigation and naval activities has been produced, however, by Christophe Picard.[264]

[256] See [pseudo-]Severus, *History of the Patriarchs*, PO 5, p. 71.

[257] More below on the Copts' dislike of such compulsory services.

[258] Theophanes, *Chronicle*, p. 546.

[259] The earlier translator of Theophanes' *Chronicle*, Harry Turtledove, did not commit himself to any interpretation "The Egyptians of the two expeditions [...]."

[260] See Bell, *Greek Papyri in the British Museum*, introduction, vol. 6, pp. xxxii–xxxv ("The Naval Organization of the Khalifate"). Bell (and, in addition, C. H. Becker and Adolph Grohmann) also wrote several studies on individual papyri of this collection; they will be cited below. Bell's publication of these Greek Papyri in this volume (henceforth P. Lond.) was followed by his publishing translations of a selection of them in a series of articles in *Der Islam* (see *Bibliography*), all under the same title: "Translations of the Greek Aphrodito Papyri in the British Museum." Below the papyri will be referred to with their numbers in P. Lond., and the translations will be indicated with their place in *Der Islam* without the articles' titles.

[261] Fahmy's book was re-published under a different title in Cairo, 1966; see *Bibliography*.

[262] In his monumental work *L'Islam et la mer*, as one can easily see in his footnotes on issues related to the early Islamic period, which he discusses only briefly. Despite its impressive scope and the amazing amount of information it provides, de Planhol's book, as far as the early period which interests us here is concerned, repeats essentially one basic, sweeping, and indiscriminating thesis: that there is a fundamental disinterest and weakness in the Muslims' attitude toward the sea (p. 24; also p. 26) and that "all the techniques of the sea were provided by the local Christian population" (p. 25; also pp. 26, 32, 50–51, 453). See the excellent review of de Planhol's book by Conrad, "Islam and the Sea."

[263] In his 2008 article "Role of the Copts," mentioned above.

[264] He has published extensively on the subject. See most recently his *La mer des califes*.

The main texts of these papyri that concern us are those that talk about sailors (Arabic *nawātī, nawātiyya*, sing. *nūtī*); they occur either in letters from the Muslim governor of Egypt to the (Christian) pagarch of Aphrodito requesting sailors, or in accounts indicating payments received in the treasury relating to these sailors. From these texts it is fully clear that the legal basis for the service of the sailors in the Muslim fleet was the compulsory "public service" required of the Egyptians as part of their tribute to the Islamic state[265] — as was the case of the people of Nessana. This service, as we learn from the papyri, could be with or without constant flow of instructions from the government,[266] but the most informative papyri are those that tell us about the required services with specific instructions from the government. Many of these are fleet related, given that Egypt housed two of the main arsenals in the empire for ship construction and fleet preparation: in (the island of) Babylon (*jazīrat/ṣināʿat* al-Rawḍa, on the Nile near al-Fusṭāṭ) and in Clysma (al-Qulzum = Suez, on the Red Sea), in addition to the naval bases in Alexandria, Damietta, and Rosetta, from where the fleets set sail.[267] The numerous references in the papyri requisitioning goods and equipment for the ships, or provisions and supplies for the Muslim fighters, need not detain us here, for we are concerned only with the human element, with the people who manned the fighting ships.

According to Bell, the crews of the ships of the Muslim fleets based in Egypt were divided into two groups. The first represented the military part of the crew and consisted of "Muhājirūn" and "mawālī"; the second consisted of "rowers, helmsmen, etc."[268] We are concerned here with the sailors of the second group and must try to find out more about them.

First and foremost, the papyri are clear in indicating that these sailors were Egyptian Christians, overwhelmingly Copts. This can be concluded from the names of such sailors mentioned in some papyri, of which two should suffice here. P. Lond. 1434, an account, mentions the names of four sailors; they are John son of Apa Têr, Phoebammon son of Ġamoul, Phoebammon son of Dionysius, and George son of Bartholomew.[269] P. Lond. 1449, another account, mentions thirteen sailors whose names are Isaac son of Apollo, Papas son of George, Zacharaias son of Apa Têr, Psacho son of Dianos, Theodosius son of Koutos, Mark son of Abraham, Samuel son of Enôch, Isaac son of Mercurios, Philemmos son of Philip, George of Ermaôt[...], George son of Dionysius, Helias son of Thi[.]tos, and Joseph son of Ermos.[270]

Second, the papyri give the impression that the number of these sailors was enormous. P. Lond. 1393, a letter, requests sixty-nine sailors; P. Lond. 1450, an account, talks about

---

[265] See Bell, "The Aphrodito Papyri," p. 112. This is why I doubt that the word "recruitment," used by Fahmy (*Muslim Sea-Power*, pp. 98ff.) and accepted by Muhammad ("Role of the Copts," pp. 6ff.) is the correct term to use for the Muslims literally requesting [= ordering] the services of the local Christians. Bell is more careful; he talks about "choosing" and "requisitioning" the sailors (pp. 112–13).

[266] As in P. Lond. 1338, 1339, translated in *Der Islam* 2 (1911), pp. 272, 273: "[...] and if you had had any proper sense you would not have required many letters from us on this account" and "[...] therefore do not require another letter from us on this matter after the present one," respectively.

[267] See Bell, *Greek Papyri in the British Museum*, p. xxxiii; idem, "The Aphrodito Papyri," pp. 112–13. Babylon and Clysma are mentioned frequently in these papyri, as will be clear shortly, Alexandria rarely; Damietta and Rosetta are mentioned in P. Lond. 1449, translated in *Der Islam* 17 (1928), p. 8. Fahmy, when discussing the Egyptian arsenals and dockyards (*Muslim Sea-Power*, pp. 23–50), lists also Tinnīs (Tenessos; pp. 34–35); but whether it was already operating in the Umayyad period is uncertain.

[268] Bell, *Greek Papyri in the British Museum*, p. xxxiv.

[269] Ibid., p. 320; translation in *Der Islam* 4 (1913), p. 92.

[270] Ibid., p. 372. I am indebted to François Gaudard, of the Oriental Institute, University of Chicago, for assistance in deciphering these names.

sixty-eight sailors, and another account, P. Lond. 1497, about forty-six sailors; and the bilingual (Arabic and Greek) letter requesting sailors for the army of ʿAbdallāh b. Mūsā b. Nuṣayr heading to Pentapolis (Barqa) in Ifrīqiya in 95/714 specifies ninety-five and a half sailors.[271] More striking are P. Lond. 1434 and 1435, which are both accounts. They deal with four indictions (tax cycles: the 12th, 13th, 14th, and 15th indictions) covering part of the years 96 and 97 (714–716). In this short period of a few months, the following sets of sailors are recorded: four sailors; five sailors; twenty-nine sailors; seven sailors; and four sailors, in the former papyrus; and in the latter: four sailors; five sailors; another five sailors; sixteen sailors; and two sailors. This gives us a total of eighty-one sailors.[272] Even more striking is P. Lond. 1433, which is an account of miscellaneous taxes dated in the year 88 (706–707) for one indiction (the 5th) only. Among many other things, it mentions the following about sailors:

- 31 sailors for 7 months with their supplies,
- 1 sailor for 1 month for Clysma,
- 1 sailor for 8 months for the ships at Clysma,
- 4 $^{1}/_{3}$ sailors for the raiding fleet of the Orient with their supplies for 4 months,
- 8 sailors for the raiding fleet of the Orient with their supplies for 4 months,
- 7 $^{2}/_{3}$ sailors for the raiding fleet of Egypt and that of the Orient with their supplies for 6 months,
- 3 $^{1}/_{3}$ sailors with their supplies for the raiding fleet of Egypt,
- 14 sailors,
- 79 sailors for the raiding fleet of Egypt with their supplies for one month and for the fare of the ship which carried them, and
- freight on the ship which carried 79 sailors and their supplies for 7 months.[273]

Now if we remember that these papyri deal almost exclusively with only a small administrative district in Upper Egypt, we can imagine how large was the number of sailors requisitioned from all the villages and towns of Egypt. To say that they were in the thousands is probably a conservative estimate.[274] And the papyri do provide evidence that the sailors were requested from all parts of Egypt.[275]

Third, in most of the cases in which sailors are mentioned, a time period is specified for the duration of the service required of the sailors, as we can see in the just cited lines of P. Lond. 1433. The service period is defined by months and ranges mostly between one and six months; only in a few cases do we get seven months, as in the lines cited above. This clearly has to do with the amount of tribute/tax required of the people addressed by the specific

[271] The letter, on this last papyrus, located in Berlin, not in the British Museum, is addressed from Qurra b. Sharīk to the people of Antinoe (Anṣinā, in Arabic); see Becker, "Papyrusstudien," p. 150, and (for a more accurate reading of the Greek part) Bell, "The Berlin Ḳurrah Papyrus." For further comments, see Abū Ṣafiyya, *Bardiyyāt Qurra ibn Sharīk al-ʿAbsī*, no. 41.

[272] P. Lond. 1434 is translated in *Der Islam* 4 (1913), pp. 87–92; P. Lond. 1435 is translated in *Der Islam* 4 (1913), pp. 92–96.

[273] P. Lond. 1433 is translated in *Der Islam* 3 (1912), pp. 369–73.

[274] Bell's remarks, *Greek Papyri in the British Museum*, p. xxxv, where the evidence of the papyri leads him to believe that "the fleets maintained by the Khaliphate were of considerable size [...]" and that "large drafts of sailors are made."

[275] See Muhammad, "Role of the Copts," pp. 7, 11.

text payment requests. A similar consideration certainly lies behind the occasional request of fractions of sailors, as in three cases mentioned above. How exactly half or one-third of a sailor was translated on the ground is nowhere given. Fahmy's explanation, however, is convincing: "[...] a third of a sailor [...] meant that three small places were called on to provide a man between them, each paying a third of his wages, the man himself being presumably chosen by arrangements between the local chiefs of the hamlets [...]." [276]

Fourth, and as was mentioned by Bell, the sailors received wages (*ajr*) and an allowance of food (*maʿīsha*), that is, provisions;[277] and for that there is sizeable evidence in the papyri.[278] The wages ranged between one-half (gold) *solidus* and one *solidus*, as most of the accounts that mention wages say,[279] and provisions included those which the sailors needed "on the journey as far as the mouth of the Nile," as is mentioned several times in P. Lond. 1434,[280] meaning on the journey that took them to their place of duty.

Fifth, the papyri indicate that the sailors served on all kinds of ships and in the various fleets starting sail from Egypt, as well as on the ships stationed there for one reason or another. Of the ships that are mentioned in the papyri, the following are identified; *carabi, dramonaria, acatia, acatenaria*, two-banked galleys, and castellated ships.[281] The fleets that are most often mentioned there are the fleet of Egypt and the fleet of the East, although a fleet that headed to Africa (= Ifrīqiya) is also mentioned.[282] The sailors were also asked to report to duty at the ships stationed in the two shipbuilding centers in Egypt: the island of Babylon and Clysma.[283]

Sixth, and as insinuated by Bell in the text cited above, those Egyptian sailors were non-military, whence Bell has estimated they were employed as "rowers, helmsmen, etc." Since this matter lies at the heart of the topic at hand, we must try to determine if it is completely accurate. And, in fact, the evidence provided by the papyri supports the claim that the Christian Egyptian sailors were not a fighting force. For one thing, the only textual reference to the job of the sailors on the ships is that of "manning" them.[284] For another, the requisition

---

[276] Fahmy, *Muslim Sea-Power*, p. 101; copied verbatim in Muhammad, "Role of the Copts," p. 11.

[277] Bell, *Greek Papyri in the British Museum*, p. xxxiv; idem, "The Aphrodito Papyri," p. 112.

[278] Fahmy (*Muslim Sea-Power*, pp. 109–12) has composed useful (but now not comprehensive) tables, based on the papyri, for the wages of sailors and artisans, cost of provisions, and cost of materials. See also Muhammad, "Role of the Copts," pp. 19–21.

[279] See in particular P. Lond. 1433, translated in *Der Islam* 3 (1912), pp. 369–73; P. Lond. 1434, translated in *Der Islam* 4 (1913), pp. 87–92; P. Lond. 1435, translated in *Der Islam* 4 (1913), pp. 92–96. See also, for a papyrus from a collection other than that of the British Museum, PERF 572, published by Grohmann in his "Greek Papyri of the Early Islamic Period," no. 13, pp. 38–39.

[280] Translated in *Der Islam* 4 (1913), pp. 87–92.

[281] P. Lond. 1434, translated in *Der Islam* 4 (1913), pp. 87–92; P. Lond. 1435, translated in *Der Islam* 4 (1913), pp. 92–96; P. Lond. 1441, translated in *Der Islam* 17 (1928), pp. 4–6; P. Lond. 1449, translated in *Der Islam* 17 (1928), pp. 6–8. Fahmy's informative chapter on "Mediterranean Muslim Warships" (*Muslim Sea-Power*, pp. 115–42) deals overwhelmingly with the post-Umayyad, ʿAbbāsid period, and hence is not germane to this study.

[282] See the papyri mentioned in the previous note and P. Lond. 1350, translated in *Der Islam* 2 (1911), p. 279. One presumes that the ships of the fleet heading to Ifrīqiya would dock at Tunis (see above); but Pentapolis (Barqa) is also mentioned as a destination in the bilingual Aphrodito papyrus from Berlin. See also Bell, "The Aphrodito Papyri," p. 115. Those fleets at times had to time their movement so that it uses the Canal of Trajan before it got blocked; see P. Lond. 1346, translated in *Der Islam* 2 (1911), p. 277.

[283] See P. Lond. 1433, translated in *Der Islam* 3 (1912), pp. 369–73; P. Lond. 1336, translated in *Der Islam* 2 (1911), pp. 271–72.

[284] P. Lond. 1449, translated in *Der Islam* 17 (1928), pp. 6–8.

of sailors is often connected with the requisition of workmen or skilled workmen.[285] For a third, we have a Greek papyrus bearing a heading in Arabic that identifies the requisitioned sailors by the word "nawātiyya": *ilā ṣāḥib ashqūh fī ajr nawātiyya min nawātiyyat al-maᶜbar jihat* [...],[286] that is, by the loanword from Greek which means sailor or seaman.

But the most conclusive evidence comes from four texts in the papyri that make the fleet composed of two clearly distinct groups: "fighting men" and "sailors," the first group referring obviously to the Muslims, and the second to the Egyptian (Christian) local labor force that provides services and supplies to both groups. Thus, in a letter from Qurra b. Sharīk, the governor of Egypt, to Basilius, the pagarch of Aphrodito, the latter is asked "to convey the sailors and skilled workmen — with their supplies *and those of the fighting men* —who were requisitioned of your administrative district for the raiding fleet of Egypt."[287] And in another letter, the pagarch is informed that demand notes have been sent to him "for the requisition of sailors and skilled workmen and their supplies *and those of the fighting men of the raiding fleet of Egypt*," and the docket at the bottom of the papyrus repeats this information: "concerning supplies for *the fighting men and sailors of the raiding fleet of Egypt*."[288] With this textual distinction between sailors and fighting men, it is clear that the Egyptian *nawātiyya* were not a combat force. At this point, one cannot help but remember Saḥnūn's statement, cited in the introduction of this study, that, although he is opposed to the participation of non-Muslims in the battles of the Muslims, he had no objection to the former serving as "sailors (*nawātiyya*) or servants (*khadam*)."[289] A native of the coastal province of Ifrīqiya, Saḥnūn could very well have had firsthand knowledge that such participation did indeed occur.

The last thing we have to mention about the sailors is how they looked upon their assignment, given that we had met in (pseudo-)Severus a text that indicated deep dislike of this job by the monks.[290] This dislike, however, was almost certainly shared by the lay population as well, since several papyri speak about sailors fleeing their duties and somehow disappearing. One entry in an account records the amount spent on "the expenses of Nuᶜaimān *maulā* of ᶜAbd Allāh the all-honoured Governor, who went down with a letter concerning sailors of the *carabi* who fled [...]."[291] Another mentions fugitives from Fayyūm who are probably sailors,[292] and still another, in Arabic this time, asks Basilius to send back the sailor who fled, together with the rather hefty fine of $4^1/_3$ *solidi*.[293] Two fragments clearly talk about forty-one sailors

---

[285] See P. Lond. 1351, translated in *Der Islam* 2 (1911), pp. 279–80; P. Lond. 1353, translated in *Der Islam* 2 (1911), pp. 280–81; P. Lond. 1410, translated in *Der Islam* 3 (1912), pp. 132–33; P. Lond. 1414, translated in *Der Islam* 3 (1912), p. 137; P. Lond. 1441, translated in *Der Islam* 17 (1928), pp. 4–6; P. Lond. 1451; P. Lond. 1452; P. Lond. 1454. Sometimes the sailors are not mentioned in the text, but the context is clearly a naval one. Such workmen, skilled or otherwise, working on ships while at sea are not always the same as the workmen working on the ships when the ships are aground in the shipyards, as will be mentioned below.

[286] P. Lond. 1450. Another papyrus, now an Arabic one, namely Becker, "Arabische Papyri des Aphroditofundes," no. 8, pp. 84–86, has been read by Becker thus: *li-jaysh sanat iḥdā wa-tisᶜīn nabaṭiyyayn dhawbajayn wa-najjāran* [...]. Becker, clearly cognizant of a naval context, translated *nabaṭiyyayn* as "zwei [...] Schiffszimmerleute." For comments and the correct reading (*nawbaj*) of the word *dhawbajayn* in this papyrus, see Abū Ṣafiyya, *Bardiyyāt*, no. 40, p. 210.

[287] P. Lond. 1351, translated in *Der Islam* 2 (1911), pp. 279–80.

[288] P. Lond. 1353, translated in *Der Islam* 2 (1911), pp. 280–81.

[289] See above, at n. 15.

[290] See above, at n. 258.

[291] P. Lond. 1441, translated in *Der Islam* 17 (1928), p. 5. The following entry also seems to talk about the same issue.

[292] See Bell, "The Aphrodito Papyri," pp. 111–12.

[293] See Becker, "Neue arabische Papyri des Aphroditofundes," no. 10; republished in Grohmann, *Arabic Papyri in the Egyptian Library*, no. 152.

who have fled[294] — a sizeable number. And from one papyrus, we learn that sailors who had fled had been sent back to Babylon.[295] From another, however, a letter from the governor to Basilius, we learn that the government did not know a lot about its sailors, those who fled, but others as well:

> We do not know the number of the sailors who returned to your administrative district of those who went out with the raiding fleet to Africa with ʿAṭāʾ b. Rifāʿa and were sent back by Mūsā b. Nuṣayr, nor those who remained of them in Africa. Thus when you receive this letter write to us the number of the sailors who returned to your administrative district, asking them about the sailors who remained in Africa and for what reason they stayed there, and the number of those who died in Africa, and the number of those who died on the journey after their discharge.[296]

Bell and most later scholars[297] identified this expedition as the one to Sicily or Sardinia, about which we know from Ibn ʿAbd al-Ḥakam and pseudo-Ibn Qutayba, and which I discussed in an earlier work.[298] The importance of this papyrus for our purposes here lies not in its destination but in its uncovering of concern on the part of the government that sailors were fleeing their duties and just disappearing, and that the government had no information about them, hence the need to resort to the local official in charge, the pagarch, in order to fill in the blanks. The papyrus also implies that the number of sailors involved was not small, that many could die while on duty, while still others opt to disappear in the place the ships dock, even if that meant settlement in a foreign land. All of this, perhaps in addition to another papyrus,[299] indicates that, given the chance, the sailors conscripted by the Muslim government could be desperate enough to leave their homes in return for not serving as sailors in the Muslim fleet.

It is probably in this context that we can understand better, at least in part, the preference of local Egyptians to pay cash in lieu of sending sailors in person to serve in the fleet.[300] This cash, called "money composition," was legitimate and is mentioned even in some accounts and requisitions of sailors by the government.[301] There were cases, however, in which the government insisted on, and expected compliance with, receiving the services in person.[302]

---

[294] P. Lond. 1438 and P. Lond. 1484.

[295] This is P. Lond. 1433, in particular lines 323, 401; see Bell, "An Official Circular of the Arab Period," p. 83.

[296] P. Lond. 1350, translated in *Der Islam* 2 (1911), p. 279.

[297] See Bell, *Greek Papyri in the British Museum*, p. 24; idem, "The Aphrodito Papyri," p. 115; Fahmy, *Muslim Sea-Power*, pp. 64–69; Muhammad, "Role of the Copts," pp. 15–16, 18.

[298] See al-Qāḍī, "Population Census and Land Surveys," p. 394 and n. 181.

[299] This is P. Lond. 1374, translated in *Der Islam* 2 (1911), pp. 375–76. It concerns the wages of seven sailors who "remained" in the Orient, which the people of Aphrodito are requested to pay. It is not clear, though, from the text whether the sailors remained in the Orient with the knowledge of the government or without it, and for what reason. Unlike P. Lond. 1350, though, here the government knows at least their number.

[300] See Bell, "The Aphrodito Papyri," p. 112; Fahmy, *Muslim Sea-Power*, p. 100; Muhammad, "Role of the Copts," p. 14.

[301] See P. Lond. 1336, translated in *Der Islam* 2 (1911), p. 272. An entry in an account, P. Lond. 1433, translated in *Der Islam* 3 (1912), p. 371, has a sum "for sailors for the raiding fleet of the Orient, with their supplies, for 6 months, viz. by money composition for 2 months in kind for 4 months [...] 8 sailors with their supplies for 4 months in kind and for 2 months by money composition [...]." See also P. Lond. 1410, translated in *Der Islam* 3 (1912), p. 133.

[302] See P. Lond. 1393, in Bell, "Two Official Letters," p. 279: "Let us not find that you have sent a money composition for any [...] whatever, but only the person himself; (otherwise) we shall in requital visit you with a retribution which will be to your detriment,

Before concluding this part, it is important to mention two other categories of people who were involved in auxiliary functions with the Muslim fleet, and on whom the papyri provide invaluable information. The first category consists of the people who worked on the ships while the ships were not at sea, but rather on the ground, stationed in the two main shipbuilding centers in Egypt, at Clysma or the island of Babylon.[303] The papyri mention three such groups within this category: laborers, workmen, and skilled workmen; in particular it mentions carpenters, caulkers, blacksmiths, ironworkers, and sawyers. The jobs that they did are identified there as building, cleaning, fitting up, and hauling and repairing those damaged of them.[304] These workmen's service, like that of the sailors, was clearly part of the tribute that the local population had to pay to the Muslims, and, like the sailors also, they were requisitioned for specific periods of time (in months) and were paid wages and assigned provisions.[305] These varied, presumably depending on the skill needed for the requested service, although the payments within one category of workers could vary too.[306] Again as in the case of sailors, a money composition could be paid in lieu of these workmen's services,[307] although the government could insist on workmen doing the work personally.[308] Fleeing their work was a noticeable phenomenon among workmen on the ships,[309] and there is a papyrus written on the occasion of the flight of caulkers working on the *carabi* in Babylon which indicates that the government met the fleeing of workmen with great severity, assigning on them huge financial penalties that could reach 1,000 *solidi.*[310]

---

since you have no excuse whatever with regard to the personal service." See also Bell, "The Aphrodito Papyri," p. 112; Fahmy, *Muslim Sea-Power*, pp. 101–02; Muhammad, "Role of the Copts," pp. 14–15.

[303] Cf. Bell, "The Aphrodito Papyri," p. 114. One must be careful in using the papyri for identifying these workmen, making sure, to the extent possible, that they are textually connected with the docked ships "in Clysma" or "in Babylon," since many workmen mentioned in the papyri were requisitioned for non-navy-related purposes, on which see ibid., p. 116. In some cases, a maritime context helps identify these workmen as working on ships (as when they are mentioned alongside sailors); but here there is always a chance that those workmen could be serving on sailing ships, not stationary ones.

[304] See P. Lond. 1336, translated in *Der Islam* 2 (1911), pp. 271–72; P. Lond. 1346, translated in *Der Islam* 2 (1911), p. 277; P. Lond. 1371, translated in *Der Islam* 2 (1911), p. 375; P. Lond. 1376, translated in *Der Islam* 2 (1911), pp. 376–77; P. Lond. 1386, translated in *Der Islam* 2 (1911), pp. 380–81; P. Lond. 1410, translated in *Der Islam* 3 (1912), pp. 132–33; P. Lond. 1414, translated in *Der Islam* 3 (1912), p. 137; P. Lond. 1433, translated in *Der Islam* 3 (1912), pp. 369–73; P. Lond. 1434, translated in *Der Islam* 4 (1913), pp. 87–92; P. Lond. 1435, translated in *Der Islam* 4 (1913), pp. 92–96; P. Lond. 1441, translated in *Der Islam* 17 (1928), p. 6.

[305] Most of the papyri mentioned in the previous note include references to these matters. An interesting entry in P. Lond. 1414 (translated in *Der Islam* 3 [1912], p. 137), an account, talks about the "cost of oil and salt for the maintenance of skilled workmen employed on the *carabi* at Babylon [...]." Muhammad ("Role of the Copts," pp. 21–22) correctly notes that the wage of a (presumably skilled) carpenter could be higher than that of a sailor.

[306] See the table composed by Fahmy, *Muslim Sea-Power*, pp. 109–10. It has to be noted, though, that the table shows a maximum of 1 $^1/_3$ *solidi* for a carpenter, while P. Lond. 1410 (translated in *Der Islam* 3 [1912], p. 133) shows a carpenter's service could be valued at 2 *solidi*.

[307] P. Lond. 1410, translated in *Der Islam* 3 (1912), p. 133: "[...] 4 skilled workmen with their supplies for three months [...] and if you compound in money, pay for their wages and supplies as above." See also P. Lond. 1435, translated in *Der Islam* 4 (1913), p. 94, which talks about the money composition of the laborer who fled; P. Lond. 1512 (dated A.D. 709), a Coptic papyrus, talks about 2 $^1/_2$ *solidi* being received "partly in lieu of workmen."

[308] P. Lond. 1393, in Bell, "Two Official Letters," p. 279, cited above, concerns both sailors and skilled workmen (artisans [*sic*] in Bell's translation), and see Bell's comments cited in Crum's introduction to the Coptic papyrus P. Lond. 1508. See also Bell, "Two Official Letters," p. 276; idem, "The Aphrodito Papyri," pp. 112–13; Muhammad, "Role of the Copts," pp. 10, 14–15.

[309] In P. Lond. 1435, translated in *Der Islam* 4 (1913), p. 94, a "labouror who fled from the *carabi*."

[310] See Bell, "An Official Circular," p. 77.

By the second category I mean the administrative capability in which some non-Muslims served in an auxiliary capacity the activities of the Muslim fleet. This is a broad topic that needs separate research. What can be mentioned here is that the papyri provide the name of one Christian who had a high administrative naval position, namely Theodore the Augustal, who was stationed in Alexandria.[311] He could be the same person mentioned by (pseudo-) Severus as *mutawallī dīwān al-iskandariyya tilka al-ayyām tāwudrūs* (Theodore, the official in charge of the registers of Alexandria in those days).[312] If this is correct, this puts his tenure of this important administrative position during the governorship of Qurra b. Sharīk (90–96/708–715).

Conclusions

The above shows that there is no doubt that non-Muslims of various faiths and ethnicities served in the Muslim armies during the conquests, in practically all of the lands these armies undertook expeditions, and the same applies to the Muslim fleets of Egypt, the East, and Africa. They served there either as individuals or as groups, although the latter was almost certainly more frequent and surely more effective; and they served in a variety of capacities, assisting the Muslims as couriers, guides, lookouts, spies, advisors, laborers, workmen, technicians, sailors, and mercenaries. While some were intentionally brought into the ranks of the Muslim armies by the Muslim government through its commanders in the field, or forced to serve as part of the compulsory public service requirement of the tribute, others came forward voluntarily to the aid of the Muslims for a variety of motives, ranging from fear to profit. They sometimes actually fought alongside the Muslims in battle, while in others they did not (as in the fleet), and they also were sometimes compensated for their work, while others they were not – the sources, all of them, do not allow for making an estimate about the ratio of one practice to the other. This compensation could come in the form of money or provisions – in one case, even women – and perhaps even some prestige; it could, however, come indirectly, especially in the form of exemption from paying the tribute.

Most of the ways in which the non-Muslims aided the Muslim armies may have been improvised by the Muslims due to need, especially at the beginning of the conquests. For the non-Muslims, however, these ways were not that new, as they had been through them during the rule of the previous empires, especially as the non-Muslim sources point out. Indeed, our study has shown that there was a great deal that did not change for both governments and people of the Near East under the young Islamic empire. Just like the Byzantines and the Sasanians before them, the Muslims not only made use of the services of the local populations to support their military operations, employing them as guides, spies, and mercenaries, but also took them with them to battle to fight in their wars. Like them, too, they made non-Muslims help their military campaigns by drafting people into auxiliary works to promote their war effort under the legal tax cover of compulsory public service, and they moved whole populations from one place to another for defense and other purposes, manning posts on the frontiers with advance guards composed of indigenous, mostly unconverted, people. This is yet another facet of the continuity between the pre-Islamic and Islamic Near East.

---

311 P. Lond. 1392, translated in *Der Islam* 2 (1911), p. 381. See also Bell, *Greek Papyri in the British Museum*, p. xxxiii; Fahmy, *Muslim Sea-Power*, pp. 28, 30.

312 [Pseudo-]Severus, *History of the Patriarchs*, PO 5, p. 57.

The study has further shown a strong relationship between theory and practice in the attitude of the Muslims toward using non-Muslims in the Muslim armies, as the early Muslim jurists seemed attuned to the reality of things on the ground as they were reported by historians. Whereas the early jurists formulated their opinions on the basis of the Prophet's *sunnas*, they also based their rulings on the actions of the leaders of the Muslim community, some of whom had fought in the battles of the Muslims, just as the Prophet himself had done. And when there were discrepancies between traditions on the participation of non-Muslims in the Muslim army, some prohibiting and some permitting it, the traditions that reflected the reality on the ground trumped those that were more "pure" and "ideal." It is, furthermore, noteworthy that the two most outspoken early *ḥadīth* scholars/jurists who supported the broadest inclusion and remuneration of non-Muslims either came from Syria (al-Awzāʿī) or lived in Syria (al-Zuhrī), that is, in a frontier province by both land and sea. And it was al-Awzāʿī, as we have seen, who objected, *on legal grounds*, to al-Walīd II's transfer of the Cypriots to Syria, causing, perhaps, the reversal of al-Walīd's action by his successor, Yazīd III. This is one instance that shows the strong relationship between the theoreticians of the law and the practitioners of it on the ground.

Mention of the law brings us to two historiographical issues that the above study helps us reflect on. The first is the enormous usefulness of diversifying sources when studying early Islamic history. Whereas there is no doubt that the Islamic sources remain by far the vastest and most important resource for information about that period, there is equally no doubt that depending solely on these sources, and ignoring the non-Islamic sources and documentary materials, deprives the scholar of a mine of information that could be, even when not extensive, always enriching and sometimes crucial. Without this latter information, for example, our knowledge of the sailors who manned the Muslim fleet and the workers who worked on the ground on Muslim ships would be much less, and our understanding of the dynamics of defection from the Byzantine army to the Muslims much impoverished. Consulting the non-Islamic sources also allows us to hear the voice of the people who constituted the majority of the population of the expanding Muslim empire in the early period, a voice that the Islamic sources generally do not record, not out of malice, but simply out of lack of interest – except in specific situations. But this voice is extremely important to listen to in order to gain a broader, more comprehensive vision of how the Muslim ruling government was viewed by all the people it ruled, from all sectors of society, not only those people and sectors whose attitudes the Islamic sources are interested in tracing. And these attitudes, as we have seen in the above study, could have a crucial effect at times, perhaps, in deciding the outcome of the government's actions. The failure of Maslama's extended campaign against Constantinople had innumerable reasons, of course. But the statement of a Greek source that the defection of Egyptian Christian sailors to the Byzantine side, and their informing on the Muslims' ships, were decisive in ending the campaign with defeat, while it has to be examined on its own, is an invaluable addition that opens our eyes to new vistas of historical vision, and makes us wonder about how those sailors collectively felt when they were drafted, through what amounts to compulsory service, to serve aboard Muslim ships in foreign, faraway lands, and in situations in which their lives were endangered, without perceptible gain for themselves to compensate for the potential loss of life. Overall, thus, allowing sources of varying provenances and inclinations to feed our knowledge of history broadens our horizons while giving us a better grasp of what could have happened in early Islamic history.

The second historiographical issue on which the above study sheds light concerns the questionable authenticity of the reports in the Islamic historical tradition about early Islam. In this study, I have not attempted to evaluate single traditions and to subject them to rigorous examination, for my intention was to report the historical image as it was presented in the sources. And that historical image is not of the making of the Islamic sources alone, but of the non-Islamic as well, even when the latter are earlier, sometimes contemporaneous with the events they report on. The most striking thing that the study has shown is that the Islamic and non-Islamic sources, as well as the documentary materials, complement each other and hardly ever contradict themselves;[313] indeed, they often agree with each other, and when they do agree, this is truly remarkable, since the agreement comes despite each side bringing to each description of events its own intellectual, moral, and political baggage with it. Robert Hoyland's impressively broad study of Islam as seen by non-Muslims has shown that "[i]f what the non-Muslims say the Muslims were saying in the seventh century agrees with what the Muslims wrote down in the ninth century, then it is likely that this is what the Muslims were saying from the beginning, or at least from the time of the relevant non-Muslim witness. And if they did not agree, then this should be investigated, for the very fact that there are so many instances of agreement means that discrepancies deserve our attention."[314] Such an approach is encouraging, for it tells us that a dialogue of the sources is not necessarily destructive, but, rather, intrinsically, constructive. It also tells us that there is still much more work to be done in early Islamic history.

Abbreviation

P. Lond. Bell, H. I. *Greek Papyri in the British Museum*, Vol. 4: *The Aphrodito Papyri.*

Bibliography

ᶜAbd al-Razzāq b. Hammām al-Ṣanᶜānī. *Al-Muṣannaf.* Edited by Ḥabīb al-Raḥmān al-Aᶜẓamī. 2nd edition. Beirut, 1403/1983.

Abū al-ᶜArab al-Qayrawānī, Muḥammad b. Aḥmad b. Nuᶜaym. *Ṭabaqāt ᶜulamāʾ Ifrīqiya wa-Tūnis.* Edited by ᶜAlī al-Shabbī and Naᶜīm Ḥasan al-Yāfī. Tunis, 1968.

Abū Dāwūd, Sulaymān b. al-Ashᶜath. *Sunan Abī Dāwūd.* Edited by ᶜIzzat ᶜUbayd al-Daᶜᶜās and ᶜĀdil al-Sayyid. Beirut, 1388/1969.

Abū Ṣafiyya, Jāsir ibn Khalīl. *Bardiyyāt Qurra ibn Sharīk al-ᶜAbsī.* Riyadh, 2004.

Abū ᶜUbayd al-Qāsim b. Sallām. Kitāb *al-Amwāl.* [al-Qāhirah]: Maktabat al-Kullīyāt al-Azharīyah, [1968].

———. *Kitāb al-kharāj.* Edited by Muḥammad Khalīl Harrās. Cairo, 1388/1968

Abū ᶜUbayd al-Bakrī, ᶜAbdallāh b. ᶜAbd al-ᶜAzīz. *Al-Mughrib fī dhikr bilād Ifrīqiya wa-al-Maghrib* (Description de l'Afrique septentrionale). Reprint of the Algiers 1913 edition, Cairo, n.d.

---

[313] On the need to stop opposing Muslim and non-Muslim sources, see Borrut, *Entre mémoire et pouvoir,* pp. 137ff.

[314] Hoyland, *Seeing Islam as Others Saw It*, p. 592.

Abū Yūsuf, Yaʿqūb b. Ibrāhīm al-qāḍī. *Kitāb al-kharāj*. Edited by Iḥsān ʿAbbās. Beirut and Cairo, 1985.

————. *Al-Radd ʿalā siyar al-Awzāʿī*. Edited by Abū al-Wafā al-Afghānī. Beirut, [1357/1938].

Agapius of Manbij. *Kitāb al-ʿunwān*. Edited and translated by Alexandre Vasiliev, *Kitab al-Unvan, Histoire universelle*, Part II/2. Patrologia Orientalis 8. Paris, Firmin-Didot, 1912.

Anonymous. *Akhbār majmūʿa (ajbar machmuâ)*. Edited by Emilio Lafuente y Alcantara. Madrid, 1867.

ʿAthamina, Khalil. "Non-Arab Regiments and Private Militias during the Umayyad Period." *Arabica* 45/3 (1998): 347–78.

al-Balādhurī, Aḥmad b. Yaḥyā b. Jābir. *Kitāb futūḥ al-buldān*. Edited by M. J. de Goeje. Leiden: Brill, 1866.

al-Bayhaqī, Abū Bakr Aḥmad b. al-Ḥusayn. *Al-Sunan al-kubrā*. Edited by Muḥammad ʿAbd al-Qādir ʿAṭā. Mecca, 1414/1994/Edited by Muḥammad ʿAbd al-Qādir ʿAṭā. Beirut, 1999.

————. *Al-Sunan al-ṣughrā*. Edited by ʿAbd al-Muʿṭī Amīn Qalʿajī. Al-Manṣūra [Egypt], 1410/1989.

Becker, C. H. "Arabische Papyri des Aphroditofundes." *Zeitschrift für Assyriologie* 20 (1907): 68–104.

————. "Neue arabische Papyri des Aphroditofundes." *Der Islam* 2 (1911): pp. 245–68.

————. "Papyrusstudien." *Zeitschrift für Assyriologie* 22 (1909): 137–54.

Bell, H. I. "The Aphrodito Papyri." *Journal of Hellenic Studies* 28 (1908): 97–120.

————. "The Berlin Ḳurrah Papyrus." *Papyrusforschung* 5 (1909–1913): 189–91.

————. *Greek Papyri in the British Museum*, Vol. 4: *The Aphrodito Papyri*. London: British Museum, 1910.

————. "An Official Circular of the Arab Period." *Journal of Egyptian Archaeology* 31 (1945): 75–84.

————. "Translations of the Greek Aphrodito Papyri in the British Museum." *Der Islam* 2 (1911): 269–83, 372–84; 3 (1912): 132–40, 368–73; 4 (1913): 87–96; 17 (1928): 4–8.

————. "Two Official Letters of the Arab Period." *Journal of Egyptian Archaeology* 12 (1926): 265–81.

Borrut, Antoine. "L'espace maritime syrien au cours des premiers siècles de l'Islam (viie-xe siècle): le cas de la région entre Acre et Tripoli." *Tempora. Annales d'histoire et d'archéologie* 10–11 (1999–2000): 1–33.

————. *Entre mémoire et pouvoir: l'espace syrien sous les derniers Omeyyades et les premiers Abbassides (v. 72–193/692–809)*. Leiden: Brill, 2011.

Brock, Sebastian P. "Syriac Views of Emergent Islam." In *Studies in the First Century of Islamic Society*, edited by G. H. A. Juynboll, pp. 1–21. Papers on Islamic History 5. Carbondale: Southern Illinois University Press, 1982.

al-Bukhārī, Muḥammad b. Ismāʿīl. *Ṣaḥīḥ al-Bukhārī*. Reprint of the Cairo edition. Beirut, 1405/1985.

Conrad, Lawrence I. "Islam and the Sea: Paradigms and Problematics." *Al-Qanṭara* 23 (2002): 123–54.

Crone, Patricia. *Slaves on Horses: The Evolution of the Islamic Polity*. Cambridge: Cambridge University Press, 1980.

al-Dabbāgh, Abū Zayd ʿAbd al-Raḥmān b. Muḥammad. *Maʿālim al-īmān fī maʿrifat ahl al-Qayrawān*. Edited by Ibrāhīm Shabbūḥ. Cairo, 1968.

Donner, Fred M. "The Bakr b. Wāʾil Tribes and Politics in Northeastern Arabia on the Eve of Islam." *Studia Islamica* 51 (1980): 5–38.

————. *The Early Islamic Conquests*. Princeton: Princeton University Press, 1981.

————. "From Believers to Muslims: Confessional Self-Identity in the Early Islamic Community." *Al-Abhath* 50–51 (2002–2003): 9–53.

————. *Muhammad and the Believers: At the Origins of Islam*. Cambridge: Harvard University Press, 2010.

Fahmy, Aly Mohamed. *Muslim Sea-Power in the Eastern Mediterranean from the Seventh to the Tenth Century A.D.* [London], 1950; re-published, with no changes to the text or pagination, as *Muslim Naval Organisation in the Eastern Mediterranean from the Seventh to the Tenth Century A.D.* Cairo, 1966.

Grohmann, Adolf. "Greek Papyri of the Early Islamic Period in the Collection of Archduke Rainer." *Études de Papyrologie* 8 (1957): 9–40.

———. *Arabic Papyri in the Egyptian Library.* 6 volumes. Reprint of the first Cairo edition. Cairo, 1994.

Guillaume, A., trans. *The Life of Muhammad.* Oxford: Oxford University Press, 1955.

Ḥamīdullāh, Muḥammad. *Al-Wathāʾiq al-siyāsiyya li-l-ʿahd al-nabawī wa-l-khilāfa al-rāshida.* 3rd edition. Beirut, 1969.

Hourani, George F. *Arab Seafaring in the Indian Ocean in Ancient and Early Medieval Times.* Princeton Oriental Studies 13. Princeton: Princeton University Press, 1951.

Hoyland, Robert G. *Seeing Islam as Others Saw It: A Survey and Evaluation of Christian, Jewish, and Zoroastrian Writings on Early Islam.* Studies in Late Antiquity and Early Islam 13. Princeton: Darwin Press, 1997.

———. *Theophilus of Edessa's Chronicle and the Circulation of Historical Knowledge in Late Antiquity and Early Islam.* Translated Texts for Historians 57. Liverpool: Liverpool University Press, 2011.

Humphreys, R. Stephen, trans. *The Crisis of the Caliphate.* The History of al-Ṭabarī 15. Albany: State University of New York Press, 1990.

———. *Muʿawiya ibn Abi Sufyan: From Arabia to Empire.* Makers of the Muslim World. Oxford: Oneworld, 2006.

Ibn ʿAbd al-Ḥakam, Abū al-Qāsim ʿAbd al-Raḥmān b. ʿAbdallāh. *Kitāb futūḥ Miṣr wa-akhbārihā.* Edited by Charles C. Torrey. Yale Oriental Series, Researches 3. New Haven: Yale University Press, 1922.

Ibn Abī Ḥātim al-Rāzī, ʿAbd al-Raḥmān b. Muḥammad. *Al-Jarḥ wa-al-taʿdīl.* Reprint of the Hyderabad edition. Beirut, 1952.

Ibn Abī Shayba, Abū Bakr ʿAbdallāh b. Muḥammad. *Muṣannaf Ibn Abī Shayba.* Edited by Kamāl Yūsuf al-Ḥūt. Beirut, 1409/1989.

Ibn al-ʿAdīm, Kamāl al-Dīn ʿUmar b. Aḥmad b. Abī Jarāda. *Zubdat al-ḥalab fī tārīkh Ḥalab.* Edited by Suhayl Zakkār. Beirut, [1988].

Ibn ʿAsākir, Abū al-Qāsim ʿAlī b. al-Ḥasan. *Tārīkh madīnat Dimashq.* Edited by ʿUmar ibn Gharāma al-'Amrawī. 80 vols. Beirut, 1415–1421/1995–2000.

Ibn Aʿtham al-Kūfī, Abū Muḥammad Aḥmad. *Kitāb al-futūḥ.* Reprint of the Hayderabad edition. Beirut, n.d.

Ibn Duqmāq. *Al-Intiṣār li-wāsiṭat ʿiqd al-amṣār.* Reprint of the Cairo edition. Beirut, n.d.

Ibn Ḥajar al-ʿAsqalānī, Shihāb al-Dīn Aḥmad b. ʿAlī. *Al-Iṣāba fī tamyīz al-ṣaḥāba.* Reprint of the 1328 Cairo edition. Cairo, n.d.

Ibn Ḥazm, Abū Muḥammad ʿAlī b. Aḥmad. *Al-Muḥallā.* Edited by Aḥmad Muḥammad Shākir. Beirut, 1969.

Ibn ʿIdhārī al-Marrākushī, Aḥmad b. Muḥammad. *Kitāb al-bayān al-mughrib fī akhbār Ifrīqiya wa-l-Maghrib.* Edited by G. S. Colin and É. Lévi-Provençal. Reprint of the Leiden edition. Beirut, n.d.

Ibn al-Qūṭiyya, Abū Bakr Muḥammad b. ʿUmar. *Tārīkh iftitāḥ al-Andalus.* Edited by Ibrāhīm al-Ibyārī. Beirut, 1982.

[Pseudo-]Ibn Qutayba. *Al-Imāma wa-l-siyāsa.* Edited by Ṭāhā Muḥammad al-Zaynī. Cairo, n.d.

Ibn Yūnus. *Tārīkh ibn Yūnus al-miṣrī.* Edited by ʿAbd al-Fattāḥ Fatḥī ʿAbd al-Fattāḥ. Beirut, 1421/2000.

John bar Penkayē. *Chronicle of John bar Penkayē*. In *Sources syriaques*, edited and translated by Alphonse Mignana. Leipzig: Harrassowitz, [1908].

John, Bishop of Nikiu. *Chronicle*. Edited by R. H. Charles, *The Chronicle of John, Bishop of Nikiu*. Text and Translation Society Series 3. Oxford: William & Norgate, 1916.

Kaegi, Walter E. *Byzantium and the Early Islamic Conquests*. Cambridge: Cambridge University Press, 1992.

Khalīfa b. Khayyāṭ. *Tārīkh Khalīfa ibn Khayyāṭ*. Edited by Akram Ḍiyāʾ al-ʿUmarī. Beirut, 1397/1977.

Khaṣāwinah, Sāmī ʿAbd Allāh, ed. *Conference on Orientalism: Dialogue of Cultures*. Amman: al-Jāmiʿah al-Urdunīyah, 2004.

al-Kindī, Abū ʿUmar Muḥammad b. Yūsuf. *Kitāb al-wulāt wa-kitāb al-quḍāt*. Edited by Rhuvon Guest, *The Governors and Judges of Egypt*. London: Luzac & Co., 1912.

Kraemer, Casper J. *Excavations at Nessana:* Vol. 3: *Non-Literary Papyri*. Princeton: Princeton University Press, 1958.

Lammens, Henri. "Les Perses du Liban et l'origine des Métoualis." *Mélanges de la faculté orientale de l'Université Saint-Joseph de Beyrouth* 14 (1929): 21–39.

La Vaissière, Étienne de. *Samarcande et Samarra: élites d'asie centrale dans l'empire abbasside*. Studia Iranica, Cahier 35. Paris: Association pour l'avancement des études iraniennes, 2007.

al-Mālikī, Abū Bakr ʿAbdallāh b. Muḥammad. *Riyāḍ al-nufūs fī ṭabaqāt ʿulamāʾ al-Qayrawān wa-Ifrīqiya*. Edited by Bashīr al-Bakkūsh. Beirut, 1983.

al-Maqrīzī, Taqī al-Dīn Aḥmad b. ʿAlī. *Kitāb al-mawāʿiẓ wa-al-iʿtibār bi-dhikr al-khiṭaṭ wa-al-āthār*, known as *al-Khiṭaṭ al-maqrīziyya*. Būlāq, 1870.

Michael the Syrian. *Chronicle*. Edited and translated by Jean-Baptiste Chabot, *Chronique de Michel le Syrien*. 4 vols. Paris: Academie des inscriptions et belles-lettres, 1899–1910. Reprinted Brussels: Culture et Civilisation, 1963; Toronto: Gorgias Press, 2008.

Morony, Michael G. *Iraq after the Muslim Conquest*. Princeton: Princeton University Press, 1984.

Muhammad, Tarek M. "The Role of the Copts in the Islamic Navigation in the 7th and 8th Centuries: The Papyrological Evidence." *Journal of Coptic Studies* 10 (2008): 1–32.

Muslim b. al-Ḥajjāj. *Al-Jāmiʿ al-ṣaḥīḥ*. Edited by Muḥammad Fuʾād ʿAbd al-Bāqī. Reprint of the Cairo edition. Beirut, n.d.

Palmer, Andrew. *The Seventh Century in the West-Syrian Chronicles*. Translated Texts for Historians 15. Liverpool: Liverpool University Press, 1993.

Picard, Christophe. *La mer des califes: une histoire de la Méditerranée musulmane (viie–xiie siècle)*. Paris: Ed. du Seuil, 2015.

Planhol, Xavier de. *L'Islam et la mer: la mosquée et le matelot, VIIe–XXe siècle*. Paris: Perrin, 2000.

al-Qāḍī, Wadād. "Madkhal ilā dirāsat ʿuhūd al-ṣulḥ al-islāmiyya zaman al-futūḥ." In *Proceedings of the Fourth International Congress of the History of Bilād al-Shām (Bilād al-Shām fī ṣadr al-Islām), Jordanian University, 1985*, edited by Muḥammad ʿAdnān al-Bakhīt and Iḥsān ʿAbbās, vol. 2, pp. 193–269. Amman, 1987.

———. "Population Census and Land Surveys under the Umayyads (61–132/661–750)." *Der Islam* 83 (2008): 341–416.

al-Raqīq al-Qayrawānī, Abū Isḥāq Ibrāhīm b. al-Qāsim. *Tārīkh Ifrīqiya wa-l-Maghrib*. Edited by al-Munjī al-Kaʿbī. Tunis, 1968.

al-Ṣafadī, Ṣalāh al-Dīn Khalīl b. Aybak. *Al-Wāfī bi-l-wafayāt*. Edited by Sven Dedering. Beirut and Wiesbaden: F. Steiner, 1974.

Saḥnūn, ʿAbd al-Salām b. Saʿīd al-Tanūkhī. *Al-Mudawwana al-kubrā*. Edited by Ḥamdī al-Dimirdāsh Muḥammad. Ṣaydā [Lebanon], 1419/1999.

Sauvaget, Jean. "Notes de topographie omeyyade." *Syria* 24 (1944–1945): 96–112.

Sebeos. *The Armenian History*. Translated by R. W. Thomson and James Howard-Johnston, *The Armenian History Attributed to Sebeos*. 2 vols. Translated Texts for Historians 31. Liverpool: Liverpool University Press, 1999.

[Pseudo-]Severus, *History of the Patriarchs of the Coptic Church of Alexandria*. Edited and translated by B. Evetts. Paris: Firmin-Didot, 1907 (Patrologia Orientalis 1) and 1910 (Patrologia Orientalis 5).

al-Shāfiʿī, Muḥammad b. Idrīs. *Kitāb al-umm*. Edited by Muḥammad Zuhrī al-Najjār. Reprint of the Cairo edition. Beirut, n.d.

al-Shaybānī, Muḥammad b. al-Ḥasan. *Kitāb al-siyar al-kabīr*, with the commentary of al-Sarakhsī. Edited by Ṣalāḥ al-Dīn al-Munajjid and ʿAbd al-ʿAzīz Aḥmad. Cairo, 1971–1972.

al-Shīrāzī, Abū Isḥāq Ibrāhīm b. ʿAlī. *Al-Muhadhdhab fī fiqh al-imām al-Shāfiʿī*. Edited by Muḥammad al-Zuḥaylī. Damascus and Beirut, 1417/1996.

al-Ṭabarī, Muḥammad b. Jarīr. *Tārīkh al-Ṭabarī*.

- Edited by Muḥammad Abū al-Faḍl Ibrāhīm. Cairo, 1960–1969.
- Edited by M. J. de Goeje, *Tārīkh al-rusul wa-l-mulūk*. Leiden: Brill, 1879–1901.

Theophanes. *Chronicle*. Translated by Cyril Mango and Roger Scott, *The Chronicle of Theophanes Confessor: Byzantine and Near Eastern History, A.D. 284–813*. Oxford: Clarendon Press, 1997 (earlier translation by Harry Turtledove. Philadelphia: University of Pennsylvania Press, 1982).

al-Tirmidhī, Muḥammad b. ʿĪsā. *Sunan al-Tirmidhī*. 2nd edition. Beirut, 1403/1983.

Whitby, Michael. "Recruitment in Roman Armies from Justinian to Heraclius (ca. 565–615)." In *The Byzantine and Early Islamic Near East*, Vol. 3: *States, Resources and Armies*, edited by Averil Cameron, pp. 61–124. Princeton: Darwin Press, 1995.

al-Yaʿqūbī, Aḥmad b. Abī Yaʿqūb b. Wāḍiḥ. *Tārīkh al-Yaʿqūbī*. Beirut, [1960].

Yāqūt b. ʿAbdallāh, Shihāb al-Dīn. *Muʿjam al-buldān*. Beirut, n.d.

Yarbrough, Luke. "I'll not Accept Aid from a *mušrik*." In *The Late Roman and Early Islamic Mediterranean and Near East: Authority and Control in the Countryside*, edited by A. Delattre, M. Legendre, and P. Sijpesteijn. Princeton, forthcoming.

Zakeri, Mohsen. *Sāsānid Soldiers in Early Muslim Society: The Origins of ʿAyyārān and Futuwwa*. Wiesbaden: Harrassowitz, 1995.

6

Al-Akhṭal at the Court of ʿAbd al-Malik: The *Qaṣīda* and the Construction of Umayyad Authority

Suzanne Pinckney Stetkevych, Georgetown University

This study proposes to examine the role of the Christian poet al-Akhṭal al-Taghlibī (ca. 20/640–before 92/710) as panegyrist to the court of the Umayyad caliph ʿAbd al-Malik ibn Marwān. It argues that, as with other insignia of authority — such as the construction of the Dome of the Rock in Jerusalem and the minting of Umayyad coinage — poetry played an essential role in the consolidation and construction of Umayyad authority and legitimacy after the end of the *Fitna* of ʿAbd Allāh ibn al-Zubayr and the Marwānid Restoration. I will not rehearse here the biography and bibliography of al-Akhṭal al-Taghlibī.[1] Rather, I will focus on the examination of several key poems and anecdotes that have been oft cited or repeated in both classical Arabic literary compendia and modern Arabic and Western literary studies, but have not, in my view, been interpreted in such a way as to reveal the performative aspect of court poetry in constructing and consolidating caliphal power and authority and articulating an ideology of Islamic rule, and, further, have not been adequately discussed in terms of the broader issues of Umayyad history and the formation of the Umayyad state.

It is advisable to begin with a summary of the religious and political situation of the period at hand — the so-called Marwānid Restoration — which we might more appropriately term the Marwānid "Usurpation" of the Umayyad caliphate from the original Sufyānid branch, or of the claims to the caliphate put forth by the ʿAlids and Zubayrids, as well as, of course, the Khārijites, and the role of the Arab Christian tribe of the Banū Taghlib, and its master-poet al-Akhṭal, in it. The facts that seem pertinent to me are, in summary: that the Umayyads, in moving the capital of the Islamic state from the cities of the Ḥijāz, Mecca and Medina, to Syria — and Damascus — had moved from the autochthonous Arab cultic center of Islam to a grand historic cosmopolitan center. That is to say, in Arab-Islamic myth and cult, Mecca was autochthonously Arab/Arabic and proto-Islamic (*maqām Ibrāhīm*, etc.), whereas Damascus had been captured from the Byzantine empire by Khālid ibn al-Walīd in 14/635 and was a seat of Greek administration and Syriac religious scholarship. In this sense Damascus became what we might term a cosmopolitan imperial seat as opposed to Medina, the religious and administrative seat of the Prophet, an Arab-Islamic cultic seat for the Islamic state.[2] The Umayyad

[1] For a brief biography, classical sources, and modern bibliography of al-Akhṭal (Ghiyāth ibn Ghawth ibn al-Ṣalt, Abū Mālik), see Sezgin, *Geschichte des Arabischen Schrifttums*, vol. 2: *Poesie*, pp. 318–21.

[2] On post-conquest Damascus, see now Khalek, *Damascus after the Muslim Conquest*. See also more broadly Humphreys, *Muʿawiya ibn Abi Sufyan*.

land holdings in Damascus, as well as Muʿāwiya's long governorship there, conferred upon the Umayyads a more cosmopolitan and imperial outlook than the more parochial perspective of, for example, their major rival for the caliphate, ʿAbd Allāh ibn al-Zubayr.[3]

Whatever their vision, the Banū Umayya ibn ʿAbd Shams had better claims to Arab than to Muslim loyalties. As is well established, not only was Abū Sufyān long hostile and a latecomer to Islam, but in the course of the First and Second *Fitnas*, the Banū Umayya had alienated both the principals and the followers of major "faith-based" constituencies — the Ṣaḥāba, the Anṣār, and the ʿAlids. Both the Sufyānid victory in the First *Fitna* and the Marwānid Restoration of Umayyad rule in the Second *Fitna* were accomplished by force of arms against fellow Muslims and "Islam" — shedding Muslim blood and destroying the Kaʿba — an awkward base upon which to construct a claim for legitimate Islamic authority. Clearly the Banū Umayya had to construct authority and legitimacy, and had to seek allies and supporters, where they could. In this respect the tribal range wars between the Qaysīs (Muḍar) and Kalbīs/Yamanīs in al-Jazīra (northern Mesopotamia) became absorbed into the struggle for the caliphate as the Yamanī faction, and with them the powerful Christian tribe of the Banū Taghlib, sided with the Banū Umayya while the Qaysī faction sided with the Zubayrids — most directly fighting for Muṣʿab ibn al-Zubayr in Iraq.[4] As we shall see, this enmity and the concomitant bloodshed between the Banū Taghlib and especially the Qaysī tribe of the Banū Sulaym continued well after the pacification of Iraq and the various stages of incorporation of the Qaysī tribes into the Umayyad state.

The pertinent names and dates for our purposes are:

- 65/684: Umayyads recognize Marwān ibn al-Ḥakam as caliph.
- 1 Muḥarram 65/18 August 684: The final Battle Day of Marj Rāhiṭ, a plain northwest of Damascus: Marwān ibn al-Ḥakam is supported by the Kalbī/Yamanī tribes; al-Akhṭal's tribe, the Banū Taghlib, have sided with them in support of the Umayyads. The Marwānids and their supporters inflict a decisive defeat upon al-Daḥḥāk ibn Qays al-Fihrī, the head of the Qaysī tribes, and supporter of the rival caliphate of ʿAbd Allāh ibn al-Zubayr. Al-Daḥḥāk is slain and his severed head presented to Marwān. Umayyad control of Syria is reestablished. Zufar ibn al-Ḥārith al-Kilābī escapes and holds out in Qirqīsiyāʾ.
- 65/685: Marwān ibn al-Ḥakam dies and his son ʿAbd al-Malik accedes to the (shaky and highly contested) caliphate.
- 69/689: ʿAbd al-Malik makes a ten-year truce with the Byzantine emperor in return for annual tribute.
- 70/689: Yawm Tharthār at the al-Ḥashshāk River: the Banū Taghlib defeat the Qaysī and pro-Muṣʿab ibn al-Zubayr tribe of the Banū Sulaym, slay its leader ʿUmayr ibn al-Ḥubāb, and send his severed head to ʿAbd al-Malik.
- 71/690–691: Defeat of Zufar ibn al-Ḥārith, the Qaysī supporter of Muṣʿab ibn al-Zubayr, at Qirqīsiyāʾ; he agrees to a negotiated truce with ʿAbd al-Malik.
- 72/691: Defeat of Muṣʿab ibn al-Zubayr in Iraq.

[3] See *EI*[2] s.v. "Umayyads" (G. R. Hawting).

[4] Ibid.

- 17 Jumādā I or II 73/4 October or 3 November 692: After a six-month siege of Mecca by the notorious general al-Ḥajjāj ibn Yūsuf, during which the city and even the Kaʿba were bombarded, ʿAbd Allāh ibn al-Zubayr is defeated and slain on the battlefield. = ʿĀm al-Jamāʿa (Year of [Re]unification of the Community).
- 73/692: Yawm Bishr: al-Jaḥḥāf, leader of the Qaysī tribe of the Banū Sulaym, now Umayyad clients, massacres the Banū Taghlib.
- 73/692: ʿAbd al-Malik resumes wars with the Byzantines.
- 86/705: Death of ʿAbd al-Malik.

Recent work in the fields of history, art history, and numismatics has undertaken a fruitful cooperation, or integration, that has significantly advanced and nuanced our understanding of the formation and construction of the Marwānid state. Literature, especially poetry, has not played an adequate role, and it is this situation that I would like to redress in this paper.[5] Particularly pertinent to the present discussion is the extensive body of work on ʿAbd al-Malik's construction of the Dome of the Rock (Qubbat al-Ṣakhra) in Jerusalem. However varied and disputed the particular interpretations of the geographical, religious, architectural, inscriptional, pictorial, historical, and political symbolisms involved in this complex and unique structure, one thing is clear: that the choice within a sacred city of a site itself long sacred to Christians and Jews (and probably in the Near Eastern folk culture in general) that had been incorporated (and would in the course of time be further incorporated) into Islamic myth and cult (*ūlā al-qiblatayn* [the first of the two qiblas], *al-Isrāʾ wa-al-Miʿrāj* [the Night Journey and Ascension], *thālith al-Ḥaramayn* [the third of the Two Sanctuaries], etc.) was part of a plan to co-opt all those symbolic languages for the expression of Umayyad authority and, further, that the co-optation of all those symbols of authority and addition of specifically Islamic ones amounted to the subsuming and subduing of the authority of their former masters (beginning with Solomon and ending with the Byzantines). I believe it is also certainly correct to understand ʿAbd al-Malik's Jerusalem project as, on the one hand, a contingency plan (including redirecting the Islamic pilgrimage to Jerusalem) for temporary use until the Zubayrids were defeated, or even for permanent use as the cultic site of a second Islamic state with its administrative capital at Damascus (à la Mecca and Medina) if he could not prevail against them.[6] We need to note, too, that the various languages of symbols that ʿAbd al-Malik co-opted in his Jerusalem project and Dome of the Rock were

[5] I have begun this endeavor in Stetkevych, "Umayyad Panegyric," and *Poetics of Islamic Legitimacy*, pp. 80–143. Crone and Hinds, in *God's Caliph*, recognize to some degree the importance of poetry in the formation of the Umayyad conception of the caliphate, but are hampered by their view of court poetry as "sycophantic" (p. 56) and the lack of any sense of the performative and ceremonial functions of the *qaṣīdāt al-madḥ* as a literary form. They nevertheless provide numerous and useful citations from Umayyad poetry of caliphal titles and attributes (see esp. pp. 4–57). Although I do not agree with her identification of Arabic poetic images with the column on Umayyad coinage that replaces the cross on Byzantine coinage, I find Jamil's work on the development of Jāhilī poetic images of authority into Islamic and Umayyad ones extremely important. Her study of the development of three select sets of Arabic poetic imagery — the celestial imagery of the pole, the hand-mill, and the well-pulley — from the pre-Islamic through the Umayyad is extremely original and important, both for the history of poetry, material culture, and Umayyad ideology (Jamil, "Caliph and Quṭb").

[6] For a recent attempt at reconciling the various hypotheses with regard to the erection of the Dome of the Rock, see Elad, "ʿAbd al-Malik and the Dome of the Rock."

essentially or originally non-Arab non-Islamic ones. The Dome of the Rock inscription associating it (whether, as is disputed, at the initiation or completion of the building) with the year 72/691–692 demonstrates its association with the consolidation of legitimate authority during and after the Second *Fitna*.[7] The building of the Dome of the Rock and ʿAbd al-Malik's Jerusalem project in general have been rightly associated with his consolidation, co-optation, and Islamization of coinage in his new minting campaign (72–78/ 692–698).[8]

The year 72–73/691–692 is, furthermore, the date of *Khaffa al-qaṭīnu* (*Qaṣīda I*, below), al-Akhṭal's most celebrated panegyric to ʿAbd al-Malik ibn Marwān and one that is both contextually and textually recognized as the premier poetic construction of Umayyad authority, in particular in the person of ʿAbd al-Malik.[9] What is curious in the context of the present volume is that the subject of the poet's religion is nowhere indicated or suggested in the text of the poem itself and yet is the explicit subject of the anecdotes in the classical literary tradition that serve to introduce, contextualize, and, therefore, interpret the poem.

An anecdote from al-Iṣbahānī's (d. 356/967) *Al-Aghānī* does not refer specifically to the poem under discussion, but provides an indication of the authority that this Christian poet from the tribe of the Banū Taghlib wielded at the Umayyad court:

> A man once said to Abū ʿAmr, "How amazing al-Akhṭal was! A Christian infidel who composed invective against Muslims!" "O you wretched fool!" he replied, [Don't you know that] al-Akhṭal could come clad in a silken gown and a silken girdle, wearing around his neck a golden chain from which hung a golden cross, and with wine dripping from his beard, and thus present himself, without asking permission, before ʿAbd al-Malik ibn Marwān!"[10]

Part of the reference here is the politico-religious situation that first brought al-Akhṭal into the service of the Umayyads, when Yazīd, still during the reign of his father Muʿāwiya, wanted a poet to compose invective against the Anṣār. No Muslim could be found to inveigh against those who had aided and defended the Prophet, but this Christian poet, whose invective talents had already been recognized, had no such scruples. So scathing — which is to say, effective — was his invective, that the caliph Muʿāwiya ordered his tongue to be cut out, and he was saved only by the intercession of his son and successor Yazīd.[11] The main question we have to address, however, is what made this poet so valuable and powerful that ʿAbd al-Malik is depicted as allowing him with such exaggerated religious effrontery to, unbidden, enter his court?

To answer this, we have to give more serious interpretative attention to the many classical Arabic literary critical anecdotes — such as the many recorded in *Kitāb al-Aghānī* — and particularly those regarding the classical literary dispute concerning who, of the formidable Umayyad poetic triumvirate, was the best poet: al-Akhṭal, al-Farazdaq, or Jarīr. Al-Akhṭal is repeatedly singled out as *al-amdaḥ*, the best panegyrist of the three, and, indeed, one anecdote cites his rival al-Farazdaq as naming al-Akhṭal not merely the best panegyrist of the

---

[7] On these aspects, see Rabbat, "The Meaning of the Umayyad Dome of the Rock"; the various studies included in Raby and Johns, eds., *Bayt al-Maqdis I* (esp. Elad, "Why Did ʿAbd al-Malik Build the Dome of the Rock?") and Johns, ed., *Bayt al-Maqdis II*; Grabar, *The Shape of the Holy*, *passim*. More generally on the construction of authority and the state in the reign of ʿAbd al-Malik, see Robinson, *ʿAbd al-Malik*, *passim*.

[8] See Bacharach, "Signs of Sovereignty," and references.

[9] See Stetkevych, *Poetics of Islamic Legitimacy*, pp. 86–88; Lammens, "Le chantre des Omiades," at p. 162, ref.

[10] Al-Iṣbahānī, *Al-Aghānī*, vol. 8, p. 3045.

[11] Lammens, "Le chantre des Omiades," pp. 131–40; al-Ḥāwī, ed., *Sharḥ Dīwān al-Akhṭal*, pp. 38–42.

Islamic period, but, moreover, *amdaḥu al-ʿArabi*, the best praise poet of the Arabs.[12] At this point it is crucial, as I have called for in much of my other work, on the one hand, to dispense with the common disparagement of the dominant classical Arabic poetic genre — *qaṣīdat al-madḥ* — as nothing but sycophantic flattery, and, on the other, to move well beyond the well-meaning but limited/ing and ultimately facile interpretation of the panegyric ode as a "mirror for princes."

Incorporating my own earlier work on the ritual and ceremonial aspects of the *qaṣīdat al-madḥ* (rite of passage, gift exchange, etc.) with further work on performance theory[13] and performative theory,[14] my 2002 book *Poetics of Islamic Legitimacy* emphasizes the composition and presentation of the *qaṣīdat al-madḥ* in terms of a court ritual of supplication in which the poet declares his allegiance to the patron who, in return, promises protection and support. The poet in this ritual serves as a synecdoche for all the ruler's subjects. Above and beyond this, I argue that the *qaṣīdat al-madḥ*, as a verbal structure, constructs legitimate authority, that in its ceremonial presentation or recitation it enacts the subject–ruler relationship, and that it thereby confers authority and legitimacy upon the patron. Finally, as with all ritual and ceremony, the individual *qaṣīdat al-madḥ* combines a tradition-honored repeated form, revered as authentic and timeless, with new (though sometimes their novelty is denied, or at least disguised) elements that negotiate contemporary disputes. However felicitous a choice al-Akhṭal may have proved for lampooning the Anṣār, it is his unrivalled talent at *madīḥ* — as we now understand it as the construction and conferral of legitimate authority — that made him indispensable for ʿAbd al-Malik.

The Arabic(-Islamic) literary tradition deals with the awkward issue of al-Akhṭal's being an infidel, Christian, through a lively anecdote of transgression and redemption recorded in al-Iṣbahānī's *Kitāb al-Aghānī*. The poem cited in the anecdote is precisely *Khaffa al-qaṭīnu*, our *Qaṣīda I* of the present study (below):

> Al-Akhṭal came before ʿAbd al-Malik ibn Marwān who asked him to recite for him. "My throat is dry," responded the poet, "Order someone to bring me a drink." "Bring him some water," ordered the Caliph. "That's for donkeys," said al-Akhṭal, "and we have plenty of it." "Then give him milk." "I've long since been weaned!" "Then give him honey." "That's for the sick!" "Well, what *do* you want?" "Wine, O Commander of the Faithful!" "Have you ever known me to serve wine, you bastard?! If it weren't for the inviolable bond (*ḥurma*) between us, O what I would do to you!" So al-Akhṭal left and came upon one of ʿAbd al-Malik's attendants. "Damn you," he said to him, "the Commander of the Faithful ordered me to recite, but my voice was hoarse. Give me some wine!" So he did. Then al-Akhṭal said, "Match it with another!" So he did. "You have left the two of them fighting in my stomach, better give me a third!" So he did. "Now you've left me listing to one side, give me a fourth for balance." The servant gave it to him, and al-Akhṭal went before ʿAbd al-Malik and recited:
>
> *Those that dwelt with you have left in haste*
> *departing at evening or at dawn,*
> *Alarmed and driven out by fate's caprice*
> *they head for distant lands.*

[12] Al-Iṣbahānī, *Al-Aghānī*, vol. 8, p. 3032.

[13] Most useful is Bauman, *Verbal Art as Performance*.

[14] Especially pertinent is Austin, *How to Do Things with Words*. Further on the use of performance theory and performative theory in the interpretation of Arabic literature, see Stetkevych, "Qaḍāyā al-Qaṣīda al-ʿArabiyya."

> When he finished the poem, ʿAbd al-Malik said to a servant boy, "Take him by the hand, boy, and help him out, heap robes of honor upon him, and reward him generously." Then he proclaimed, "Every people has its poet, and the poet of the Banū Umayya is al-Akhṭal."[15]

The transgression consists of being a Christian and of affronting the dignity of the Islamic caliph by requesting wine in his presence. It is, ʿAbd al-Malik declares, only the sacred bond (of client-patron protection, à la Jāhiliyya) that prevents him from killing the poet on the spot. Unrepentant and undeterred by the caliph's oath, the poet leaves, finds some caliphal attendants to supply him with the refreshment he requires, and then returns, compounding his transgression by performing the *qaṣīdat al-madḥ* presentation ceremony in an inebriated state (as we can deduce from the caliph's having to ask a servant boy to help al-Akhṭal out). The poet's redemption is the poem itself. Clearly in ʿAbd al-Malik's estimation the "dignity" — that is, the legitimacy — that the poem confers upon the caliph far outweighs the "indignity" of a Christian appearing in his presence intoxicated. When the caliph then "pronounces" al-Akhṭal the poet laureate of the Banū Umayya, we must understand that it is because al-Akhṭal, through his poem, has (in the full performative sense of the word) "pronounced" the Banū Umayya the legitimate rulers of the Islamic Umma. Furthermore, we must understand that in forgiving, rewarding, and protecting the subject who has just declared his allegiance and submitted to him, the caliph is "enacting" or "performing" his role as legitimate moral authority (the protector and defender of those that recognize and submit to him) and, in specifically Arabic terms, the virtue of *ḥilm* (forbearance, clemency).

What is essential here is that the change of status, which is the essence of every ritual, is, for the poet, from an infidel flagrantly transgressing against Islam to an indispensable mainstay of the Umayyad Islamic caliphate. It is to be understood that ʿAbd al-Malik, and with him the Banū Umayya, has also undergone a change of status — from doubtful legitimacy to established and recognized legitimacy. How has al-Akhṭal accomplished this?

First, it is evident that his verbal performance of *qaṣīdat al-madḥ* has been perceived by the caliph as a ceremonial and ritual (that is, performative) success. For this, we have to understand, as I have tried to demonstrate in earlier work, that since pre-Islamic times the *qaṣīdat al-madḥ* and *fakhr* had performed precisely this courtly function of constructing, conferring, and performing or enacting legitimate authoritative rule, in a tribal context, through its ceremonial presentation and subsequent recitations.[16] That is, the conceptual bases for legitimate Islamic (caliphal) rule are not, as many historians claim, derived from post-Islamic Persian sources, and so on, but are already fully articulated in the pre-Islamic *qaṣīda*, which however autochthonously Arabic and Arab was, in a deeper and broader sense, also the product of a rich Near Eastern subsoil containing Jewish, Christian, Persian, and so on, nutrients. The fact that these concepts or principles of legitimacy have been expressed through the highly mnemonic rhetorical and ritual structure of the oral-formulaic ode, rather than the expository or narrative prose genres, should not blind us to the fact that, however more readable we find the latter, it was the *qaṣīdat al-madḥ* in literature and in courtly and political practice that formulated both the pre-Islamic and Islamic Arab concepts of legitimate rule and, with the spread of the *qaṣīdat al-madḥ* to virtually all other Muslim societies, Islamic rule in general. It is important to reiterate here that the *qaṣīdat al-madḥ* was

[15] Al-Iṣbahānī, *Al-Aghānī*, vol. 8, p. 3040.

[16] This is the gist of my book *Poetics of Islamic Legitimacy*.

not a rhymed and metered treatise on the concepts of legitimate rule, rather it was a verbal and ceremonial performance that enacted allegiance and submission to legitimate authority and through which that authority was verbally and bodily constructed and conferred ("acted out"). This means, as I have argued at length elsewhere, that we must examine the full psychological and moral trajectory of the *qaṣīda* as a literary form, including the expression of loss and nostalgia in the elegiac prelude, the patron- or tribe-directed liminal quest of the journey section, and the celebration of and submission to the monarchic or tribal virtue and authority in the "praise" (*madīḥ*) or "boast" (*fakhr*) section. Again, the *qaṣīda* does not propose to compose a treatise on legitimate rule, rather it ceremonially enacts the allegiance of the subject to the ruler, and the legitimate exercise of power by that ruler.[17]

Let us look with a keener eye at the many classical literary critical anecdotes and opinions that tie al-Akhṭal so closely to the great (court) poets of the Jāhiliyya. Not only is he repeatedly compared to the great court panegyrists al-Nābigha al-Dhubyānī and Aʿshā Maymūn,[18] but the celebrated Basran philologist Abū ʿAmr (ibn al-ʿAlāʾ, d. 154/770) is quoted as saying that if al-Akhṭal had lived even one day in the Jāhiliyya, he would not have ranked any of the other poets above him.[19] Further, his poetry is compared to theirs — especially the *madīḥ* of al-Nābigha and the wine descriptions of al-Aʿshā — the undisputed pre-Islamic master in that regard. In modern times, Henri Lammens refers to a "renaissance" of poetry in the Umayyad era, and Wahb Rūmiyya refers, though sometimes disparagingly as "blind imitation," to the resurgence in the Umayyad period of the courtly pre-Islamic *qaṣīdat al-madḥ*.[20] The point in the context of the present argument is that the resurgence of the high courtly Jāhilī *qaṣīdat al-madḥ*, as well as other genres, *hijāʾ* (lampoon, invective), after a period of poetic decline generally recognized by literary critics from the appearance of Islam through the Rāshidūn period, occurs precisely at the period of greatest crisis in and competition for legitimate rule of the Islamic community. Modern Arab literary historians, especially in the 1960s and 1970s, such as Shawqī Ḍayf and Nuʿmān al-Qāḍī, have produced literary historical studies emphasizing the highly politicized and factional poetry of the Umayyad period, but without appreciating either the poetic or ceremonial dimensions involved.[21] More to the point, al-Akhṭal, as not merely one of the undisputed top three poetic talents of his time, but as the best of them at *madīḥ* and the closest of them to the poetry of al-Nābigha and al-Aʿshā, was uniquely placed in terms of his poetic talent to perform the job ʿAbd al-Malik most needed done. Al-Akhṭal constructs Umayyad caliphal authority, then, by reprising the master *qaṣīda*s of the Jāhiliyya, thereby invoking or reactivating their authority-conferring power, and by implicating into them those elements of legitimacy that distinguish the Banū Umayya from their rivals and competitors for the caliphate. Lammens seems to have had some sense of this when he relates ʿAbd al-Malik's particular enthusiasm for panegyric poetry and the verses of al-Nābigha al-Dhubyānī, as well as of al-Akhṭal.[22]

Here we must note once more that, as with all ritual and ceremony, each *qaṣīda* is not a mere rehearsal of generic requirements, but rather a nuanced negotiation between

---

[17] Again, these ideas are examined at length throughout my book, *Poetics of Islamic Legitimacy*.

[18] Al-Iṣbahānī, *Al-Aghānī*, vol. 8, pp. 3032, 3039.

[19] Ibid., pp. 3031, again, 3032.

[20] Lammens, *Études sur le siècle des Omayyades*, pp. 220–21; and idem, "Le chantre des Omiades," pp. 144–45; Rūmiyya, *Qaṣīdat al-Madḥ*, pp. 304–05 and 299–502 *passim*; and the discussion in Stetkevych, *Poetics of Islamic Legitimacy*, pp. 81–82, 337.

[21] See Ḍayf, *Al-Taṭawwur wa-al-Tajdīd*; al-Qāḍī, *Al-Firaq al-Islāmiyya*; and the discussion in Stetkevych, *Poetics of Islamic Legitimacy*, pp. 80–84, 337.

[22] Lammens, "Le chantre des Omiades," p. 140 and references.

contemporary needs and traditional values. The authority of tradition is subtly adjusted even as it is brought to bear on the relevant present. We must also bear in mind that al-Akhṭal is not abstractly concerned with Umayyad legitimacy, rather he is exploiting the Jāhilī-style *qaṣīdat al-madḥ* to advance and negotiate not only his own poetic standing at court, but the political-military status of the Banū Taghlib in the Umayyad power structure vis-à-vis other contenders for power and influence. With these considerations in mind, let us look briefly at the panegyric ode that forms the basis for the anecdote we have discussed.

Qaṣīda I: al-Akhṭal's *Khaffa al-qaṭīnu*

Al-Akhṭal's celebrated Rāʾiyya that begins *Khaffa al-qaṭīnu*[23] (The tribe has departed) opens with a masterfully executed elegiac prelude (*nasīb*) in which the poet uses the theme of the departure of his beloved's tribe from their campsite as a tie-in to a wine scene, then a further nostalgia-tinged depiction of the poet's mind's eye following the departed women (vv. 1–17). The effect is to invoke the authority of the master poets of the Jāhiliyya while at the same time, through his mastery of their forms and themes, assuming their authority for himself. Further, although this *qaṣīda* does not feature the supplicatory journey section (*raḥīl*) and the self-abasement of the poet before the patron that it so often expresses, al-Akhṭal nevertheless, eluding explicit self-abasement through the use of the third person and other indirection "whose gifts do not elude us," establishes ʿAbd al-Malik as the source of bounty for those in need, verses 17–18.

17. They alighted in the evening,
 and we turned aside our noble-bred camels:
 For the man in need, the time had come
 to journey

18. To a man whose gifts do not elude us,
 whom God has made victorious,
 So let him in his victory
 long delight!

He thereby presents the caliph as the object of supplication while not directly depicting himself as the supplicant. Within the Arabic poetic tradition this ruse suggests, on the one hand, the high status and confidence of the poet, while on the other hand pointing to the use of the same technique, for the same purpose, in the celebrated *Qāfiyya* of the Jāhilī master Zuhayr ibn Abī Sulmā in a panegyric to Harim ibn Sinān:

Harim's supplicants and those that seek his bounty
Have beaten pathways to his doors.[24]

---

[23] For further references, full translation, and analysis along lines somewhat different from the present argument, and further primary and secondary sources, see Stetkevych, "Umayyad Panegyric," and idem, *Poetics of Islamic Legitimacy*, pp. 80–109, 336–42; my translation follows the text, commentary, and notes of Qabāwa, ed., *Shiʿr al-Akhṭal*, vol. 1, pp. 192–211; I have also consulted Ṣāliḥānī, *Shiʿr al-Akhṭal*, pp. 160–79.

[24] Thaʿlab, *Sharḥ Dīwān Zuhayr ibn Abī Sulmā*, pp. 33–55, v. 36. See partial translation and discussion of this poem in Stetkevych, *The Mantle Odes*, pp. 22–28.

At the same time, verse 18 serves as a formal felicitation of the caliph on his victory and confirmation of his divine appointment "whom God has made victorious." As will be stressed further below in the discussion of *Qaṣīda III*: al-Akhṭal's *La-ʿamrī la-qad ʾasraytu*, the declaration that ʿAbd al-Malik's victory is God-given, not merely the result of brute force, constitutes a claim to legitimacy. In this ethical code, might does not in itself confer right. Rather, the opposite must be claimed: the (divine) right is the source of military might and, therefore, of legitimate rule. We must understand that congratulations and felicitations are a form of declaration of support and allegiance and that the failure to perform this ceremonial obligation would indicate a withdrawal of allegiance and breaking of political ties. Verse 19 further confers title and authority: "Caliph of God" (*khalīfat Allāh*), the conduit between his subjects and cosmic power, "through whom men pray for rain"; further, verse 21, "In him the common weal resides."[25]

19. He who wades into the deep of battle,
auspicious his augury,
The Caliph of God
through whom men pray for rain.

. . . .

21. In him the common weal resides,
and after his assurance
No peril can seduce him
from his pledge.

Verses 18–21 define the credentials required for legitimate rule: victory, and its correlate, divine appointment, military courage and prowess, cosmic/intercessory powers, service to the common good, honoring one's pledge. Of course, these are also precisely the qualities that the client or subject requires from his ruler. What is crucial poetically and ritually is that this is not an expository description of legitimate rule, but rather a performative recognition and declaration of allegiance to a ruler for whom the poet claims, or confirms, these qualities.

The extended simile comparing the caliph in awe and generosity to the mighty Euphrates at flood stage at once imparts a stunning cosmic dimension, the ruler as a "force of nature," and at the same time invokes the majestic poetic authority of, for example, al-Nābigha al-Dhubyānī in his celebrated *Dāliyya* poem of apology to the Lakhmid king al-Nuʿmān ibn al-Mundhir, whose Euphrates simile serves as a recognized model for al-Akhṭal's.[26]

22. Not even the Euphrates when its tributaries
pour seething into it
And sweep the giant swallow-wort from its two banks
into the middle of its rushing stream,

[25] Here and below, see the discussion of Crone and Hinds on the Umayyads distancing their concept of the caliphate from the Prophet Muḥammad and their use of the title *khalīfat Allāh*; Crone and Hinds, *God's Caliph*, pp. 4–23.

[26] See Stetkevych, *Poetics of Islamic Legitimacy*, ch. 1, esp. pp. 24, 41–42.

23. And the summer winds churn it
 until its waves
Form agitated puddles
 on the prows of ships,

24. Racing in a vast and mighty torrent
 from the mountains of Byzance
Whose foothills shield them from it
 and divert its course,

25. Is ever more generous than he is
 to the supplicant
Or more dazzling
 to the beholder's eye.

The effect of this passage, as indeed of al-Akhṭal's Jāhilī-derived *qaṣīdat al-madḥ* as a whole, is to create, borrowing Paul Connerton's term, a "mythic concordance" between the tradition-revered poet and king of pre-Islamic Hīra and the poet and caliph of Umayyad Damascus.[27] The authority of sacred kingship immortalized in al-Nābigha's master panegyrics to al-Nuʿmān – divine appointment, Solomonic virtue and cosmic power, Euphrates-like natural force of destruction and abundance, and so on – is in general through the "performance" of the *qaṣīdat al-madḥ* as literary genre and courtly ceremony and in particular through immediately recognizable literary allusions to the Jāhilī master panegyrists transferred to the new Islamic ruler. Al-Akhṭal's verse 30, the caliph's army, "the like of which no man or jinn has ever seen," proffers a subtle but clear comparison of ʿAbd al-Malik's army with that of Solomon.[28]

The aspect of the performative *qaṣīdat al-madḥ* as a nuanced negotiation directed to (the poet's) immediate political ends comes to the fore in other parts of the poem. The poet is swearing allegiance, but at the same time negotiating the terms of the relationship. In terms of political-military history, the problem of the Banū Taghlib – especially after the defeat of the Zubayrids (actually, after their defeat at Marj Rāhiṭ in 65/684 many of the Qaysīs technically submitted to the Umayyads) – was that the former supporters of Muṣʿab ibn al-Zubayr, especially the Qaysī tribe of the Banū Sulaym, have now become fellow clients of the Banū Umayya and therefore rivals of the Banū Taghlib for favor and position in the Umayyad hierarchy, as we can gather from verses 26–34 on ʿAbd al-Malik's pacification of Iraq.

Verses 35–43 demonstrate to us another aspect of the poet's construction of legitimate authority. He brings his panegyric skills to bear specifically on the Quraysh, the tribe of the Prophet Muḥammad, as the recipients of God-given good fortune and victory and the highest exemplars of every virtue:

35. In the mighty Nabʿ-tree of Quraysh
 round which they gather,

[27] On this term, see Connerton, *How Societies Remember*, p. 43 and *passim*. I have adapted his term broadly to the study of the *qaṣīda*, especially in Stetkevych, *Poetics of Islamic Legitimacy*.

[28] On the use of the Solomonic model by the Umayyads, see Borrut, *Entre mémoire et pouvoir*, pp. 217ff.; in Jāhilī poetry, see Stetkevych, *Poetics of Islamic Legitimacy*, pp. 35–37.

No other tree can top
    its lofty crown.

36. It overtops the high hills,
    and they dwell in its roots and stem;
They are the people of generosity,
    and, when they boast, of glory,

37. Rallying behind the truth, recoiling from foul speech,
    disdainful;
If adversity befalls them,
    they bear it steadfastly.

38. If a darkening cloud casts its pall
    over the horizons,
They have a refuge from it
    and a haven.

39. God allotted to them the good fortune
    that made them victorious,
And after theirs all other lots
    are small, contemptible.

40. They do not exult in it
    since they are its masters;
Any other tribe, were this their lot,
    would be exultant, vain.

41. Ruthless toward their foe,
    till they submit;
In victory,
    the most merciful of men.

42. Those that harbor rancor toward them
    cannot endure their battle-wrath;
When their rods are tested
    no flaw is found.

43. It is they who vie with the rain-bearing wind
    to bring sustenance
When impoverished supplicants
    find scant food.

What is interesting about this passage is that its contents are entirely Jāhilī. Perhaps the closest comparison that comes to mind is Labīd's boast of the God-given virtue and superiority of his tribe in his Muʿallaqa:

83. Be then content, O enemy, with what the S/sovereign allotted you;
For virtues were allotted us by H/him who knows them.

84. When trusts were apportioned to the tribes,
The A/apportioner allotted us the greatest share.

85. He built for us a high-roofed edifice,
To which the tribesmen mount, both youths and full-grown men.

86. They are the first to act when the tribe is stricken:
In war its horsemen; in disputes, its arbiters.

87. They are a spring-time to those that seek refuge,
And to indigent women, their food stores exhausted,
while the year stretches long.[29]

But of course, in historical-political context, it is the Banū Umayya's belonging to Quraysh that is essential to their claim to the Islamic caliphate. On the one hand, this celebration of the unique God-given superiority of the Quraysh is aimed against Khārijite ideas; at the same time, by emphasizing Qurashī lineage alone over direct descent from the Prophet Muḥammad or belonging to the Saḥāba, the unique claims of the ʿAlids (in particular at this time al-Mukhtār's support of Muḥammad ibn al-Ḥanafiyya) and Zubayrids are dismissed. Although we should not forget the power and high status in pre-Islamic times of the Umayya ibn ʿAbd Shams clan of Quraysh vis-à-vis the Banū Hāshim of the Prophet or the Banū ʿAbd al-ʿUzza of the Zubayrids, it seems to me that since the ʿAlids, Zubayrids, and Umayyads are all Qurashīs, the ultimate clincher for divine appointment rests in victory, which, apparently, at the time of the composition of this *qaṣīdat al-madḥ*, ʿAbd al-Malik could claim.

The extent to which such "Jāhilī" Arab virtues as celebrated in this passage were considered constitutive of legitimate Islamic authority can be gleaned from the anecdote cited in al-Aghānī: the first ʿAbbāsid caliph al-Saffāḥ (r. 132–136/750–754) was asked, "A poet has composed some panegyric for you. Do you want to hear his poem?" He replied, "What could he possibly have to say about me after the son of the Christian woman [al-Akhṭal] said of the Banū Umayya:

[41.] Ruthless toward their foe, till they submit;
In victory, the most merciful of men."[30]

The passage that extends from verse 44 to 57 is especially pertinent to the present argument. Here the poet turns from the third to the second person to apostrophize the Banū Umayya and in doing so to simultaneously declare Taghlibī allegiance and stake the Taghlibī claim to highest status among the competing client tribes. Verse 44 is to be read as a statement of recognition and allegiance, even gratitude and submission. In verses 45–47 the poet states his personal claim: that the Banū Umayya are indebted to him for the *hijāʾ* (invective) of the Anṣār that effectively silenced their enemies.[31] In verses 48–50 he warns the Banū Umayya of the treacherous character of their erstwhile foe turned client, the Qaysī chieftain

---

[29] Translation from Stetkevych, *The Mute Immortals Speak*, p. 17.

[30] Al-Iṣbahānī, *Al-Aghānī*, vol. 8, p. 3048; Hārūn al-Rashīd is said, likewise, to have considered this the best line of panegyric composed for any Umayyad or ʿAbbāsid; see reference in Lammens, "Le chantre des Omiades," p. 166. On the issue of pre-Islamic as proto-Islamic, see Stetkevych, *The Mute Immortals Speak*, pp. 42–45; idem, *The Mantle Odes*, pp. 29–30.

[31] As Lammens has pointed out, v. 45 is a parody of the famous line by Ḥassān ibn Thābit; see Lammens, "Le chantre des Omiades," p. 235.

Zufar ibn al-Ḥārith, a supporter of Muṣʿab ibn al-Zubayr, who held out in his fortress at Qirqīsiyāʾ until in 71/690–691 he was besieged by ʿAbd al-Malik and negotiated a truce — a warning that, as it turned out, was well founded.[32] The remaining verses restate the Umayyad indebtedness to Taghlibī force of arms. Verse 51 states quite explicitly that ʿAbd al-Malik, here addressed as "Commander of the Faithful" (*amīr al-muʾminīn*), owes his victory to the Banū Taghlib. The poet rehearses the Taghlibī defeat of the Qaysī tribe Banū Sulaym, supporters of Muṣʿab ibn al-Zubayr on Yawm al-Ḥashshāk/Yawm al-Tharthār[33] of the year 70/689, a victory crowned by the Banū Taghlib's slaying of the chieftain of the Banū Sulaym, ʿUmayr ibn al-Ḥubāb, whose severed head they then presented to the caliph in al-Ghūṭa of Damascus. Verse 57 drives the poet's point home "thanks to us [the Banū Taghlib] ...." Al-Akhṭal's point is that the Banū Taghlib are the ones who subdued the tribes of Qays ʿAylān, the supporters of Muṣʿab ibn al-Zubayr, and forced them to submit to ʿAbd al-Malik, thus contributing to the Umayyad victory in the Second *Fitna*. The point is that now that Qays ʿAylān have submitted to and sworn allegiance to ʿAbd al-Malik, the caliph should remember to whom he owes his victory and not now favor the tribes of Qays ʿAylān over the Banū Taghlib. As we know from the history of the ensuing period of consolidation of Marwānid power, al-Akhṭal was quite right to be concerned — as when in the year 73 A.H. the Qaysī tribe of the Banū Sulaym, led by al-Jaḥḥāf, massacred the Banū Taghlib in the surprise attack of Yawm al-Bishr, the subject of al-Akhṭal's plea for restitution in his powerful and beautiful *Lāmiyya* that opens *ʿAfā Wāsiṭun* (*Qaṣīda II*, discussed below). This point is further brought home later in the present poem when the Qaysī support of Muṣʿab ibn al-Zubayr is referred to as "error" (v. 58) and "Satan's snares" (v. 60).

The remainder of the poem, verses 71–84, lampoons, above all, al-Akhṭal's poetic rival, Jarīr, and his tribe the Banū Yarbūʿ, a branch of Tamīm, with the goal of establishing their baseness and lack of status, that is, unworthiness to compete with al-Akhṭal and the Banū Taghlib for Umayyad favor. The combination of *madīḥ*, *fakhr* (personal and tribal boast), and *hijāʾ* (lampoon, invective, satire) within the framework of what is structurally the *madīḥ* section of this ode is subsumed under the overarching purpose of the *qaṣīdat al-madḥ*, that is, to ceremonially restructure the community after a crisis.[34] Thus, in what is essentially a victory ode, al-Akhṭal's role as panegyrist is not merely to declare, but to legitimize, the *mamdūḥ*'s victory — that is, to establish the legitimacy of ʿAbd al-Malik's rule, to discredit or dismiss other contenders and their supporters, and, above all, for the poet, to secure the best possible position for his tribe among the now enlarged company of Umayyad clients. While our current historical interest may lie more with Marwānid claims vis-à-vis their rivals to the caliphate, we must also understand that for the victorious caliph's subjects the internal politics of the empire were a matter not merely of political power and prestige, but, as the inter-tribal intrigue and bloodshed during and after the Second *Fitna* and the "pacification" of Iraq indicate, a matter of life and death (see below, *Qaṣīda II*).

In sum, in *Khaffa al-qaṭīnu* we see al-Akhṭal harnessing the authority and prestige of the Jāhilī *qaṣīdat al-madḥ* to construct Umayyad Islamic authority through the subtle extension of pre-Islamic virtues and concepts of legitimate and divinely appointed rule into what has become an Islamic environment. By invoking the Banū Umayya as Quraysh, al-Akhṭal confers

---

[32] See Lammens, "Le chantre des Omiades," pp. 384–98.

[33] See Qabāwa, *Shiʿr al-Akhṭal*, vol. 1, pp. 72–77.

[34] On this process, see Stetkevych, *Poetics of Islamic Legitimacy*, pp. 105–09.

Islamic legitimacy without even mentioning Islam per se. More significantly, he omits all mention of other (competing) clans of Quraysh whose historic Islamic credentials are stronger than those of the Banū Umayya and whose lineage is closer to the Prophet — the Banū Hāshim of the Prophet and hence the ʿAlids, and the Zubayrids of Banū ʿAbd al-ʿUzzā (ʿAbd Allāh ibn al-Zubayr's mother was Asmāʾ, the daughter of Abū Bakr and sister of the Prophet's wife ʿĀʾisha). In other words, rhetorically at least, al-Akhṭal limits, or narrows, Quraysh to the Banū Umayya. He compounds his declaration of legitimate rule through conferring what are by this time the recognized titles for the leader of the Islamic state: "Caliph of God" (v. 19) and "Commander of the Faithful" (v. 28) and through attributing ʿAbd al-Malik's victory (over, at least, Muṣʿab ibn al-Zubayr), and later "Qurashī" victory more broadly, to God (vv. 18, 39). Further, the poet, in negotiating the position of himself and the Banū Taghlib, offers recognition of and allegiance to the Banū Umayya, with the express demand that they, too, recognize the loyal service that al-Akhṭal and his tribe have performed and the unrivalled status they should be accorded in the hierarchy of Umayyad clients. We should note, too, that the poet subtly manipulates the identities of proper names and Islamic titles. ʿAbd al-Malik, the *mamdūḥ* of the ode, is never mentioned by name, but in the third then second person. Rather, he is defined or identified by associations and titles: "whom God has made victorious," "Quraysh," "God made them victorious," "Banū Umayya," "Caliph of God," "Commander of the Faithful," with the effect that all of these become identified with one another and with legitimate authority.

Finally, in this regard, we should note what the poet has left unsaid: in composing his verbal monument to Umayyad legitimacy, he has given no hint in the poetic text of rival claimants or claims to the caliphate, nor of any disruption of Qurashī-Umayyad rule, that is, the transfer of power from the Sufyānids to the Marwānids. Above all, our point in investigating al-Akhṭal's panegyrics to ʿAbd al-Malik ibn Marwān should not be merely to single out particular "Islamic" proper names and titles, "Quraysh," "Caliph of God," and so on, but rather to understand that, as with the appropriation of symbols of legitimacy and authority witnessed in the minting of coins and construction of the Dome of the Rock, al-Akhṭal has appropriated the Jāhilī courtly *qaṣīdat al-madḥ* as a verbal ceremonial and ritual performance of legitimate, God-given authority to construct and confer legitimate Islamic authority upon ʿAbd al-Malik and the Banū Umayya.

Qaṣīda II: al-Akhṭal's *ʿAfā Wāsiṭun*

We should turn briefly to what I consider al-Akhṭal's most beautiful and powerful poem, his *Lāmiyya* that opens *ʿAfā Wāsiṭun*[35] (Wāsiṭ lies deserted). I take it from the fact that it is the first poem in both versions of al-Sukkarī's recension of the *dīwān* of al-Akhṭal that my high estimation of the poem is hardly original. Composed in the aftermath of the slaughter by al-Jaḥḥāf (the chieftain of the Qaysī Banū Sulaym) of the Banū Taghlib at Yawm Bishr[36] in the year 73/692–693, the poem challenges rather than confirms Marwānid authority and legitimacy,

[35] For a full translation and discussion, along somewhat different lines from the present argument, and further primary and secondary sources, see Stetkevych, *Poetics of Islamic Legitimacy*, pp. 110–43. I have followed the edition, commentary, and notes of Qabāwa, *Shiʿr al-Akhṭal*, vol. 1, pp. 13–38, and consulted Ṣāliḥānī, *Shiʿr al-Akhṭal*, pp. 1–11; al-Ḥāwī, *Sharḥ Dīwān al-Akhṭal*, pp. 259–73.

[36] Qabāwa, *Shiʿr al-Akhṭal*, vol. 1, pp. 35–38; al-Iṣbahānī, *Al-Aghānī*, vol. 12, pp. 4364–69.

rebukes the caliph for failure to fulfill his sacred obligation to defend loyal clients under his protection, and threatens to withdraw Taghlibī allegiance. In contrast to the golden cross and silk robes in which, literary tradition tells us, al-Akhṭal routinely appeared before ʿAbd al-Malik, we are told he presented this *qaṣīda* clad in rags, still covered in dirt and blood.[37] Not simply a dramatic detail, this should draw our attention to a crucial component of Jāhilī-based Arab virtue: that the strong and noble are measured by how they treat their clients and those under their protection (refugees etc.). For al-Akhṭal to come to court in silks and a solid gold cross was an indication of the level of protection and dignity the Umayyads conferred upon their (even Christian, infidel) clients. To have one's client in rags is a disgrace — not to the client, but to the liege-lord who is honor bound to protect him. Further, the panegyric is addressed not to the caliph himself, but to an Umayyad prince, Khālid ibn ʿAbd Allāh ibn Khālid ibn Asīd, presumably with the idea that he will intercede with the caliph to obtain the bloodwite, status, and protection that are the due of loyal clients. At the same time, I think we are given to understand not merely that al-Akhṭal has lost status at the caliphal court, but that the caliph on his part has proven himself unworthy of the highest praise, which is now conferred on the famously munificent Khālid. In this respect, I take verse 50 to mean that the Banū Umayya in general and the Marwānids in particular are at Khālid's disposal and will not refuse his request. This should be understood as a rebuke (in Arabic poetic parlance, *ʿitāb*) and a challenge to ʿAbd al-Malik.

I will confine myself here to those aspects most pertinent to the present argument. The first is the extremely extended *raḥīl*, desert journey, section, which is to be understood as an expression of the poet's supplicatory stance and ends in the arrival of the poet's camel caravan at Khālid the "bestower of grace" (v. 42), "in whom to place one's hopes" (v. 43). Second, in terms of the poetic symbolic idiom of legitimate rule and God-given prosperity (i.e., the proof of divine appointment), the poet invokes a long and particularly beautiful image of pastoral prosperity that is rhetorically structured in the form of a benediction or blessing. Exactly as when you give change to a beggar, he says, "God bless you," the supplicant-poet calls down a blessing upon the one he supplicates — the idea being that it will be fulfilled when and if the *mamdūḥ* awards the poet or fulfills his request. The sense of the verb in the perfect form seems to shift in this passage from *duʿāʾ* (optative) to the *māḍī* (past tense) — as though the poet is calling for a continuation of a bounty and blessing that already exists, and therefore testifies to Khālid's (and by extensions the Marwānid-Umayyad) legitimate rule. My point is that God-given legitimacy and authority are not represented merely by titles such as "Caliph of God" or "Commander of the Faithful" but can also be evoked even more effectively in the poetic tradition through the sublime lyricism of this storm passage:

52. May God water a land
    the best of whose people is Khālid,
With a cloud whose spouts disgorge
    abundant rain.

53. When the east wind
    cuts through its crotches,

[37] Lammens, "Le chantre des Omiades," p. 392; al-Iṣbahānī, *Al-Aghānī*, vol. 12, p. 4376.

Its water-laden lower parts
flow like milk.

54. When the wind shakes it,
it drags its trains,
Like the ponderous gait of newly-calved she-camels
tending their young.

55. Pouring incessantly, the lightning-bolts on its sides
like lamps aglow in the darkness
Or the flanks of piebald steeds
in panic bolting.

56. Then, when it turned and headed
toward al-Yamāma,
The south wind called out to it,
and it turned back, sluggishly.

57. It watered Laʿlaʿ and al-Qurnatayn
and barely bore
Its heavy loads away
from Laʿlaʿ.

58. It left al-Ḥazn's hilltops
floating above the floodwater
Like a cluster of slender steeds
kept tethered by the tents.

59. Incessantly raining it headed east
to al-Dahnā
Like a camel laden with textiles,
decked with bells, heavily burdened.

60. At al-Maʿrasāniyyāt it alighted
and from it in Grouse Meadow
The she-camels, full-uddered, newly calved,
Yearn gently over their young.

The third point reverts once more to the matter of titles, as witnessed in the verses in which al-Akhṭal issues his challenge to Umayyad authority and threatens to withdraw Taghlibī allegiance:

61. At al-Bishr, al-Jaḥḥāf
launched an attack
From which complaints and cries for help
rose to Allāh!

62. So ask the Banū Marwān:
Why is a bond of protection
And a weak rope
still connected

63. To the leap of a thief [al-Jaḥḥāf]
after Muṣʿab passed by Ashʿath,
[And was then left dead], neither deloused,
nor washed.

64. Was it al-Jaḥḥāf who brought you [Muṣʿab's head]
so that you ordered him
Against those under your protection,
that they be massacred in the midst of their abodes?

65. Trusting in a bond of clientage/pact of protection so sure
that if you invoked it to call the mountain goats
Down from the steep peaks
they would descend.

66. If Quraysh by their sovereign authority
do not change this,
There will be withdrawal and departure
from Quraysh.

After citing the outrage of al-Jaḥḥāf, the former supporter of Muṣʿab ibn al-Zubayr now slaughtering long-term loyal Umayyad clients, the poet declares, "So ask [sing.] the Banū Marwān" about this (v. 62). It seems to me that the imperative singular and following interrogative here has a double sense: one an impersonal rhetorical expression of outrage addressed to any and all hearers of the poem, but also much more explicitly, the poet's demand to Khālid that he seek from his Marwānid kinsmen justice for their loyal clients, "trusting in an inviolable covenant." What strikes me in the ensuing passage of challenge, indeed threat, of withdrawal of allegiance from the Marwānids is that none of what we could probably term the "titles of legitimate Islamic rule" of this period are invoked: no "Caliph of God," no "Commander of the Faithful"; only the might or dominion (*mulk*) of Quraysh. It seems as if the cries that rose to God of verse 61 have not been answered by the Banū Marwān and, until they do, not only is the poet threatening to withdraw Taghlibī allegiance (v. 66), but also, rather than conferring legitimate Islamic authority as he did in the previous and coming *qaṣīdat al-madḥ*, the poet demonstrates here his power to withhold and withdraw it.

Qaṣīda III: al-Akhṭal's *Bāʾiyya: La-ʿamrī la-qad asraytu*[38]

1. By my life, I have journeyed by night — no night for a weakling —
On a she-camel with sunken eyes and hollow flanks,

[38] I have followed the recension of Qabāwa. In my interpretation and identification of proper names I have consulted the commentaries and editors' notes of the following editions of al-Akhṭal's *dīwān*: Qabāwa, *Shi'r al-Akhṭal*, vol. 1, pp. 39–53; Ṣāliḥānī, *Shi'r al-Akhṭal*, pp. 17–26; and al-Ḥāwī, *Sharḥ Dīwān al-Akhṭal*, pp. 180–92. Ṣāliḥānī's v. 47 follows Qabāwa's v. 31; Qabāwa notes additional *Naqāʾiḍ* verse after v. 35; see additional verse after v. 46 in Qabāwa's notes; in Ṣāliḥānī v. 46 comes after Qabāwa's v. 51. There are occasional variants in words and especially in vocalization. In my translation, for readability, I have not used brackets for interpolations, except in cases where the identity of proper names or antecedents of pronouns is open to question.

2. Built like a camel-stallion, the other white-hued camels cannot keep up with
her swift pace,
When, like bent pulley-rods, they list under their riders' weight.

3. Racing the hollow-eyed gaunt camels, she urgently sought the bounty
Of a pasture that is neither too sparse nor too coarse.

4. As if the camels' shaking *mays*-wood saddles were mounted
On drought-stricken sand-grouse of ʿĀlij,

5. Sand-grouse emaciated by the blazing noontime heat of mirage-pale days,
Hastening to drink at the spring of ʿUbāgh,

6. When they bear in their gullets water from the sand-mounds
To the hidden nest where their downy chicks,

7. All alike, like sets of twins, in a stifling land, seek shelter
In the dried *khidrāf* plants and desiccated thorns of *ʿirb*.

8. When the camel-driver urges on his beasts,
You see how long they are from lips to base of tail.

9. How many a desert like a sea did these camels cross,
how many a night did they plunge into
To reach you, O Commander of the Faithful,
how many a barren waste?

10. Listing from exhaustion they shun mankind,
As if they saw in them a band of blond Slavs,[39]

11. Avoiding the plain of al-Ṣaḥṣaḥān where the Bedouin tents
Of the Banū Numayr and the Banū Kalb had appeared,

12. They headed right from the highland of al-ʿUqāb, and then light-hued camels
Bore us left from ʿAdhrāʾ, the abode of the Banū al-Shajb,

13. Hastening with long strides to keep us far from everything,
As if we were mute, unable to bid "Peace!" or introduce ourselves.

14. When al-ʿAyyūq rose in the night-time sky and the Pleiades plunged their
necks
Between Arcturus and Spica Virginis and the heart of Leo,

15. To you, O Commander of the Faithful, I rode my she-camel,
With an auspicious augury,
with a spacious and welcoming place to alight.

---

[39] This verse is cited as the earliest Arab written reference to the Slavs (*al-Ṣaqāliba*). According to Byzantine sources, in A.S. 6156/664–665 some 5,000 Slavs defected to the Umayyads and settled near Apamea, and during ʿAbd al-Malik's reign, A.S. 6184/692–693, the commander of Slavic recruits was bribed by the Arabs and came over to the Arab side with 20,000 of them. See *EI*[2] s.v. "al-Ṣaḳāliba" (P. B. Golden, C. E. Bosworth, and P. Guichard).

16. To a believer whose radiant countenance dispels
The clouds of cares and grief,

17. Where men in need kneel down their camels, seeking the bountiful rain
Of a noble man's gift of prisoners and spoils.

18. You see the pure iron rings of an ample coat of mail that flows
Over a man who scoffs at calamities and war,

19. War's brother, when it raises its tail, biting,
like a she-camel resisting a stallion,
He mounts her in any case, easy or hard,

20. An Imam who leads forth the cavalry until the ropes tremble
On the necks of travel-wearied steeds with jutting hipbones.

21. Fixing their gaze, each one a blood-steed, kept tethered by the tent,
Readied for battle or else led beside the riding-camels.

22. Though lean, they have grown used to every splendid thing:
Egyptian robes for horse-cloths and sweet perfumed spoils.

23. Refractory, they turn off from the hard rough road because of their sore
hooves;
Despite their injuries they amble, bent to one side,
like men whose shoulders ache.

24. If they are forced to go far, there is always a crow
Over a limping one or a [new-born/aborted] foal.

25. Every year you conduct against the Byzantines a campaign
Far-reaching in its hoof-prints and in its road.

26. At the border pass the battle-mares cast forth fetuses like new-born lambs,
As if the placentas were red-dyed robes ripped open.

27. Daughters of the stud-stallion Ghurāb, they did not reach full term,
But aborted from the constant jostling of being pulled through distant wastes.

28. They have two sorts of days: a day of rest and a day when they complain
Of stones caught in their hooves from the perilous border-pass.

29. [ʿAbd al-Malik] plunges through dark starless nights, whose dawns break
to reveal a wrathful man,
Relentless in pursuit of his enemies, never flagging, never cowardly.

30. [Marwān] Ibn Abī al-ʿĀṣī's lineage is on all sides from Quraysh,
He is of their core, not of their lowly hangers-on.

31. God placed the caliphate among you [pl.], bestowing it upon
A noble man, whose food tray is never bare nor barren.

32. You are aggrieved at us, Qays ʿAylān, all of you,
But what enemy of ours have we not left aggrieved?

33. Surely those tribes knew that we are energetic, decisive,
The ones who cut the stake-rope and let loose discord.

34. Then if the war of the two sons of Nizār (Muḍar and Rabīʿa) has died down,
It is only after we have been found guiltless for punishing
the Banū Kilāb and Banū Kaʿb.

35. And the Wild Asses (al-Ḥuqb), the riff-raff of Qays,
We left their corpses stacked like firewood at the bend of Wadī al-Tharthār.

36. [Just as, of old, the Banū Taghlib] made Jazʾ ibn Ẓālim taste death
With a sharp blade that penetrated between his ribs and guts.

37. The Banū al-Ṣamʿāʾ,[40] their swords notched in defeat, sought refuge
With every woman whose arms and heels were stained with grease and dirt.

38. Because of your error, [O Banū al-Ṣamʿāʾ], the two days of Marj Rāhiṭ brought
The annihilation of the [Qaysī] tribes, a grievous affair.

39. Through the two sons of Muḥārib and the horsemen of the Banū al-ʿAjlān —
How [ill] they sufficed you as riders! —
You vied [in vain] for glory with the People of Truth,

40. The camel stallions of Abū al-ʿĀṣī, who, on the morning Damascus was in
uproar,
Were [so black with weapons that they looked] like scabby camels daubed with
tar,

41. Leading forth a vast wave of the Banū Umayya that had not tarried
In the abodes of Sulaym in al-Hijāz nor in al-Haḍb.

42. Kings, rulers, men of valor! If anyone tries to make trouble for them,
They know how to make worse trouble!

43. You [pl.] appeared like the new moon, entering the sacred month
[al-Muḥarram][41]
And became rulers of a dominion, neither new-gained nor usurped.

44. While the horses of the foe charged again,
The spear-tips, flashing like meteors in the hands of the death-seeking
warriors, repelled them.

45. My eye has never seen a dominion like the one that brought you
Neither spear-thrust nor sword-blow,

46. [But brought you instead] the black-assed horsemen of [the wounded] Muslim
[ibn ʿAmr al-Bāhilī], [surrendering]
On the morning when he, still alive but in agony, tried to ward off death.

---

[40] Al-Ṣamʿāʾ is the black [slave] mother or grandmother of ʿUmayr ibn al-Ḥubāb.

[41] The Marwānid victory at Marj Rāhiṭ was on 1 Muḥarram 65.

47. But Allah considered you [sing.] the place to put His truth,
Despite enemies and mendacious deniers.

48. May Allah bring shame upon a band of [Jarīr's clan] the Banū Kulayb,
Who are like kids of al-Ḥijāz seeking the shelter of their reed goat-pens.

49. Remote in their pasture-lands, the place they alight is not wide;
They cannot even protect or defend their own herds.

50. O Banū Kalb [Sons of a Dog, = Kulayb?], were it not that [Farazdaq's tribe] the Sons of Dārim protect you
In times of calamity and war,

51. You would have to protect yourselves from the Banū Mālik by paying tribute,
For thus, despite himself, the vile man pays.

52. Surely she who, moaning in pain, gave birth to Jarīr,
Had adulterous eyes and a wanton heart.

53. Guests do not enjoy alighting at her [tent]
When the acacia tops are white [with snow] like ash-colored brood-mares,

54. Jarīr's kinsmen say, "Defend us from behind, O Jarīr!"
But Jarīr is not one to defend or stand fast.

To get some idea of how minutely nuanced the *qaṣīdat al-madḥ* is to its contemporary circumstances and how subtly the grounds of legitimacy can shift, we turn now to a slightly later panegyric of al-Akhṭal to ʿAbd al-Malik. The *Bāʾiyya* that opens *La-ʿamrī la-qad ʾasraytu* (By my life, I have journeyed by night) should be dated to several years later than *Qaṣīda I: Khaffa al-qaṭīnu* (probably from 72 or 73/691 or 692–693) and *Qaṣīda II: ʿAfā Wāsiṭun* (73/692–693) and reflects the poetic and political circumstances particular to that period in both its structure and themes. As its opening description of the poet's journey to the caliphal court indicates, it is from the somewhat later period in al-Akhṭal's career, after the end of the Second *Fitna* and the pacification of Iraq, when al-Akhṭal lived most of the year with the Banū Taghlib in their tribal lands in al-Jazīra (northern Mesopotamia) and came to ʿAbd al-Malik's court at Damascus only at specified times to deliver his panegyrics.[42] These poems can be understood as a form of tribute and declaration or reaffirmation of allegiance on the part of the poet and his tribe to their liege-lord, the Umayyad caliph. Further, although during the period of the Second *Fitna* ʿAbd al-Malik had paid tribute to the Byzantines rather than try to fight on two fronts, with his victory over the Zubayrids, he resumed annual campaigns against the Byzantines, 73/692. The poet's reference in verse 25 to ʿAbd al-Malik's annual Byzantine campaigns suggests a date for the poem several years after the resumption of Umayyad-Byzantine hostilities.

The poem does not feature the traditional opening elegiac prelude (*nasīb*) of abandoned campsite and lost beloved, but opens rather with what is normally the central journey section (*raḥīl*) (vv. 1–15), here construed as the poet's night journey by she-camel through the badlands and deserts that separate the tribal lands of the Banū Taghlib in al-Jazīra from the

[42] Lammens, "Le chantre des Omiades," pp. 405–06.

Umayyad court at Damascus. His she-camel outpaces and races the other emaciated camels, which are then compared to desert sand-grouse desperately racing through the noonday heat carrying water in their gullets from the spring of ʿUbāgh for their thirsting chicks (vv. 1–7). Of particular note is the clearly metaphorical intent of verse 3, in which the urgent search for rich pasture is clearly a metaphor for the poet's, and other supplicants', seeking caliphal bounty. In this respect, too, the emaciated she-camels that the poet's mount outstrips refer to the poet's political and poetic rivals — a topic that al-Akhṭal treats explicitly in the final section of the poem, verses 48–54, an invective (*hijāʾ*) against his poetic rival, Jarīr (see below) — and their competing poems. The metaphor of verse 3 is explicated, as it were, in verse 9.

Especially distinctive of this *raḥīl*, too, is the description of the hostile tribal lands through which the camel caravan and the poet on his she-camel make their way, avoiding contact. As if to build suspense, the poet addresses ʿAbd al-Malik as "Commander of the Faithful" (*amīr al-muʾminīn*) in verse 9 as the goal of the journey, but it is not until verse 15, where he is again addressed with this caliphal title, that the poet and his she-camel arrive. The proper names of places[43] and tribes in verses 11–12 serve as witnesses that trace the poet's treacherous journey, thereby vouching for his dedication and determination and serving to authenticate the poem as message and the poet as its messenger.

The arrival, which serves as the transition (*takhalluṣ*) from the *raḥīl* section to the *madīḥ* (praise), spans verses 15–17. Of particular interest is verse 17: as in *Qaṣīda I: Khaffa al-qaṭīnu*, al-Akhṭal does not directly present himself as a first-person supplicant, but rather, the caliph's court is "Where men in need kneel down their camels." More interesting still, the "rain of bounty" sought in this poem is specified as a figurative expression for "gifts of prisoners and spoils." As Muslims, even if enemies, could not be described in such terms, this can only refer to Byzantine prisoners and spoils.

It is not surprising then that the *madīḥ* section proceeds in verses 17–29 to present ʿAbd al-Malik as a warrior leading the battle-steeds on military campaigns, which, as verse 25 indicates, are annual campaigns against the Byzantines (this also points to a date for the poem several years beyond the resumption of Byzantine-Umayyad hostilities in 73/692). The presentation of ʿAbd al-Malik as a robust and tireless warrior together with the references to prisoners and rich spoils may be understood to counter the humiliation of having had to pay tribute to the Byzantines during the Second *Fitna*.[44] The power and beauty of this passage derive from the metonymic description of the battle-steeds for the caliph and his army, and even then, not on their performance in battle, but rather the hardships of the journey through the border lands, the stones injuring their hooves and constant jolting and exhaustion causing the mares among them to abort their fetuses.[45] As we noted in some of the most poetically striking of the passages in the two other odes by al-Akhṭal in this study — the wine scenes in both, the Euphrates simile and description of (tribal) virtues in *Qaṣīda I: Khaffa al-qaṭīnu*, the storm scene in *Qaṣīda II: ʿAfā Wāsiṭun* — in this poem, too, the dramatic description of the suffering and determination of ʿAbd al-Malik's battle-mares evokes a Jāhilī

---

[43] For which see editor's notes, Ṣāliḥānī, *Shiʿr al-Akhṭal*, pp. 18–19.

[44] The ignominy of ʿAbd al-Malik's Byzantine truce and tribute payments is emphasized by Robinson, *ʿAbd al-Malik*, pp. 28–29, 41.

[45] It is of note that this description of battle-steeds on a distant military campaign resembles the camel-journey sections of others of al-Akhṭal's poems, such as *ʿAfā Wāsiṭun*, above. See vv. 25–41, translation, Stetkevych, *Poetics of Islamic Legitimacy*, pp. 123–25.

poetic precedent, for example, the description of Harim ibn Sinān's battle-mares in Zuhayr ibn Abī Sulmā's celebrated *Qāfiyya*:[46]

37. The leader of horses whose hoofs have broken edges,
That are bridled with leather straps or strips of flax.

38. They leave on raids fat and return emaciated, their young aborted,
When before, full bodied and big-bellied, they were led beside the camels,

39. So that he brings them back matted and ungroomed,
Suffering from pain in their hoofs, sciatic nerves and peritoneum.

It is interesting for us, too, in our examination of the consolidation of Marwānid power that, in contrast to *Qaṣīda I: Khaffa al-qaṭīnu*, here in verse 30 al-Akhṭal specifically invokes the Marwānids' pure Qurashī lineage, through Marwān's father al-Ḥakam Ibn Abī al-ʿĀṣī, as the "core" or "spine" of Quraysh, not lowly hangers-on. With this, he seems to be dismissing, on the one hand, the Zubayrids, scions of a lesser branch, the ʿAbd al-ʿUzza, as opposed to the Umayyad clan of the powerful ʿAbd Shams, but apparently also the Sufyānid branch of the Umayyads. The declaration in verse 31 that "God placed the caliphate in you" (pl.) must then be understood as a specific reference to the Banū Marwān — an element quite consciously absent from the two earlier poems discussed above.

What me might term the First Movement of the *madīḥ* section, verses 15–31, thus constructs specifically Marwānid Umayyad authority on the basis of (victorious, or at least persistent) military campaigns against the Byzantines by a Qurashī of the Umayyad line of Ibn Abī al-ʿĀṣī (i.e., ʿAbd al-Malik ibn Marwān ibn al-Ḥakam ibn Abī al-ʿĀṣī ibn Umayya ibn ʿAbd Shams),[47] in whom God has bestowed the caliphate upon a man of noble character whose prosperity and generosity guarantee the common weal (v. 31).

The passage from verses 32–47 is especially pertinent to the present argument. It features a brilliantly forged combination of Taghlibī tribal *fakhr* and Marwānid *madīḥ* that reprises the Marwānid rise to power in a manner that legitimizes, this time, specifically Marwānid rule, reiterates the now historical Taghlibī loyalty and support, while at the same time reminding ʿAbd al-Malik of the historic hostility of the now trucially allied tribes of Qays ʿAylān. Obviously, the poet's concern is not so much for history as for contemporary politics: to pay homage to his liege-lord in a manner that strengthens the Marwānid-Taghlibī alliance at the expense of their traditional foes and competitors for Marwānid favor, the Qaysīs.

Al-Akhṭal begins by taunting the Qaysīs and rejecting their grievances against the Taghlibīs — what we can assume are contemporary grievances that the Qaysīs have brought before the caliph. The poet first claims that, now that hostilities have died down, the Banū Taghlib have been found guiltless in their actions against the Qaysī tribes of Kilāb and Kaʿb, but he then shifts directly back to the Taghlibī slaughter of Qaysīs on the bank of the Wadī al-Tharthār, that is, Yawm al-Ḥashshāk, in the year 70/689, when they slew ʿUmayr Ibn al-Ḥubāb of the Banū Sulaym, a supporter of Muṣʿab ibn al-Zubayr, and sent his severed head to ʿAbd al-Malik. He then uses a reference to the pre-Islamic glory of the Banū Taghlib (v. 36) as a frame for lampooning the lowly black (= slave) mother or grandmother of Ibn al-Ḥubāb

[46] Thaʿlab, *Sharḥ Dīwān Zuhayr ibn Abī Sulmā*, pp. 33–55. For English translation, see Stetkevych, *The Mantle Odes*, p. 26.

[47] See the genealogy in *EI*², s.v. "Umayya b. ʿAbd Shams" (G. Levi Della Vida [and C. E. Bosworth]).

(v. 37). In verses 38–41 he moves further back, to the battle of Marj Rāhiṭ (65/684). This is especially politically important for al-Akhṭal because that battle staked the tribes of Qays ʿAylān who backed ʿAbd Allāh ibn al-Zubayr against the Kalbī/Yamanī tribes — and with them the Banū Taghlib — who backed Marwān ibn al-Ḥakam. The latter are presumably the referent of the "People of Truth" (*ahl al-ḥaqq*) of verse 39, but, more importantly for us, as the "camel stallions of the Abū al-ʿĀṣī" and the [Banū] Umayya in verses 40–41. In terms of the construction of legitimacy, the effect of these three verses is to once more identify the true caliphate specifically with the Marwānid branch of the Banū Umayya. Also of note is the parallelism or analogy established between Taghlibī and Umayyad victories over the tribes of Qays ʿAylān. It is also crucial to the construction of legitimate authority that al-Akhṭal does not merely celebrate military prowess and victory — especially at Marj Rāhiṭ, the military victory that marks the Marwānid "Restoration" of the Umayyad caliphate and marks them as "Kings, rulers, men of valor" (v. 42) — but the poet constantly balances temporal military victory with timeless divine appointment or right. Thus, verse 43 depicts, through the verb *ahallū* (cf. *hilāl* "new moon"), the Marwānid Restoration as the appearance of the new moon marking the beginning of the sacred month (Muḥarram, a reference to the battle of Marj Rāhit). This simile combines the sacred and the cosmic to describe Marwānid accession to (or usurpation of) power as a "restoration" or reappearance, like the appearance of the new moon. Al-Akhṭal clinches the claim to long-established divinely appointed legitimacy, as opposed to mere military power grab, in closing the verse by declaring Marwānid-Umayyad "dominion, neither new-gained nor usurped."

How important it was to the construction of legitimate authority that it be cast in terms of God-given right is reflected in the critical estimation, as recounted in *Al-Aghānī*, of both al-Akhṭal and ʿAbd al-Malik, of precisely this verse:

> Someone recited to ʿAbd al-Malik a poem by Kuthayyir in which was the verse:
>
> They did not abandon it forced out because of love,
> But rather he requested it with the edge of the Mashrafī blade.
>
> He was pleased with it, but then al-Akhṭal said to him, "O Commander of the Faithful, what I said to you was better." "What was that?" he replied." "I said," said the poet:
>
> "You entered the month of Muḥarram like the new moon and became
> Masters of a dominion neither new-gained nor usurped.
>
> I made it yours by right, while he had you take it by force." "You're right," said the caliph.[48]

Verses 45–46 refer to the surrender to ʿAbd al-Malik of the warriors of the wounded Muslim ibn ʿAmr al-Bāhilī, a supporter of Muṣʿab ibn al-Zubayr, who was brought before ʿAbd al-Malik and died in his presence. The idea seems to be that they surrendered rather than fighting on, so that ʿAbd al-Malik achieved victory even without force of arms, or perhaps rather that ʿAbd al-Malik emerged completely unscathed while his wounded enemy died defeated in captivity and his followers, rather than fighting heroically to the death, surrendered. The passage closes with a verse (47) that singles out the *mamdūḥ*, ʿAbd al-Malik, as God's choice as the Repository of divine Truth/Right, and we can see that, in the logic of

---

[48] Al-Iṣbahānī, *Al-Aghānī*, v. 8, p. 3034.

the verse, the "enemies and mendacious deniers" of the second hemistich deny not merely ʿAbd al-Malik, but God's Truth, that is, ʿAbd al-Malik's divine right to dominion.

The final verses of the poem, as we saw in *Qaṣīda I: Khaffa al-qaṭīnu*, consist of *hijāʾ* directed against al-Akhṭal's rival and potential competitor as ʿAbd al-Malik's favorite, Jarīr, who was otherwise the poet of ʿAbd al-Malik's (in)famous governor of Iraq, al-Ḥajjāj ibn Yūsuf. The performative purpose of this closing section of invective is to promote the view that Jarīr is so morally base, both personally and in his family and tribe, that it would be beneath the caliph's dignity to have him at the caliphal court.

What is striking about this poem in the context of the present argument is al-Akhṭal's promotion of a specifically Marwānid claim to caliphal authority, one that is conspicuously absent from the general Umayyad claims he put forth in *Qaṣīda I: Khaffa al-qaṭīnu*, only a few years earlier. Also noteworthy is the way in which the poet is able to virtually identify the Qays ʿAylān as the implacable common enemy of both the Banū Umayya and the Banū Taghlib in a way that binds the latter two together at the expense of the rival Umayyad client. Most essential for the present argument are the means by which al-Akhṭal has constructed or reconstructed the Marwānid rise to power in such a way as to define and refine their exclusive right to the caliphate and which, in ways well understood and appreciated by the Arab-Islamic poetic tradition, define legitimate Islamic authority as deriving not from brute force but from divine appointment.

I hope that this discussion of three major *qaṣīdas* by al-Akhṭal to ʿAbd al-Malik ibn Marwān has amply demonstrated the role of Arabic poetry, and the *qaṣīdat al-madḥ* in particular, in conferring and confirming — but also, when necessary, challenging — Islamic, and particularly Marwānid/Umayyad, legitimacy and thereby articulating an ideology of legitimacy specific to Islamic caliphal rule. Furthermore, we can begin to understand how the *qaṣīda* is used not merely to invoke the time-honored values and traditions that are encoded in it, but also as a refined and subtle tool of negotiation and renegotiation of rank and status for both the poet and the patron in the light of unfolding political and military events. Thus we see even in just the three poems selected for discussion in the present study, the trajectory of al-Akhṭal's *qaṣīdas* in tandem with the consolidation of Marwānid power. Above all, just as ʿAbd al-Malik's construction of the Dome of the Rock in Jerusalem co-opted and redirected for the Arab and Islamic Umayyad dynasty ancient Near Eastern, Jewish, and Christian sites and symbols of cosmic, religious, moral, and political authority, so too did his patronage of the *qaṣīdat al-madḥ*, especially as composed by al-Akhṭal, serve to co-opt and redirect toward the Banū Umayya, and then more specifically the Marwānid branch, the legitimizing force of the autochthonous Arab poetic tradition.

Bibliography

al-Akhṭal. *Dīwān.*

- al-Ḥāwī, Īliyyā Salīm, editor. *Sharḥ Dīwān al-Akhṭal al-Taghlibī.* Beirut: Dār al-Thaqāfa, [1968?].
- Qabāwa, Fakhr al-Dīn, editor. *Shiʿr al-Akhṭal Abī Ghiyāth ibn Ghawth al-Taghlibī.* Recension of al-Sukkarī. 2 vols. 2nd edition. Beirut: Dār al-Āfāq al-Jadīda, 1399/1979.
- Ṣāliḥānī, Anṭūn [= A. Salhani], *Shiʿr al-Akhṭal.* Recension of Abū Saʿīd al-Sukkarī. 2nd edition. Beirut: Dār al-Mashriq (al-Maṭbaʿa al-Kāthūlīkiyya), 1969 [reprint of 1891 edition].

Austin, J. L. *How To Do Things with Words.* New York: Oxford University Press, 1965.

Bacharach, Jere L. "Signs of Sovereignty: The Shahāda, Qurʾānic Verses, and the Coinage of ʿAbd al-Malik." *Muqarnas* 27 (2010): 1–30.

Bauman, Richard. *Verbal Art as Performance.* Prospect Heights: Waveland Press, 1984.

Borrut, Antoine. *Entre mémoire et pouvoir: l'espace syrien sous les derniers Omeyyades et les premiers Abbassides (v. 72–193/692–809).* Leiden: Brill, 2011.

Connerton, Paul. *How Societies Remember.* Cambridge: Cambridge University Press, 1989.

Crone, Patricia, and Martin Hinds. *God's Caliph: Religious Authority in the First Centuries of Islam.* University of Cambridge Oriental Publications 37. Cambridge: Cambridge University Press, 1986.

Donner, Fred M. *Muhammad and the Believers: At the Origins of Islam.* Cambridge: Harvard University Press, 2010.

Ḍayf, Shawqī. *Al-Taṭawwur wa-al-Tajdīd fī al-Shiʿr al-Umawi.* 2nd edition. Cairo: Dār al-Maʿārif, 1959.

Elad, Amikam. "Why Did ʿAbd al-Malik Build the Dome of the Rock? A Re-examination of the Muslim Sources." In *Bayt al-Maqdis I: ʿAbd al-Malik's Jerusalem*, edited by Julian Raby and Jeremy Johns, pp. 33–58. Oxford Studies in Islamic Art 9. Oxford: Oxford University Press, 1992.

———. "ʿAbd al-Malik and the Dome of the Rock: A Further Examination of the Muslim Sources." *Jerusalem Studies in Arabic and Islam* 35 (2008): 167–226.

Grabar, Oleg. *The Shape of the Holy: Early Islamic Jerusalem.* Princeton: Princeton University Press, 1996.

Grabar, Oleg, and Benjamin Z. Ḳedar, editors. *Where Heaven and Earth Meet: Jerusalem's Sacred Esplanade.* Jerusalem: Yad Ben-Zvi Press; Austin: University of Texas Press, 2009.

Humphreys, R. Stephen. *Muʿawiya ibn Abi Sufyan: From Arabia to Empire.* Makers of the Muslim World. Oxford: Oneworld, 2006.

al-Iṣbahānī, Abū al-Faraj. *Al-Aghānī.* Edited by Ibrāhīm al-Abyārī. 32 vols. Cairo: Dār al-Shaʿb, 1969–1979.

Jamil, Nadia. "Caliph and Quṭb. Poetry as a Source for Interpreting the Transformation of the Byzantine Cross on Steps in Umayyad Coinage." In *Bayt al-Maqdis II: Jerusalem and Early Islam*, edited by Jeremy Johns, pp. 11–58. Oxford Studies in Islamic Art 9/2. Oxford: Oxford University Press, 1999.

Johns, Jeremy, editor. *Bayt al-Maqdis II: Jerusalem and Early Islam.* Oxford Studies in Islamic Art 9/2. Oxford: Oxford University Press, 1999.

Khalek, Nancy. *Damascus after the Muslim Conquest: Text and Image in Early Islam.* Oxford: Oxford University Press, 2011.

Lammens, Henri. "Le chantre des Omiades: notes bibliographiques et littéraires sur le poète arabe chrétien Akhṭal." *Journal Asiatique* 4, 9th series (1894): 94–176, 193–241, 381–459.

———. "Le califat de Yazîd 1er." *Mélanges de la faculté orientale de l'Université Saint-Joseph de Beyrouth* 4 (1910): 233–312.

———. *Études sur le siècle des Omayyades.* Beirut: Imprimerie Catholique, 1930.

al-Qāḍī, Nuʿmān. *Al-Firaq al-Islāmiyya fī al-Shiʿr al-Umawī.* Cairo: Dār al-Maʿārif, 1970.

Rabbat, Nasser. "The Meaning of the Umayyad Dome of the Rock." *Muqarnas* 6 (1989): 12–21.

Raby, Julian, and Jeremy Johns, editors. *Bayt al-Maqdis I: ʿAbd al-Malik's Jerusalem.* Oxford Studies in Islamic Art 9. Oxford: Oxford University Press, 1992

Robinson, Chase F. *ʿAbd al-Malik.* Oxford: Oneworld, 2005.

Rūmiyya, Wahb. *Qaṣīdat al-Madḥ ḥattā Nihāyat al-ʿAṣr al-Umawī: Bayn al-Uṣūl wa-al-Iḥyāʾ wa-al-Tajdīd.* Damascus: Manshūrāt Wizārat al-Thaqāfa wa-al-Irshād al-Qawmī, 1981.

Sezgin, Fuat. *Geschichte des Arabischen Schrifttums,* Vol. 2: *Poesie bis ca. 430 H.* Leiden: Brill, 1975.

Stetkevych, Suzanne Pinckney. *The Mantle Odes: Arabic Praise Poems to the Prophet Muḥammad.* Bloomington: Indiana University Press, 2010.

———. *The Mute Immortals Speak: Pre-Islamic Poetry and the Poetics of Ritual.* Ithaca: Cornell University Press, 1993.

———. *The Poetics of Islamic Legitimacy: Myth, Gender, and Ceremony in the Classical Arabic Ode.* Bloomington: Indiana University Press, 2002.

———. "Qaḍāyā al-Qaṣīda al-ʿArabiyya: al-Manāhij wa-al-Manhajiyya: Taṭbīq Naẓariyyat al-Adāʾ ʿalā Saqṭ al-Zand wa-al-Luzūmiyyāt: Madkhal fī Shiʿr Abī al-ʿAlāʾ al-Maʿarrī." In *Al-Nadwa al-Duwaliyya: Qaḍāyā al-Manhaj fī al-Dirāsāt al-Lughawiyya wa-al-Adabiyya: al-Naẓariyya wa-al-Taṭbīq,* pp. 333–49. Riyadh: Jāmiʿat al-Malik Saʿūd, 1431/2010.

———. "Umayyad Panegyric and the Poetics of Islamic Hegemony: al-Akhṭal's *Khaffa al-Qaṭīnu* ('Those that Dwelt with You Have Left in Haste')." *Journal of Arabic Literature* 28/2 (1997): 89–122.

Thaʿlab, Abū ʿAbbās Aḥmad ibn Yaḥyā ibn Zayd al-Shaybānī. *Sharḥ Dīwān Zuhayr ibn Abī Sulmā.* Cairo: Al-Dār al-Qawmiyya lil-Ṭibāʿa wa-al-Nashr, 1964 [photo offset of Cairo: Dār al-Kutub, 1944].

7

ʿUmar II's *ghiyār* Edict: Between Ideology and Practice

Milka Levy-Rubin, The National Library of Israel

In my book *Non-Muslims in the Early Islamic Empire: From Surrender to Coexistence*, I attempt to trace the emergence of the regulations regarding the status of non-Muslims under Muslim rule beginning with the initial agreements signed at the time of the conquest and continuing into the seventh to ninth centuries, a period in which the relationship between the Muslim rulers and the numerous populations of conquered peoples was formed. It was during this latter period that endeavors were made to create a consistent policy regarding the conquered population, and the document of *Shurūṭ ʿUmar*, which was to become canonic, was drawn up.

One of the main questions that came up was: When did a structured code or set of rules, rather than sporadic regulations, begin to take shape? The first thing to come to mind is naturally ʿUmar II's edict, which appears in various sources containing a series of regulations related first and foremost to the external appearance of *ahl al-dhimma*, that is, to the *ghiyār*.

The *ghiyār* element stands also at the basis of the general uniform *Ṣulḥ* documents[1] written around 800 that propose to define the regulations regarding non-Muslims, including those of Abū Yūsuf, al-Shāfiʿī, and most famous of all *Shurūṭ ʿUmar*. The roots of the main part of *Shurūṭ ʿUmar*, that of the *ghiyār*, are indeed to be found in ʿUmar II's edict. Moreover, Abū Yūsuf's text and *Shurūṭ ʿUmar* adduce a list of restrictions regarding the external appearance of the non-Muslims that is more detailed than the one found in ʿUmar II's edict. Thus, for example, Abū Yūsuf describes in detail the *zunnār*, the variegated *qalānis*, and their distinctive saddles; he mentions the prohibition on wearing turbans (*ʿamāʾim*), and on wearing the hair long, and not cutting the forelocks. One may therefore naturally assume the existence of a process of development throughout the eighth century, starting with ʿUmar's edict, and ripening toward the end of the century into full-blown documents, reflecting a developed policy.

However, when one reads carefully the relevant sources regarding the treatment of the *dhimmīs*, this is not the impression one gets. The next time ʿUmar's edict comes up is in Abū Yūsuf's *Kitāb al-kharāj* when he cites this edict, which was transmitted to him by ʿAbd al-Raḥmān b. Thābit b. Thūbān (d. A.H. 165), a well-known Damascene transmitter of his own

[1] See Levy-Rubin, *Non-Muslims*, ch. 2.

day, an ascetic (*zāhid*),[2] who heard it from his father. As is clearly emphasized in the edict itself, ʿUmar II found it difficult to enforce it during his own reign:

> ʿUmar b. ʿAbd al-ʿAzīz wrote to one of his governors: "Regarding the matter at hand: you shall not permit a cross to be manifested, that is not smashed or effaced; a Jew or a Christian shall not ride on a saddle (*sirj*), but shall ride on a pack-saddle (*ikāf*); their women shall not ride on leather saddles (*riḥāla*), they shall ride on a pack-saddle (*ikāf*). Order this expressly, and prevent those who are under your authority [from letting] a Christian wear a *qabāʾ*, a silk garment, or a turban (*ʿaṣb*).
>
> I have been told that many of the Christians under your authority have returned to wearing turbans (*ʿamāʾim*), have given up wearing the girdles (*manāṭiq*)[3] on their waists, and have begun to wear their hair long and to neglect cutting it [i.e., their forelocks. — M.L.R.]. I swear that if anyone under your authority does so, this attests to your weakness, inability, and flattery, and when they go back to this [i.e., their former costumes and habits. — M.L.R.] they know what you are. Look out for everything which I have prohibited and prevent it from being carried out. Goodbye."[4]

A survey of the sources, both Muslim and non-Muslim alike, describing the period between ʿUmar II and Abū Yūsuf, exhibits no real trace of this *ghiyār* policy. Is this due just to lack of material regarding this issue or to some accidental oversight, or does this reflect the reality of the time? In other words, was the *ghiyār* edict attributed to ʿUmar II genuine, or was it attributed to him by later generations? If it was genuine, was it in fact enforced after his days? What was the effectual policy regarding non-Muslims under Umayyad rule and during the beginning of ʿAbbāsid rule until the end of the eighth century, when the *ghiyār* concept seems to have become the norm? In chapter three of my book, I attempt to demonstrate that, despite the inclination to cast doubt on their veracity, the Muslim sources are correct in attributing the first code regarding the attire and behavior of non-Muslims in Muslim society to the caliph ʿUmar II and that this code was indeed part of a planned and deliberate policy that was a result of his ideology regarding the ascendancy of Islam over the other religions.[5] I will summarize briefly here the main claims adduced in that chapter.

Although the sources all attribute the creation of the *ghiyār* to the caliph ʿUmar b. ʿAbd al-ʿAzīz (r. 99/717–101/720), one can very easily — perhaps somewhat too easily — dismiss this traditional claim as part of the myth in which ʿUmar b. ʿAbd al-ʿAzīz's figure is shrouded.[6] As is well known, he was conceived in later generations as *al-khalīfa al-ʿādil* "an exemplar of the Muslim virtues of piety, equity and humility."[7] Hawting suggests that ʿUmar II's pious image was a means of attaining continuity from the Rāshidūn through the Umayyads to the ʿAbbāsids, and for rejecting Shīʿite claims.[8] In general, it is believed that a large part of

---

[2] See Ibn ʿAsākir, *Taʾrīkh madīnat Dimashq*, vol. 34, pp. 236–59; al-Mizzī, *Tahdhīb*, vol. 17, pp. 12–18.

[3] The usual term is *zunnār*, the term used indeed by Abū Yūsuf himself in the previous paragraph describing the prohibitions of his day. The use of the term *minṭaqa*, which was later used exclusively for military and honorary belts, may point to the early date of this tradition, before a clear distinction was made between these two terms. See Levy-Rubin, *Non-Muslims*, pp. 154–57.

[4] Abū Yūsuf Yaʿqūb b. Ibrāhīm, *Kharāj*, pp. 127–28.

[5] Ibid., pp. 88–98.

[6] See, e.g., Hawting, *The First Dynasty of Islam*, pp. 15–18, 76–81. For avid support of ʿUmar II as a devout and pious Muslim, a vehement critique of the Umayyads, and an adamant follower of the *Rāshidūn*, see Murad, "Was ʿUmar II 'a True Umayyad'?"

[7] See *EI*[2] s.v. "ʿUmar b. ʿAbd al-ʿAzīz" (P. M. Cobb); on the prevalence of this topos see Borrut, "Entre tradition et histoire," pp. 329–36.

[8] Hawting, *The First Dynasty of Islam*, pp. 18, 77: "While there is no doubt that the acceptance of ʿUmar as a genuine caliph (*khalīfa*), unlike the other Umayyads who count only as kings (*mulūk*), is based to some

Umayyad history was successively reconstructed throughout the ninth and tenth centuries. It is thus tempting to claim that the traditional attribution of the creation of a code of rules to ʿUmar b. ʿAbd al-ʿAzīz is part of the myth that surrounded the actual person.

However, two main claims encourage the rejection of this approach. The first is the unanimity of the sources regarding the edict issued by ʿUmar and the fact that they exhibit a strong linguistic similarity when citing the core of the edict;[9] the second and more significant claim is the fact that the edict, as cited in the *risāla* cited in Ibn ʿAbd al-Ḥakam's *Sīra*, does not stand alone but is presented as a concrete expression of the manifest ideology that was promoted by ʿUmar II. I will not repeat here the proofs for the authenticity of the *rasāʾil*, as these are all adduced in chapter three of my book.[10] I will relate only to the ideology itself, which is crucial for the present thesis.

A short comment is needed here: in his paper in the present volume, as well as in another paper he published,[11] Luke Yarbrough has cast serious doubts on the authenticity of these *rasāʾil*, as well as on most of the other sources that adduce ʿUmar II's edict regarding the non-Muslims. In fact, although Yarbrough's suggestion "to read the epistles as pseudepigrapha composed by Muslim officials for an audience of ʿAbbāsid ruling elites" is indeed based on thorough research and is tempting, I believe that there is enough evidence to support their authenticity. In addition to the evidence provided in my book (my statement, which is cited questioningly by Yarbrough on page 51 of his article, that "there is no reason to doubt the authenticity of these documents" is actually preceded by the words "given these considerations," all of which are provided by me in detail beforehand) one should also take into account the following: ʿUmar II's image as a persecutor of the non-Muslims who refused to convert to Islam, who forbade the testimony of a Christian against a Muslim, forbade wine in the cities, and sent a "letter concerning religion" to the emperor Leo is found in the *Chronicle* of Theophanes,[12] which was written in Byzantium in the first years of the ninth century at the latest. Theophanes is the earliest extant witness of "Theophilus" or the Syriac Common Source. Unlike the other sources citing Theophilus which were written later under Muslim rule, his *Chronicle* is not affected by later concepts. All of the facts mentioned by Theophanes appear in fact in Michael the Syrian's chronicle as well.[13] On pages 34–35 Yarbrough himself admits that if Michael the Syrian's evidence does indeed go back to this source then it is strong evidence. The additional details given by Michael the Syrian (the prohibition to raise their voices in prayer, to strike the *nāqūs*, to ride on a saddle, and the diminution of the punishment on the murder of a Christian) are corroborated also in the *Chronicle of 1234*[14] which, as noted by Yarbrough following Hoyland, is surprisingly divergent from Michael. Thus, while Michael's position is unequivocally negative regarding ʿUmar II, the *Chronicle of 1234* adheres to the ambivalent image. ʿUmar's dual image of a just and good ruler versus the persecutor of Christians, which Yarbrough views as incoherent and as a proof of later editing, is not

extent on historical facts and on this caliph's personality and actions, it is also clear that much of the traditional writing about him should be regarded as pious and moralistic story-telling in keeping with the needs and outlook of tradition."

[9] Levy-Rubin, *Non-Muslims*, pp. 89–92.

[10] Ibid., pp. 92–98.

[11] Yarbrough, "Origins of the *ghiyār*."

[12] Theophanes, *Chronicle*, ed. De Boor, p. 399; trans. Mango and Scott, p. 550.

[13] Michael the Syrian, *Chronicle*, 11.XIX, pp. 455–56/488–89; for English translation of these sources see Hoyland, *Theophilus of Edessa's Chronicle*, pp. 215–17.

[14] *Chronicle of 1234*, ed. Chabot, CSCO 109, *pp. 307–08 (Latin trans.); for English, see Hoyland, *Theophilus of Edessa's Chronicle*, p. 217.

incomprehensible if we consider the state of mind of Christians living under Muslim rule. They often adopt the Muslim historiographic stance, yet in this case also preserve independent Christian memory, which granted, does not always appear similarly in all chronicles.

Another case in point is Abū Yūsuf's report, which precedes al-Mutawakkil by more than half a century. Abū Yūsuf (d. 795 C.E.), also writing at about the same time, specifically mentions the edict issued regarding the *ghiyār* in his time and differentiates between the latter and the edict which was issued in ʿUmar's time only to be neglected.[15]

I would like to stress also that the edict concerning the Christians is perfectly in line with ʿUmar's revolutionary policy: converts to Islam are for the first time exempt from the *jizya*, while those choosing to remain Christians now have to bear the consequences of their choice and live in *dhull wa-al-ṣaghār,* a state of humiliation. The edict should not therefore be considered premature for its time, as Yarbrough claims.

As regards the ousting of Christian officials, there is evidence that is prior to al-Mutawakkil. The first unsuccessful threat to their standing appears as early as al-Walīd's days when Theophanes mentions that he "forbade that the registers be written in Greek"[16] while al-Manṣūr "actually expelled the Christians from the government chanceries for a short time."[17] The point here is not whether this move succeeded but rather whether these restrictions befit the atmosphere of the eighth century.[18] Well, apparently, they certainly did! Many other steps, such as breaking crosses, killing pigs, forbidding vigils, and raising of taxes, all occurred from ʿAbd al-Malik's days onward.

I would now like to return to ʿUmar's ideology. The two *rasāʾil* in ʿAbd al-Ḥakam's *Sīra* emphasize the idea that the publication of the edict regarding the non-Muslims was part of ʿUmar's promotion of the ideology of the exaltation of Islam and the degradation of the non-Muslims.

The concept of the "chosen people," which was central in Jewish and Christian theology, was adopted by Muḥammad; it is well represented in the Qurʾān and is even more prominent in later tradition. Its adoption is naturally coupled with the degradation of unbelievers.[19] The idea that God has chosen the Muslims and will now exchange their misery with bounty and victory is expressed in ʿUmar II's pious accession epistle[20] and is supported there by Sura 24:55: "God has promised those of you who believe and do righteous deeds that He will surely make you successors in the land, even as He made those who were before them successors, and that He will surely establish their religion for them that He has approved for them, and will give them in exchange, after their fear, security."[21]

---

[15] Abū Yūsuf Yaʿqūb b. Ibrāhīm, *Kharāj*, p. 127.

[16] Theophanes, *Chronicle*, ed. De Boor, p. 376; trans. Mango and Scott, p. 524; Agapius (Maḥbūb) of Manbij, *Kitāb al-ʿunwān*, p. 498; Michael the Syrian, *Chronicle*, 11.XVII, p. 451/481; *Chronicle of 1234*, CSCO 109, *pp. 298–99. For English translation, see Hoyland, *Theophilus of Edessa's Chronicle*, pp. 199–200.

[17] See Theophanes, *Chronicle*, ed. De Boor, p. 431; trans. Mango and Scott, p. 596.

[18] Yarbrough, "Origins of the *ghiyār*," pp. 26–27.

[19] See Qurʾān 3:110–12, 3:139, 2:61, 17:111, 42:45, 47:35. On this subject, see Ben-Shammai, "The Idea of Election in Early Islam" (in Hebrew); Friedmann, *Tolerance and Coercion in Islam*, pp. 34–39, esp. p. 35, and n. 115, citing al-Bukhārī, *Ṣaḥīḥ*, vol. 1, pp. 339–40: "Islam is exalted and nothing is exalted above it" (*al-Islām yaʿlū wa lā yuʿlā*).

[20] Abū al-Qāsim ʿAbd al-Raḥmān b. ʿAbd al-Ḥakam, *Sīrāt ʿUmar b. ʿAbd al-ʿAzīz*, pp. 79–82.

[21] Translated in Arberry, *The Koran Interpreted*, vol. 2, p. 53.

The lowly and humiliating position of those who had been deprived of their previous advantages, according to this theology, needs to be guarded and preserved by Islam. This idea is emphasized in an edict cited by Ibn ʿAbd al-Ḥakam, which, according to him, was sent by ʿUmar b. ʿAbd al-ʿAzīz to his governors. The edict opens with the statement "The *mushrikūn* are impure since God has made them the army of Satan."[22] The term *mushrikūn* here clearly denotes non-Muslims in general rather than pagans, as becomes clear in the following sentences.[23] It goes on to speak about *ahl al-shirk*, who had so far aided the Muslims, levying taxes and serving as officials and administrators under Muslim rule, a situation that was brought to an end by *Amīr al-Muʾminīn*. The conclusion is,

> Any official or administrator that I am informed of in your district who is not a Muslim should be dismissed by you and a Muslim should be placed in his stead. The annihilation of their deeds is the annihilation of their religions! It is fitting for them to be reduced to the degree of humility and contempt (*dhull wa-al-ṣaghār*) to which God had reduced them. Do that and write to me of the action you took.[24]

It is especially significant that this declaration forms the prelude to the edict we have cited above regarding the riding restrictions. The next edict, directly following this, concerns the dress regulations:[25]

> ʿUmar wrote to the provinces (*āfāq*): a Christian must be distinguished by his [trimmed] forelocks (*mafrūq al-nāṣiya*);[26] he shall not wear a *qabāʾ*,[27] he shall not walk about except with a leather belt (*zunnār min julūd*),[28] nor [shall he wear] a Persian mantle (*ṭaylasān*), nor trousers with anklets (*sarāwīl dhāt khadama*) nor shoes with straps (*ʿadhaba*); arms shall not be found in his home.

Thus, the *ghiyār* edict is a direct consequence of the exaltation of Islam and the state of humility and degradation that was to be imposed upon non-Muslims.[29]

In chapter five of my book, I have attempted to demonstrate that the concept of displaying social hierarchy via codes of dress and appearance, which forms the basis of the *ghiyār*, was inspired by the Sasanian ethos, where each class had its own dress code. The declaration that the non-Muslims need "to be reduced to the degree of humility and contempt (*dhull wa-al-ṣaghār*)" is thus in concert with the aristocratic ethos adopted by the Muslims from the

---

[22] وانّ المشركون نجس حين جعلهم الله جند الشيطان, ibid., p. 159.

[23] On the use of *mushrikūn* for non-Muslims in general as a polemical term, and reflecting, in fact, the original Qurʾānic tone, see Hawting, "Idolatry and Idolators," pp. 477 and 479.

[24] See a *ḥadīth* expressing the same message and attributed to ʿUmar in *Shurūṭ al-naṣāra* from the tenth or eleventh century C.E., in Cohen, "What Was the Pact of ʿUmar?" p. 148: افلا اتخذت كاتبا حنيفا يكتب لك قال يا امير المومنين ما لي وله له دينه ولي كتابه وقال عمؤ لا تامنهم اذ خوّنهم الله ولا تكرمهم اذ اهانهم الله ولا تدناهم اذ اقصاهم الله. This tradition is repeated in later literature; see al-Qurṭubī, *Tafsīr*, vol. 6, p. 179; al-Maqdisī, *Al-Mughnī*, vol. 1, p. 270; vol. 6, p. 326.

[25] Abū al-Qāsim ʿAbd al-Raḥmān b. ʿAbd al-Ḥakam, *Sirāt ʿUmar b. ʿAbd al-ʿAzīz*, p. 160.

[26] See above, n. 13; Bravmann, "Ancient Arab Background."

[27] The *qabāʾ* was "a luxurious sleeved robe slit in front with buttons (*muzarrar*) made of fabric such as brocade (*dībāj*), and apparently of Persian provenance"; see Stillman, *Arab Dress*, p. 12 and n. 17; see also Dozy, *Supplément aux dictionnaires arabes*, pp. 352–62.

[28] Here literally "a belt made of leathers," perhaps meaning that the belt could be made of various kinds of leather: Ibn ʿAsākir, *Taʾrīkh madīnat Dimashq*, vol. 2, p. 180, has *zunnār min jild* in the singular.

[29] Regarding the infiltration of Sasanian clothes items into Muslim society already during the Umayyad period, see Levy-Rubin, *Non-Muslims*, pp. 96–97, 133–35.

Sasanians, according to which the nobility must be dressed in appropriate attire, while the lower class should wear the dress of baseness or humility (*libās al-madhalla*) in accordance with its humiliated condition.[30]

There is no question here of trying to achieve mere technical distinction between Muslims and non-Muslims, meant essentially to distinguish the Muslims from the non-Muslim majority (rather than degrade the latter), as suggested by Noth,[31] but rather a fulfilment or implementation of the notion expressed in Qurʾān 2:61 that all non-believers shall be "struck by humiliation and misery" (*al-dhilla wa-al-maskana*; see also Suras 3:112, 42:45).

The policy adopted in this case by ʿUmar II, establishing the superiority of Muslims over the non-Muslims who were still in control in many vital places, tallies perfectly with his image as a *mahdī* in his time, who walks in the footsteps of his great ancestor ʿUmar I, called *al-fārūq*, akin to Syriac *pāroqā* "savior, redeemer."[32]

This same doctrine and structure, put differently (a fact that indicates the independence of the two edicts), is repeated 130 years later, in al-Mutawakkil's edict. First he expounds upon the concept of the Muslims as the chosen people, exalted through their faith and religion as long as they fulfill the commandments of Islam. He then goes on to say, "The Muslims through God's favor by which he has elected them, and the superiority he gave them by the religion he chose for them, are distinguished from members of other religions by their righteous laws, their fine and upright statutes, and their evident proof." Only then does he proceed to supply the detailed instructions regarding the *ghiyār*, a direct consequence of the distinction made previously.[33]

It should be noted that this concept, usually represented by the *hendiadys al-dhull wa-al-ṣaghār*, used in the edict, is reiterated in the *tafsīr* and *ḥadīth* literature wherein the non-Muslim is justly doomed to a life of misery and humiliation.[34]

The Evidence during the Following Decades

ʿUmar's exaltation ideology and the *ghiyār* edict that stemmed from it were an important part of ʿUmar II's policy. Yet, there is no evidence of the implementation of the *ghiyār* regulations by the subsequent Umayyad caliphs.[35] Moreover, even these restrictions are not noted by all

---

[30] See Levy-Rubin, *Non-Muslims*, ch. 5, pp. 137–42, esp. p. 140.

[31] Noth, "Abgrenzungsprobleme."

[32] Regarding the epithet *fārūq*, see Levi Della Vida, in his review of volume V of L. Caetani's *Annali*; *EI*[2] s.v. "ʿUmar (I) b. al-Khaṭṭāb" (G. Levi Della Vida [and M. Bonner]); Crone and Hinds, *God's Caliph*, pp. 113–14; Crone and Cook, *Hagarism*, pp. 5–6; Barthold, "Caliph ʿUmar II," pp. 73–75; Bashear, "The Title '*Fārūq*'"; Donner, "La question du messianisme."

[33] See al-Ṭabarī, *Taʾrīkh*, vol. 3, pp. 1392–93; Kraemer, *The History of al-Ṭabarī*, vol. 34: *Incipient Decline*, pp. 92–93.

[34] See al-Ṭabarī, *Tafsīr*, vol. 4, p. 51; Ibn Kathīr, *Tafsīr*, vol. 2, p. 350; al-Qurṭubī, *Tafsīr*, vol. 1, p. 430; al-Nīsābūrī, *al-Mustadrak ʿala al-ṣaḥīḥayn*, vol. 4, p. 477; Ibn Abī Shayba, *Muṣannaf*, vol. 4, p. 216, no. 19437.

[35] It should be noted, however, that the *Zuqnīn Chronicle* attributes to Yazīd II measures which are attributed to ʿUmar II by Michael the Syrian and Theophanes including the prohibition of the testimony of a "Syrian," i.e., Christian, against an "Arab" and the setting of the blood-value of an Arab at double the value of a Syrian. (*Zuqnīn Chronicle*, ed. Chabot, p. 164, trans. and annot. Harrak, p. 155; Michael the Syrian, *Chronicle*, vol. 4, p. 456 (text), vol. 2, pp. 488–89 (trans.); Theophanes reports about the prohibition on wine in the cities, the forced conversion of Christians, the prohibition of the testimony of a Christian against a Muslim, and ʿUmar II's letter to the Byzantine emperor Leo. He does not mention the issue of the *ghiyār*; see Theophanes, *Chronicle*, ed. De Boor, p. 399; trans. Mango and Scott, p. 550.

Christian chronicles. Thus, for example, in the Byzantine-Arab chronicle, Agapius and Eutychius do not relate to the latter at all, and present ᶜUmar as in Muslim tradition as the just Caliph.[36]

On the other hand, when reading the non-Muslim sources relating to the Umayyad period and the early ᶜAbbāsid rule from ᶜAbd al-Malik's reign onward, we do have a substantial amount of information regarding other forms of the behavior of Muslim authorities toward the non-Muslim inhabitants. We hear of orders to remove and efface crosses on various occasions starting already in the days of the caliph ᶜUthmān.[37] There are also numerous reports regarding the intervention of Muslim authorities in the appointment of patriarchs and other church dignitaries and their involvement in various church matters.[38]

However, the most common reports one hears about are the census (*taᶜdīl*) followed by the levying of the *jizya*, often coupled with sealing, stamping, and branding of the non-Muslim inhabitants. This starts with ᶜAbd al-Malik's famous census followed by the levying of the *jizya* (signifying capitation tax and not tax generally) for the first time according to the *Zuqnīn Chronicle*[39] and continues with the census of 708/9, when Maslama took control of Mesopotamia and had the lands measured and the vineyards and crops counted, as well as animals and persons. In addition, Maslama is reported to have "hung lead seals on everyone's necks."[40] In the year 721/2, Dhaḥḥāk, emir of Mesopotamia, conducted a census unknown before.[41] Hishām is reported to have oppressed the people with excessive exactions and tribute, higher than all those before him (in this case the sources do not refer specifically to the *jizya*).[42] The chaos in the Umayyad caliphate following Hishām's rule, which ended with the fall of the dynasty, seems to have either obscured similar cases, or maybe even aided the local non-Muslim population to evade heavy taxation. The next we hear about this is during al-Manṣūr's reign, when this phenonmenon seems to have reached its climax. We have numerous descriptions of al-Manṣūr's treatment of the non-Muslims. One report is based on the Syriac Common Source identified with Theophilus of Edessa.[43] The fullest version of this seems to appear in the *Chronicle of 1234*:[44]

---

[36] *Chronicle of 819*, CSCO 81, p. 15 (text), CSCO 109, p. 11 (Latin trans.); Eutychius (Saīd b. Biṭrīq), *Annales*, pp. 43–44; Agapius, *Kitāb al-ᶜunwān*, pp. 502–03; *Byzantine-Arab Chronicle from 741*, §40; trans. in Hoyland, *Seeing Islam as Others Saw It*, p. 625.

[37] See Michael the Syrian, *Chronicle*, vol. 4, pp. 421–22 (text), vol. 2, p. 432 (trans.); Palmer, *West-Syrian Chronicles*, pp. 169–70; regarding ᶜAbd al-Malik, see Dionysius of Tell-Maḥrē in Palmer, *West-Syrian Chronicles*, text no. 12, AG 1015, p. 78; see Michael the Syrian, *Chronicle*, vol. 4 (text), p. 447, vol. 2, p. 475 (trans.), who reports in the same context about an order to remove all crosses.

[38] Theophanes, *Chronicle*, ed. De Boor, p. 416; Michael the Syrian, *Chronicle*, vol. 4, p. 467 (text), vol. 2, p. 511 (trans.); *Theophanes continuaatus*, ed. Migne, Patrologia graeca 109, col. 68 = Michael the Syrian, *Chronicle*, vol. 4, p. 461 (text), vol. 2, pp. 495–96 (trans.); vol. 4, p. 524 (text), vol. 2, p. 75 (trans.); *Zuqnīn Chronicle*, ed. Chabot, pp. 247–49, trans. Harrak, pp. 219–20.

[39] *Zuqnīn Chronicle*, ed. Chabot, p. 154, trans. Harrak, p. 147.

[40] *Chronicle of 1234*, CSCO 109, *p. 299 = *Chronicle of 819*, CSCO 81, p. 15 (text), CSCO 109, p. 10 (Latin trans.).

[41] *Chronicle of 819*, CSCO 81, p. 16 (text), CSCO 109, p. 11 (Latin trans.).

[42] Michael the Syrian, *Chronicle*, vol. 4, p. 457 (text), vol. 2, p. 490 (trans.); *Chronicle of 1234*, CSCO 109, * p. 309.

[43] Conrad, "The Conquest of Arwād"; see also Hoyland, *Theophilus of Edessa's Chronicle*, pp. 1–41.

[44] *Chronicle of 1234*, CSCO 81, p. 340 (text), trans. by Hoyland in *Theophilus of Edessa's Chronicle*, p. 308. See also *Chronicle of 819*, CSCO 81, p. 20 (text), CSCO 109, p. 14 (Latin trans.), where it is stated that Mūsa b. Musᶜab was a Jew, and that he branded (*karked*; see Brockelmann, *Lexicon Syriacum*, col. 346A) rather than cut off Christians' thumbs; see also Michael the Syrian, *Chronicle*, vol. 4, pp. 476–77, vol. 2, pp. 526–67 (trans.), who mentions the heavy taxation without the sealing and the thumbs; Theophanes says that "ᶜAbdallah ordered that Christians and Jews should be marked on their hands." See also Agapius, *Kitāb al-ᶜunwān*, p. 546, who also emphasized the heavy taxation.

> Abu Ja'far appointed over Mosul Musa ibn Musᶜab,[45] a wicked and merciless man, and an enemy of the Christians. He thought up torments which the world had never seen before. He increased tribute and multiplied exactions. He attached lead seals to men's necks and cut off the thumbs of their hands. He demanded tax (*gzītā*) even for windows and doors with the result that people were digging up old graves to extract gold and silver. In addition, there was a great famine and pestilence in his days. Men were perishing (so fast) that there was no one to do the burying. Wolves went about and devoured many men. One had to pay a whole silver coin (*zūzā*) for a donkey or a bull or three or four eggs or two or three handfuls of wheat, for this harsh famine was (everywhere) in the world.

The most detailed report of this event is to be found however in the *Zuqnīn Chronicle*. The *Chronicle* informs in detail of the appointment of the wicked and greedy Mūsā b. Muṣᶜab as governor of Mosul, and the affliction he brought about.[46] It then goes on to provide an exhaustive description of the *taᶜdīl* conducted by al-Manṣūr, who "wanted to subject more people to the capitation tax (*ksef rīsha*)."[47] Everything was measured, and whatever was not registered in the census was registered as crown property. His tax agents were everywhere overtaxing wherever possible. Having described all this in great detail the chronicle goes on to say,

> The Caliph also appointed another agent in order to brand and stamp people on the neck, like slaves. The prophet says: *Everyone who had not received the mark of that beast on the forehead* (Rev. 20:4). But here, not only did they bear it on the forehead, but also on both hands, on the chest, and even on the back. When this official came, he aggravated the land by his arrival more than all his predecessors, because he had been ordered to mark people on the hand with a mark that would not go away or be erased for the rest of their lives.[48]

He returns to this somewhat later, this time adding the following:

> After each one had brought his people into the city, they were branded. They wrote the name of the town on the right hand, and on the left hand "Gazīra"; they hung two seals on the neck, one branded with the name of the town, and the other with the name of the province.... At this point as Daniel the Prophet and John the Apostle said: *All the people received the mark of the beast on their hands, breasts and backs.*[49]

This phenomenon of sealing, branding, and stamping has been reviewed extensively by Chase Robinson in his article "Neck-Sealing in Early Islam." Robinson has demonstrated that it "has its origins in a tradition of humiliating neck-sealing, to which slaves and captives had long been subjected in pre-Islamic Iraq and (apparently) Iran, the symbolic connection with slavery and captivity being signaled by associated branding and tattooing."[50] According to Robinson, neck-sealing, associated with tax payment, is only secondary. More significant is the fact that it identified and stigmatized. In the Bible tagging by an ear hole, through which a ring with a tag may have been strung, marked human chattel (Exod. 21:6).[51] There

---

[45] On him, see *Zuqnīn Chronicle*, trans. Harrak, p. 223 n. 3.

[46] *Zuqnīn Chronicle*, ed. Chabot, pp. 252–57, trans. Harrak, pp. 223–26.

[47] *Zuqnīn Chronicle*, ed. Chabot, p. 265, trans. Harrak, p. 234.

[48] *Zuqnīn Chronicle*, ed. Chabot, p. 268, trans. Harrak, p. 236.

[49] *Zuqnīn Chronicle*, ed. Chabot, p. 292, trans. Harrak, pp. 254–55.

[50] Robinson, "Neck-Sealing," p. 434.

[51] Ibid., p. 408.

is Talmudic evidence that slaves wore metal and clay sealings around their necks. In the Persian and Byzantine world, captives had their necks sealed with *boullae*.[52] Although there is no evidence regarding pre-Islamic Arabia, Robinson notes, interestingly, that this is what may explain in Arabic the semantic overlap between *raqaba* as both "neck" and "slave."[53] Robinson adduces numerous examples of the neck-sealing and tattooing of slaves and captives under Muslim rule.[54] In certain cases this practice is applied to Muslim Arabs for purposes of subjugation and humiliation as well. Thus, when al-Ḥajjāj defeats Ibn al-Zubayr in Mecca, he humiliates the Zubayrid supporters by setting lead seals on their necks or their wrists.[55] In its extensive description of the year 773/4, the *Zuqnīn Chronicle* tells the following episode: an Arab tax agent by the name of Razīn had found out that his agents were robbing and pillaging. Consequently, "he brought them and pierced their nostrils in which he placed a ring, as is done to camels. He also made a hole between their eyes in which he attached a seal; he prepared chains so that they might be pulled by them."[56]

It is thus quite evident that Arab Muslims in the eighth century viewed the sealing as a sign of humiliation that was identified with slavery and captivity. The coupling of the payment of the *jizya* with sealing was therefore much more than technical. Just as the cutting of the forelock was a sign of the humiliation of the captive,[57] so was sealing, branding, and tattooing. The payment of the *jizya* was indeed considered a humiliation. During the conquest the people of Darband actually asked for their tribute to be military assistance, saying expressly that they preferred this to the option that the Arabs would "humiliate [them] with the [payment of] *jizya*."[58] The *jizya* was indeed considered among many Muslim jurists as an *ʿuqūba*, that is, punishment, rather than as an *ujrā*, payment.[59] As already noted by many classical scholars, the payment of the *jizya* by the conquered was inseparably attached to their *ṣaghār*, as is indeed strongly emphasized already in Qurʾān 9:29.[60] Thus, even if we accept Kister's claim[61] that the term "*ʿan yadin*" in this same passage was in fact "*ʿan ẓahri yadin*" and meant "according to their ability" and not "by force" or "by humiliation" as the later jurists thought, the passage as a whole signified the humiliation of the conquered people who were now considered captives of the Muslim victors.

I will return now to ʿUmar II's *ghiyār* regulations: since we do not have here a case of "silent sources" that provide us with no information regarding the question at hand, we might be tempted to suppose that ʿUmar's edict was a whistle in the dark, that is, that since ʿUmar was an exceptional figure among his predecessors and successors and had reigned three years only, his edict regarding the *dhimmīs* had not struck roots in the next decades. Indeed, the evidence seems to point instead to the continuity of an ancient custom that was prevalent in the Near East and was adopted by the Muslims. Its implementation awarded the authorities

---

[52] Ibid., pp. 408–09.

[53] Ibid., pp. 409–10.

[54] Ibid., pp. 411–17.

[55] Ibid., p. 415.

[56] *Zuqnīn Chronicle*, ed. Chabot, p. 355, trans. Harrak, p. 303.

[57] See Bravmann, "Ancient Arab Background," pp. 413–14 and n. 59; Levy-Rubin, *Non-Muslims*, p. 153.

[58] See Pourshariati, *Decline and Fall of the Sasanian Empire*, pp. 274–75; al-Ṭabarī, *Taʾrīkh*, vol. 1, p. 2664, trans. in Rex Smith, *The History of al-Ṭabarī*, vol. 14: *The Conquest of Iran*, p. 35; جزيتنا اليكم النصر... فلا تذلّونا بالجزية ("Our tribute to you will be the military assistance we render you ... but do not humiliate us with tribute").

[59] Kister, "ʿAn Yadin (IX, 29)."

[60] See Cahen, "Coran IX-29"; Bravmann, "A propos de Qurʾān IX-29" (for the three articles of Kister, Cahen, and Bravmann together, see Paret, *Der Koran*, pp. 288–303).

[61] Kister, "ʿAn Yadin (IX, 29)."

not only with an ample amount of taxes that filled their coffers, but with continuous control over the local conquered population who were in fact treated as captives and slaves were.

However, an examination of both policies, that is, ʿUmar II's policy as reflected in his edict, and the policy prevalent throughout the eighth century (attributed to ʿUmar I himself by Muslim sources),[62] clarifies that although the means may be different, their purpose is one and the same: to manifest humiliation.

There is, nevertheless, one very significant difference. Despite what we are often led to think by the later Muslim sources, the leading principle behind the payment of the *jizya* coupled with the sealing was not the religious identity of the payer but, as we have just seen, his identity as a captive, and therefore "slave" of the Muslims, as well as his non-Arab ethnicity. In some cases, there is in fact a lack of clarity regarding the identity of those included in this category of "the humiliated conquered." Are Arab Christians included in this category? They certainly did not think so, refusing to pay the humiliating *jizya* and opting for a double *ṣadaqa* instead.[63] Were *mawālī*, non-Arab Muslims who were originally part of the conquered population, free from the *jizya*? As is well known, this was not something that was taken for granted; al-Ḥajjāj b. Yūsuf's treatment of the *mawālī* is well known, and according to Ibn ʿAbd al-Ḥakam, the caliph ʿAbd al-Malik had actually ordered ʿAbd al-ʿAzīz, who was governor of Egypt, to collect the *jizya* from those *dhimmīs* who had converted to Islam.[64] During this period *mawālī* were in fact treated as second-class citizens in many other respects.[65] Many of the attributes of the position of the *mawālī* in Muslim society actually resemble those that are to be found in the *Shurūṭ* regarding non-Muslims.[66] Thus, *mawālī* were prohibited from marrying Muslim women, and the life of a *mawlā* was worth less than that of an Arab. They were also, at least formally, considered unsuitable for holding official positions in the government.[67] In addition, as in the case of the non-Muslims, there were explicit status symbols that differentiated them from the Arab Muslims: they were not to use a *kunya*, but *ism* only, precisely as is stated in the *Shurūṭ*;[68] they were not to walk alongside Muslims, and in public gatherings they were allotted the last and humblest seats.[69]

What ʿUmar's regulations and the "sealing-*jizya*" policy had in common is the fact that they both aimed at humiliation (*al-dhull wa-al-ṣaghār*). The difference is, however, that ʿUmar aimed for the first time to draw the line not between conqueror and conquered, or Arab and non-Arab, but between Muslim and non-Muslim. ʿUmar's reforming policy regarding the *jizya* and the *kharāj*, and his retraction of al-Ḥajjāj's order, do not need to be dwelt upon here. The

[62] See Robinson, "Neck-Sealing," pp. 414–15, with references to various sources, who believes that tax sealing of the non-Muslims appeared only in the first decades of the eighth century, despite its traditional attribution to the time of the conquest.

[63] See al-Ṭabarī, *Taʾrīkh*, vol. 1, pp. 2508–11; Friedmann, "Classification of Unbelievers"; idem, *Tolerance and Coercion in Islam*, pp. 63–66; Robinson, *Empire and Elites*, pp. 60–62.

[64] See ʿAbd al-Raḥmān b. ʿAbdallah b. ʿAbd al-Ḥakam, *Kitāb futuḥ Miṣr wa-akhbāriha*, pp. 155–56; al-Maqrīzī, *Al-Mawāʿiz wa-al-iʿtibār*, vol. 1, p. 208; see Dennett, *Conversion and the Poll Tax*, pp. 182–83.

[65] See Goldziher, *Muhammedanische Studien*, vol. 1, pp. 101–46 (ed. and trans. by Barber and Stern as *Muslim Studies*, pp. 98–136); *EI*[2] s.v. "Mawlā" (P. Crone); Levy, *The Social Structure of Islam*, pp. 53–67; see Crone, "The Significance of Wooden Weapons," p. 178, who notes: "All non-Arabs were 'slaves' in Arab eyes whatever their formal status.... A slave was a non-Arab, a non-Arab was a slave, literal or metaphorical, past or present, Muslim or otherwise."

[66] See Levy-Rubin, *Non-Muslims*, pp. 142–43.

[67] See Crone, "Mawlā," regarding marriage, *diya*, and positions, and references there.

[68] See Goldziher, *Muhammedanische Studien*, vol. 1, p. 267 = Barber and Stern, *Muslim Studies*, p. 242.

[69] See Levy, *Social Structure of Islam*, p. 59; al-Mubarrad, *Kitāb al-kāmil*, pp. 711–12.

point that needs to be made is that ʿUmar II did not in fact retract or change the praxis and the significance of levying the *jizya*. The principle of humiliation tallied perfectly with his views. He was no advocate of the non-Muslims, but of Islam and the newly converted, and even the latter could not hold on to their land.[70] There is therefore no reason to think that he wanted to cancel the tax-sealing policy. Indeed, the new regulations did not annul this policy, as is clear not only from the sources but from the archaeological evidence as well[71] — rather, it supplemented it.

The tax-sealing policy was well fitted to the majority of the non-Muslims living in the rural areas, in villages and small towns, which, according to the surrender agreements, were allowed to go on as before and in which Muslim presence seems to have still been minimal during the eighth century. All that was demanded of these non-Muslims, in fact, was to accept their humble status as captives and pay their taxes.

Who then were the new regulations aimed at? As has been noted already by Antoine Fattal, it is quite likely that first and foremost ʿUmar II wanted to prevent the non-Muslims from looking like "Muslim soldiers," as indeed stated by Bar Hebraeus.[72] Since there were indeed a significant number of newly converted *dhimmīs* who, as demonstrated by Patricia Crone, had joined the Muslim army just in order to be given the chance to become a part of Muslim society, it was especially important to be able to differentiate between these and other *dhimmīs* who pretended to pass as such.[73] However, this edict was no doubt relevant to all non-Muslims living in the *amṣār*, the garrison cities, as well as in the major cities of the *ajnād*, and included women as well as men. The most likely candidates were the *dihqāns* and the *kuttāb* and their families, who were to be dismissed from office according to the edict. However, dismissed or not, they could still be walking around clad in smart Sasanian clothes, exuding status and rank. This had to be mended. The aim of ʿUmar II's edict was to create a state in which only Muslims could appear in dress and paraphernalia signifying social superiority.

ʿUmar II's edict reflected a well-founded ideology of the exaltation of Islam and the Muslims over the other religions and their adherents. This constituted a change in comparison to the existing approach which confused the superiority of Islam, with the superiority of the Arab and of the conqueror.

When implementing his ideology, ʿUmar II employed two means: the first, the well-known method of the tax-sealing that was in use for the rural and peripheral population of non-Muslims, excluding now the converted *mawālī*; and the second, a new set of regulations which applied in reality to the higher strata of the non-Muslims who lived in *amsār al-muslimīn*, whose members often served in government offices (another phenomenon which ʿUmar II attempted to terminate) and dressed just as the upper Muslim strata did. The issue of the presence and the behavior of non-Muslims in *amṣār al-muslimīn* was indeed a very sensitive one during this period, and it abounds in the sources.[74] Obviously, the coexistence of Muslims and non-Muslims exacerbated the need to emphasize the superiority of the Muslim over the non-Muslim and to avoid the possibility of confusion or mix-up between the two.

---

[70] On this, see Décobert, "Notule sur la patrimonialisme omeyyade," pp. 237–39.

[71] Robinson, "Neck-Sealing," pp. 423–27.

[72] Fattal, *Le statut légal*, pp. 98–99; Bar Hebraeus, *Chronicon ecclesiasticum*, p. 117.

[73] Crone, "The Pay of Client Soldiers"; Hasson, "Les *mawālī* dans l'armée musulmane." See also Wadād al-Qāḍī's article in this volume.

[74] On this issue, see Levy-Rubin, "*Shurūṭ ʿUmar* and Its Alternatives"; idem, *Non-Muslims*, pp. 58–86.

This is exactly the purpose of the *ghiyār* regulations; it did not aim at replacing the humiliating ceremony of collecting the *jizya*, but added an additional tier to it.

Since the *ghiyār* affected only a limited, albeit growing, number of non-Muslims mainly in *amṣār al-muslimīn*, it is not surprising that we hear less of it than of the tax-sealing process that was intended for the broad strata of non-Muslims. The best evidence that ʿUmar II's *ghiyār* regulations were not a passing phase is Abū Yūsuf's reference to it.[75] Before citing ʿUmar II's edict he presents the *ghiyār* regulations that were accepted in his days. It is interesting to point out that the first thing he notes is the procedure of breaking the seals that hung on the *dhimmīs*' necks. Then follow the *ghiyār* regulations: as mentioned already above, these include details regarding specific items of clothing, their shape, their colors, and so on, which demonstrate that the regulations had become much more defined and detailed. Also by his time, there is no confusion anymore, as is the case in ʿUmar II's edict as cited by Abū Yūsuf (see above, n. 4) between the term *minṭaqa*, which by Abū Yūsūf's day was reserved exclusively for the special official or military belt worn by the Muslims, and the *zunnār*, which was a mandatory item of dress worn by the *dhimmīs*.[76]

By Abū Yūsuf's time, ʿUmar II's *ghiyār* regulations seem to have indeed become well established at least in the Muslim *amṣār*, while the tax-sealing procedure seems to have become more symbolic and refined, at least in the case of the upper strata of the non-Muslims. As noted by Robinson, Abū Yūsuf describes a formal procedure in which the non-Muslim puts on the seal before the payment of the *jizya* and breaks it immediately following it, an act that he rightly reads as "an attempt to frame the practice as a tax procedure."[77] It follows that, although non-Muslims by definition were a social class or *ṭabaqa* inferior to that of the Muslims,[78] and therefore humiliated, members of the upper strata of non-Muslims were not actually treated as captives or slaves. Indeed, the tax-sealing procedure seems to have faded away during the tenth century,[79] while the *ghiyār* acquired a central place as the most significant code that represented the status of the non-Muslims.

If we are to judge by the policy toward non-Muslims in the following centuries, ʿUmar II's policy, which was based on his ideology of the exaltation of Islam rather than the superiority of the Arab conqueror, was immensely effective, first by limiting the tax-sealing procedure to non-Muslims only, and even more significantly later, when his *ghiyār* policy pushed the tax-sealing procedure to the background and became entrenched as the hallmark of non-Muslims in Islamicate society for generations to come.

---

[75] Abū Yūsuf, *Kharāj*, p. 127.

[76] See Levy-Rubin, *Non-Muslims*, pp. 154–57.

[77] Robinson, "Neck-Sealing," p. 421.

[78] On this, see Levy-Rubin, *Non-Muslims*, ch. 5, esp. pp. 141–62.

[79] Robinson, "Neck-Sealing," p. 417.

Bibliography

Abū Yūsuf Yaʿqūb b. Ibrāhīm. *Kitāb al-kharāj*. Cairo, A.H. 1352.

Agapius (Maḥbūb) of Manbij. *Kitāb al-ʿunwān*. Edited and translated by Alexandre Vasiliev, *Kitab al-Unvan, Histoire universelle*. Patrologia Orientalis 8/3. Brepols: Turnhout, 1911.

Arberry, A. J. *The Koran Interpreted*. 2 vols. London: Allen & Unwin; New York: Macmillan, 1955.

Bar Hebraeus. *Chronicon ecclesiasticum*. Edited and translated by Jean Baptiste Abbeloos and Thomas Joseph Lamy. 3 vols. Leuven: Peeters, 1872–1877.

Barthold, W. W. "Caliph ʿUmar II and the Conflicting Reports on His Personality." *Islamic Quarterly* 15/2-3 (1971): 69–95.

Bashear, Suliman. "The Title 'Fārūq' and Its Association with ʿUmar I." *Studia Islamica* 72 (1990): 47–70.

Ben-Shammai, Haggai. "The Idea of Election in Early Islam." In *Chosen People, Elect Nation and Universal Mission*, edited by S. Almog and Michael Heyd, pp. 147–77. Jerusalem: Zalman Shazar Center, 1991. [in Hebrew]

Borrut, Antoine. "Entre tradition et histoire: genèse et diffusion de l'image de ʿUmar II." *Mélanges de la faculté orientale de l'Université Saint-Joseph de Beyrouth* 58 (2005): 329–78.

Bravmann, Meir M. "A propos de Qurʾān IX-29: *Ḥatta yuʿtū l-ǧizyata ʿan yadin wa-hum ṣāghirūna*." *Arabica* 10 (1963): 94–95.

———. "The Ancient Arab Background of the Qurʾānic Concept al-Jizyatu ʿan Yadin." *Arabica* 13 (1966): 307–14.

Brockelmann, Carl. *Lexicon Syriacum*. 2nd ed. Halle: Niemeyer, 1928.

Al-Bukhārī, Muḥammad b. Ismāʿīl. *Ṣaḥīḥ*. Edited by Ludolf Krehl. Leiden: Brill, 1864.

Byzantine-Arab Chronicle from 741. Edited by Juan Gil, *Corpus Scriptorum Muzrabicorum*. 2 vols. Manuales y anejos de "Emérita" 28. Madrid: Instituto Antonio de Nebrija, 1973.

Cahen, Claude. "Coran IX-29: *Ḥatta yuʿtū l-jizyata ʿan yadin wa-hum ṣāghirūna*." *Arabica* 9 (1962): 76–79.

Chronicle of 819 (Anonymous). Edited by Jean-Baptiste Chabot, *Chronicon anonymum ad A.D. 819 pertinens*. Appended to *Anonymi Auctoris Chronicon ad Annum Christi 1234 pertinens*. CSCO 81 (Scriptores Syri 36) and CSCO 109 (Scriptores Syri 56). Paris: Gabalda, 1920, 1937.

Chronicle of 1234 (Anonymous).

- Syriac text, edited by Jean-Baptiste Chabot, *Anonymi Auctoris Chronicon ad Annum Christi 1234 pertinens*. 2 vols. CSCO 81 (Scriptores Syri 36) and CSCO 82 (Scriptores Syri 37). Paris: Gabalda, 1920, 1916.
- Latin translation of vol. 1 by Jean-Baptiste Chabot, *Anonymi Auctoris Chronicon ad Annum Christi 1234 pertinens, I*. CSCO 109 (Scriptores Syri 56). Paris: Gabalda, 1937.
- French translation of vol. 2 by Albert Abouna, with introduction, notes, and index by Jean-Maurice Fiey, *Anonymi Auctoris Chronicon ad A.C. 1234 pertinens, II*. CSCO 354 (Scriptores Syri 154). Leuven: Peeters, 1974.
- Reprint of all four volumes, CSCO 81, 82, 109, and 354 (Scriptores Syri 36, 37, 56, 154), Leuven: Durbecq, 1952–.

Cohen, Mark R. "What Was the Pact of ʿUmar? A Literary-Historical Study," *Jerusalem Studies in Arabic and Islam* 23 (1999): 100–57.

Conrad, Lawrence I. "The Conquest of Arwād: A Source-Critical Study in the Historiography of the Early Medieval Near East." In *The Byzantine and Early Islamic Near East*, Vol. 1: *Problems in the Literary*

Source Material, edited by Averil Cameron and Lawrence I. Conrad, pp. 317–401. Studies in Late Antiquity and Early Islam 1. Princeton: Darwin Press, 1992.

Crone, Patricia. "The Pay of Client Soldiers in the Umayyad Period." *Der Islam* 80 (2003): 284–300.

———. "The Significance of Wooden Weapons in al-Mukhtār's Revolt and the ʿAbbāsid Revolution." In *Studies in Honour of Clifford Edmund Bosworth*, Vol. 1: *Hunter of the East: Arabic and Semitic Studies*, edited by Ian Richard Netton, pp. 174–87. Leiden: Brill, 2000.

Crone, Patricia, and Michael Cook. *Hagarism: The Making of the Islamic World*. Cambridge: Cambridge University Press, 1977.

Crone, Patricia, and Martin Hinds. *God's Caliph: Religious Authority in the First Centuries of Islam*. University of Cambridge Oriental Publications 37. Cambridge: Cambridge University Press, 1986.

Décobert, Christian. "Notule sur la patrimonialisme omeyyade." In *Umayyad Legacies: Medieval Memories from Syria to Spain*, edited by Antoine Borrut and Paul M. Cobb, pp. 213–54. Islamic History and Civilization, Studies and Texts 80. Leiden: Brill, 2010.

Dennett, Daniel C. *Conversion and the Poll Tax in Early Islam*. Harvard Historical Monographs 22. Cambridge: Harvard University Press, 1950.

Donner, Fred M. "La question du messianisme dans l'islam primitif." In "Mahdisme et millénarisme en Islam," edited by M. García-Arenal. *Revues des Mondes Musulmans et de la Méditerranée* 91–92–93–94 (2000): 17–28.

Dozy, Reinhart P. A. *Supplément aux dictionnaires arabes*. 2 vols. Beirut: Librairie du Liban, 1991. Reprint of Leiden: Brill, 1881.

Eutychius of Alexandria (Saʿīd b. Biṭrīq). *Annales*. [*Taʾrīkh al-majmūʿ ʿala al-taḥqīq wa-al-taṣdīq* or *Naẓm al-jawhar*]. Edited by Louis Cheïkho, Bernard Carra de Vaux, and Habib Zayyat, *Eutychii patriarchae Alexandrini annales*. 2 vols. Corpus Scriptorum Christianorum Orientalium 50–51 (Scriptores Arabici III, 6–7). Leuven: Peeters, 1906, 1909.

Fattal, Antoine. *Le statut légal des non-musulmans en pays d'Islam*. Recherches publiées sous la direction de l'Institut de lettres orientales de Beyrouth 10. Beirut: Imprimerie catholique, 1958.

Friedmann, Yohanan. "Classification of Unbelievers in Sunni Muslim Law and Traditions." *Jerusalem Studies in Arabic and Islam* 22 (1998): 171–72.

———. *Tolerance and Coercion in Islam: Interfaith Relations in the Muslim Tradition*. Cambridge: Cambridge University Press, 2003.

Goldziher, Ignaz. *Muhammedanische Studien*. 2 vols. Halle: Niemeyer, 1889–1890. Edited and translated by C. R. Barber and S. M. Stern as *Muslim Studies*. 2 vols. London: Allen & Unwin, 1968.

Hasson, Isaac. "Les *mawālī* dans l'armée musulmane sous les premiers Umayyades." *Jerusalem Studies in Arabic and Islam* 14 (1991): 176–213.

Hawting, Gerald R. "Idolatry and Idolators." In the *Encyclopaedia of the Qurʾān*, pp. 475–84. Leiden: Brill, 2002.

———. *The First Dynasty of Islam: The Umayyad Caliphate A.D. 661–750*. 2nd ed. London: Routledge, 2000.

Hoyland, Robert G. *Seeing Islam as Others Saw It: A Survey and Evaluation of Christian, Jewish and Zoroastrian Writings on Early Islam*. Studies in Late Antiquity and Early Islam 13. Princeton: Darwin Press, 1997.

———. *Theophilus of Edessa's Chronicle and the Circulation of Historical Knowledge in Late Antiquity and Early Islam*. Translated Texts for Historians 57. Liverpool: Liverpool University Press, 2011.

Ibn ʿAbd al-Ḥakam, ʿAbd al-Raḥmān b. ʿAbdallah. *Kitāb futuḥ Miṣr wa-akhbāriha*. Edited by Charles C. Torrey. Yale Oriental Series, Researches 3. New Haven: Yale University Press, 1922.

Ibn ʿAbd al-Ḥakam, Abū al-Qāsim ʿAbd al-Raḥmān. *Sirāt ʿUmar b. ʿAbd al-ʿAzīz*. Cairo: Dār al-Faḍīla, 1994.

Ibn Abī Shayba, ʿAbdallāh Muḥammad. *Muṣannaf Ibn Abī Shayba al-Kūfī*. Riyadh, A.H. 1409.

Ibn ʿAsākir, Abū al-Qāsim ʿAlī b. al-Ḥasan. *Taʾrīkh madīnat Dimashq*. Edited by Muḥib al-Dīn Abī Saʿīd b. Gharāma al-ʿImrawī. 80 vols. Beirut: Dār al-Fikr, 1995–2001.

Ibn Kathīr, Abū al-Fidāʾ, ʿImād al-Dīn Ismāʿīl b. ʿUmar. *Tafsīr al-Qurʾān al-ʿāẓīm*. Beirut, A.H. 1401/1980.

Kister, Meir J. "ʿAn Yadin (IX, 29)." *Arabica* 11 (1964): 272–78.

Kraemer, Joel L., annotator and translator. *The History of al-Ṭabarī*, Vol. 34: *Incipient Decline: The Caliphates of al-Wāthiq, al-Mutawakkil, and al-Muntaṣir A.D. 841–863/A.H. 227–248*. Albany: State University of New York Press, 1989.

Levi Della Vida, G. Review of Volume V of L. Caetani's *Annali*. *Rivista degli studi orientali* 4 (1911): 1074–76.

Levy, Reuben. *The Social Structure of Islam: Being the Second Edition of the Sociology of Islam*. Cambridge: Cambridge University Press, 1957.

Levy-Rubin, Milka, "*Shurūṭ ʿUmar* and Its Alternatives: The Legal Debate throughout the Eighth and Ninth Centuries over the Status of the Dhimmīs." *Jerusalem Studies in Arabic and Islam* 30 (2005): 170–206.

———. *Non-Muslims in the Early Islamic Empire: From Surrender to Coexistence*. Cambridge: Cambridge University Press, 2011.

al-Maqdisī, ʿAbdallāh b. Aḥmad b. Qudāma. *Al-Mughnī*. Beirut: Dar al-Fikr, A.H. 1405.

al-Maqrīzī, Aḥmad b. ʿAlī b. ʿAbd al-Qādir. *Al-Mawāʿiz wa-al-iʿtibār fī dhikr al-khiṭaṭ wa-al-āthār*. Edited by A. F. Sayyid. London: Muʾāssasat al-furqān li-al-turāth al-islāmī, 2002.

Michael the Syrian. *Chronicle*. Edited and translated by Jean-Baptiste Chabot, *Chronique de Michel le Syrien*. 4 vols. Paris: Academie des inscriptions et belles-lettres, 1899–1910. Reprinted Brussels: Culture et Civilisation, 1963.

al-Mizzī, Jamāl al-Dīn Abū al-Ḥajjāj Yūsuf. *Tahdhīb al-kamāl fī asmāʾ al-rijāl*. Beirut, 1992.

al-Mubarrad, Muḥammad b. Yazīd. *Kitāb al-kāmil*. Edited by W. Wright. Leipzig: G. Kreysing, 1864.

Murad, Hasan Q. "Was ʿUmar II 'a True Umayyad'?" *Islamic Studies* 24 (1985): 325–48.

al-Nīsābūrī, Muḥammad b. ʿAbdallah. *Al-Mustadrak ʿala al-ṣaḥīḥayn*. 6 vols. Beirut: Dar al-Maʿrifa, 1998.

Noth, Albrecht. "Abgrenzungsprobleme zwischen Muslimen und nicht-Muslimen: Die 'Bedingungen ʿUmars (*aš-šurūṭ al-ʿumariyya*)' unter einem anderen Aspekt gelesen." *Jerusalem Studies in Arabic and Islam* 9 (1987): 290–315; translated by M. Muelhaeusler in R. G. Hoyland, ed., *Muslims and Others in Early Islamic Society*, pp. 103–24. Burlington: Ashgate, 2004.

Palmer, Andrew. *The Seventh Century in the West-Syrian Chronicles*. Translated Texts for Historians 15. Liverpool: Liverpool University Press, 1993.

Paret, Rudi. *Der Koran*. Darmstadt: Wissenschaftliche Buchgesellschaft, 1975.

Pourshariati, Parvaneh. *Decline and Fall of the Sasanian Empire: The Sasanian-Parthian Confederacy and the Arab Conquest of Iran*. London: I. B. Tauris, 2008.

al-Qurṭubī, Abū ʿAbd Allāh Muḥammad b. Aḥmad al-Anṣārī. *Tafsīr al-Qurṭubī: al-jāmiʿ li-aḥkām al-Qurʾān*. Cairo, A.H. 1372.

Rex Smith, G. *The History of al-Ṭabarī*, Vol. 14: *The Conquest of Iran A.D. 641–643/A.H. 21–23*. Albany: State University of New York Press, 1994.

Robinson, Chase F. *Empire and Elites after the Muslim Conquest: The Transformation of Northern Mesopotamia*. Cambridge: Cambridge University Press, 2000.

———. "Neck-Sealing in Early Islam." *Journal of the Economic and Social History of the Orient* 48/3 (2005): 401–41.

Stillman, Yedidah Kalfon. *Arab Dress: A Short History from the Dawn of Islam to Modern Times*. Leiden: Brill, 2000.

al-Ṭabarī, Muḥammad b. Jarīr. *Taʾrīkh al-rusul wa-al-mulūk*. Edited by M. J. de Goeje et al. 15 vols. Leiden: Brill, 1879–1901.

———. *Jāmiʿ al-bayān ʿan taʾwīl al-Qurʾān (Tafsīr)*. 30 vols. Beirut, A.H. 1405/1984.

Theophanes. *Chronicle*.

- Edited by Carl De Boor, *Theophanis Chronographia*. 2 vols. Leipzig: Teubner, 1883–1885.
- English translation by Cyril Mango and Roger Scott, *The Chronicle of Theophanes Confessor. Byzantine and Near-Eastern History A.D. 284–813*. Oxford: Clarendon Press, 1997.

Theophanes continuaatus. Migne, Jacques Paul, editor. *Historiae Byzantinae scriptores post Theophanem, ex editione Francisci Combefisii*. Patrologia graeca 109. Paris: J.-P. Migne, 1863.

Yarbrough, Luke. "Origins of the *ghiyār*." *Journal of the American Oriental Society* 134/1 (2014): 113–21.

Zuqnīn Chronicle (Anonymous).

- Edited by Jean-Baptiste Chabot, *Incerti Auctoris chronicon anonymum pseudo-Dionysianum*. CSCO 104 (Scriptores Syri 53). Leuven: Peeters, 1933.
- Translated and annotated by Amir Harrak, *The Chronicle of Zuqnīn*, Parts III and IV, *A.D. 488–775*. Toronto: Gorgias Press, 1999.

8

Did ᶜUmar b. ᶜAbd al-ᶜAzīz Issue an Edict Concerning Non-Muslim Officials?

*Luke Yarbrough, Saint Louis University**

Introduction

The Umayyad caliph ᶜUmar (II) b. ᶜAbd al-ᶜAzīz died in early February of the year 720. So ended his reign of about 29 solar months over the largest polity then in existence. He was buried on a plot of land purchased from a monk at a Christian monastery in the *jund* of Ḥimṣ.[1] One month later a much humbler transaction took place several hundred miles away. Peter, village headman of Jeme in Upper Egypt, signed for the receipt of a *solidus*: the poll tax of one Johannes son of Mena.[2] A scribe named Anastasios wrote the receipt in Coptic on an ostracon. The signatures of both men were accompanied by crosses.

This latter transaction would have irked the ᶜUmar II whom we find depicted in certain historical accounts, modern as well as medieval. As part of a multifarious Islamization program, this ᶜUmar II issued an edict that non-Muslims were not to hold positions of political or administrative authority as, for instance, scribes or tax collectors. One piece of evidence adduced for this edict — a sentence in the work of the historian al-Kindī (d. 350/961) — has often been taken to mean that local Coptic headmen in Egypt were replaced with Muslims. Yet here we glimpse a Coptic headman and scribe in action immediately after ᶜUmar II's death. Another ostracon shows Peter in the same role a year earlier.[3] Such dissonance pervades the evidence for the edict, as we shall see. How should historians understand such disagreement? The most common approach is to affirm the historicity of the edict without scrutinizing the evidence too closely or critically.[4] Another is to allude warily to evidence of the

* I am grateful to Michael Cook, Patricia Crone, Christian Sahner, Lev Weitz, and the conference participants for their comments on drafts of this paper. They bear no responsibility for faults that remain.

[1] On his burial place at Dayr Simᶜān, see Dickie, "Appendix." Anecdotes surrounding the purchase are found in Ibn ᶜAsākir, *Taʾrīkh madīnat Dimashq*, vol. 45, p. 254; Ibn Saᶜd, *Kitāb al-ṭabaqāṭ al-kabīr*, vol. 7, p. 392; al-Iṣbahānī, *Ḥilyat al-awliyāʾ*, vol. 5, p. 14; for a report that he inherited the plot from his mother, and another that he merely happened to be in the neighborhood at the time of his death, see al-Yaᶜqūbī, *Taʾrīkh*, vol. 1, p. 318. A few sources name a different monastery; see Borrut, *Entre mémoire et pouvoir*, pp. 304f.

[2] See Wilfong, "Greek and Coptic Texts," pp. 91f. (O.O.I. 30023, dated 15 March 720).

[3] Ibid., pp. 92f. (O.O.I. 30025, dated 28 January 719). Wilfong's dating of 30023, but not 30025, is tentative.

[4] The edict was treated this way in Tritton, *Caliphs*, pp. 21f., and Fattal, *Le statut légal*, p. 248. The former is cited by Keating, *Defending the People of Truth*, p. 77, the latter by Cohen, *Under Crescent and Cross*, p. 66; Eddé, Micheau, and Picard, *Communautés chrétiennes*, p. 146. See also independent adoptions of this method in Lewis, *The Arabs in History*, p. 77; Baron, *A*

edict.[5] A third is to express in passing vague misgivings about the reliability of that evidence.[6] Or it may simply be left unmentioned.

Much legendary material is shot through the sources on which we rely for our knowledge of the reign of ʿUmar II.[7] Yet it is difficult to tell how much. On its own the vast scale of the writings attributed to ʿUmar II in comparison with Umayyads who reigned for much longer signals that he had become a literary as well as a historical figure.[8] Historians may feel entitled to doubt that wolves mixed amicably with sheep during his rule,[9] that he carried on a conversation with the dirt of a graveyard[10] and with a genie in the form of a snake,[11] that he played host to al-Khaḍir,[12] and even that he objected to the employment of administrators whose *fathers* had been non-Muslims (Manicheans or Christians),[13] to give but a few examples. Yet accounts of these events are found alongside relatively believable reports and carry *isnāds* of ostensibly equal authority. Too often the evidence for the reign of ʿUmar II — and for the Umayyad period in general — is sifted by discreetly discarding legendary material and treating the plausible remainder as more or less reliable. Unless one takes a literary detour around the problem of historical accuracy, however, it is only by focused and source-diverse study of an event that one can begin to assess its historicity. The edict of ʿUmar II regarding non-Muslim officials has not received such study.

This essay thus presents and evaluates the evidence that ʿUmar II issued an edict forbidding agents of the Umayyad state to employ non-Muslims. Its argument is that the evidence is intractable, allowing historians neither to confidently assess the nature of the policy nor even to be certain that it was formulated at all. By taking a considered stand for intractability we avoid unwarranted credulity and skepticism alike; by presenting all known evidence and identifying its difficulties we formulate problems that future work may succeed in solving, with or without the help of new evidence.

The method proposed here is applicable to other problems in early Islamic history: exhaustively to study an insoluble problem by collecting all available evidence and setting maximal (credulous) and minimal (skeptical) bounds to a range of plausible readings. Modern

Social and Religious History of the Jews, vol. 3, pp. 151f.; Levy-Rubin, *Non-Muslims*, pp. 94f. I find no basis for Tritton's description elsewhere of the edict's fate (*EI*[1] s.v. "Naṣārā"): "ʿUmar II gave orders to dismiss all *dhimmīs* from government service, but such confusion resulted that the order was soon afterwards ignored."

5 Lewis, *The Jews of Islam*, pp. 46f.

6 Richard Gottheil remarked that the extant texts of the edict insofar as they "breathe hatred to all non-Muḥammadans" have "little verisimilitude." Jean-Maurice Fiey viewed them similarly: "les pièces attribuées à ce calife, lettres et 'conditions' aient bien des chances d'être beaucoup plus tardives" (Gottheil, "Dhimmis and Moslems in Egypt," p. 359; Fiey, *Chrétiens syriaques*, p. 4).

7 The heavily hagiographical posthumous construction of ʿUmar II is the subject of the classic study by W. W. Barthold: "Caliph ʿUmar II and the Conflicting Reports on His Personality," and arises in *EI*[2] s.v. "ʿUmar (II) b. ʿAbd al-ʿAzīz" (P. M. Cobb) as well as (most recently and thoroughly) in Borrut, "Entre tradition et histoire" (updated in Borrut, *Entre mémoire et pouvoir*, pp. 283–320), an inspiration for the present essay.

8 See Crone and Hinds, *God's Caliph*, pp. 77f., esp. n. 22. The later caliph Hishām reigned eight times longer than ʿUmar II but is credited with about half the official correspondence.

9 Ibn ʿAsākir, *Taʾrīkh madīnat Dimashq*, vol. 45, p. 223; al-Ājurrī, *Akhbār Abī Ḥafṣ*, p. 50; Ibn al-Jawzī, *Sīra*, p. 70.

10 Ibn ʿAsākir, *Taʾrīkh madīnat Dimashq*, vol. 45, pp. 232f.

11 Ibn ʿAsākir, *Taʾrīkh madīnat Dimashq*, vol. 45, p. 146; Ibn al-Jawzī, *Sīra*, p. 30.

12 Ibn al-Jawzī, *Sīra*, pp. 43f.

13 Al-Iṣbahānī, *Ḥilya*, vol. 5, p. 273; Ibn al-Jawzī, *Sīra*, p. 62.

scholarship on the Umayyads has shown occasional tendencies to advance credulous or skeptical interpretations of evidence doggedly to the exclusion of alternatives, cheerfully to ignore serious flaws in the sources, or to maintain a studied silence about insoluble problems that does little to advance the field. The method of setting bounds to a plausible range of readings might, as one tool among many, open new avenues in Umayyad studies. The reign of ᶜUmar II alone offers numerous problems on which it might be tested.

The minimal reading of the evidence for the edict of ᶜUmar II maintains that no edict was in fact issued. The several epistles that purport to give the text of the edict are equally likely to represent pseudepigraphical political critique composed later. Because the historicity of the edict has not been critically examined and is usually assumed, I give more space to development of the minimal reading in this essay. The maximal reading holds that reports of the edict must refer to some event(s) of his reign. It is a version of this reading that Milka Levy-Rubin adopts in her essay in this volume. In my view, however, even the maximal reading does not permit us to conclude very much about what that event was. More precisely, it does not align with the notion that ᶜUmar II dismissed non-Muslim officials in accordance with some early version of the Islamic legal prohibition against such officials that would be formulated by Muslim jurists during the centuries that followed.

Historians who use the edict of ᶜUmar II to explain other events (e.g., changes in the onomastic profile of the papyri or a turning point in the career of John of Damascus) or as a point of departure for surveys of the political rights of non-Muslims should be aware that they are assenting to a strong version of the maximal reading of the evidence.

I. Evidence for the Edict of ᶜUmar II

I have argued elsewhere that proto-Sunnī Arab transmitters in second-/eighth-century Kūfa originated reports that the second caliph, ᶜUmar (I) b. al-Khaṭṭāb (d. 34/644), spoke out against non-Muslim officials. If this is so, then his grandson, ᶜUmar II, is the next candidate for first Muslim ruler actually to enact such a policy.[14] ᶜUmar II's edict in fact represents the only known attempt to purge Christians, Jews, and Zoroastrians as such from the Umayyad administration. Evidence for the edict may be divided into three categories. The first category consists of texts purporting to be epistles that the caliph sent to his lieutenants; these are found in early as well as late Muslim sources. The second consists of two allusions to the edict in Muslim sources, one explicit and one that is much less clear. The third consists of passages found in late Christian sources that might refer to the edict.

A. The Epistles

1. Ibn ᶜAbd al-Ḥakam

One epistle is found in the caliph's *sīra*, usually ascribed to ᶜAbdallāh b. ᶜAbd al-Ḥakam (d. 214/829) but available only in a recension transmitted by his son Muḥammad (d. 268/882).

[14] Yarbrough, "Upholding God's Rule." The language reforms usually associated with ᶜAbd al-Malik (d. 86/705) may have led to the dismissal of non-Muslim officials. But these reforms do not seem primarily to have targeted the religious affiliation of officials as such.

Muḥammad appears to have shaped the work to some degree.[15] Like most early Islamic literature, this *sīra* is composed of discrete reports. However, those reports are not supplied with the usual individual *isnāds*: lists of the individuals who purportedly transmitted each one. Our epistle (here termed Ep.[IAḤ]) thus lacks an *isnād*. It occurs some pages after a disjuncture in the *sīra*; after reports surrounding ʿUmar II's death an *isnād* is given (for the first time since the work's opening, some eighty pages before), beginning again with Muḥammad b. ʿAbdallāh b. ʿAbd al-Ḥakam.[16] The epistle may thus be part of a secondary addition. Its text is in several places problematic, and the following translation is thus provisional.

> ʿUmar b. ʿAbd al-ʿAzīz wrote to his administrators: "Now then, 'the associators are unclean' (Qurʾān 9:28), inasmuch as God declared them the host of the devil (cf. Qurʾān 4:76, 26:95), and declared them 'the greatest losers in their works whose striving goes astray in the present life, while they think that they are working good deeds' (Qurʾān 18:103). By my life, they are among those who, on account of their striving, deserve God's curse, and [indeed] the curse of all who curse (cf. Qurʾān 2:159, which refers to *ahl al-kitāb*). In times past, when the Muslims would come to a country in which associators (*ahl al-shirk*) were found, they would seek their assistance, because of their knowledge of taxation, scribal practice, and administration. They had their day, but now God has put an end to it by the Commander of the Faithful.[17] I know of no non-Muslim scribe or administrator in any part of your district but that I have dismissed him, and replaced him with a Muslim. Verily, to blot out their works is to blot out their religions. Indeed, it is most fitting that they be lowered to their station of humiliation and abasement to which God has lowered them. Therefore, do that, and write to me how you have done. See that no Christian rides upon a saddle; let them ride upon pack saddles.[18] None of their women is to ride in a litter; let her ride upon a pack saddle. Let them not straddle riding animals, but rather ride side-saddle. Forward this to your administrators, wherever they be, and write to them an epistle stressing it, and spare me [the trouble]. There is no strength except with God."[19]

2. *Al-Balādhurī*

The lengthy *vita* of ʿUmar II in the genealogical history by Aḥmad b. Yaḥyā al-Balādhurī (d. 279/892f.), *Ansāb al-ashrāf*, contains two more such epistles. Unlike the preceding they are supplied with *isnāds*. To my knowledge they have not been noted in modern studies. One (termed Ep.[B1]) is textually related, if distantly, to Ep.[IAḤ]:

---

[15] See the *isnāds* in the work of Ibn ʿAbd al-Ḥakam, *Sīrat*, pp. 19, 100, and Brockopp, *Early Mālikī Law*, pp. 24–26.

[16] Ibn ʿAbd al-Ḥakam, *Sīra*, p. 100.

[17] A variation of this notion whereby ʿUmar II is credited with ending non-Muslims' employment, not by fiat but because there were now enough skilled Muslims to take their place, is found in the work of the Mālikī jurist Jalāl al-Dīn ʿAbdallāh Ibn Shās (d. 616/1219), *ʿIqd al-jawāhir al-thamīna*, vol. 3, p. 495. See also the similarly late, vague reference in Gottheil, "A Fetwa on the Appointment of Dhimmis to Office," p. 212.

[18] For this translation of *ikāf* (pl. mult. *ukuf*), see Levy-Rubin, *Non-Muslims*, p. 90.

[19] Ibn ʿAbd al-Ḥakam, *Sīrat*, pp. 135f. This epistle was reproduced in modified forms by later writers. The version given by Fattal (*Le statut légal*, p. 248) is Belin's translation from the *Madhamma* of Ibn al-Naqqāsh ("Fetoua relatif à la condition des zimmis"), itself dependent upon the *Aḥkām ahl al-dhimma* of Ibn al-Qayyim. It belongs to a somewhat longer passage clearly excerpted from this work of Ibn ʿAbd al-Ḥakam.

> Manṣūr b. Abī Muzāḥim[20] related to me from Shuʿayb b. Ṣafwān,[21] saying, ʿUmar b. ʿAbd al-ʿAzīz wrote, "Now then, the Muslims must demote the associators and unbelievers as God has demoted them, and lower them to their station of humiliation and abasement to which God has lowered them. They must not take them into their confidence, or give them authority over the people of Islam, such that [the non-Muslims'] statutes are applied to [the Muslims], and they employ them in greed for what they have, and use them to fill their own needs, cheating and despoiling them. Therefore, dismiss absolutely everyone in your employ who does not follow the religion of Islam, and replace him with a Muslim of whose religion, trustworthiness, and uprightness you approve. Oblige them to wear belts, and ride upon pack saddles, and tonsure their heads. Obey God, and fear Him, for you shall have neither sanctuary nor ability to resist if you disobey Him. Peace."[22]

The other epistle presented by al-Balādhurī (termed Ep.^{B2}) contains only indistinct echoes of the two preceding:

> al-Madāʾinī[23] from Maslama [b. al-Muḥārib][24] and others, said: ʿUmar b. ʿAbd al-ʿAzīz wrote to one of his administrators, "Now then, God has used Islam to honor its people, to ennoble and uphold them, but [He has] imposed humiliation and abasement upon all others. He made [the Muslims] 'the best nation ever brought forth to men' (Qurʾān 3:110). Therefore, do not under any circumstances appoint over the affairs of any Muslim anyone from the people of their pact (*ahl dhimmatihim*) and their tax (*kharājihim*). Their hands and tongues would stretch out against them, and they would humiliate them when God has upheld them, insult them when God has honored them, and expose them to their craftiness and arrogance against them, not to mention the inevitable fraud. Indeed, God says, '[O you who] believe, take not for your intimates outside yourselves. Such men spare nothing to ruin you; they yearn for you to suffer.' (Qurʾān 3:118) And He says, 'Take not Jews and Christians as friends they are [friends to one another] (Qurʾān 5:51).'"[25]

3. *Al-Ṭurṭūshī*

The political-advice treatise of al-Ṭurṭūshī (d. 520/1126), *Sirāj al-mulūk*, gives additional witness to what now begins to look like an epistolary campaign:

[20] This and the following are state officials in Kufa and Baghdad. Manṣūr (d. 235/849) was a Turkish captive and *mawlā* of Azd. See Elad, *Medieval Jerusalem and Islamic Worship*, p. 83 n. 32, and al-Khaṭīb, *Taʾrīkh Madīnat al-Salām*, vol. 15, pp. 91–93.

[21] Abū Yaḥyā al-Thaqafī (d. 170–93/786–809), who is described as a *kātib* in the *dīwān* in Baghdad and an unreliable transmitter. See Ibn Abī Ḥātim al-Rāzī, *Kitāb al-jarḥ wa-al-taʿdīl*, vol. 4, p. 348, no. 1522; al-Bukhārī, *al-Taʾrīkh al-kabīr*, vol. 2, p. 223, no. 2586; al-Khaṭīb, *Taʾrīkh Madīnat al-Salām*, vol. 10, pp. 329f., no. 4766.

[22] Al-Balādhurī, *Ansāb al-ashrāf*, vol. 7, pp. 137f.

[23] *EI*^{2} s.v. "al-Madāʾinī" (U. Sezgin).

[24] Maslama was "a major informant" of al-Madāʾinī. He had pro-Umayyad leanings, though chiefly toward his Sufyānid forebears. Madelung, without direct reference to this epistle, characterizes his reports about the later Marwānids as "factual" and "detached." Madelung, "Maslama b. Muḥārib: Umayyad Historian."

[25] Al-Balādhurī, *Ansāb al-ashrāf*, vol. 7, p. 104. This epistle is reproduced nearly verbatim, introduced by *qīla* ("it was said") in Ibn al-Athīr, *al-Kāmil fī l-taʾrīkh*, vol. 5, p. 66 and, introduced by *kataba ilā ʿummālihi nuskhatan wāḥida* ("he wrote a single copy to his administrators"), in al-Nuwayrī, *Nihāyat al-arab fī funūn al-adab*, vol. 21, p. 321. I do not consider these separately. They name no source and since Ibn al-Athīr certainly used the *Ansāb* (and perhaps even the work of al-Madāʾinī) and shares much material with al-Nuwayrī it is quite likely that the *Ansāb* was in fact their source. See Brockelmann, *Das Verhältnis*, pp. 34, 44f., 53.

> ʿUmar b. Asad[26] said, "There came to us an epistle of ʿUmar b. ʿAbd al-ʿAzīz to Muḥammad b. al-Muntashir:[27] 'Now then, I am informed that there is in your employ a man, called Ḥassān b. Yazīd, who is not of the religion of Islam. But God [...] says, "O believers, take not as your friends those of them, who were given the Book before you, and the unbelievers, who take your religion in mockery and as a sport. And fear God, if you are believers" (Qurʾān 5:57). Therefore, when my epistle reaches you summon Ḥassān b. Yazīd to Islam. If he converts he is one of us. But if he refuses, do not seek his assistance, or that of anyone not of the people of Islam, in any task of the Muslims (*ʿalā shayʾin min aʿmāli*[28] *al-muslimīn*).' Then he read to him the epistle and he converted. So he taught him ritual purity and prayer.

It may be stated at this juncture that the evidence cited by Fattal from the *Mustaṭraf* of al-Ibshīhī is, *pace* Fattal, entirely irrelevant to ʿUmar II.[29]

B. References in Islamic Historiography

Apart from the epistles themselves we can point to only two mentions of this edict in early historical works by Muslims. One is a report in al-Balādhurī's work that follows immediately upon Ep.[B2]. It informs us on the same authority as Ep.[B2] (al-Madāʾinī and Maslama b. Muḥārib) that ʿUmar II wrote instructing his governor in Baṣra, ʿAdī b. Arṭāt, to dismiss non-Muslim (*dhimmī*) administrators. Ibn Raʾs al-Baghl[30] and Ibn "Zādhānfarrūj" [read Zādhān Farrūkh] b. Bīrī[31] were dismissed, but "Zādhmir" [read Āzādmard] b. al-Hirbidh[32] was retained. ʿUmar II wrote again to order Āzādmard's dismissal, this time successfully.

The other allusion, which has been used most frequently by Arabic papyrologists (below, n. 83), is found in the work of the historian al-Kindī (d. 350/961) and is less clear:

> Ibn Qudayd[33] related to me, from ʿUbayd Allāh b. Saʿīd,[34] from his father,[35] from Ibn Lahīʿa,[36] [who] said, "ʿUmar b. ʿAbd al-ʿAzīz wrote to [the governor] Ayyūb b. Shuraḥbīl concerning the army pay (*farīḍat al-jund*), saying, 'Attach it to the houses of noble and righteous lineage, for people are mines,[37] and portion out to debtors 25,000 dinars.'" The [troops sent against] Constantinople returned, and over the

[26] This figure is obscure. He is perhaps to be identified with the ʿUmar b. Asad, a native of Cordoba, who heard *ḥadīth* in Egypt at the mosque of Qulzum (Clysma). See Ibn al-Faraḍī, *Taʾrīkh ʿulamāʾ al-Andalus*, vol. 1, p. 421, no. 962. Other editions give different permutations of the name.

[27] Governor of Wāṣit under ʿUmar II and later caliphs; see Ibn Saʿd, *Kitāb al-ṭabaqāt*, vol. 8, p. 422, no. 3207.

[28] A polysemous homonym that can also denote "territories," "lands," etc.

[29] Fattal, *Le statut légal*, p. 248 n. 59; al-Ibshīhī, *Kitāb al-mustaṭraf*, p. 135. All of Ibshīhī's evidence relates in fact to ʿUmar I.

[30] See below, §II.B.

[31] See Sprengling, "Persian to Arabic," pp. 185ff.; Justi, *Iranisches Namenbuch*, pp. 377f.

[32] See below, §II.B.

[33] Ibn Qudayd (d. 312/925) was the source of more than half the traditions in this work; see al-Kindī, *Kitāb*, ed. Guest, p. 18.

[34] This individual "serves almost entirely as an intermediary between his father and Ibn Qudaid" (al-Kindī, *Kitāb*, ed. Guest, p. 21).

[35] Saʿīd b. Kathīr b. ʿUfayr (d. 226/841), a prominent Mālikī, may have written a book transmitted by his son from which al-Kindī drew reports such as this one (al-Kindī, *Kitāb*, ed. Guest, p. 26).

[36] He died in 174/790. See EI^2 s.v. "Lahīʿa" (F. Rosenthal). If the birthdates in the late 90s are to be believed, he was a very small child during the reign of ʿUmar II.

[37] This phrase parallels a well-known *ḥadīth*; see references in Wensinck, *Handbook of Early Muhammadan Tradition*, vol. 4, p. 156 (to the *Ṣaḥīḥ*s of Bukhārī and Muslim and the *Musnad* of Aḥmad b. Ḥanbal). Cf. Ibn ʿAsākir, *Taʾrīkh madīnat Dimashq*, vol. 65, p. 212, where the report ends with "mines."

> Egyptian contingent was Abū ʿUbayda b. ʿUqba b. Nāfiʿ al-Fihrī. The estates of the Copts were wrested from the pagarchies, Muslims were employed over [the Copts],[38] and women were banned from the baths.[39]

If the word "estates" (*mawārīth*) is actually to be read "headmen" (*mawāzīt*) then a case could be made for linking this account to the epistles of ʿUmar II. The passage is difficult to interpret, however, and will be discussed further below.

C. Christian Sources

1. The History of the Patriarchs of Alexandria

Three relatively late works by Christian authors might lend support to the historicity of the edict. The earliest is the *History of the Patriarchs of Alexandria* (*HP*), a voluminous account of the Coptic Church from its earliest days to the eleventh century, when it was compiled and redacted from earlier accounts by the Alexandrine Copt Mawhūb b. Manṣūr b. Mufarrij.[40] *HP* paints an ambivalent picture of the rule of ʿUmar II in Egypt:[41]

> This ʿUmar b. ʿAbd al-ʿAzīz did great good before men, [but] did evil before God [cf. Luke 16:15]. He commanded that there be no tax upon the estates (*awāsī*) of the Church, and the bishops. He invalidated taxation and rebuilt the cities that were in ruins. The Christians were in security and calm, as were the churches. Then after that he began to do evil. He wrote a letter to Egypt, full of woe. In it was written: ʿUmar commands and says, he who wishes to remain in his condition (primitive recension: "kingdom") and lands, let him be of Muḥammad's religion like me. And let him who does not wish, depart from my lands.[42] Then the Christians submitted to him that of which they had disposal, and "they trusted in God," and submitted their service to the Muslims (primitive recension: "and the Muslims received their service"), and "they became an example to many" [Ps. 71:7]. The hand [of oppression?] entered upon the Christians in every place, whether great or insignificant, rich or poor, from the governors, the administrators (primitive recension: "and the Muslims"). He ordered and said that the poll tax be taken from all the people who did not become Muslims, though their custom had not been to do so. God did not long abide him, but swiftly destroyed him, and did not allow him to rule because he was like the Antichrist.

The text is frequently obscure, but the overall picture is clear enough: in his 29-month rule ʿUmar II first pursued policies beneficial to the Copts, then abruptly changed course and instituted measures unfavorable to them. These appear to have involved a choice between conversion and some kind of dispossession or expulsion. It is certainly possible (though not necessary) to read here reference to expulsion from state employ. In fact, this account is among the strongest pieces of evidence for the edict.

---

38 *Wa-nuziʿat mawārīthu al-qibṭi ʿani l-kuwari wa-stuʿmila l-muslimūna ʿalayhim.* The readings (and meanings) of some terms in this sentence are uncertain. This translation follows the edition closely. See further below, §II.B.

39 Al-Kindī, *Kitāb*, ed. Guest, pp. 68–69; cf. al-Kindī, *Kitāb*, ed. Naṣṣār, pp. 89f.

40 See den Heijer, *Mawhūb ibn Manṣūr ibn Mufarriǧ*.

41 Translation based upon the "Vulgate" version of the *HP* as edited by Evetts, *History of the Patriarchs*, pp. 71–72, with attention to variants found in the "primitive recension" as published by Seybold, *Severus ibn al-Muqaffaʿ*, pp. 143f.

42 Can also mean "employ"; see n. 28, above.

2. Michael the Syrian

A phrase that pertains more clearly to an edict of ʿUmar II is found in the work of the chronicler and Syrian Orthodox patriarch known as Michael the Syrian (d. 1199):[43]

> ʿUmar, as soon as he took up the rule over the Arabs, began to mistreat the Christians and that for two reasons: firstly, because he wanted to honour and to affirm the laws of the Muslims; secondly, because of Constantinople, which the Arabs were unable to capture and before which many of them died [with loss of much] wealth. Rancour filled in his heart and he was very opposed to Christians in every way. He was declared to be a zealot for their laws and was considered to be God-fearing and he was averse to evil. He ordered oppression of the Christians in every way to make them become Muslims. He legislated that every Christian who became a Muslim would not pay poll tax and many converted. He also decreed that Christians should not testify against Muslims, *act as governors*, raise their voices for prayer, strike the sounding-board (to call people to prayer), wear the overcoat, or ride in a saddle and (that) if an Arab killed a Christian he could not be executed for it, but just paid compensation of 5,000 silver coins. He forbade and terminated the exactions from dwellings, inheritances, and portions of the revenues from lands [, which were taken from][44] churches, monasteries, and poor people. He also forbade Arabs to drink wine or must.

Amidst another largely negative account of ʿUmar II's policies we learn that Christians were not to act as governors.

3. John of Damascus

Modern surveys of the life of John of Damascus (d. ca. 132/750) often assert that he was dismissed from public office, which his forebears had occupied, by the edict of ʿUmar II.[45] This notion seems to have originated with Nasrallah, one of John's modern biographers.[46]

---

[43] I use the translation of Hoyland (*Theophilus of Edessa's Chronicle*, pp. 216f.); emphasis is mine. For the text, see Michael the Syrian, *Chronicle*, ed. Ibrahim, pp. 458–59. The crucial phrase is absent from another version of Michael's chronicle: the modern French rendition of an early Armenian translation. See Michael the Syrian, *Chronicle*, trans. Langlois, pp. 252f.

[44] Hoyland translates the bracketed phrase "exactions [...] levied in favour of" (Chabot: "le prélèvement [...] qu'on prélevait au profit des [...]"). The sentence is difficult. The grammatical subject of *meshtaqlā wāth* (Hoyland's "levied," which takes "exactions" or "revenues" as its subject) is in fact "lands." Syriac *men* (from) normally cannot mean "in favour of." The sense seems instead to be that ʿUmar deprived Christian institutions of revenue by confiscating land from which they had formerly collected. If *meshtaqlā* were to refer to exactions then Michael might in fact mean that ʿUmar lightened the tax burden, as Langlois' translation of the Armenian version of Michael's chronicle suggests: "que le corps des prêtres serait exempt d'impôts pour tous ses biens."

[45] Recent examples: Glei, "John of Damascus," p. 295; Küng, *Islam: Past, Present, and Future*, p. 8; Caseau, "Sacred Landscapes," p. 50; Goodman, "Greek Impact on Arabic Literature," p. 479; Peters, *Allah's Commonwealth*, p. 117.

[46] Nasrallah, *Saint Jean de Damas*, pp. 75, 81. Following Caetani, Nasrallah noted the anti-Christian measures attributed to ʿUmar II and concluded that John could not have remained in state employ. But of the seven supporting passages Caetani cited, five represent derivations of Theophanes' material (which does not mention state employment), one refers to Agapius of Manbij (which mentions no anti-Christian measures at all), and only the third, Michael the Syrian, indicates that ʿUmar II "impone molte regole vessatorie ... sull'attività pubblica dei cristiani." See Caetani, *Chronographia Islamica*, vol. 5, p. 1243. Subsequent work on John set the *terminus post quem* of his retirement at the accession of Hishām in 724. See Sahas, *John of Damascus on Islam*, p. 45. For an important new study on the career of John of Damascus, which indicates that Muslim Arabic sources in fact make no

Robert Hoyland has questioned whether John was employed by the state to begin with, but acknowledges that a passage from the Seventh Ecumenical Council (787) might refer to John's decision to leave state service:

> John, who is insultingly called Mansour by all, abandoned all, emulating the evangelist Matthew, and followed Christ, considering the shame of Christ as a richness superior to the treasures which are in Arabia. He chose rather to suffer with the people of God than to enjoy the temporary pleasure of sin.[47]

Matthew was a tax collector, and followed Jesus' call (Matt. 9:9). John might conceivably have left state service to comply with the edict of ʿUmar II.

4. Kitāb al-Majdal

The chronicle attributed to the twelfth-century Nestorian Christian Mārī b. Sulaymān refers to ʿUmar II only in reporting his death and asking God's mercy upon him. However, his successor Yazīd is said to have "restored the Christians to his service, and honored them" (*wa-radda l-naṣārā ilā khidmatihi wa-akramahum*).[48] It may be implied here that Christians had been out of the caliph's service. The edict of ʿUmar II might be given as the reason.[49] This chronicle is "largely based upon the *Chronicle of Siirt*," which Hoyland dates to the tenth century.[50]

D. Summary of the Evidence for a Religious Criterion

We have collected the following evidence for the edict of ʿUmar II concerning non-Muslim officials: 1) four epistles that purport to be transcripts of it, textually distinct but related in their use of certain phrases; 2) an explicit allusion in a Muslim source from Iraq; 3) a possible allusion in an Egyptian Muslim source; 4) three allusions, varying in clarity, in late Christian sources from Egypt, Syria, and Iraq. If one accepts all of this evidence then several conclusions follow: 1) ʿUmar II wrote a series of different epistles to his lieutenants in various parts of the empire. This directive targeted all non-Muslims employed by the state in the scribal professions (*kitāba*), taxation (*jibāya*), and administration more broadly (*tadbīr*), not merely those given authority over Muslims (see especially Ep.^{B1}); 2) he checked up on enforcement and reapplied pressure where necessary; 3) he justified the edict by reference to the Qurʾān and to a deep antipathy to non-Muslims as such, and was interested primarily in their "humiliation and abasement" and that Muslims be hired in their stead.

II. Assessing the Evidence

Should this newly expanded assemblage of evidence in fact be accepted as reliable? There is *prima facie* warrant for a degree of suspicion. Only a fraction of Umayyad subjects in 717

---

mention of John of Damascus at all, but rather only of his father, Manṣūr b. Sarjūn, see Anthony, "Fixing John Damascene's Biography." See also Sidney Griffith's contribution to this volume.

[47] Hoyland, *Seeing Islam as Others Saw It*, pp. 481f.

[48] Anonymous, *Maris Amri et Sliba*, p. 65.

[49] To my knowledge this has not been proposed previously.

[50] Hoyland, *Seeing Islam as Others Saw It*, pp. 444, 452. On the authorship of *Kitāb al-Majdal*, see Holmberg, "A Reconsideration of the *Kitāb al-Mağdal*."

were Muslims — perhaps less than 10 percent.[51] Those Muslims were living in a conquest-driven tribute state whose full members tended to have little interest in relatively menial bureaucratic employment. An Arabic scientific and educational high culture to produce large numbers of skilled administrators was decades away at best. It was not universally agreed that non-Arabs were to be welcomed as full members of the *umma*, or that *mawālī* had to convert. The administrative machinery of the Islamic state had rested on a non-Arab, largely non-Muslim base since that state's first expansion.[52] The detailed socio-religious programs of Islamic law (which would come to include arguments against non-Muslim officials) and a class of religious professionals to advocate for them were nascent. Under these circumstances we might well wonder that a head of state aspired to purge all non-Muslim administrators, as the epistles claim. All in all ʿUmar II's religious criterion appears rather out of place in the early eighth-century setting. The evidence thus merits scrutiny.

A. The Epistles

The unique epistle presented by al-Ṭurṭūshī may be dealt with on its own. It is a distortion of an incident that according to a much more reliable source — the *Kitāb al-wuzarāʾ* of al-Jahshiyārī — took place during the caliphate of Hishām (r. 105–125/724–743). There, Hishām wrote to the same Muḥammad b. al-Muntashir concerning this Ḥassān, described as "al-Nabaṭī," a well-attested Christian official in Iraq.[53] Even al-Jahshiyārī's report may be suspect; it uses juristic terminology common in later centuries (*lā yustaʿānu bi-dhimmī*) and occurs a few lines after a report that Hishām placed the Christian "Tādhrī b. Asṭīn" over the administration of Ḥimṣ. But in any case, Hishām can scarcely have written to the same governor about a Christian official with the same name, with the same result. Al-Jahshiyārī's account is to be preferred and al-Ṭurṭūshī's is thus unreliable, at least as it pertains to ʿUmar II (whose conduct carried much more paradigmatic weight than did Hishām's). The person who misascribed it would of course have used better information about ʿUmar II if any had been available.

We may next consider the authenticity of the three related epistles (Ep.[IAḤ] and Eps.[B1 & B2]) by comparing them to one another and to similar texts from the same historical and historiographical settings. Unfortunately the three are relatively ill-suited to source-critical study. They claim no shared paths of transmission and are too divergent for exhaustive comparison. Yet there are faint echoes of intertextuality. Only one phrase — "humiliation and abasement" — is found in all three, though Ep.[B2] has it in slightly divergent form. This phrase is best known from a Prophetic *ḥadīth* transmitted with various *isnāds*.[54] All three also stress the theme that political hierarchy among humans should mirror the hierarchy of their religions as God has arranged it: Islam on top. However sensible it might seem, this theme is not inevitable and reflects a shared original milieu. Ep.[IAḤ] and Ep.[B1] are more closely linked. They share two phrases that account for roughly a fifth of their respective contents. This fact must reflect a common background.

---

[51] Conrad, "Conquest of Arwād," p. 345 n. 87, building upon the conclusions of Bulliet.

[52] For some indications, see Yarbrough, "Upholding God's Rule," p. 58 n. 145.

[53] Al-Jahshiyārī, *Kitāb al-wuzarāʾ*, p. 60. On Ḥassān, see Morony, "Aramean Population," pp. 3–4.

[54] Wensinck, *Handbook of Early Muhammadan Tradition*, vol. 2, pp. 183f.

What was this common background? It might of course have been an authentic epistle or epistles sent by ʿUmar II. The hypothesis that an actual edict of ʿUmar II was recalled separately and very imperfectly by transmitters solves two problems. First, it explains why the texts as we have them resemble one another but only faintly. Second, it explains how a protracted epistolary campaign on a very public issue is coupled with near-total silence in other veins of Muslim and Christian historiography (on which see below, §III.A). On this model there would have been no campaign but rather a single epistle, perhaps of limited diffusion, that we would not expect to have been widely reported in other sources, unlike an empire-wide edict.

It must be observed, however, that a later pseudepigraphic ascription of these texts to ʿUmar II might just as easily explain the common background; furthermore, the epistles do in fact have affinity to later texts. The affinity is most pronounced in connection with the first undisputed purge of non-Muslim administrators by a caliph: the ʿAbbāsid al-Mutawakkil, whose boon companion was al-Balādhurī, in 235/850. Al-Ṭabarī (d. 310/923) and Ibn Zabr (d. 329/940) sum up this edict with the phrase, "He forbade that they should be employed in the administrative bureaus and areas of authority *wherein their statutes would be applied to Muslims*."[55] This is a nearly verbatim reproduction of a phrase in Ep.[B1] It is uncommon in the juristic literature on the topic and thus is quite distinctive. Although the epistle that al-Ṭabarī then supplies does not mention employment, Ibn Zabr gives a separate epistle written by the high official al-Najāḥ b. Salama[56] (d. 245/860) that implemented Mutawakkil's edict on non-Muslim officials.[57] This document bears unmistakable signs of textual affinity to Ep.[B2]: the verse describing Muslims as "the best nation ever brought forth to men" (Qurʾān 3:110); the phrase "humiliation and abasement" using the form *al-dhilla wal-ṣaghār* rather than *al-dhull wal-ṣaghār* as in Ep.[IAḤ] and Ep.[B1]; and the phrase "stretch out their tongues and hands," with the verb in both cases in the seventh form rather than the first form expected from the Qurʾānic allusion (60:2), which verse is also unexpected here (unlike, e.g., Qurʾān 3:118 or 5:51). Thus Ep.[B2], which bears little textual resemblance to Ep.[IAḤ] and Ep.[B1] and whose impressive *isnād* (Maslama b. al-Muḥarib—al-Madāʾinī) gives it the best claim to authenticity of the three, turns out to bear an unmistakable resemblance to a text of the mid-ninth century, in which time the epistles' content is more at home.

There exists in later sources another epistle that purports to be an instrument by which al-Mutawakkil publicized his edict.[58] It too is shot through with language, quotations, and themes found in our epistles. If all the "Mutawakkilian" content were removed from the texts attributed to ʿUmar II there would be little left of them. One of the two phrases shared by Ep.[IAḤ] and Ep.[B1] is found verbatim near the end of this epistle (*inzālu ahli l-dhimmati manāzilahum allatī anzalahum Allāhu taʿālā bihā*), but the way in which al-Mutawakkil's epistle echoes all three of ours is pervasive. Although the sources in which this epistle of al-Mutawakkil is found also contain a version of Ep.[IAḤ] this is not simply a matter of material from Ep.[IAḤ] having been transposed into this epistle by a later compiler; language found in

---

[55] *Wa-nahā an yustaʿāna bihim fī l-dawāwīni wa-aʿmāli l-sulṭani llatī yujrā aḥkāmuhum fīhā ʿala l-muslimīn.* Al-Ṭabarī, *Taʾrīkh*, vol. 3, p. 1390; Cohen, "What Was the Pact of ʿUmar?" p. 148 (emphasis added).

[56] On al-Najāḥ, see al-Ṭabarī, *Taʾrīkh*, vol. 3, pp. 1440–46; Ibn ʿAsākir, *Taʾrīkh madīnat Dimashq*, vol. 61, pp. 451–59.

[57] Cohen, "What Was the Pact of ʿUmar?" pp. 151–53.

[58] See Ibn Qayyim al-Jawzīya, *Aḥkām ahl al-dhimma*, vol. 1, pp. 222–24; cf. al-Qalqashandī, *Subḥ al-aʿshā*, vol. 13, pp. 367f. For the source of these reports, see Yarbrough, "A Rather Small Genre."

Ep.[B1] or Ep.[B2] but not Ep.[IAH] also appears in it (e.g., Ep.[B1]: *wa-lā yushrikūhum fī amānātihim*; al-Mutawakkil *apud* Ibn al-Qayyim: *al-ishrāk lahum fī amānātihim*).

These epistles of al-Mutawakkil, issued into a setting that by comparison to the early eighth century teemed with historians, are likely to preserve the language in which al-Mutawakkil publicized his edict. But the author of this edict would naturally have called on arguments and notions current in his setting. That the language in which that reasoning was expressed is heavily reflected in the texts of our epistles suggests that they, too, might be products of early ʿAbbāsid Iraq.

Did the author of al-Mutawakkil's epistle use language from our texts in order to tap into the authority of ʿUmar II's memory? He might well have wished to adopt such precedent. Yet the advantage would have been to stress the continuity between his own policies and those of the fifth "rightly guided" caliph, ʿUmar II. Since there is no explicit reference, and since our epistles are too rare in the sources to indicate that the connection would have been immediately obvious, it is more likely that the edicts of al-Mutawakkil and those ascribed to ʿUmar II arose in parallel in the same Iraqi milieux. They drew on a common conceptual and lexical stock either to encourage the adoption of these policies or to justify their implementation.

The *isnāds* attached to the epistles in al-Balādhurī's work also suggest an Iraqi background. All individuals named lived in ʿAbbāsid Iraq. The source of Ep.[B2] — which we have seen to resemble closely a text of the mid-ninth century — is the Baṣran Maslama b. al-Muḥārib, from whom al-Madāʾinī (and al-Balādhurī) transmitted many reports. We have few opinions about his reliability because he did not transmit *ḥadīth*. Both figures attached to Ep.[B1], meanwhile, were prominent scribes in the ʿAbbāsid administration of Iraq, where they doubtless rubbed shoulders — and competed — with non-Muslim officials. Shuʿayb b. Ṣafwān was scribe to the *qāḍī* of Kūfa Ibn Shubruma (d. 144/761), and also spent time in Baghdad — he moved, that is, in precisely the same circles in which reports opposing non-Muslim officials attributed to ʿUmar I originated and grew.[59] Shuʿayb was also a companion of the ʿAbbāsid caliph al-Manṣūr (*min ṣaḥābat Abī Jaʿfar*), according to a report from Aḥmad b. Ḥanbal, and narrated a number of reports about ʿUmar II.[60] He was known as a poor transmitter of *ḥadīth*. The renowned critic Yaḥyā b. Maʿīn, one of Shuʿayb's chief detractors, referred in fact to "those long epistles via Manṣūr b. Abī Muzāḥim" as evidence of his unreliability. Manṣūr himself was a proto-Sunnī scribe, a Turkish captive who left his government post for reasons we do not know. While he might well have had opportunity to narrate from Shuʿayb, the greatest single flaw in this *isnād* is that elsewhere one finds either two or three transmitters between Shuʿayb and ʿUmar II.[61] Here there are none. Both Shuʿayb and Manṣūr might have had ample motive and opportunity to compose and/or disseminate an epistle such as Ep.[B1]. The difficulty is that we have no reliable method for distinguishing an early-ʿAbbāsid-era pseudepigraphical composition from a middle-Umayyad document, except of course comparison to other texts on the same theme. We have seen that comparison to the texts of al-Mutawakkil lends support to the later dating.

---

[59] On Ibn Shubruma, see *EI*², s.v. (J.-C. Vadet); on the Kufan circles, see Yarbrough, "Upholding God's Rule."

[60] Al-Khaṭīb, *Taʾrīkh madīnat al-salām*, vol. 10, pp. 329f., no. 4766.

[61] E.g., Ibn al-Jawzī, *Sīra*, p. 9 (three names separating Shuʿayb from ʿUmar II), p. 118 (two names separating them).

There is, finally, the matter of tone. The epistles exhibit strong antipathy toward non-Muslims; as Gottheil remarked more than a century ago, they "breathe hatred to all non-Muḥammadans."[62] But ʿUmar II is depicted in many Muslim reports as favorably inclined toward non-Muslims. An aged *dhimmī* from Ḥimṣ successfully petitioned him for justice in a property dispute with Umayyad family members by appealing to "the book of God" against an executive order written by an Umayyad.[63] One of the chief demands that ʿUmar II made of Khārijites was not to molest *ahl al-dhimma*.[64] He commanded his agents to "be kind to them" and to lift taxes from them in their old age.[65] Faced with a revenue surplus he instructed a governor to "strengthen (*qawwi*) *ahl al-dhimma* [by lifting their taxes], for we have no need of them for a year or two."[66] He was concerned on his deathbed that they be treated justly.[67] He was in the habit of buying his groceries from *dhimmī*s, to whom he insisted on paying full price.[68] He had no objection to Christians endowing churches.[69] In the Umayyad stronghold of Damascus he upheld the Christians' claim to their churches, offending the Muslim populace.[70] When he traveled to Jerusalem, he would lodge with a monk, who years later recalled how his pious tears leaked through the ceiling.[71] On another occasion, before his accession, he begged a monk for a wise maxim; the line of ascetic poetry that he received was on his lips at the moment of his appointment.[72] He left money to the monastery at which he chose to be buried.[73] These testimonia might of course be equally unreliable. To the extent that they lack a basis in authentic historical memory, we may conclude that the memory of a vituperative ʿUmar II intent on the humiliation of non-Muslims had not permeated the circles in which they were circulated. We might thus question whether the vituperative memory has itself a firm historical basis. But to the extent that the eirenic descriptions of ʿUmar II preserve authentic memories, we may conclude that the vindictive author(s) of the epistles did not share the views of the figure who inspired those memories. In either case, the cumulative effect is to call the ascription of the epistles to ʿUmar II into question.

B. References in Islamic Historiography

The report given by al-Balādhurī names three non-Muslims who were dismissed from the administration in Iraq. It is in fact the only unequivocal evidence of ʿUmar II's edict in early Muslim historiography apart from the epistles themselves. It is not, however, entirely independent of the epistles, for its *isnād* is identical to that of Ep.[B2] The first name it gives, Ibn Zādhān Farrūkh b. Bīrī, is known from other sources; his name was Mardānshāh.[74] His father, the famous Zādhān Farrūkh, died during the rebellion of Ibn al-Ashʿath (ca. 80–83/699–702).[75]

---

[62] Gottheil, "Dhimmis and Moslems in Egypt," p. 359.

[63] Al-Ājurrī, *Akhbār Abī Ḥafṣ*, p. 58; Ibn al-Jawzī, *Sīra*, pp. 104–05.

[64] Al-Iṣbahānī, *Ḥilyat al-awliyāʾ*, vol. 5, p. 310; Ibn al-Jawzī, *Sīra*, p. 77.

[65] Ibn Saʿd, *Kitāb al-ṭabaqāt*, vol. 7, p. 370; al-Balādhurī, *Ansāb al-ashrāf*, vol. 7, p. 87; Abū ʿUbayd al-Qāsim b. Sallām, *Kitāb al-amwāl*, pp. 58, 64.

[66] Ibn ʿAbd al-Ḥakam, *Sīra*, p. 58.

[67] Ibid., p. 98.

[68] Ibn al-Jawzī, *Sīra*, p. 162.

[69] Ibn Saʿd, *Kitāb al-ṭabaqāt*, vol. 7, p. 349.

[70] Abū ʿUbayd, *Kitāb al-amwāl*, pp. 223–24; Ibn ʿAsākir, *Taʾrīkh madīnat Dimashq*, vol. 2, pp. 273f.

[71] Ibn al-Jawzī, *Sīra*, pp. 185–86.

[72] Ibn ʿAsākir, *Taʾrīkh madīnat Dimashq*, vol. 45, pp. 209–10; cf. Ibn ʿAbd al-Ḥakam, *Sīra*, p. 48, where he again visits a monastery.

[73] Ibn al-Jawzī, *Sīra*, p. 295.

[74] Sprengling, "Persian to Arabic," p. 190; al-Balādhurī, *Futūḥ al-buldān*, p. 301.

[75] Sprengling, "Persian to Arabic," p. 190, to which "unequivocal and convincing evidence" add the corroborating date of 82/701 given by Khalīfa b. Khayyāṭ, *Taʾrīkh*, p. 222.

His descendants continued as Zoroastrians in service of the Umayyad and ʿAbbāsid states for at least two more generations.[76]

The other two names are also attested. Āzādmard b. al-Hirbidh was employed by the governor al-Ḥajjāj (d. 95/714).[77] There is evidence that he was dismissed and maimed by al-Ḥajjāj[78] but none that he was re-hired. Ibn Raʾs al-Baghl is more difficult to identify. An administrator of the name was reportedly imprisoned over tax revenues in the time of al-Aḥnaf b. Qays (d. 67/686–7).[79] The Greek-speaking doctor who treated the Umayyad caliph al-Walīd I (d. 96/715) on his deathbed is also named as Ibn Raʾs al-Baghl.[80] This doctor is thus probably not identical with the wealthy Zoroastrian "nobleman of China" (*dihqān al-ṣīn*) named Ibn Raʾs al-Baghl in another account, which based on accompanying names must be set in the seventh century.[81] Neither figure is thus likely to be the Javānābeh (?) Ibn Raʾs al-Baghl who helped to finance Khālid al-Qasrī (gov. Iraq ca. 105–120/723–738).[82] The name may designate a generic non-Muslim tycoon. On the whole, our assessment of the reliability of this report is inconclusive. On the encouraging side, it gives the names of non-Muslims reported independently to have participated in the administration of Umayyad ʿIrāq, though not necessarily under ʿUmar II. One also finds, however, that the onomastics are hazy, the narrative framed by topoi, and the *isnād* identical to that of the very text we wish to authenticate — the text, in fact, whose contents have been shown to correspond closely to a mid-ninth-century epistle on the same subject. Here too, absent corroborating testimonia, we have no reliable way to distinguish a sincere recollection of the Umayyad period from an ʿAbbāsid retrojection. If one wishes to treat this report as reliable, it points to a sustained campaign on the part of the caliph, inasmuch as it describes an executive order, investigation of its implementation, and its reassertion.

The sentence from the history of al-Kindī quoted in §I.B — "The estates of the Copts were wrested from the pagarchies, and Muslims were employed over them" (*wa-nuziʿat mawārīthu al-qibṭi ʿani al-kuwari wa-stuʿmila al-muslimūna ʿalayhim*) — has been read as reference to the edict of ʿUmar II.[83] But in fact the verb in the sentence is passive; there is no indication of its agent, if any. Nor, in the form we have it, does it have any connection to the dismissal of officials. This connection requires an emendation introduced by Ḥusayn Naṣṣār, who reworked[84] the 1912 edition. Naṣṣār emended *mawārīth* (heritages, estates) to *mawāzīt*

---

[76] Al-Jahshiyārī, *Kitāb al-wuzarāʾ*, p. 99; here Māgushnasp b. Bahrām b. Mardānshāh b. Zādhān Farrūkh is *kātib* to Sulaymān b. Ḥabīb (see Sprengling, "Persian to Arabic," pp. 190f.).

[77] Al-Balādhurī, *Ansāb al-ashrāf*, vol. 7, p. 364; he is perhaps to be identified with the Āzādmard Kāmkār who restructured the city of Fasā in Fārs under al-Ḥajjāj (Ḥamza al-Iṣbahānī, *Hamzae Ispahanensis Annalium Libri X*, p. 37). But see also an attestation from much earlier, where Āzādmard b. al-Hirbidh is brought to Baṣra by an appointee of Ziyād b. Abīhi (d. 53/673), Nuʿaym b. al-Thawlāʾ b. Masʿūd of the B. Nahshal (al-Balādhurī, *Ansāb al-ashrāf*, vol. 11, p. 150).

[78] Al-Balādhurī, *Ansāb al-ashrāf*, vol. 7, p. 402; al-Ābī, *Nathr al-durar*, vol. 5, p. 42; al-Tanūkhī, *Nishwār al-muḥāḍara wa-akhbār al-mudhākara*, pp. 136f. (emend patronymic from "al-Farand").

[79] Al-Balādhurī, *Ansāb al-ashrāf*, vol. 11, p. 425.

[80] Al-Balādhurī, *Ansāb al-ashrāf*, vol. 7, p. 35.

[81] Al-Iṣbahānī, *Kitāb al-aghānī*, vol. 11, p. 249. The poet to whom he lent, al-Uqayshir, died ca. 80/699. See al-Uqayshir, *Dīwān*, p. 15.

[82] Al-Balādhurī, *Ansāb al-ashrāf*, vol. 7, p. 429.

[83] Fattal, *Le statut légal*, p. 248 n. 59. It is the strongest evidence on the basis of which Frantz-Murphy (*Arabic Agricultural Leases and Tax Receipts*, pp. 24, 26 nn. 20, 69) argues that Coptic headmen were removed, in many cases permanently, under ʿUmar II. She uses it to explain patterns in the papyrological evidence. Sijpesteijn also uses the reading *mawāzīt* (*Shaping a Muslim State*, p. 103 n. 380; "The Archival Mind," p. 172, where she posits a rather sharp break in administrative practice on the basis of this datum). See also Abbott, "A New Papyrus," p. 30.

[84] Naṣṣār worked from Guest's edition, not from the British Museum MS (see al-Kindī, *Kitāb*, ed. Naṣṣār, p. 26).

(headmen), declaring that *mawārīth* "has no meaning here." The words do look alike and the emendation is plausible. Frantz-Murphy treated it as definitive. Yet it must be pointed out that competent historians have taken the reading *mawārīth* seriously. Ibn Taghrībirdī (d. 874/1470), for example, altered the passage to accommodate it: *wa-nuziḥati l-qibṭu ʿani al-kuwari wa-stuʿmila ʿalayha l-muslimūn wa-nuziʿat aydīhim ayḍan ʿani l-mawārīthi wa-stuʿmila ʿalayha l-muslimūn* ("The Copts were removed from the pagarchies and Muslims employed over [the pagarchies], and their hands were also removed from the estates, and Muslims employed over [the estates]").[85] Al-Maqrīzī (d. 845/1442) also read *mawārīth*.[86] Additional evidence for *mawārīth* is preserved by Ibn Ḥazm:[87]

> By way of Ibn Wahb,[88] from Ibn Lahīʿa, from Yazīd b. Abī Ḥabīb,[89] that ʿUmar b. ʿAbd al-ʿAzīz wrote to Hayyān b. Shurayḥ, "Make the inheritances (*mawārīth*) of the *dhimmīs* accord with Qurʾānic inheritance regulations."

This report was transmitted by some of the same Egyptian authorities with additional details (e.g., the name of the chief finance officer). It also adduces an epistle of ʿUmar II to Egypt that interfered with the *mawārīth* of non-Muslims.[90] There is no reason that al-Kindī's report should not also concern the *mawārīth* of non-Muslims as all extant witnesses say it did. The report, though still not quite transparent, indicates that the state assumed control over intestate estates. Surviving documents confirm that this happened.[91] The next phrase ("and Muslims were employed over [the Copts]") is, like that which follows it ("and women were forbidden from the baths"), not directly related, though it certainly does signal the increasing presence of Muslim officials in an administration that remained largely Christian. This is preferable to the conjectural reading *mawāzīt*. If one nevertheless wishes to link this testimony to the edict of ʿUmar II there are non-trivial implications: his edict applied not just in Iraq or to non-Muslim officials with authority over Muslims, but also to local administrators of the non-Muslim population in Egypt (the *mawāzīt* of the *kuwar*).

C. Christian Sources

1. *History of the Patriarchs of Alexandria* (*HP*)

We have seen that the evidence from *HP* is among the strongest for the edict. Yet a difficulty that it shares with the other evidence from Christian historiography is its late provenance and textual corruption. Its late provenance makes it difficult to be sure that its testimony

[85] Ibn Taghrībirdī, *Al-Nujūm al-zāhira*, vol. 1, p. 364 (Leiden); cf. the Cairo ed., vol. 1, p. 238.

[86] Al-Maqrīzī, *Kitāb al-mawāʿiẓ*, vol. 2, p. 50 (London); cf. the Cairo ed., vol. 1, p. 302.

[87] Ibn Ḥazm, *al-Muḥallā*, vol. 9, p. 307.

[88] He died in 197/812; see Muranyi, *ʿAbd Allāh b. Wahb*, pp. 17–49, 106–07 (for notes on this *isnād*).

[89] He died in 128/746; see Muranyi, *ʿAbd Allāh b. Wahb*, p. 107.

[90] To ʿUmar II are elsewhere attributed instructions concerning the disposal of *mawārīth ahl al-arḍ*: the state is not to interfere with them, save for administrators whom the imam sends with special instructions (Ibn ʿAbd al-Ḥakam, *Sīra*, p. 83). He directed that the *mīrāth* of a manumitted non-Muslim *mawlā* go to the treasury (al-Balādhurī, *Ansāb al-ashrāf*, vol. 7, p. 96).

[91] An early-eighth-century papyrus from Jeme contains the phrase *annahā mātat fa-lam yakun lahā warithun fa-a[ʿṭaw] mālahā li-amīri al-muʾminīn* ("Sie ist gestorben und hatte keinen Erben, so [haben sie gegeben] ihren Besitz an den Befehlshaber der Gläubigen"). Thus even in Upper Egypt the state confiscated intestate estates (here of a woman bearing an Arab name). Liebrenz, "Eine frühe arabische Quittung," esp. pp. 300–01.

is in fact independent evidence for the event and not, for example, a horizontal borrowing from other historiography. Its textual corruption makes it difficult to discern what it in fact says about the event. Our only control on the *HP* is the ecclesiastical chronicle (henceforth *HPY*) traditionally attributed to Yūsāb of Fūwah (d. ca. 1257–1271).[92] *HPY* is "more compact than the *HP*, with basically the same structure and contents."[93] These contents represent an "abridged paraphrase" of *HP*,[94] a summary with and without additional sources, or in some cases an independent witness to an earlier source.[95] The biography of the forty-third patriarch, Alexander, a contemporary of ʿUmar II, is textually related to that found in *HP*. The text of *HPY* here is also corrupt. It mentions neither ʿUmar II nor anything that could be construed as reference to an edict about non-Muslim officials.[96]

> *HP:* [ʿUmar commands] and says, "He who wishes to remain in his condition [or "kingdom"] and lands, let him be of Muḥammad's religion like me. And let him who does not wish, depart from my lands." Then the Christians submitted to him that of which they had disposal.
>
> *HPY:* And they had said, "He who is not of M[uḥamma]d's religion, or else [?] let him depart from our country (*bilād*)." And they took all the Christians' money.

If *HPY* is here a summary of *HP* then the compiler of *HPY* clearly did not understand *HP* as describing dismissal from government service. But it cannot be ruled out that the two derive independently from a common source. If this is the case then that source may not have envisioned such dismissal either. What might such a common source have been? This passage has been attributed to John the Deacon, who composed what became *vitae* 43–46 of *HP* in Coptic ca. 770.[97] Throughout this *vita HPY* seems a primitive rearrangement and digest of *HP*, with clear disagreements on names and facts. This suggests summary less than independent access to a less extensive common source, perhaps by John the Deacon; the expanded text of *HP* thus might be the work of the eleventh-century redactor Mawhūb b. Manṣūr or an intermediary. On this hypothesis the common source as reflected in *HPY* contained no evidence of ʿUmar II's edict. This evidence might well have been interpolated at a later time when Coptic officials were subject to the pressure to convert and the example of ʿUmar II given as justification.

Yet even if the account in *HP* is accepted as a faithful rendering of John's work there is a further difficulty. The language does not refer unambiguously to an edict of the kind we want. That it has been given as evidence of such may owe to its citation in this connection by Tritton and Fattal.[98] Evetts' translation of the passage makes no reference to administrative employment.[99] Like the compiler of *HPY* Evetts understood the consequence of refusal to convert as banishment from lands — not offices — and the Coptic response to involve payments, not resignations. The author of the Arabic *HP* knew how to speak about state employment using the usual Arabic idioms; an Athanasius was chief of the administration (*mutawallī dīwān*) of Alexandria, while a Theodore took over the affairs of (*tawallā umūr*) the same city.[100] He

92 On this ascription, see Moawad, "Zur Originalität."
93 Den Heijer, "Coptic Historiography," p. 81.
94 Ibid., p. 96.
95 Moawad, "Zur Originalität," pp. 262, 264f.
96 [Yūsāb of Fūwah], *Taʾrīkh al-ābāʾ al-baṭārika* [= *HPY*], pp. 52–54.
97 See Swanson, "John the Deacon."
98 Tritton, *Caliphs*, pp. 21f., whence Fattal, *Le statut légal*, p. 248.
99 Evetts, *History of the Patriarchs*, p. 71.
100 Ibid., pp. 48, 66.

refers to numerous Christian state scribes (*kātib*, pl. *kuttāb*), an official granted favor with the governors (*arkhun razaqahu Llāhu qabūlan ʿinda l-wulāt*), and a Christian with authority to command and forbid (*kāna dhā amrin wa-nahy*).[101] Pressure on Christian officials to convert is described unambiguously in the isolated, individual cases that preceded the reign of ʿUmar II[102] and the empire-wide decree of al-Mutawakkil.[103] We do not find here the usual language of state employment or dismissal.

Thus there is textual reason (namely, *HPY*) to wonder whether unpopular measures were attributed to ʿUmar II by the late-eighth-century deacon John or by the eleventh-century redactor Mawhūb. Further, the text of *HP* does not make clear what those measures actually were; there is no unambiguous reference to our edict. Finally, the striking juxtaposition of both glowing and bitter representations of ʿUmar II, who had only twenty-nine months to make impressions, raises the distinct possibility that an early positive account was redacted together with negative accretions. The biblical reference (Luke 16:15) to the Pharisees "who loved money" and who likewise earned human approbation but divine opprobrium suggests a conceptual bracket for combining the two depictions of ʿUmar II.

In summary, there are a number of uncertainties that bear upon the reliability of the *HP*'s testimony. Yet it cannot be categorically ruled out that it constitutes evidence of an edict of ʿUmar II; it is indeed possible to read the Arabic as relevant to the dismissal of officials. One could further conclude — conjecturally, given the current state of research — that the eighth-century Coptic source referred likewise to the dismissal of officials. If we accept its reliability, the evidence of the *HP* indicates both that the edict was promulgated well into the caliph's reign and that it was quite effective.

2. *Michael the Syrian*

How reliable is Michael the Syrian's late account of the rule of ʿUmar II, with its statement that the caliph decreed that Christians were not to "act as governors"? It is accepted that Michael relied for this period on a lost work by Dionysius of Tell-Maḥrē (d. 845), who in turn relied on an unidentified "Eastern Source" that stands in an uncertain relationship to the lost chronicle by Theophilus of Edessa (d. 785).[104] If the key statement was found in the work of Theophilus, who was a young man during the reign of ʿUmar II, then it is strong testimony indeed.[105] This, however, now appears unlikely. Hoyland, who has compared all the extant witnesses to the Eastern Source and Theophilus, doubts that this description of

---

[101] Ibid., pp. 57, 62, 64 (the last locution, at least, can hardly be a literal translation of the Coptic account by John the Deacon!).

[102] Ibid., p. 52.

[103] ʿAbd al-Masīḥ and Burmester, eds. and trans., *History of the Patriarchs*, p. 5 (Arabic text), p. 8 (English trans.).

[104] For the most recent conspectus of scholarship on this historiographical problem, see Hoyland, *Theophilus of Edessa's Chronicle*, pp. 1–41, 337; see also Conrad, "Conquest of Arwād," p. 326, and Hoyland, *Seeing Islam as Others Saw It*, pp. 400–09. Other recent contributions are Conterno, *Palestina, Siria, Costantinopoli* (I thank Dr. Conterno for making her unpublished dissertation available to me); Debié, *L'écriture de l'histoire en syriaque*.

[105] Schick, writing of the incongruities in the Syriac historiography on ʿUmar II, noted that Theophilus, "add[ed] himself the comments about anti-Christian measures.... As he wrote only a generation after these events, he was well placed to know details about them" (*Christian Communities*, pp. 88–89). Levy-Rubin makes the same assumption (*Non-Muslims*, p. 91). But since we do not have Theophilus' work, we can scarcely decide what details he knew without comparing the witnesses.

ʿUmar II's reign was found even in the work of Dionysius because it is "surprisingly divergent" from the other witness to Dionysius: the *Chronicle of 1234*. He suggests that Michael's "more hostile comments were added later, and perhaps are [his] own words."[106] It is *a fortiori* less likely that the eighth-century Christian sources on which Michael indirectly depended made any mention of acting as governors, which in any case features only in one of the two available versions of Michael's chronicle. In fact, the early Syriac historiography we possess is uniformly positive in its evaluation of ʿUmar II (see further below). There are signs that Michael's negative assessment in this passage owes to an Arabic, perhaps Muslim source: what Hoyland calls his "unusual" use of the word *mashlmānē* for Muslims, and Arabicisms like *qbāytā* = *qabāʾ*. As independent confirmation of the edict Michael's phrase is unreliable.

3. *John of Damascus*

There appears to be scant basis for the assertion that John of Damascus was dismissed by an edict of ʿUmar II. That he was remembered as having been associated with a role in state financial administration is demonstrated by the passage from the Seventh Ecumenical Council (above). This passage does not show that he served in an official capacity, however. It need refer to nothing more than his decision to become a monk rather than following his forebears in officialdom.

4. *Kitāb al-Majdal*

The passing mention in this late source of a reinstatement of Christians to caliphal service by Yazīd gives no evidence of an edict of ʿUmar II. Yet its very obliquity suggests that some Christians may have been excluded from state service during the years that preceded Yazīd's accession in 101/720. There is currently no way to know whether this exclusion involved ʿUmar II, the preceding administrative language reforms, or something else entirely.

III. Silences

As we have seen, the evidence for the edict is weighted heavily toward the epistles. The absence of other kinds of evidence is striking. Even if the foregoing discussion of reliability is ignored and the evidence read with credulous enthusiasm, the problem of silence remains. The perils of the *argumentum e silentio* are well known. Yet not all silences are alike. In *ḥadīth* studies,[107] for example, limited audiences and random patterns of transmission render dubious the argument that because a book lacks a certain *ḥadīth*, the *ḥadīth* must not have existed when the book was composed. But in the present case we are dealing not with pious sententiae murmured to disciples or with private epistles on problems of dogma[108] but with a radical public edict, promulgated, enforced, and reinforced across the largest empire in the world. We would expect a wide and fairly consistent scatter of attestations, as we have for

[106] Hoyland, *Theophilus of Edessa's Chronicle*, p. 217 n. 607.

[107] For a cogent objection to the *argumentum e silentio* in this field, see Motzki, "Dating Muslim Traditions," pp. 214–19.

[108] Cf. other epistles attributed to ʿUmar II (attributions viewed with reserve in Mourad, *Early Islam Between Myth and History*, pp. 121–39, and Cook, *Early Muslim Dogma*, pp. 124–36).

the similar measure of al-Mutawakkil. Instead, we find mostly silences, which permeate three bodies of evidence: other extended Muslim accounts of ʿUmar II's rule, non-Muslim sources treating the same, and legal opinions expressed by early authorities who both opposed the state employment of non-Muslims and were wont to cite the precedent of ʿUmar II. These silences are not proof positive against the edict. Yet their cumulative testimony should not be ignored.

A. Biographies of ʿUmar II

The early epistles cited above are found in two of the more extensive biographical treatments of ʿUmar II. Several other such treatments are available to us. None mentions an epistle or edict of this kind.[109] To my knowledge Muslim historiography preserves no other reports, however terse, that allude to this edict. Al-Ṭabarī, notably, does not mention it. Apart from the reports of al-Balādhurī and al-Kindī we are given either a text of the epistle, or nothing.

B. Non-Muslim Sources

Of the histories by non-Muslim authors that recall ʿUmar II, fewer than half mention any measures unfavorable to non-Muslims. Of these, only *HP* and Michael the Syrian make any reference to our edict.

The silences fall into two groups. The first comprises accounts textually related to *HP* and Michael. For *HP* this means *HPY*, whose witness we have considered. For Michael it means the three chronicles related to his in that they derive material by various channels from the lost "Eastern Source" and Theophilus of Edessa. The first witness is the anonymous Syriac *Chronicle of 1234*, which like Michael accessed the common sources via the work of Dionysius. This work lists the prohibitions on loud prayer, bell-ringing, and riding with a saddle, as well as the repudiation of the *lex talionis* for Muslims who murder Christians, and instatement of a (5,000 *zuzā*) blood payment instead.[110] The same source describes ʿUmar II as a "good and compassionate man, truth-loving and just, and he was averse to evil." But in fact it can now be shown that the negative aspects are later accretions. The phrase used to praise ʿUmar II in a chronicle composed in the 730s, about ten years after the caliph's death, and used by Dionysius, is redacted in order coherently to incorporate discriminatory measures, as follows:

[109] I refer to al-Iṣbahānī, *Ḥilya*, vol. 5, pp. 253–353; Ibn ʿAsākir, *Taʾrīkh madīnat Dimashq*, vol. 45, pp. 126–274; Ibn al-Jawzī, *Sīra*; Ibn Saʿd, *Kitāb al-ṭabaqāt*, vol. 7, pp. 324–97, no. 1820; I owe this lineup to Borrut, "Entre tradition et histoire," p. 331 n. 11, to which add al-Ājurrī, *Akhbār Abī Ḥafṣ*.

[110] *Chronicle of 1234*, ed. Chabot, CSCO 109, pp. 307–08. This is the work Bosworth must have meant by "Chronicle of Siʿirt" in "The Concept of Dhimma," p. 47.

Chronicles of 819/846 (witnesses to chronicle of ca. 730)[a]	***gabrā ṭābā*** *w-malkā* ***mᵊraḥmānā yatīr men*** *kulhōn* ***malkē da-qdāmaw(hy)***
	a good man and a more compassionate king **than** all **the kings before him**
Chronicle of 1234[b]	***gabrā ṭābā […] wa-mraḥmānā*** *[…] bram saggī etdalqab la-krestyānē* ***yatīr men malkē da-qdāmaw(hy)***
	a good man[…] and compassionate […] however, he was very opposed to Christians, **more than the kings before him**

[a] Hoyland, *Theophilus of Edessa's Chronicle*, pp. 316–18. Syriac from *Chronicle of 819*, ed. Chabot, CSCO 81, p. 15.
[b] Hoyland, *Theophilus of Edessa's Chronicle*, p. 217.

Bar Hebraeus (d. 1286), dependent on Michael's work, omits the crucial phrase. This omission, combined with the silence of the Armenian version, might lead one to question whether the phrase was in fact written by Michael.[111] Bar Hebraeus' abridged Arabic chronicle gives no hint of such measures, offering instead hagiographical material of obvious Muslim provenance.[112]

The second witness to Michael's source is the Arabic chronicle of Agapius of Manbij; it has only good things to say about ᶜUmar II, praising his asceticism and aversion to corruption and stating that he "lived outwardly a good life" (*aẓhara sīratan ḥasana*).[113] The third, the Greek chronicle attributed to Theophanes Confessor, states that ᶜUmar II banned wine, forced Christians to apostatize under penalty of death, and forbade the testimony of a Christian against a Muslim.[114] We find here elements of the longer list of disabilities given by Michael. But state employment is absent. The disabilities do not necessarily go back to Theophilus. It is insufficiently recognized but entirely possible that Theophanes and Dionysius may both have used the work of George Syncellus (or a different author of the "Eastern Source," ca. 780) for eighth-century events. For us this would mean that the peg on which Theophanes and Dionysius hung discriminatory restrictions would be the work not of Theophilus but of George, who was keen to stress Muslim oppression.[115] A point in favor of this hypothesis is Agapius' omission of any negative comment on ᶜUmar II; Agapius has the best claim to have accessed Theophilus' work directly.

The second category of silence in non-Muslim historiography comprises sources that cover the reign of ᶜUmar II and are textually unrelated to *HP* and to Michael. The following sources make no mention of a religious criterion for state employment. They have, moreover, no complaints to make about ᶜUmar II: 1) the *Byzantine-Arab Chronicle of 741*, which according to Hoyland has a Syrian Christian source in common with the *Hispanic Chronicle of 754*; this source states only that "he was of such great kindness and compassion that to this day as

[111] Ibn al-ᶜIbrī [Bar Hebraeus], *Chronicon syriacum*, pp. 117–18. The impending publication of additional Arabic and Armenian witnesses by Gorgias Press may help to answer this question.

[112] Ibn al-ᶜIbrī [Bar Hebraeus], *Taʾrīkh mukhtaṣar al-duwal*, pp. 114–15.

[113] Agapius of Manbij, *Kitāb al-ᶜunwān*, ed. Cheïkho, p. 358; ed. and French trans. Vasiliev, pp. 502–03.

[114] Theophanes, *Chronicle*, ed. de Boor, vol. 1, p. 399; trans. Mango and Scott, p. 550. The first statement is plausible, the second manifestly polemical, and the third without support in Muslim sources; see Crone, *Roman, Provincial, and Islamic Law*, p. 16.

[115] Palmer, *West-Syrian Chronicles*, pp. 85–104, esp. pp. 95f. See further Hoyland, *Theophilus of Edessa's Chronicle*, pp. 7–10. On George's keenness, see Theophanes, *Chronicle*, trans. Mango and Scott, p. lxi.

much honour and praise is bestowed on him by all, even foreigners, as ever has been offered to anyone in his lifetime holding the reins of power";[116] 2) the Syriac *Zuqnin Chronicle*, completed in 775; it credits the ban on Christian testimony and differential penalties for murder to Yazīd, his successor;[117] 3) the Syriac chronographies of 819 and 846, on which see the chart above in this section; 4) the eighth-century Armenian *History of Łewond*, which gives a report that ʿUmar II was "the noblest among the men of his race," and relates how he allowed Armenian Christian captives to return home;[118] 5) the universal history of the Melkite Saʿīd b. al-Biṭrīq (Eutychius of Alexandria, d. 328/940);[119] 6) the Samaritan chronicle of Abū al-Fatḥ al-Danafī, which relates the anti-*dhimmī* measures of ʿAbbāsid caliphs in detail but passes over ʿUmar II without comment;[120] 7) the terse chronography of the early eleventh-century Church of the East metropolitan Elias bar Shīnāyā, which does report anti-Jewish measures taken by Leo III, contemporary of ʿUmar II;[121] 8) the chronicle of al-Makīn b. al-ʿAmīd (d. 672/1273), himself a state official, who used both Muslim and Christian sources;[122] 9) the *Chronicon orientale* traditionally attributed to the Coptic state official Ibn al-Rāhib (d. ca. 1295).[123]

While one must acknowledge the "fair-mindedness and the plain speaking"[124] that chroniclers could display, it is difficult to believe that those who were unequivocal in their praise of ʿUmar II knew of major discriminatory disabilities imposed by him on Christians as such. Historians who mixed their praise with notice of such disabilities were not necessarily being fair-minded; it is at least as likely that they were tasked with reconciling contradictory reports. Such reports are likely to have entered non-Muslim historiography from the clouds of hagiographical material that were fast gathering around ʿUmar II in the Arabic tradition. It is noteworthy that all of the demonstrably eighth-century non-Muslim historiography (nos. 1–4 above) is complimentary to ʿUmar II and describes no discriminatory disabilities imposed by him.

C. Early Juristic Views on the State Employment of Non-Muslims

Notable early Muslim legal authorities who opposed the employment of non-Muslim officials also tended to esteem the memory of ʿUmar II. In some cases they were fond of citing his precedent to support their views. Yet they did not mention his precedent for this issue.

There is a terse opinion on the topic attributed to Mālik b. Anas (d. 179/796). Mālik had considerable affection for the legal precedent of ʿUmar II.[125] His disciple Ibn al-Qāsim

[116] "The Byzantine-Arab Chronicle of 741 and Its Eastern Source" (= "Excursus B"), in Hoyland, *Seeing Islam as Others Saw It*, pp. 423–27, 625.

[117] *Zuqnīn Chronicle*, trans. Harrak, pp. 151–55.

[118] Łewond, *History of Łewond*, trans. Arzoumanian, p. 70.

[119] Saʿīd b. Biṭrīq, *Annales*, ed. Pococke, vol. 2, pp. 378–82. On Saʿīd, see the superb article by F. Micheau in *EI*², s.v.

[120] Abū al-Fatḥ, *Kitāb al-taʾrikh*, trans. Levy-Rubin, p. 55 (on ʿUmar II), pp. 90–93 (on Abbasid restrictions on *dhimmīs*).

[121] Elias bar Shīnāyā, *Chronography*, ed. Brooks and Chabot, Latin trans. pp. 77f.

[122] Al-Makīn b. al-ʿAmīd, *Al-Majmūʿ al-mubārak*, ed. Ḥasan, pp. 176–78.

[123] Ibn al-Rāhib (attrib.), *Chronicon orientale*, ed./Latin trans. Cheïkho, vol. 2, p. 57, no. 15. The *Kitāb al-tawārīkh*, which differs textually from *Chronicon orientale*, is more likely to represent the actual work of Ibn al-Rāhib. A verdict on the matter must await the ed./trans. of *Kitāb al-tawārīkh* currently in preparation by Dr. S. Moawad.

[124] The phrase Palmer uses to explain how Dionysius of Tell-Maḥrē could both praise and impugn ʿUmar II (*West-Syrian Chronicles*, p. 99 n. 240).

[125] Borrut, "Entre tradition et histoire," pp. 359f.; al-Shāfiʿī, *al-Umm*, vol. 8, p. 550.

al-ʿUtaqī heard him say: "The *ahl al-dhimma* are not to be taken as scribes in any of the Muslims' affairs" (*fī shayʾin min umūri l-muslimīn*).[126] Later sources report that Mālik was asked whether Christians are to be hired as scribes, to which he replies, "No, I do not think so (*lā arā dhālik*). That is because scribes are consulted; is a Christian to be consulted in the affairs of Muslims? It does not please me that he should be hired as a scribe." That Mālik appears to be improvising rather tentatively is a mark in favor of the authenticity of this report.[127] That he does not mention the precedent of ʿUmar II (or, for that matter, ʿUmar I), resorting instead to *raʾy*, suggests that he was unaware of these precedents.

The same may be said of his pupil al-Shāfiʿī (d. 204/820), an Iraqi by birth who settled in Egypt.[128] Regarding the issue at hand he wrote:

> No judge or governor of the Muslims ought, in my view (*mā yanbaghī ʿindī*), to take a *dhimmī* scribe, or to place a *dhimmī* in a position whereby he is made superior to a Muslim. We ought to strengthen Muslims so that that they have no need of those not of their own religion. The judge has of all people the least excuse in this matter.[129]

Al-Shāfiʿī gives no precedent for his view, describing it as specific to himself. He leaves room for excuses and variant views. There is no sign that he knew of prominent early authorities who had already weighed in on the matter, let alone proscribed non-Muslim officials. There was of course no requirement that he or Mālik refer to ʿUmar II. Neither was there anything to prevent either from doing so. Citing his precedent would seem to have been a convenient way, however, to lend authority to their views.

Aḥmad b. Ḥanbal (d. 241/855) does cite precedent in the account reported by the effective founder of the Ḥanbalī *madhhab*, Abū Bakr al-Khallāl (d. 311/923). Asked by his disciple Abū Ṭālib[130] whether Jews and Christians are to be employed "in the Muslims' administrative positions (*aʿmāl*), such as taxation (*al-kharāj*)," Ibn Ḥanbal responds: "Their assistance is not to be sought in anything."[131] Three reports are then cited — two concerning ʿUmar I,[132] and a Medinese *ḥadīth* narrated by Mālik in which the Prophet refuses the military assistance of a *mushrik*.[133] In a later account, Ibn Ḥanbal expresses more permissive, less formulaic views.[134] A disciple named Abū ʿAlī al-Ḥusayn b. Aḥmad b. al-Mufaḍḍal al-Bajalī[135] is visiting Ibn Ḥanbal when an emissary arrives from the caliph with a question: should Muslim sectarians (*ahl al-ahwāʾ*) be hired by the state? The reply is negative, and elicits a second question: "Then the Christians and Jews are to be hired, but not them?" Ibn Ḥanbal's answer does not reflect the prohibition reported by al-Khallāl: "The Christians and Jews do not proselytize for their religions, whereas the sectarians are proselytizers."[136]

---

[126] Saḥnūn, *al-Mudawwana al-kubrā*, vol. 5, p. 146.

[127] Quoted from Ibn ʿAbd al-Barr, *Bahjat al-majālis*, vol. 1, p. 358; cf. abbreviated version in al-Qarāfī, *al-Dhakhīra*, vol. 8, p. 352.

[128] For al-Shāfiʿī's reference to the precedent of ʿUmar II, which is occasional rather than pervasive, see, e.g., al-Shāfiʿī, *al-Umm*, vol. 5, pp. 288, 607, 636.

[129] Al-Shāfiʿī, *al-Umm*, vol. 7, p. 522.

[130] Aḥmad b. Ḥumayd al-Mushkānī (d. 244/858 or 859); see al-ʿUlaymī, *al-Manhaj al-aḥmad*, vol. 1, pp. 197–98, no. 45.

[131] Al-Khallāl, *Ahl al-milal*, vol. 1, p. 195.

[132] On these, see Yarbrough, "Upholding God's Rule," §§2–5.

[133] On this, see Yarbrough, "I'll not Accept Aid from a *mushrik*."

[134] Ibn Mufliḥ, *al-Ādāb al-sharʿīya*, vol. 1, p. 275; cf. idem, *Kitāb al-furūʿ*, vol. 10, p. 248.

[135] I am unable to identify this person.

[136] According to Ibn Mufliḥ, Ibn Taymīya, who is presumably his proximate source, had this report from al-Bayhaqī's (lost?) *manāqib* work on Ibn Ḥanbal. Cf. similar accounts in Ibn al-Jawzī, *Manāqib*, pp. 184f.; al-Dhahabī, *Siyar aʿlām al-nubalāʾ*, vol. 11, p. 297.

The similar report that follows, ascribed to Muḥammad b. Aḥmad b. Manṣūr al-Marrūdhī,[137] has four emissaries from the caliph al-Mutawakkil visit Ibn Ḥanbal. They ask him whether it is better that the state hire Jahmīya[138] or Jews and Christians. It turns out that the Jahmīya are not to be hired under any circumstance. There is no harm by contrast in hiring Jews and Christians in those state affairs in which they have no authority over Muslims. After all, "the forebears hired them." Al-Marrūdhī protests, "Are the Jews and Christians to be hired, polytheists that they are, and not the Jahmīya?" Ibn Ḥanbal replies with evident irritation: "Boy (*ya-bnī*), Muslims are led astray by them, whereas Muslims are not led astray by those people." It is difficult to imagine Ibn Ḥanbal making such statements if he or his audience were aware of the strident epistles of ʿUmar II. Elsewhere in the work by al-Khallāl he cites the precedent of ʿUmar II approvingly.[139] Yet were he, Mālik, and al-Shāfiʿī ignorant of this dramatic edict, which would have been enacted in Mālik's lifetime? If they knew of it, why did none of them mention it? While it cannot be ruled out that the reason for this is that ʿUmar II's edict was lightly applied and of short duration, we will see that there are difficulties with this thesis, and it is tempting to answer these questions by postulating that ʿUmar II did not issue such an edict at all.

D. The Awāʾil Literature

A minor genre of early Arabic literature deals with "firsts": lists of the first people (*awāʾil*) known to have said or done this or that. In the most important extant example of the genre, the work of Abū Hilāl al-ʿAskarī (d. 395/1005), the first person to have ordered non-Muslims to differentiate their clothing from that of the Muslims was the ʿAbbāsid caliph al-Mutawakkil (d. 247/861). It is added in the same breath that he ordered the dismissal of non-Muslim state administrators, leading to a number of conversions (names are given).[140] But as we have seen, these measures were elsewhere ascribed to ʿUmar II. Either Abū Hilāl did not do his homework, or the information about ʿUmar II was not widely available, or it was available but for some reason he ignored it. Since the *awāʾil* collectors tended to do their homework, one would like to ask why the edict of ʿUmar II was so poorly known or evidence of it distrusted.[141]

E. Documentary Evidence

As was suggested at the outset of this essay, non-Muslim state officials attested during and immediately after the reign of ʿUmar II erode the evidentiary base for the claim that he issued an edict to dismiss such people.

I know of only three (exclusively) Arabic documents that can be securely dated to the reign of ʿUmar II. One of these (P. Séoudi 1, dated 9 Dhu l-Ḥijja 101 = 21 June 719) involves an administrator known as Abū Milla, a name which according to Werner Diem reflects not Arab but Coptic or Greek origin (his religious affiliation is of course unclear). Another

[137] = Muḥammad b. Aḥmad al-Marwarūdhī, who is described as monopolizing some of Ibn Ḥanbal's responsa (al-ʿUlaymī, *al-Manhaj al-aḥmad*, vol. 2, p. 12).

[138] *EI*² s.v. "Djahmiyya" (W. Montgomery Watt).

[139] E.g., al-Khallāl, *Ahl al-milal*, vol. 1, p. 181.

[140] Abū Hilāl al-ʿAskarī, *Kitāb al-awāʾil*, vol. 1, p. 84.

[141] I here approach the *awāʾil* much after the fashion of G. H. A. Juynboll. See his *Muslim Tradition*, pp. 10–23.

names only Muslim officials, highlighting again the fact that Muslim officials were becoming increasingly common in local administration. This fact would have made later ascription of a religious criterion for state employment to this period more plausible than to, for example, that of ʿUmar I. But it does not increase the likelihood that this change took place by fiat.[142] The third Arabic document is the letter of 99–100/718–719 from the Sogdian ruler Dēwāštīč to the Arab governor al-Jarrāḥ b. ʿAbdallāh, whom he addresses as his *mawlā*. On the basis of the pious formulae used in this letter — formulae that must be attributed to the experienced scribe who wrote it — it has been maintained that Dēwāštīč was a Muslim. This might well be doubted; the chronicles that refer to Dēwāštīč mention no conversion and he died challenging Muslim rule. Pending review of the Sogdian evidence with the question of conversion in mind, its answer should not be presumed on the basis of epistolary formulae. At any rate, an Arab official whose Sogdian letter to Dēwāštīč was also preserved at Mount Mugh (Mugh 1.I) and postdates the Arabic letter to al-Jarrāḥ does not address him as a Muslim (it does acknowledge him as "king of Sogdiana and ruler of Samarqand" and describe the official agency of non-Muslims, as "true assistants and faithful [servants]," in conveying letters among Arab and non-Arab commanders).[143] It seems probable that Dēwāštīč, like the Iṣpāhbadh,[144] was a local non-Muslim ruler on the imperial periphery who paid tribute and was loosely integrated into the state administration.

The Greek and Coptic evidence, too, is of limited quantity. In addition to the two Coptic ostraca already mentioned there is a Greek ostracon from Jeme that records the receipt of a tax (or fine - *prostimon*) and is signed by Christian officials Komes and Athanasios. It has recently been dated to 9 March 720, about a month after the death of ʿUmar II.[145] Two Greek papyri — P. Grenf. 105 and 106 (= Wessely, *Griechische Papyrusurkunden* [SPP III], no. 259) of 25 and 31 August 719 — do name a Muslim official, a Zubayr b. Ziyād, who issues an *entagion* (demand note) to a Christian. These two documents preserve a few lines of Arabic and a seal that bears a religious message: "Believe in God and his apostles." Chances are good, however, that the Greek scribe was not Zubayr, and that he was in fact a Christian; the Greek portion of P. Grenf. 106 begins with a cross.[146] It is also unlikely that the long Greek account of 716–721 (P. Lond 1413) and register of requisitions from 719 (P. Lond 1436) were written by Muslims.[147]

---

[142] Diem, "Vier Dienstschreiben," esp. pp. 240–43 (P. Louvre JDW 14 = PAL III 27 B, and P. Seoudi 1).

[143] On Dēwāštīč, see *EIr* s.v. (B. Marshak). Marshak accepts his conversion following Kratchkovsky, whose evidence was the Arabic letter (Kratchkovskaya and Kratchkovsky, "Oldest Arabic Manuscript," p. 55). The Sogdian letter to Dēwāštīč is re-edited and translated in Yakubovich, "Mugh 1.1 Revisited." Yakubovich states, again on the basis of the Arabic letter, that Dēwāštīč "(at least nominally) declared himself a Muslim" (p. 245). Strictly speaking this is not true; the king of Sogdiana is unlikely to have known much Arabic and the pious formulae should be credited to the scribe. For Kratchkovsky's judgment that the document was in "an experienced chancery calligraphist's hand," see his *Among Arabic Manuscripts*, p. 147.

[144] On whom see *EI*[2] s.v. "Dābūya" (B. Spuler). ʿUmar II affirms the local authority of the Iṣpāhbadh, "*ṣāḥib* Ṭabaristān," in al-Balādhurī, *Ansāb al-ashrāf*, vol. 7, p. 127.

[145] O. Petr. 464. See Tait, ed. *Greek Ostraca*, vol. 1, p. 151, to be read with Gonis, "Tax Receipts," p. 162. For Gonis' date revision, see his "Reconsidering Some Fiscal Documents," p. 193.

[146] Grenfell and Hunt, *New Classical Fragments*, pp. 154–56; Casson, "Tax-Collection Problems," p. 279; Gonis, "Reconsidering Some Fiscal Documents," p. 225. For two Greek tax receipts (bearing crosses) to the same individual from the reign of ʿUmar II, see SP 13269 and 132670, in Ruprecht, ed., *Sammelbuch Griechischer Urkunden*, pp. 129–30. These were surely written by Christian officials. But for an eighth-century Muslim tax collector (Sulaymān) who countersigns a Greek tax receipt (in Greek letters), see Gonis, "Reconsidering Some Fiscal Documents," p. 228.

[147] Al-Qāḍī, "Population Census and Land Surveys," p. 402 n. 214.

On the whole the picture is about as one would expect it to be on the assumption that the conversion of the administrative corps was gradual and organic. Local rulers on the frontiers are non-Muslims. Greek- and Coptic-language documents are more common than Arabic in Egypt. The majority of lower officials there are Christians but there are hints of a growing Muslim presence at these levels. It would be difficult to sustain from these documents an argument for a disjuncture in administrative personnel of the sort that the dismissal of all scribes, tax collectors, and administrators (as indicated in Ep.[IAḤ]) would occasion.

IV. Readings of the Evidence

If all qualms about reliability are allayed and, for the sake of argument, all the evidence accepted as relevant to and accurate for the edict of ʿUmar II, it becomes difficult to tell a coherent story. Assume for a moment that the caliph sent a significant number of epistles, some of whose divergent texts we are fortunate to possess. They were sent well before the end of the caliph's reign, for he had time to check after and re-apply them more than 700 miles away, as the unique report from al-Balādhurī about Baṣra makes clear. But they were also sent well after his reign began, for he needed time first to impress the Copts and others with his leniency (*HP*). Inspired by a desire to humiliate non-Muslims, he commanded unequivocally that absolutely all such officials be dismissed. The edict was quite effective, removing local Coptic headmen (al-Kindī) and Iraqi officials (al-Balādhurī, *Kitāb al-majdal*) alike.

But if the edict was so widely, persistently, and successfully applied then how to explain the lack of a single independent, clear reference to it in Muslim historiography, in the Christian historiography demonstrably prior to the eleventh century, and in the opinions of the early jurists? How to explain the coexistence of these vituperative epistles in the sources with other reports that describe the caliph's kindness and solicitude for *dhimmī*s? How to explain away the implausibility that a head of state should have proposed to leave not a single (*aḥadan min*; Ep.[B1]) non-Muslim "scribe or official" (*kātib wa-lā ʿāmil*; Ep.[IAḤ]) in the administration of an empire the vast majority of whose population was non-Muslim and which had from the first depended upon non-Muslim officials at the regional and local levels?

But perhaps the edict was only a minor, localized affair after all, for which wide attestation is not to be expected; in this case, no energy would have been put behind its enforcement. This is the explanation proposed by Milka Levy-Rubin in her article in this volume. But how then to explain the parallel reports from Iraq, Syria, and Egypt? How to explain the textual diversity of the epistles? Given the righteous indignation with which the caliph reacts to the very concept of a non-Muslim official, can he really have singled out just a few in Baṣra? Or it could be that the edict, though geographically widespread, was promulgated so briefly that it left only a light impression in the sources? What then to do with the testimony of *HP*, which bewails the tribulations of the excluded Copts, or with the only clear testimony in Muslim historiography, which has the caliph enforcing his edict against local Muslim reluctance in Iraq?

What if, however, the edict pertained only to certain non-Muslim officials: those who exercised direct authority over Muslims? This is, after all, a particular concern of the epistles and might have affected a smaller number of officials.[148] But the epistles clearly direct that

[148] One source reports that in conjunction with *ghiyār* requirements (on the historicity of which, see Yarbrough, "Origins of the *ghiyār*") ʿUmar II commanded that no non-Muslim employ a Muslim. This

every last non-Muslim official is to be dismissed. And what of the evidence of al-Kindī that has been relied upon by Arabic papyrologists? Were the *mawāzīt* in the *kuwar* of Egypt exercising authority over Muslims? This would be a significant discovery.

However it is manipulated, the evidence does not cohere. Something has to go. It is not a question of whether to discount evidence but rather of which evidence to discount. It will not do simply to assert that "there is no real reason to [...] doubt the authenticity of the documents."[149] The historian who is tempted to treat the epistles as straightforward documents must address several questions. Which documents should not be doubted? All of them? One in particular? How is it to be identified? Or is it a hypothetical underlying *Urtext* that should not be doubted? Can this be recovered? If not, are we justified in affirming the historicity of an event when we are unable confidently to authenticate any single piece of evidence for it?

It may turn out that some subset of the evidence read through a particular interpretive lens will yield a compelling account. But at present we lack the means of making the necessary judgments; it has been seen that virtually all of the evidence is of doubtful reliability (though little of it can be categorically dismissed), so we have no touchstone against which to evaluate the rest. For this purpose even a single independent, laconic reference to the edict in an early source would go a long way. In short, the evidence is intractable. More precisely, it is open to alternative readings that give accounts of its nature, quantity, and distribution that are at least as convincing as are readings that accept the evidence at face value.

The most persuasive such alternative is to read the epistles as pseudepigrapha composed by Muslim officials for an audience of ʿAbbāsid ruling elites. Professional competition in the ʿAbbāsid *dīwān* certainly provided sufficient motive for the composition of such documents; the transparent attempt found in the *Sirāj* of al-Ṭurṭūshī shows that ʿUmar II's epistles were being used in just this way. These policies were ascribed to a caliph whose example was both paradigmatic and late enough to be plausible.[150] The *isnād* of Ep.[B1], which is textually related to Ep.[IAH], cites as its earliest authority the Iraqi Muslim scribe Shuʿayb b. Ṣafwān, who was in the entourage (*ṣaḥāba*) of the caliph al-Manṣūr and reportedly died in the reign of al-Rashīd. He was very young at best in the reign of ʿUmar II. The critic Yaḥyā b. Maʿīn impugned his reliability precisely on the basis of "those long letters via Manṣūr b. Abī Muzāḥim," who is the other figure in the *isnād* and was also an early ʿAbbāsid official. There is a thin but diverse layer of evidence for a short-lived attempt by the caliph al-Manṣūr to do without non-Muslim officials,[151] suggesting that the issue was of concern in the early ʿAbbāsid setting and under al-Manṣūr in particular. Ep.[B2], which we have seen to share most of its language with an epistle of al-Mutawakkil, could well have been composed to urge or justify al-Mutawakkil's policy. Its *isnād* was also tasked with authorizing the only other clear, non-epistolary reference to

is a different issue than that with which our epistles are concerned, but the memory of such a command could conceivably have occasioned the epistles. We lack the material for further study of this question; Ibn ʿAbd Rabbih, *al-ʿIqd al-farīd*, vol. 4, p. 436.

149 Levy-Rubin, *Non-Muslims*, p. 94.

150 For his paradigmatic example, see the jibe that ʿAbbād b. Kathīr reportedly directed to al-Manṣūr: "O Commander of the Faithful, are you not ashamed that the Umayyads should produce an ʿUmar b. ʿAbd al-ʿAzīz while you [ʿAbbāsids] produce nothing of the sort?" Ibn al-Jawzī, *Sira*, p. 71. On ʿAbbād, see al-Mizzī, *Tahdhīb*, vol. 14, pp. 145ff. That lateness enhanced plausibility is clear from the sentence in Ep.[IAH], which made the obvious explicit: "In times past, when the Muslims would come to a country in which associators (*ahl al-shirk*) were found, they would seek their assistance.... They had their day, but now God has put an end to it."

151 E.g., Ibn al-Qayyim, *Aḥkām ahl al-dhimma*, vol. 1, p. 214f.; Theophanes, *Chronicle*, ed. de Boor, p. 596. On the provenance of the former account, see Yarbrough, "A Rather Small Genre."

ʿUmar II's edict in all of Muslim historiography, to which it was juxtaposed by al-Balādhurī, himself a bureaucrat and boon companion of al-Mutawakkil.

On this reading, evidence that was baffling can be explained. The dissemination of the epistles along limited scholarly channels explains both the imbalanced distribution of evidence and the silences that hem it round. Here it was the epistles that generated "memories" of the event and not the reverse. Thus it is unsurprising that the epistles form the backbone of the evidence and that other evidence is rare and isolated but linked to the epistles. Since the pseudepigraphic epistles could not have been widely known at an early date it is unsurprising that early Muslim and non-Muslim historiography is silent about such a measure under ʿUmar II. But since they formed a *locus classicus* that could be invoked later, it is unsurprising that late historians – including the non-Muslims most affected – eventually became aware of them. This would have occurred with the isolated cases of *HP* and Michael the Syrian and with later Muslim historians like Ibn al-Athīr and al-Nuwayrī who depended ultimately on al-Balādhurī, as well as the cluster of texts that includes Ibn al-Qayyim's work and which depended for this account ultimately on Ibn ʿAbd al-Ḥakam. Most importantly, by supposing that the epistles were authored by disgruntled ʿAbbāsid bureaucrats we can understand their harsh tone and avoid the *prima facie* implausibility of a wholesale purge actually having been promulgated as Umayyad policy.

This alternative reading gives an account of the evidence that is in many respects more coherent than the credulous reading. Yet neither is provable. This alternative may be said to form a minimal (skeptical) bound to a range of plausible readings of the evidence. The maximal reading, by contrast, could yield the conclusion that ʿUmar II must have done something. A maximalist cannot, however, simply affirm all of the evidence, which has been shown to present internal contradictions that render it intractable. Instead, historians inclined to the maximal reading must discount or reinterpret some portion of the evidence to make sense of the rest. At present we do not possess the means to establish reliable data on the basis of which to undertake this operation. One hopes that new evidence will appear to clear things up. The effect of this bounding operation is to neutralize evidence pertaining to the edict until a satisfactory solution can be found. The edict should not be used to explain other events or trends. The epistles, for instance, are important in that they record ideas that originate in the second or third century A.H. As such they may be analyzed, but not attached securely to ʿUmar II. It is equally likely that they are the work of ʿAbbāsid bureaucrats. The reading tallies with G. R. Hawting's views on the "fiscal rescript" of ʿUmar II, often considered among the most reliable pieces of his reign's documentary residue: "There is too the danger that the information represents anachronistic reading back of later conditions into the time of ʿUmar II ... in spite of the general acceptance of its authenticity, its ascription to ʿUmar as a whole can only be impressionistic and open to question."[152]

What has this essay added to our knowledge of Christians and others in the Umayyad state? We have studied the only known attempt to purge non-Muslims as such from the administration of that state: an edict ascribed to ʿUmar II. All known evidence – much of it not previously considered – has been presented and critically analyzed. I have argued that the evidence is, because of its doubtful reliability or relevance and its internal inconsistency, intractable. I have also proposed minimal and maximal bounds to a range of plausible readings. A minimal reading would suggest that the epistles are pseudepigrapha composed

---

[152] Hawting, *The First Dynasty of Islam*, p. 78.

in the ʿAbbāsid period, and the other evidence either irrelevant or inspired by the epistles themselves. A maximal reading would suggest that ʿUmar II took some measure(s) adversely affecting non-Muslim bureaucrats under the Umayyads. Pending new evidence or analysis, however, it is not possible to say with confidence what it was.

Abbreviations

HP — *History of the Patriarchs of the Coptic Church of Alexandria*, Vol. 3: *Agathon to Michael I (766)*. Edited and translated by Basil Evetts. Patrologia Orientalis 5. Paris: Firmin-Didot, 1910.

HPY — [Yūsāb of Fūwah]. *Taʾrīkh al-ābāʾ al-baṭārika.* Edited by S. al-Suryānī and N. Kāmil. Cairo: n.p., 1992.

Bibliography

Abbott, Nabia. "A New Papyrus and a Review of the Administration of ʿUbaid Allāh b. al-Ḥabḥāb." In *Arabic and Islamic Studies in Honor of Hamilton A. R. Gibb,* edited by George Makdisi, pp. 21–35. Leiden: Brill, 1965.

ʿAbd al-Masīḥ, Yassā, and O. H. E. Burmester, editors and translators. *History of the Patriarchs of the Egyptian Church,* Vol. 2, Part 1. Cairo: Société d'archéologie copte, 1943.

al-Ābī, Manṣūr b. Ḥusayn. *Nathr al-durar.* Edited by M. ʿA. Qurna. 8 vols. Cairo: al-Hayʾa al-Miṣrīya al-ʿĀmma li-al-Kitāb, 1980–.

Abū al-Fatḥ al-Sāmirī al-Danafī. *Kitāb al-taʾrīkh.* Translated by Milka Levy-Rubin, *The Continuatio of the Samaritan Chronicle of Abū l-Fatḥ al-Sāmirī al-Danafī.* Princeton: Darwin Press, 2002.

Abū Hilāl al-ʿAskarī, al-Ḥasan b. ʿAbd Allāh. *Kitāb al-awāʾil.* Edited by M. al-Miṣrī and W. Qaṣṣāb. 2 vols. Damascus: Wizārat al-Thaqāfa wa-al-Irshād, 1975.

Abū ʿUbayd al-Qāsim b. Sallām. *Kitāb al-amwāl.* Edited by M. Kh. Harrās. Cairo: Maktabat al-Kullīyāt al-Azharīya, 1968.

Agapius of Manbij. *Kitāb al-ʿunwān.*
- Edited by L. Cheïkho, *Agapius episcopus Mabbugensis. Historia Universalis.* CSCO 65 (Scriptores Arabici III/10). Beirut: E Typographeo Catholico, 1912.
- Edited and translated by Alexandre Vasiliev, *Kitab al-ʿunvan, Histoire universelle*, part 2, fasc. 2, pp. 397–550. Patrologia Orientalis 8. Paris: Firmin-Didot, 1912.

al-Ājurrī, Abū Bakr Muḥammad b. al-Ḥusayn. *Akhbār Abī Ḥafṣ ʿUmar ibn ʿAbd al-ʿAzīz.* Beirut: Muʾassasat al-Risāla, 1979.

Anthony, Sean. "Fixing John Damascene's Biography: Historical Notes on His Family Background." *Journal of Early Christian Studies* 23/4 (2015): 607–27.

al-Balādhurī, Aḥmad b. Yaḥyā. *Ansāb al-ashrāf.* Edited by M. al-F. al-ʿAẓm et al. 26 vols. Damascus: Dār al-Yaqaẓa, 1996–2010.

———. *Futūḥ al-buldān.* Edited by M. J. de Goeje, *Liber expugnationis regionum.* Leiden: Brill, 1866.

Bar Hebraeus. *See* Ibn al-ʿIbrī, Abū al-Faraj

Baron, Salo. *A Social and Religious History of the Jews.* 2nd ed., 18 vols. New York: Columbia University Press, 1957.

Barthold, W. W. "Caliph ʿUmar II and the Conflicting Reports on his Personality." *Islamic Quarterly* 15/2–3 (1971): 69–95.

Borrut, Antoine. *Entre mémoire et pouvoir: l'espace syrien sous les derniers Omeyyades et les premiers Abbassides (v. 72–193/692–809)*. Leiden: Brill, 2011.

———. "Entre tradition et histoire: genèse et diffusion de l'image de ʿUmar II." *Mélanges de la faculté orientale de l'Université Saint-Joseph de Beyrouth* 58 (2005): 329–78.

Bosworth, C. E. "The Concept of Dhimma in Early Islam." In *Christians and Jews in the Ottoman Empire: The Functioning of a Plural Society,* edited by Benjamin Braude and Bernard Lewis, vol. 1, pp. 37–54. New York: Holmes & Meier, 1982.

Brockelmann, Carl. *Das Verhältnis von Ibn-El-Aṯīrs Kâmil Fit-Ta'riḫ zu Ṭabaris Aḫbâr Errusul wal Mulûk.* Strassburg: Karl J. Trübner, 1890.

Brockopp, Jonathan. *Early Mālikī Law: Ibn ʿAbd al-Ḥakam and His Major Compendium of Jurisprudence.* Leiden: Brill, 2000.

al-Bukhārī, Muḥammad b. Ismāʿīl. *Al-Taʾrīkh al-kabīr.* 9 vols. Hyderabad: n.p., 1960.

Caetani, Leone. *Chronographia Islamica.* 5 vols. Paris: P. Geuthner, 1912–.

Caseau, Beatrice. "Sacred Landscapes." In *Late Antiquity: A Guide to the Postclassical World,* edited by G. W. Bowersock, Peter Brown, and Oleg Grabar, pp. 21–59. Cambridge: Harvard University Press, 1999.

Casson, Lionel. "Tax-Collection Problems in Early Arab Egypt." *Transactions and Proceedings of the American Philological Association* 69 (1938): 274–91.

Chronicle of 819 (Anonymous). Edited by Jean-Baptiste Chabot, *Chronicon anonymum ad A.D. 819 pertinens.* Appended to *Anonymi Auctoris Chronicon ad Annum Christi 1234 pertinens.* CSCO 81 (Scriptores Syri 36) and CSCO 109 (Scriptores Syri 56). Paris: Gabalda, 1920, 1937.

Chronicle of 1234 (Anonymous).

- Syriac text, edited by Jean-Baptiste Chabot, *Anonymi Auctoris Chronicon ad Annum Christi 1234 pertinens.* 2 vols. CSCO 81 (Scriptores Syri 36) and CSCO 82 (Scriptores Syri 37). Paris: Gabalda, 1920, 1916.
- Latin translation of vol. 1 by Jean-Baptiste Chabot, *Anonymi Auctoris Chronicon ad Annum Christi 1234 pertinens, I.* CSCO 109 (Scriptores Syri 56). Paris: Gabalda, 1937.

Cohen, Mark R. *Under Crescent and Cross.* Princeton: Princeton University Press, 1994.

———. "What Was the Pact of ʿUmar? A Literary-Historical Study." *Jerusalem Studies in Arabic and Islam* 23 (1999): 100–57.

Conrad, Lawrence I. "The Conquest of Arwād: A Source-Critical Study in the Historiography of the Early Medieval Near East." In *The Byzantine and Early Islamic Near East*, Vol. 1: *Problems in the Literary Source Material*, edited by Averil Cameron and Lawrence I. Conrad, pp. 317–401. Studies in Late Antiquity and Early Islam 1. Princeton: Darwin Press, 1992.

Conterno, Maria. Palestina, Siria, Costantinopoli: la "Cronografia" di Teofane Confessore e la mezzaluna fertile della storiografia nei «secoli bui» di Bisanzio. Unpublished Ph.D. dissertation, Istituto di studi umanistici dell'Università di Firenze, 2011.

Cook, Michael. *Early Muslim Dogma: A Source-Critical Study.* Cambridge: Cambridge University Press, 1981.

Crone, Patricia. *Roman, Provincial, and Islamic Law.* Cambridge: Cambridge University Press, 1987.

Crone, Patricia, and Martin Hinds. *God's Caliph: Religious Authority in the First Centuries of Islam*. University of Cambridge Oriental Publications 37. Cambridge: Cambridge University Press, 1986.

Debié, Muriel. *L'écriture de l'histoire en syriaque: transmissions interculturelles et constructions identitaires entre hellénisme et islam*. Leuven: Peeters, forthcoming.

den Heijer, Johannes. *Mawhūb ibn Manṣūr ibn Mufarriǧ et l'historiographie copto-arabe.* Leuven: Peeters, 1989.

———. "Coptic Historiography in the Fāṭimid, Ayyūbid, and Early Mamlūk Periods." *Medieval Encounters* 2/1 (1996): 67–98.

al-Dhahabī, Shams al-Dīn Muḥammad b. Aḥmad. *Siyar aʿlām al-nubalāʾ.* 25 vols. Beirut: Muʾassasat al-Risāla, 1981–.

Dickie, James. "Appendix on the Tomb of ʿUmar b. ʿAbd al-ʿAzīz." *Islamic Quarterly* 16/1–2 (1972): 80.

Diem, Werner. "Vier Dienstschreiben an ʿAmmār: Ein Beitrag zur arabischen Papyrologie." *Zeitschrift der Deutschen Morgenländischen Gesellschaft* 133/2 (1983): 239–62.

Eddé, Anne-Marie, Françoise Micheau, and Christophe Picard. *Communautés chrétiennes en pays d'islam.* Paris: SEDES, 1997.

Elad, Amikam. *Medieval Jerusalem and Islamic Worship: Holy Places, Ceremonies, Pilgrimage.* Leiden: Brill, 1995.

Elias bar Shīnāyā. *Chronography.* Edited by E. W. Brooks and Jean-Baptiste Chabot, *Eliae metropolitae Nisibeni opus chronologicum.* 2 vols. in 1. Paris: E Typographeo Republicae, 1909–1910.

Evetts, Basil, editor and translator. *History of the Patriarchs of the Coptic Church of Alexandria*, Vol. 3: *Agathon to Michael I (766).* Patrologia Orientalis 5, pp. 1–215. Paris : Firmin-Didot, 1910.

Fattal, Antoine. *Le statut légal des non-musulmans en pays d'islam.* 2nd ed. Beirut: Dar el-Machreq, 1995.

Fiey, Jean-Maurice. *Chrétiens syriaques sous les Abbassides surtout à Bagdad (749–1258).* CSCO 420. Leuven: Secrétariat du CSCO, 1980.

Frantz-Murphy, Gladys. *Arabic Agricultural Leases and Tax Receipts from Egypt.* Vienna: Hollinek, 2001.

Glei, Reinhold F. "John of Damascus." In *Christian-Muslim Relations: A Bibliographical History*, edited by David Thomas and Barbara Roggema, vol. 1, pp. 295–301. Leiden: Brill, 2009.

Goodman, L. E. "The Greek Impact on Arabic Literature." In *Arabic Literature to the End of the Umayyad Period,* edited by A. F. L. Beeston, et al., 460–82. The Cambridge History of Arabic Literature. Cambridge: Cambridge University Press, 1983.

Gonis, Nikolaos. "Reconsidering Some Fiscal Documents from Early Islamic Egypt." *Zeitschrift für Papyrologie und Epigraphik* 137 (2001): 225–28.

———. "Reconsidering Some Fiscal Documents from Early Islamic Egypt II." *Zeitschrift für Papyrologie und Epigraphik* 150 (2004): 187–93.

———. "Tax Receipts on Coptic and Greek Ostraca Re-Read." *Zeitschrift für Papyrologie und Epigraphik* 147 (2004): 157–63.

Gottheil, Richard. "Dhimmis and Moslems in Egypt." In *Old Testament and Semitic Studies in Memory of William Rainey Harper,* edited by Robert Francis Harper, Francis Brown, and George Foot Moore, pp. 353–414. Chicago: University of Chicago Press, 1908.

———, editor. "A Fetwa on the Appointment of Dhimmis to Office." *Zeitschrift für Assyriologie und verwandte Gebiete* 26 (1912): 203–14.

Grenfell, Bernard P., and Arthur S. Hunt. *New Classical Fragments and Other Greek and Latin Papyri.* Greek Papyri, ser. II. Oxford: Clarendon Press, 1897.

Ḥamza al-Iṣbahānī. *Hamzae Ispahanensis Annalium Libri X.* Edited by I. M. E. Gottwald. Leipzig: Vogel, 1844.

Hawting, Gerald R. *The First Dynasty of Islam: The Umayyad Caliphate A.D. 661–750.* 2nd ed. London: Routledge, 2000.

Holmberg, B. "A Reconsideration of the Kitāb al-Maǧdal." *Parole de l'Orient* 18 (1993): 255–73.

Hoyland, Robert G. *Seeing Islam as Others Saw It: A Survey and Evaluation of Christian, Jewish and Zoroastrian Writings on Early Islam*. Studies in Late Antiquity and Early Islam 13. Princeton: Darwin Press, 1997.

————. *Theophilus of Edessa's Chronicle and the Circulation of Historical Knowledge in Late Antiquity and Early Islam*. Translated Texts for Historians 57. Liverpool: Liverpool University Press, 2011.

Ibn ʿAbd al-Barr, Yūsuf b. ʿAbdallāh al-Namarī. *Bahjat al-majālis wa-uns al-mujālis wa-shaḥdh al-dhāhin wa-al-hājis*. 2 vols. Cairo: al-Dār al-Miṣrīya, 1967–1970.

Ibn ʿAbd al-Ḥakam, ʿAbd Allāh. *Sīrat ʿUmar b. ʿAbd al-ʿAzīz*. Edited by A. ʿUbayd, 2nd ed. Cairo: Maktabat Wahba, 1983.

Ibn ʿAbd Rabbih, Aḥmad b. Muḥammad. *Al-ʿIqd al-farīd*. Edited by A. Amīn et al. 6 vols. Cairo: Lajnat al-Taʾlīf wal-Tarjama, 1940–1949.

Ibn Abī Ḥātim al-Rāzī, ʿAbd al-Raḥmān. *Kitāb al-jarḥ wa-al-taʿdīl*. 9 vols. Hyderabad: Maṭbaʿat Jamʿīyat Dāʾirat al-Maʿārif al-ʿUthmānīya, 1942–.

Ibn ʿAsākir, ʿAlī b. al-Ḥasan. *Taʾrīkh madīnat Dimashq*. Edited by ʿA. Shīrī. 80 vols. Beirut: Dār al-Fikr, 1995–1998.

Ibn al-Athīr, ʿIzz al-Dīn. *Al-Kāmil fī al-taʾrīkh*. 13 vols. Beirut: Dār Ṣādir, 1965–1967.

Ibn al-Faraḍī, ʿAbdallāh b. Muḥammad. *Taʾrīkh ʿulamāʾ al-Andalus*. Edited by B. ʿA. Maʿrūf. 2 vols. Tunis: Dār al-Gharb al-Islāmī, 2008.

Ibn Ḥazm, ʿAlī b. Aḥmad. *Al-Muḥallā*. Edited by M. Munīr al-Dimashqī. 11 vols. Damascus: Idārat al-Ṭibāʿa al-Munīrīya, 1964.

Ibn al-ʿIbrī, Abū al-Faraj [Bar Hebraeus]. *Chronicon syriacum*. Edited by P. Bedjan, *Gregorii Barhebraei Chronicon Syriacum*. Paris: Maisonneuve, 1890.

————. *Taʾrīkh mukhtaṣar al-duwal*. Beirut: Catholic Press, 1958.

Ibn al-Jawzī, ʿAbd al-Raḥmān b. ʿAlī. *Sīrat ʿUmar b. ʿAbd al-ʿAzīz*. Cairo: Maṭbaʿat al-Muʾayyad, 1913.

————. *Manāqib al-Imām Aḥmad b. Ḥanbal*. Edited by ʿA. M. ʿUmar. Cairo: Maktabat al-Khānjī, 2009.

Ibn Mufliḥ, Muḥammad al-Maqdisī. *Al-Ādāb al-sharʿīya*. Edited by ʿI. al-Ḥaristānī. 3 vols. Beirut: Dār al-Jīl, 1997.

————. *Kitāb al-furūʿ*. Edited by ʿA. A. al-Turkī. 12 vols. Beirut: Muʾassasat al-Risāla, 2003.

Ibn al-Naqqāsh, Muḥammad b. ʿAlī. "Fetoua relatif à la condition des zimmis." Translated by F. A. Belin. *Journal Asiatique*, 4ᵉ sér., 18 (1851): 417–516.

Ibn Qayyim al-Jawzīya, Muḥammad b. Abī Bakr. *Aḥkām ahl al-dhimma*. Edited by Ṣ. Ṣāliḥ. 4th ed. 2 vols. Beirut: Dār al-ʿIlm lil-Malāyīn, 1994.

Ibn al-Rāhib, Buṭrus b. al-Muhadhdhab (attributed). *Chronicon orientale*. Edited with Latin translation by L. Cheïkho, *Petrus ibn Rahib: Chronicon orientale*. 2 vols. in 1. CSCO 45–46 (Scriptores Arabici III/1). Beirut: E Typographeo Catholico, 1903.

Ibn Saʿd, Muḥammad. *Kitāb al-ṭabaqāt al-kabīr*. Edited by ʿA. M. ʿUmar. 11 vols. Cairo: Maktabat al-Khānjī, 2001.

Ibn Shās, Jalāl al-Dīn ʿAbdallāh. *ʿIqd al-jawāhir al-thamīna fī madhhab ʿālim al-Madīna*. Edited by M. Abu l-Ajfān and ʿA. al-Ḥ. Manṣūr. 3 vols. Beirut: Dār al-Gharb al-Islāmī, 1995.

Ibn Taghrībirdī, Jamāl al-Dīn Abu l-Maḥāsin. *Al-Nujūm al-zāhira fī mulūk Miṣr wal-Qāhira*. 2 vols. Leiden: Brill, 1851; Cairo: al-Muʾassasa al-Miṣrīya al-ʿĀmma, 1963–1971.

al-Ibshīhī, Muḥammad b. Aḥmad. *Kitāb al-mustaṭraf fī kull fann mustaẓraf*. Būlāq: n.p., 1868.

al-Iṣbahānī, Abū al-Faraj ʿAlī b. al-Ḥusayn. *Kitāb al-aghānī.* Edited by ʿA. al-S. al-Farrāj. 8th ed. 25 vols. Beirut: Dār al-Thaqāfa, 1990.

al-Iṣbahānī, Abu Nuʿaym. *Ḥilyat al-awliyāʾ wa-ṭabaqāt al-aṣfiyāʾ.* 10 vols. Cairo: Maktabat al-Khānjī, 1932–1938.

al-Jahshiyārī, Muḥammad b. ʿAbdūs. *Kitāb al-wuzarāʾ wa-al-kuttāb.* Edited by M. al-Saqqā et al. Cairo: Muṣṭafā al-Bābī al-Ḥalabī, 1938.

Justi, Ferdinand. *Iranisches Namenbuch.* Marburg: N. G. Elwert, 1895.

Juynboll, G. H. A. *Muslim Tradition.* Cambridge: Cambridge University Press, 1983.

Keating, Sandra Toenies. *Defending the People of Truth in the Early Islamic Period: The Christian Apologies of Abū Rāʾiṭa.* Leiden: Brill, 2006.

Khalīfa b. Khayyāṭ. *Taʾrīkh.* Edited by S. Zakkār. Beirut: Dār al-Fikr, 1993.

al-Khallāl, Abū Bakr Aḥmad b. Muḥammad. *Ahl al-milal wa-al-ridda wa-al-zanādiqa wa-tārik al-ṣalāt wa-al-farāʾiḍ.* Edited by I. b. Ḥ. b. Sulṭān. 2 vols. Riyadh: Maktabat al-Maʿārif, 1996.

al-Khaṭīb al-Baghdādī, Aḥmad b. ʿAlī. *Taʾrīkh Madīnat al-Salām.* Edited by B. ʿA. Maʿrūf. 17 vols. Beirut: Dār al-Gharb al-Islāmī, 2001.

al-Kindī, Abū ʿUmar Muḥammad b. Yūsuf. *Kitāb al-wulāt wa-kitāb al-quḍāt.*

- Edited by Rhuvon Guest, *The Governors and Judges of Egypt.* London: Luzac & Co., 1912.
- Edited by Ḥusayn Naṣṣār, *Wulāt Miṣr.* Beirut: Dār Ṣādir, 1959.

Kratchkovskaya, V. A., and I. J. Kratchkovsky. "The Oldest Arabic Manuscript From Central Asia." In *Sogdiiskii Sbornik: Sbornik Statei o Pamyatnikakh Sogdiiskogo Iazyka i Kultury Naydennykh na gore Mug v Tadzhikskoiy SSR*, pp. 52–90. Leningrad: Akademiia Nauk SSR, 1934.

Kratchkovsky, I. J. *Among Arabic Manuscripts: Memories of Libraries and Men.* Translated by Tatiana Minorsky. Leiden: Brill, 1953.

Küng, Hans. *Islam: Past, Present, and Future.* Translated by J. Bowden. Oxford: Oneworld, 2007.

Levy-Rubin, Milka. *Non-Muslims in the Early Islamic Empire: From Surrender to Coexistence.* Cambridge: Cambridge University Press, 2011.

Lewis, Bernard. *The Jews of Islam.* Princeton: Princeton University Press, 1984.

———. *The Arabs in History.* Rev. ed. New York: Harper & Row, 1967.

Łewond. *History of Łewond, The Eminent Vardapet of the Armenians.* Translated by Zaven Arzoumanian. Wynnewood: St. Sahag and St. Mesrob Armenian Church, 1982.

Liebrenz, Boris. "Eine frühe arabische Quittung aus Oberägypten." *Archiv für Papyrusforschung und verwandte Gebiete* 56/2 (2010): 294–314.

Madelung, Wilferd. "Maslama b. Muḥārib: Umayyad Historian." *The Arabist: Budapest Studies in Arabic* 24–25 (2002): 203–14.

al-Makīn b. al-ʿAmīd. *Al-Majmūʿ al-mubārak.* Edited by ʿA. B. Ḥasan, *Tarikh al-Makin: Tarikh al-Muslimin min sahib shariʿat al-Islam Abi al-Qasim Muhammad hattá al-dawlah al-Atabikiyah.* Cairo: Dār al-ʿAwāṣim, 2010.

al-Maqrīzī, Taqī al-Dīn Aḥmad. *Kitāb al-mawāʿiẓ wa-al-iʿtibār bi-dhikr al-khiṭaṭ wa-al-āthār.* Edited by A. F. Sayyid. 5 vols. London: Muʾassasat al-Furqān, 2002–; Cairo: Maktabat al-Thaqāfa al-Dīnīya, 1987.

Maris Amri et Sliba, De Patriarchis Nestorianorum Commentaria [*Kitāb al-majdal*] (Anonymous). Edited by H. Gismondi. Rome: F. de Luigi, 1896–1899.

Michael the Syrian. *Chronicle.*

- Edited by G. Y. Ibrahim, *The Edessa-Aleppo Syriac Codex of the Chronicle of Michael the Great.* Texts and Translations of the Chronicle of Michael the Great 1. Edited by G. Kiraz. Piscataway: Gorgias Press, 2009.
- Translated by Victor Langlois, *Chronique de Michel le grand, patriarche des syriens jacobites, traduite par la première fois sur la version arménienne du prêtre Ischôk.* Venice: Typographie de l'Académie de Saint-Lazare, 1868.

al-Mizzī, Yūsuf b. al-Zakī. *Tahdhīb al-kamāl fī asmāʾ al-rijāl.* 35 vols. Beirut: Muʾassasat al-Risāla, 1992.

Moawad, Samuel, "Zur Originalität der Yūsāb von Fūwah zugeschriebenen Patriarchengeschichte." *Le Muséon* 119/3–4 (2006): 255–70.

Morony, Michael G. "The Aramean Population in the Economic Life of Early Islamic Iraq." *Aram* 3/1–2 (1991): 1–6.

Motzki, Harald. "Dating Muslim Traditions: A Survey." *Arabica* 52/2 (2005): 204–53.

Mourad, Sulaiman. *Early Islam Between Myth and History: al-Ḥasan al-Baṣrī (d. 110H/728CE) and the Formation of His Legacy in Classical Islamic Scholarship.* Leiden: Brill, 2006.

Muranyi, Miklos. *ʿAbd Allāh b. Wahb (125/743-197/812): Leben und Werk / al-Muwaṭṭa: Kitāb al-muḥāraba.* Wiesbaden: Harrassowitz, 1992.

Nasrallah, P. Joseph. *Saint Jean de Damas: Son époque, sa vie, son oeuvre.* Harissa: Imp. Saint Paul, 1950.

al-Nuwayrī, Shihāb al-Dīn Aḥmad. *Nihāyat al-arab fī funūn al-adab.* 33 vols. Cairo: Al-Muʾassasa al-Miṣrīya al-ʿĀmma, 1964–1998.

Palmer, Andrew. *The Seventh Century in the West-Syrian Chronicles.* Translated Texts for Historians 15. Liverpool: Liverpool University Press, 1993.

Peters, F. E. *Allah's Commonwealth.* New York: Simon & Schuster, 1973.

al-Qāḍī, Wadād. "Population Census and Land Surveys under the Umayyads (41–132/661–750)." *Der Islam* 83 (2008): 341–416.

al-Qalqashandī, Aḥmad b. ʿAlī. *Subḥ al-aʿshā fī ṣināʿat al-inshāʾ.* 14 vols. Cairo: Al-Muʾassasa al-Miṣrīya al-ʿĀmma, 1964.

al-Qarāfī, Aḥmad b. Idrīs. *Al-Dhakhīra.* Edited by M. Ḥajjī. 14 vols. Beirut: Dār al-Gharb al-Islāmī, 1994.

Ruprecht, Hans Albert, editor. *Sammelbuch Griechischer Urkunden aus Ägypten, XVIII.* Wiesbaden: Harrassowitz, 1993.

Sahas, Daniel. *John of Damascus on Islam.* Leiden: Brill, 1972.

Saḥnūn, Abū Saʿīd ʿAbd al-Salām b. Saʿīd. *Al-Mudawwana al-kubrā.* 6 vols. Beirut: Dār Ṣādir, 1975.

Saʿīd b. Biṭrīq (Eutychius of Alexandria). *Annales.* [Ar. *Taʾrīkh al-majmūʿ ʿala al-taḥqīq wa-al-taṣdīq* or *Naẓm al-jawhar*]. Edited by E. Pococke and John Selden, *Contextio gemmarum, sive, Eutychii patriarchæ Alexandrini annales.* 2 vols. Oxford: Excudebat H. Hall, 1654–1656.

Schick, Robert. *The Christian Communities of Palestine from Byzantine to Islamic Rule.* Princeton: Darwin Press, 1995.

Seybold, C. F. *Severus ibn al-Muqaffaʿ: Alexandrinische Patriarchengeschichte von S. Marcus bis Michael I, 61–767.* Hamburg: L. Gräfe, 1912.

al-Shāfiʿī, Muḥammad b. Idrīs. *Al-Umm.* Edited by R. F. ʿAbd al-Muṭṭalib. 11 vols. Mansura: Dār al-Wafāʾ, 2008.

Sijpesteijn, Petra M. "Landholding Patterns in Early Islamic Egypt." *Journal of Agrarian Change* 9/1 (2009): 120–33.

———. "The Archival Mind in Early Islamic Egypt: Two Arabic Papyri." In *From al-Andalus to Khurasan: Documents from the Medieval Muslim World*, edited by Petra Sijpesteijn, L. Sundelin, et al., pp. 163–86. Leiden: Brill, 2007.

———. *Shaping a Muslim State: The World of a Mid-Eighth-Century Egyptian Official.* Oxford: Oxford University Press, 2013.

Sprengling, M. "Persian to Arabic." *The American Journal of Semitic Languages and Literatures* 56/2 (1939): 175–224.

Swanson, Mark N. "John the Deacon." In *Christian-Muslim Relations: A Bibliographical History*, edited by David Thomas and Barbara Roggema, vol. 1, pp. 317–21. Leiden: Brill, 2009.

al-Ṭabarī, Muḥammad b. Jarīr. *Taʾrīkh al-Rusul wa-l-Mulūk.* Edited by M. J. de Goeje, *Annales quos scripsit Abu Djafar Mohammed ibn Djarir at-Tabari.* 16 vols. Leiden: Brill, 1879–1901.

Tait, John Gavin, editor. *Greek Ostraca in the Bodleian Library at Oxford and Various Other Collections.* 3 vols. London: Egypt Exploration Society, 1930.

al-Tanūkhī, al-Muḥassin b. ʿAlī. *Nishwār al-muḥāḍara wa-akhbār al-mudhākara.* Edited by Abood Shalchy. 8 vols. Beirut: Dār Ṣādir, 1971–.

Theophanes Confessor. *Chronicle.*

- Edited by Carl De Boor, *Theophanis Chronographia.* 2 vols. Hildesheim: G. Olms, 1963. Reprint of the Leipzig: Teubner, 1883–1885 edition.
- English translation by Cyril Mango and Roger Scott, *The Chronicle of Theophanes Confessor. Byzantine and Near-Eastern History A.D. 284–813.* Oxford: Clarendon Press, 1997.

Tritton, A. S. *The Caliphs and their Non-Muslim Subjects.* London: Oxford University Press, 1930.

al-ʿUlaymī, ʿAbd al-Raḥmān b. Muḥammad. *Al-Manhaj al-aḥmad fī tarājim aṣḥāb al-Imām Aḥmad.* Edited by ʿA. al-Q. al-Arnāʾūṭ. 6 vols. Beirut: Dār Ṣādir, 1997.

al-Uqayshir al-Asadī. *Dīwān al-Uqayshir al-Asadī.* Edited by Muḥammad ʿAlī Diqqa. Beirut: Dār Ṣādir, 1997.

Wensinck, A. J. *A Handbook of Early Muhammadan Tradition.* 8 vols. Leiden: Brill, 1927.

Wessely, Carl. *Griechische Papyrusurkunden kleineren Formats.* Studien zur Palaeographie und Papyruskunde 3. Leipzig: Avenarius, 1904.

Wilfong, Terry G. "Greek and Coptic Texts from the Oriental Institute Exhibition 'Another Egypt.'" *Bulletin of the American Society of Papyrologists* 29 (1992): 85–95.

al-Yaʿqūbī, Aḥmad b. Abī Yaʿqūb. *Taʾrīkh.* Edited by M. Th. Houtsma, *Ibn Wādhih qui dicitur al-Jaʿqūbī, Historiae.* 2 vols. Leiden: Brill, 1883.

Yakubovich, Ilya. "Mugh 1.1 Revisited." *Studia Iranica* 31 (2002): 231–53

Yarbrough, Luke. "A Rather Small Genre: Arabic Works against Non-Muslim State Officials." *Der Islam* 93: 1.

———. "I'll not Accept Aid from a *mušrik*." In *The Late Roman and Early Islamic Mediterranean and Near East: Authority and Control in the Countryside*, edited by A. Delattre, M. Legendre, and P. Sijpesteijn. Princeton: Darwin Press, forthcoming.

———. "Origins of the *ghiyār*." *Journal of the American Oriental Society* 134/1 (2014): 113–21.

———. "Upholding God's Rule: Early Muslim Juristic Opposition to the State Employment of Non-Muslims." *Islamic Law and Society* 19/1 (2012): 11–85.

[Yūsāb of Fūwah]. *Taʾrīkh al-ābāʾ al-baṭārika.* Edited by S. al-Suryānī and N. Kāmil. Cairo: n.p., 1992. = *HPY*

Zuqnīn Chronicle (Anonymous). Translated and annotated by Amir Harrak, *The Chronicle of Zuqnīn, Parts III and IV, A.D. 488–775.* Toronto: Pontifical Institute of Mediaeval Studies, 1999.

Index